Income Support

Maryland Studies in
Public Philosophy

Edited by PETER G. BROWN

Also in this series

BOUNDARIES
National Autonomy and Its Limits
Edited by
PETER G. BROWN and HENRY SHUE

Income Support

CONCEPTUAL AND POLICY ISSUES

edited by

Peter G. Brown

Conrad Johnson

Paul Vernier

ROWMAN AND LITTLEFIELD
Totowa, New Jersey

First published in the United States 1981 by Rowman and Littlefield, 81 Adams Drive, Totowa, New Jersey 07512.

Distributed in the U.K. and Commonwealth by George Prior Associated Publishers Limited 37-41 Bedford Row London WC1R 4JH, England

Library of Congress Cataloging in Publication Data
Main entry under title:

Income support.

    (Maryland studies in public philosophy)
    Includes bibliographies and index.
    1. Public welfare—United States—Ad-
dresses, essays, lectures. 2. Income
maintenance programs—United States—Ad-
dresses, essays, lectures. 3. United States—
Social policy—Addresses, essays, lectures.
I. Brown, Peter G.   II. Johnson, Conrad.
III. Vernier, Paul.   IV. Series.
HV91.I45   1981   362.5'82   80-26540
ISBN 0-8476-6969-6   AACR1

Printed in the United States of America

Contents

Preface

The Center for Philosophy and Public Policy was established in 1976 with the purpose of investigating conceptual and ethical aspects of public policy formulation and debate. This emphasis complements the dominant concern now given to empirical research in the formation and evaluation of public policy.

This volume is the product of a project undertaken by the Center during 1977–79. The primary purpose of the volume is to examine basic moral and conceptual issues underlying recent welfare reform efforts as well as any future attempts to appraise or modify income support policies in this country.

The authors were chosen because of their individual expertise and to represent the wide range of disciplines and organizations concerned with income support policy. They met as a working group three times in 1977–78 to review and discuss the essays in the volume. They gave generously of their time in participating in these meetings and in writing individual essays. They graciously accepted the many requests of the editors for revisions in the interests of a coherent and well-balanced book.

The editors also wish to express their appreciation for the valuable help given by the project's advisory panel which consisted of the following members:

Professor Gerald Dworkin
Department of Philosophy
University of Illinois at Chicago Circle

Professor Joel Feinberg
Department of Philosophy
University of Arizona

Mr. Leslie Lendowsky
Director of Research
Smith Richardson Foundation

Mr. William A. Morrill
Mathematica Policy Research, Inc.
Princeton, New Jersey

Dr. John Palmer
Department of Health and Human Services
Washington, D.C.

Dr. Lester Salamon
Senior Research Associate
The Urban Institute

Professor Lester C. Thurow
Department of Economics
Massachusetts Institute of Technology

Dr. Joseph Vigilante
Dean, School of Social Work
Adelphi University

Financial support for the project was provided by the Ford Foundation and the Rockefeller Foundation. For this support and general support for the Center from the Rockefeller Brothers Fund the editors are most grateful.

To the staff of the Center, including Elizabeth Cahoon, who served as administrative manager of the project, Claudia Mills, the Center's editorial associate, and Louise Collins and Virginia Smith, who performed the secretarial and typing functions, the editors offer their warmest thanks.

The contents of each essay are solely the responsibility of the individual author. The views expressed do not necessarily represent those of the Center for Philosophy and Public Policy, the project's sponsors, the organizations with which the authors are associated, or individual members of the advisory panel.

A companion to this volume by Paul Vernier, Research Associate of the Center for Philosophy and Public Policy, is now in preparation. This companion volume is concerned with the failure of the present income support system to provide benefits on a universal basis to all those who are able-bodied and expected to work, but who lack employment and are in need. It argues that all such individuals and their dependents have a clear moral right to be covered by the system of economic support programs.

Introduction

What is the responsibility of government for the poor: *(1)* Nothing, with the role of support resting solely on charitably minded private individuals? *(2)* An obligation to provide an adequate standard of living to every poor person? *(3)* Something more than *(1)* but less than *(2)*? If there is such an obligation, what kind of obligation is it, and on what grounds does it rest?

These are practical questions that *no* nation, *especially* no advanced industrial nation, can avoid. They are practical because how they are answered will directly or indirectly affect the lives of every member of society. They are unavoidable because no nation can tax and spend without answering them, if not explicitly, then by default. The issue is not, therefore, whether we should pay attention to these questions but how well considered our reflections will be. Will our policy choices be justified by rigorous argument, or will they rest on assumptions made without serious reflection? It is the purpose of this volume to address these questions in an explicit and considered manner in the context of recent and current attempts to reform existing programs.

Income support programs are part of a much larger and more expensive system of transfer payments made by governmental bodies in the United States to its citizens. This larger system includes, among other programs, the social insurances (Old-age and Survivors' Insurance, Unemployment Insurance, and Workmen's Compensation) and compensation to veterans with service-connected disabilities. The income support system, as understood in the essays in this volume, includes only those programs which are "needs-tested," that is, programs in which economic need is both a condition of eligibility and the basis on which benefits are computed. (A brief description of each of the most important of these programs is contained in Appendix A.)

In recent years there have been two major efforts by the federal government, in 1969–72 and 1977–78, to discontinue the existing "needs-tested" programs and replace them with a new, modern system. Congress reached no working consensus on what should be done in either instance, although important alterations came out of the first attempt.

It has been a characteristic of the welfare reform debate since the 1960s first to concentrate attention on the criticisms that are leveled at the existing income support system, and then to generate new program models and policy proposals that are responsive to these criticisms. For example, the present system fails to respond to the economic need of some

ix

important segments of the population, such as the families of unemployed workers in most states and those whose earnings fall below some recognized measure of poverty. In response to this criticism, the major proposed reforms would have broadened the scope of coverage to encompass some or all of these excluded individuals.

Behind such criticisms, however, lie questions of moral principle which themselves are not generally made explicit and debated. And the substance and justification of moral principles often depend upon how we have conceptualized the world around us—the names we have given to the persons, places, and things that make up our universe. Calling a set of arrangements equitable, for instance, carries with it the notion that it is at least prima facie morally acceptable. It is, however, just on these conceptual issues and issues of social morality that the real disagreements blocking welfare reform have arisen.

The present volume seeks to make explicit such questions and issues and to examine the answers that can be given to them. Its contribution lies not only in its articulation and discussion of these fundamental issues. It goes beyond this by means of a careful examination of different answers, and, when particular answers are urged by the authors, they are supported by arguments.

The first three sections of this volume consider different aspects of these issues. The first, "Moral Authority and Proper Goals of the State," addresses the issues of why the state should be concerned with income distribution at all, the limits on state intervention in personal life, and the relative responsibilities of the federal government and the several states. The second section concerns how we should decide among the various objectives of income support policy, e.g., equity, adequacy, efficiency, and creation of work incentives—objectives which cannot be simultaneously maximized. The third considers the question of whether there are welfare rights, how they could or could not be justified, and how they should be understood. The fourth discusses the nature of the present policy debate and locates it with reference to past, current, and prospective trends.

Underlying the issues and problems discussed in all these sections is the fundamental question: What primary goal or goals should the income support program attempt to achieve? The importance of this question is that the answer given to it establishes our basic perspectives on the moral foundations of income support policy.

Consider, for example, this description of the general function of income support: Income support programs bridge existing gaps between income and need for those whose own sources of support fall below some established standard of living. These programs help to make up this deficit for those families and individuals who satisfy the conditions of eligibility set for these programs.

This description of the function of income support, it is important to note, tells us almost nothing about the possible social goals which income support programs should have. Because appraisals of existing programs and proposals for their reform are necessarily made from the perspective of one or more of these goals, an understanding of them is of substantial importance.

Four such goals have been prominently debated in recent years (together with a fifth which is a denial that government has any responsibility for income support, and which may be called the "private charity" approach). These are:[1]

1. To meet the current economic needs of persons whose incomes fall below some minimum standard of living.
2. To establish a guaranteed universal minimum income as a national floor.
3. To contribute to the goal of reducing or eliminating poverty.
4. To contribute to a program of redistributing income in the interests of social justice (for example, to achieve greater equality of income).

In one respect, these four possible goals are closely related. All are concerned with improving the economic resources of those at the bottom. Why and how one attempts to improve the circumstances of this group, however, depends importantly upon which of the four goals is taken to be primary.

One significant, and potentially confusing, interrelation among these goals is that achieving any of them will almost always incidentally advance the others. To see how this occurs, we need to distinguish conceptually between primary goals and residual consequences, and then see how this distinction brings the issue to light. If the first goal is chosen as primary, and thus the attempt is made only to provide help for those in need, the means of doing so requires the existence of an income transfer system, i.e., a system of transferring taxes collected from one group to another group. Such a system is a form of income redistribution from those who are taxed to those who are in need. Again, payments of support to the needy necessarily reduce the net incidence of poverty to some extent. Moreover, since public income support programs generally function on the basis of standard measures of need for the eligible group, and this standard determines the amount of support received, there is an approximation of a guaranteed income for that group at least—such a "guarantee" being supported by the fair hearing provisions in federal and joint federal-state programs.[2] Similar interconnections can be traced with respect to each of the other three goals when selected as primary.

No doubt many would wish to see all four of these goals accomplished and would support efforts in all four directions. This is a possibility, since these goals are not mutually incompatible. If this is so, why should it be important to identify and examine each of the goals separately? The importance is two-fold. First, each of the goals, when chosen as primary, introduces different criteria for measuring a program's success, and the resulting appraisals may therefore be divergent. These different criteria imply different social values, as well, each requiring its own justification in light of ethical principles. Second, policies for income support programs will be determined by the primary goal. Let us briefly look at some examples of ways in which different primary goals give rise to different policies.

1. Meeting economic need. How adequate is the standard of living on which the measurement of need is based? Is program coverage comprehensive, that is, are all groups of needy people included? Are the special needs of those with particular problems provided for (e.g., expensive diets for the ill)?

2. Guaranteed minimum income. Is program coverage universal? Is there a minimum floor of income below which no one is permitted to fall? How adequate is this income level for meeting everyone's economic needs?

3. Reducing poverty. How do we define poverty? How far does this program take us toward the elimination of poverty for those who will be its beneficiaries? To what extent are all poor persons covered?

4. Redistributing income. To what degree will this program help to correct injustices in the way income is distributed?

These perspectives shape the discussions of policy issues and their moral foundations found in the articles in this volume. Jodie Allen, David Lindeman, Martha Phillips, Robert Fersh, and Henry Aaron are each concerned mainly with questions arising from the first goal cited, that of meeting the economic needs of those with insufficient income. The four papers in the section on welfare rights are closely linked to the second goal of a guaranteed minimum income, since if there are moral rights to income support, such rights are typically translatable into the right to a guaranteed minimum.

The third goal of reducing or eliminating poverty is touched upon in a number of papers, including those by Barbara Bergmann, Richard B. Brandt, Geoffrey Brennan and David Friedman, and Norman Daniels. These papers, in one way or another, consider the question of who has what responsibilities for alleviating the problem of poverty in the United States.

Finally, the problem of justice in the distribution of income in relation to income support policy is discussed, directly or indirectly, in the papers by Brandt, Brennan and Friedman, Bergmann, Daniels, Conrad Johnson, and Baruch Brody. Brandt's paper presents and defends the widely held theory of utilitarianism—that social policy should be directed toward maximizing the welfare of the entire community. Brennan and Friedman argue in support of an alternative theory of justice, that of libertarianism.[3]

PGB

Notes

1. A short bibliography of books which adopt or argue for each of these primary goals is as follows:

1. *Income Support to Provide for Those in Need*

Martin Anderson, *Welfare–The Political Economy of Welfare Reform in the U.S.* (Stanford, Calif.: Hoover Press, 1978). Lester Salamon, *Welfare–The Elusive Consensus* (New York: Praeger Publishers, 1978), Chapter 4. M. Barth, G. J. Carcagno, J. L. Palmer, *Toward an Effective Income Support Program* (Madison: Institute for Research on Poverty, 1974).

2. *Income Support to Establish a Universal Guaranteed Minimum Income Floor*

Robert Theobald (ed.), *The Guaranteed Income—Next Step in Economic Evolution?* (Garden City, N.Y.: Doubleday & Co., 1965). Daniel P. Moynihan, *The Politics of a Guaranteed Income* (New York: Random House, 1973), Chapter VIII.

3. *Income Support as a Factor in Eliminating or Reducing Poverty*

Robert Plotnick and Felicity Skidmore, *Progress Against Poverty* (N.Y.: Academic Press, 1975), Chapter 7. Lowell Gallaway, *Poverty in America* (Columbus, Ohio: Grid, Inc., 1973), Chapter 10.

4. *Income Support as a Factor in Redistribution of Income*

Alvin L. Schorr, *Jubilee for Our Times—A Practical Program for Income Equality* (New York: Columbia University Press, 1977), Chapter 6, S. M. Miller and Pamela Roby, *The Future of Inequality* (New York: Basic Books, 1970), Chapter 5.

2. Payment levels and eligibility coverage in these programs are subject to change, however, since they depend on appropriations, legislation, and agency policy, all of which may be modified with not much warning.

3. A social contract theory of economic justice has recently been the subject of wide discussion as the result of the publication by John Rawls of *A Theory of Justice* (Cambridge, Mass.: Harvard University Press, 1971). Treatment of those at the bottom is an important subject of Rawls's book, particularly in Chapters II and V.

PART ONE

The Moral Authority and Proper Goals of the State With Respect to Income Support Policy

Introduction

Income support policy is a matter of recurrent debate—sometimes acrimonious, sometimes reflective. It is no wonder. For the policy of supporting the incomes of some almost invariably means taking from the incomes of others. Disagreements about the details of different programs and legislative proposals may often appear to be nothing more than disagreement about the facts of political power (who "has the votes") or about the behavioral, sociological, and economic impact of those programs. But these disagreements often mask deeper differences of fundamental philosophical conviction.

In thinking about the normative philosophical questions of welfare policy, and in the service of putting those questions in the broader framework of political and social philosophy, it is helpful to keep these two [kinds of] distinctions in mind: that between the *authority* and the *proper goals* of the state; and that between the different *levels* at which questions about authority and goals can be raised. Thus if the state does not have the authority, say, to redistribute income, the redistribution of income cannot be a proper goal for the state to adopt. There are many goals the state might have the authority to pursue, however, though these might be improper for some other reason: perhaps because self-defeating; not the most efficient means to an end; dangerous to the stability of important institutions, or whatever. And questions both about authority and about proper goals appear at different levels. Thus the authority that the U.S. Congress has to enact legislation is very different from the authority that a parent has over a child, and different from the authority that the administrator of an agency of the government has over that agency. (Though both a parent and the U.S. Congress have authority affecting the welfare of others, Congress has wide-ranging responsibility concerning the welfare of the nation as a whole while an individual parent clearly does not have this responsibility in the first instance.) Correspondingly, the goals that it is proper for each of these entities to adopt differ greatly. The papers in this section all confront one or both of these normative questions about authority and goals, some focusing on the more macro and abstract, others on the more specific.

Brandt's paper, "Utilitarianism and Welfare Legislation," is an attempt to show how utilitarian theory, which he holds is a theory about what people morally ought to do, applies as well to institutions and laws and, in particular, to the formation and evaluation of income support policy. Brandt presents utilitarian theory as a general theory to guide the design

3

both of the grand political institutions and of specific legislation, as well as the actions of particular individuals, even when they are not acting in some role that has special authority. Utilitarianism, so conceived, sets up a general goal—the maximization of good consequences (happiness, on Brandt's view)—as the proper goal for individuals, the state, and the institutions of the state. Brandt's paper applies the principle of utility to such questions as welfare rights, tax rates, the provision of jobs, and the imposition of work requirements for payments above the subsistence level.

The Brennan and Friedman paper, "A Libertarian Perspective on 'Welfare'," provides some of the main features of a libertarian perspective. Though individual libertarians do not agree on all the details, what is central to the political philosophy that has today come to be called "libertarian" is a very critical stance toward the authority and power of the state. Libertarians hold either that the state has no legitimate role to play and that all functions we associate with the modern state must be left to individuals, in their voluntary dealings with one another, or that the legitimate role of the state is quite small indeed and does not include the authority to redistribute wealth through taxation, or (what is closely related) to provide for the basic needs of the poor via explicit taxation, inflation of the currency, or any such expedient that does not depend on the voluntary cooperation of all who must make the needed sacrifices. Their conclusions are thus very different from Brandt's: Given Brandt's view about the fundamental goal of maximizing utility, combined with his view of the diminishing marginal utility of income, maximizing utility requires income support programs with the attendant redistributive effects.

This greatly circumscribed role of the state has been argued for in different ways, some of which emerge in their paper. One approach is simply to argue that certain functions, such as the redistribution of wealth or taxation to provide for a welfare system, simply go beyond the authority of the state; that individuals have rights to dispose of and use their property in the ways they choose, and that taxation for redistribution (as opposed to taking voluntary donations) would violate those rights. Another approach focuses less on the authority of the state than on the supposed unwisdom of the state's getting involved in such activities. For, it might be argued, though it is the proper goal of the state to maximize happiness or liberty, this goal is very badly served by centralizing power and by instituting state-enforced centralized charity rather than by leaving it all to individual choice. Though the state might have the moral authority to impose such demands, this more specific goal of centralizing and enforcing charity is improper because unwise. Brennan and Friedman give both these kinds of argument, and they survey some of the possibilities for a system of welfare payments that libertarians of at least some stripe might be able to accept.

Gerald Dworkin's paper, "Paternalism and Welfare Policy," examines an important question regarding the authority of the state. This is the question whether the state is justified in limiting the liberty of individuals *for their own good*. The question is one that arises frequently for welfare policy. For it is clear that some people will not use whatever "benefits" are given them in a way that actually does redound to their own good. Benefits in kind (rather than in cash) are sometimes argued for on grounds that, if the government decides to give people nutritious food rather than cash, that is some insurance at least that they will use what is given to them in a way that will genuinely benefit them. Philosophical questions about this include: Does the provision of an in-kind rather than cash benefit constitute coercion? Does it constitute paternalism? Is it within the authority of the state to impose this kind of restriction on the giving of benefits? Dworkin's paper examines the notion of paternalism and whether it is justified, and he applies some of his general ideas to specific aspects of income support policy.

Thomas Ault's paper, "Federal-State Relations and Income Support Policy," illuminates some central and politically controversial issues in the implementation of income support policy. These concern the relationship between federal and state governments, and particularly how the responsibility for pursuing welfare policy objectives is to be divided between the federal government and the states. For it is clearly not enough to decide, in the abstract, that some objective (say, providing well for the needy, and doing so in a way that satisfies the requirements of horizontal and vertical equity) ought to be pursued; we must also know how that objective and its various subordinate objectives are to be parceled out in our system of federal and state governments. (For example, Ault compares grant-in-aid and federal-entitlement approaches, and assesses their respective merits and disadvantages from the standpoints of administrative efficiency, adequacy, and the dangers of centralized authority, among others.) Indeed, the very nature of the objectives we ought to pursue, and whether they are mandatory or even desirable, may from the outset depend in significant part on how the responsibilities are apportioned among state and federal governments.

CJ

1

UTILITARIANISM AND WELFARE LEGISLATION

RICHARD B. BRANDT

Utilitarianism is a theory about what people morally ought to do and, hence, is at least indirectly about which laws and institutions (since people can affect them) are morally acceptable. I wish to focus on the implications of this theory for legislation on income distribution, primarily with respect to legislation to improve the lot of the economically deprived segments of society.

It may seem quixotic to suppose that reflection on utilitarianism can throw any light on how to resolve the baffling practical dilemmas which legislators and administrators face in trying to devise welfare programs which will meet diverse and seemingly conflicting objectives. But there is some theoretical interest in seeing how tax-welfare legislation fits into a utilitarian philosophy of government and society. And taking a broad view could have the practical effect of suggesting options which otherwise would not have been thought of, or of making the dilemmas seem less serious by placing them in perspective.

What is Utilitarianism?

The heart of utilitarianism has been its thesis about which acts are morally right: that the moral rightness of actions is fixed, somehow or other, by optimality of consequences. It has also been a theory about the conditions under which institutions are morally acceptable: Epicurus considered a law just if and only if it is a beneficial law; Jeremy Bentham made optimal consequences the standard for an acceptable system of criminal justice; and recent proposals of the American Law Institute are, similarly, very utilitarian in spirit. (The utilitarian need not say that an institution is morally unacceptable just because it is short of optimal; but he must say that it is morally unacceptable if, by utilitarian standards, it can be improved and if there is an unsatisfied moral obligation on those who can improve it to do so.)

Utilitarianism as a theory of right *action*—which seems to have appeared first in the work of Richard Cumberland around 1672—must be divided into two types. Some utilitarians, now called "act-utilitarians," think an act is right only if its net actual benefit or its expectable benefit[1], is as great as that of any other act the agent might perform. Other, historically earlier utilitarians, now called "rule-utilitarians," have argued that an act is right roughly if and only if it is of a kind which would have the best or best expectable consequences for a moral code to permit. For instance, rule-utilitarians think it is right to keep a certain kind of promise, even when it does more harm than good in the case at hand, because it would be required by the moral code it would have best consequences to have in force in the society. Some utilitarians saw the Ten Commandments or the requirements of conscience in this light, as laws laid down by God because he wanted the happiness of mankind and saw that promulgation of these laws would best achieve it.

But what is to count as the "benefit" or "good" that is to be maximized? Utilitarians disagree on this point. Until the present century, there was virtual unanimity among utilitarians that only one kind of consequence is a benefit or good in itself (further consequences aside), and that is happiness, enjoyment, or an experience which makes the subject want to continue or repeat it, for itself, at the time. There is frequent complaint that this conception of "good" or "benefit" is much too narrow; but many experiences are enjoyable in the stated sense—not only eating and sex, but running, playing chess, reading books, and solving problems. What do utilitarians who object to the happiness conception want to add? Some of them, occasionally called "ideal utilitarians," want to count as goods to be maximized just for themselves such benefits as knowledge, good character, and the distribution of happiness according to merit. One trouble with this is that each person must determine by his or her own intuition how much pleasure is just as good as how much knowledge or virtue. It has been seriously debated whether the benefits in enjoyment (etc.) that might result from successfully bribing a guard in a war-time prison camp could equal the loss in debasing the character of the guard by exposing him to temptation. In contrast, the happiness theory asserts that only one sort of thing is to be maximized, so that determining which course of action is optimal becomes a purely factual question, however great the problems of measurement and interpersonal comparisons may be. There is also the currently popular *desire* or *preference* theory which holds that some state of affairs is a good, or a benefit, in itself, just to the extent that someone *wants* it to obtain. This theory permits many things to be intrinsically good—pleasure, knowledge, art galleries, social and economic equality—but only in that someone wants them. Sometimes the following qualification is added: Something is good in itself only if somebody *would* want it to obtain *if* he had full information, clearly in mind, on what it would be like for that state of affairs to obtain. As with the happiness theory, this theory avoids reliance on intuitions and makes the determination of the optimal course of action a factual matter because, although there are serious problems in measuring and comparing intensity of desire, it is supposed that observation will determine the course of action that will maximize desire-satisfaction.

The happiness and the desire theories are not very far apart, since human psychology is such that we tend to want the recurrence of conditions we have enjoyed in the past, but they do differ to some extent. For simplicity I shall view the dispute as an in-house controversy, and view both as possible forms of utilitarian theory. I happen to prefer the currently unpopular happiness theory, and I shall think in terms of that theory rather than the desire or "ideal utilitarian" theory. For our purposes it makes little difference if I do that.

To understand utilitarianism as a general theory, it is important to identify the competing theories which it denies. When we look at these theories we begin to see that different general theories may well have different implications for tax-welfare legislation.

A feature which the competing theories have in common is that they assume there are factors, other than consequences for good or ill, which are relevant to the moral rightness of an action or institution. Some influential philosophers have thought that promises ought to be kept, the truth told, injuries recompensed by the responsible party, generous deeds gratefully recognized in some manner, and moral worth rewarded by a corresponding degree of happiness (by God if not by man), for no further reason whatsoever—and especially not because it would maximize welfare if these rules were followed. This view strikes a responsive chord in many people who think these things simply should be done, and do not think good consequences are the reason. More important for our interests are some similar principles which have been asserted with respect to property and income. John Locke, for instance, asserted that "every man has a 'property' in his own 'person.' This nobody has any right to but himself. The 'labor' of his body and the 'work' of his hands, we may say, are properly his. Whatsoever, then, he removes out of the state that Nature hath provided and left it in, he hath mixed his labor with it, and joined to it something that is his own, and thereby makes it his property . . . at least where there is enough, and as good left in common for others."[2] The exegesis and conceptual background of this affirmation are doubtless controversial, but it seems clear that Locke says one has an absolute right over one's own body (except that one may not contravene the natural law which, for example, prohibits suicide) and over one's labor. Probably he thought that if one invents something, one is free to keep it for one's self, regardless of how important it is to others that it be shared. This conception is doubtless widely held. Would the utilitarian agree with such an absolute moral right? He might, depending on his appraisal of the benefits of having such a rule in force. But he might not.

Another principle which reputable persons, including William Frankena and Nicholas Rescher, find persuasive is a requirement—distinct from *maximizing* welfare—to ensure some *equality* of welfare. In similar vein, A. K. Sen has criticized utilitarianism because that theory, as he sees it, provides that handicapped persons should receive less income than the normal person because income to a handicapped person will buy less happiness than it will for the normal person. Sen's intuitions are that a person who is handicapped at least should not be disadvantaged in income.[3]

Still others think that an industrious person's money income should be greater in order to reward his greater effort or industry (loafers should have less than those who work). Others have thought that superior talent or skill should have an economic reward (so the more intelligent should be more highly paid—if not college professors, at least intelligent persons in industry). Or some may think that a person's income should be greater if his output or contribution is greater for whatever reason; thus the rapid typist obviously deserves more income than the slowpoke. Most of these principles are not just darlings of philosophers but enjoy wide acceptance among people generally.

This is not the place to assess the merits of these alternative principles, although when we spell them out in detail and inquire exactly how they should be applied, it appears that there are problems for all of them, and the claim that these are obviously acceptable principles loses its appeal. The purpose of introducing these principles here is to illustrate what utilitarianism rejects as *basic* principles. Introducing them also serves to make clear the standing these principles can have as secondary rules in a utilitarian conception of the ideal social and economic order. We should emphasize that the utilitarian can accept these principles either as ones which should usually be followed or as principles which should be incorporated into the moral or legal code without qualification, since welfare would be maximized if they were. However this may be, if we accept utilitarianism as the *basic* theory from which these secondary principles can be derived, a major consequence follows: If one should question precisely how one of these rules is to be formulated or what its relative *weight* will be, the utilitarian has at hand a procedure that will provide an answer. The procedure is to determine exactly which principle or priority schedule would maximize social welfare, and then adopt that principle or priority schedule. Not that doing this is an easy matter, but at least the principle is clear: The rule and its relative force are fixed by the prospective benefits for all, provided the rule is recognized or in force.

This feature of utilitarianism is of special interest to some persons concerned with welfare legislation, because in their view, certain principles of "vertical" and "horizontal" equity are at least as weighty as are the principles mentioned above, in devising an acceptable welfare system. That is, it is felt that persons with the same need should receive the same degree of relief (horizontal equity), and that a person initially worse off should not receive so much relief that he is better off than the person who receives little or no help because he has a job and is working (vertical equity). These equity principles express intuitive moral preferences on the part of those concerned with welfare legislation.

But while both principles seem plausible, each has its drawback. With the first, it is complexity (should welfare allocations vary with the cost of living in different areas of the country, or in rural versus urban areas?). The drawback of the second is cost (to provide adequate help at the lower level while preserving vertical equity would require considerably increased payments at the upper levels, where it may not really be needed, and it would conflict with the principle of horizontal equity). I shall return later to this and related problems of conflicting priorities for the welfare system.

However, it is clear at once that, in principle, the utilitarian theory gives advice on how the weight of these principles is to be assessed. The first step is to inquire into the utility gain (and utility cost) of incorporating each of these principles into the system, *or* some specific compromise between them.[4] When that has been done, and we have estimates of the relative optimality of various systems, in terms of their probable degree of utility, we must ask a second question: whether some of these systems are morally required or are morally unacceptable. From the utilitarian point of view, this question is whether utility would be maximized by introducing and keeping in place a *moral* code which permitted, required, or prohibited some particular action on the part of persons in a position to influence the welfare system. Answering this second question is again not a simple matter, but it seems very unlikely that the *optimal* (utility-maximizing) welfare system would turn out to be morally objectionable, although it is just possible that the optimal moral code would place such weight on equity that the utility-maximizing *moral code* might not favor a *welfare system* that promised to be utility-maximizing. This sounds complicated, but so are the problems. At a later stage I shall suggest that these matters are in fact not overwhelmingly complex.

Utilitarianism and Rights

If utilitarianism is the thesis that maximally beneficial consequences are what directly or indirectly determine what conduct is morally right and what institutions are morally justified, one might still ask whether it is a thesis about moral *rights*, and if so, what the thesis is. This should be of interest to persons concerned about tax-welfare programs, since many people (and articles 22–27 of the United Nations *Universal Declaration of Human Rights*) affirm that all adults have a right to economic security, to equal pay for equal work, to remuneration sufficient to provide an existence worthy of human dignity, including a standard of living adequate to provide food, clothing, housing, and medical care, and so on.

The first thing to notice is that utilitarianism is not a metaethical theory about what it *is* for a person to have a right (what the term "moral right" means or should mean in clarified discourse); it is a normative theory about *which* rights people have. Utilitarians often say nothing at all about what it is to have a right; they take the concept of a "right" as something which is agreed on or argued over among philosophers whether or not they are utilitarians. The normative thesis of utilitarianism on rights is that the moral rights people have are roughly the ones whose incorporation into the moral code is maximally beneficial to society.

To see the relationship between the utilitarian thesis about rights and their general thesis, it is necessary to consider some metaethical theory about what it is to have a right. What I propose to do is outline the view of rights proposed by J. S. Mill in *Utilitarianism*—not exactly, but only roughly, since he confused some things, such as the concept of justice with the concept of a right. As modified, I think his view is substantially correct.

Consider the claim that X has a right to Y (e.g., to *do* something, enjoy something, be secured in having something). Mill does not mean that X has a right to Y merely because it would be *nice* or *beneficial* for X to do Y or enjoy Y. Rather, it is his view (widely held) that what it is for X to have a right to Y is for some person or persons to be *morally bound* or *obligated* not to interfere with his doing Y, but rather to make it possible for him to enjoy Y or be secure in having Y. One person's right thus coincides with a moral obligation on the part of others. And for Mill, what makes a person *morally bound* to do something is that this action is *required* in the sense that it is morally justified that he be punished either by law or public opinion, or, at least, by his conscience, if the action is not forthcoming. But this is not yet quite enough to establish a moral right, because people can sometimes be morally obligated to do something when there is no corresponding right. For example, a contribution to charity may be a moral obligation, but a potential recipient may not have a right to it—if the donor's obligation is only to do *something* charitable. When a person has a right, there is a moral obligation to do something specifically for *him*. So, for X to have a moral right to Y is for other people to be morally bound to do, or refrain from doing, something specifically for X. But, according to Mill, we do not say that a person has a right to something unless that person will be hurt or deprived—in an important way[5]—if the corresponding obligatory behavior is not forthcoming.[6] So Mill says that "rights" (or he should say this—in fact he says "justice") concern "certain classes of moral rules, which concern the essentials of human well-being more nearly, and are therefore of more absolute obligation, than any other rule for the guidance of life." To which he adds: "To have a right, then, is, I conceive, to have something which society[7] ought to defend me in possession of. If the objector goes on to ask, why it ought? I can give him no other reason than general utility." The last words of this sentence, of course, express his utilitarianism.

One might add or subtract a bit. One might suggest as an addition that when a person has a right, he essentially has the capacity to waive it (and hence to that degree can *control* how others treat him). That is, the right-holder has the power to release others from the obligation toward him that they otherwise would have. (This addition might be contested for some rights on the ground, say, that another's duty not to take away the life—at least where that would be an injury—of a person cannot be nullified by the person's consent to his doing so.) Or, one might add that whenever X has a right to Y, he need not feel embarrassed or ashamed about making a claim to Y in his own behalf.

If this account of a "right" is substantially correct, then we shall have to admit that X's right to Y may sometimes conflict with Z's to W, and hence we must make another distinction. We can avoid admitting the possibility of such a clash by saying that there is only one right—a very abstract right, to whatever the justified system of morality or law would secure one. Once we mention more specific rights, though, we are in for conflict, because the right to a certain level of economic welfare may well conflict with the right to procreate—at least the U. N. *Declaration* speaks of such a right. Or one person's right to privacy may conflict with another person's right to get evidence helpful to him in a criminal trial. Then how can a person have a right in the sense explained, when it is incompatible with a conflicting right which another person has? Most philosophers get around the difficulty by holding that most, or even all, rights are prima facie in the sense that they must sometimes give way to some more urgent moral claim or right. One could say that a person's right is absolute only in the specific situation where his right is *paramount*. Thus, when we say that a person has a right to freedom of speech, we ought not to claim that free speech must be secured to him unconditionally. What we may seriously claim is that securing it to him is a very high priority, but that there can be morally more weighty considerations which sometimes stand in the way. To have a right to Y is to enjoy very high moral priority on being secured in Y, but not necessarily to hold the highest priority in all situations. Mill did not make this distinction.

There are many such rights that society cannot sustain unconditionally. But what happens if a society cannot sustain a certain purported right at all? The U. N. *Declaration* says a person has a right "to a standard of living adequate for the health and well-being of himself and of his family, including food, clothing, housing and medical care and necessary social services, and the right to security in the event of unemployment, . . . old age," and so on.

But what about India, which may be simply unable to provide these things, even with indefinite sacrifice on the part of the better-off? Then, if we agree with Kant that "ought" implies "can," where something is impossible it is not morally obligatory; and if it is not morally obligatory, then by our conception there is no right. This thinking may lead us to conclude that the U. N. *Declaration* was a bit profligate in its list of rights. But should we think this way? Maybe what is a right is not a matter of what the individual's own government can provide. Perhaps it is enough if a world government could provide it. Of course, there isn't a world government. So perhaps what is meant is that if all persons were to do what they perfectly well can do—namely, get together in a united effort—then it could be done. It appears that there is vagueness here and that to have a clear concept of "a right" we need to make up our minds what we want to say, what kind of claim we want to make.[8]

The implications of utilitarianism for rights should now be clear, for utilitarianism is a proposal about what people are morally bound to do, and what people are morally bound to do is *logically* tied to what people's rights are. So, for the utilitarian, a person's moral rights are roughly what would be secured for him by the justified moral code (or morally justified law) of his country (or the world, or whatever); and what is to be secured for him is fixed by the probable social benefits of getting and keeping that moral and legal code in place.

Welfare Rights, Tax Rates, and Utilitarianism

One might suppose that on grounds of maximizing utility, a utilitarian would straightaway advocate a moral system requiring income-transfers from the rich to the poor to the point where the marginal utility of the income of everyone would be the same, and that such transfers would be the *right*, or at least the prima facie right, of the less well off. Historically this has certainly not been the case—and, as we shall see, for good reason.

Mill took some steps in the direction of what might seem the thorough-going utilitarian stance, for he thought taxes should be levied on the principle of "least sacrifice."[9] Nevertheless, although he conceded that the marginal utility of income continues to decline no matter how large that income, he could not bring himself to support a graduated tax rate, since the marginal utility of income is not "capable of being decided with the degree of certainty on which a legislator or a financier ought to act."[10] Moreover, seeming to backslide to a nonutilitarian principle, he says that "to tax the larger incomes at a higher percentage than the smaller is to lay a tax on industry and economy; to impose a penalty on people for having worked harder and saved more than their neighbors."[11] He agreed that some disparities of income derive from unequal initial opportunities, but thought that if the government does what it can to eliminate these, no one can take offense at large differences in earnings. (He did, however, favor steep inheritance taxes, since the beneficiary has not earned his advantage.) Mill's utilitarian concession to the declining marginal utility of income was to advocate a personal exemption from taxation, but a small one: "sufficient to provide the number of persons ordinarily supported from a single income with the requisites of life and health, and with protection against habitual bodily suffering, but not with any indulgence." Doubtless he would have approved the present exemption in the U. S. tax plan. As for actual welfare grants for the unemployed or unemployable, although Mill *wrote*[12] that "Since no one is responsible for having been born [hardly a utilitarian consideration!], no pecuniary sacrifice is too great to be made by those who have more than enough, for the purpose of securing enough to all persons already in existence," nevertheless he thought that such grants should be made unpleasant, lest there be a disastrous increase in the birth-rate among the poor, with a consequent over-supply of labor and further reduction of wage-rates. Indeed, Mill did not object to confining the poor to workhouses, where indeed he thought all sexual activity should be prohibited on the ground that it would only breed more paupers. Mill's view of population growth and the relation of wage-rates to population size led him to think that grants to the poor, except when made unpleasant to the recipient, would in the long run do more harm than good. Mill evidently would have said that the poor have a right only to be kept uncomfortably alive, although free from pain. Henry Sidgwick, the most careful and systematic of the utilitarians, writing a quarter-century later, was not very different.[13]

Mill and Sidgwick read as if they are in the distant past: in an era with no labor unions and with a rather simple-minded economic theory, before the lesson of the 1930s that unemployment is not a function merely of lack of industry, and before a time when people began to live with a graduated income tax and became convinced it was at least a necessary evil. If we move them into the present, keeping their basic assumption that morality, law, and economic and political institutions are to be tested by their contribution to welfare, where will they come out?

The first question I want to raise is what level of income support, for the working poor, the unemployable, and the involuntarily unemployed, can be said to be a moral *right*, prima facie or otherwise? Mill and Sidgwick evidently set this level very low, Sidgwick wanting government to mitigate "the harshest inequalities in the present distribution of incomes,"[14] but evidently not to do more. What level of income, then, from a consistent utilitarian point of view, is a moral right at present?

It is convenient to make the simplifying assumption that there soon will no longer be serious dispute that this country should have universal medical service. Such service will incidentally remove one of the most inequitable "notch"[15] problems of the present welfare system. So, medical care aside, what about level of income?

It is widely agreed among economists that—*other things being equal*, which they are not—the most efficient (utility-productive) division of the national income would be one which made the marginal utility of all incomes equal. Equality of marginal utility is hardly an identifiable target, however, in view of the general unreliability of our comparative judgments about the utility curves of individuals. But it was shown some years ago by A. P. Lerner and others that, given *ignorance* of individual utility curves, the most utility-productive way to distribute money income is *probably* to distribute it equally, again *other things being equal*.

But other things are not equal: A system providing exactly equal money incomes would be counterproductive, not only because there are *some* persons (such as the ill and the handicapped) about whom we know (that much is known about some utility curves) that a more than equal income is required to bring their marginal utility up to that of the normal person, but also because, more importantly, we know that inequality of income is necessary both to provide work incentives and to channel the supply of labor into the places where it is needed.

The utilitarian thus has a complicated question for the economist, which he will want answered so a decision can be made about which income-welfare system is optional. The question for an ideally omniscient economist is how income would be distributed in the total population on the basis of various tax-and-welfare schemes, or, more broadly if you like, on the basis of economic systems including tax-and-welfare schemes (with different proportions of total national income allocated for the welfare system, with different degrees of progressivity, different exemptions, different schemes of welfare allocation, and, especially, different levels of tax credits combined with work requirements). If the answer is provided, the utilitarian will then try to estimate what level of total social welfare would go along with these various schemes—given that he has been told how many will get how much, for each scheme. In making this judgment of welfare, he will be helped by information about the cost of a modest but adequate diet (some clue to which is given by how much the average person spends on food), since the disutility of inadequate nutrition is so manifest that an income which secures a reasonable diet will be deemed the bread, which is more important than a great deal of cake for the better off. Having identified the scheme that will produce the greatest social welfare, he can declare that that scheme of distribution—with its proposals for the shares of the jobless, the handicapped, the unskilled worker, and so on—is, on the evidence, *optimal*.[16]

Is anything less than the optimal system of distribution *morally unacceptable?* To show that it is, the utilitarian must show that the utility-maximizing moral code would *require* the expectable-welfare-maximizing distribution system. One might ask whether an optimal moral code would contain *any* requirement about the *distribution* of goods. Obviously our actual moral code does, since it contains injunctions about treating members of one's family equally, and it contains (I think) an injunction that one relieve the distress of others when this can be done at little cost to one's self. I think myself that an optimal moral code would contain a general injunction to do what one can to bring about an optimal distribution,[17] but this could be debated. Let us assume, for the moment, that an optimal moral code would require effort to approximate to an optimal system of distribution of economic goods.

The question still remains whether everyone has a *moral right* to the share he would get according to the optimal scheme of distribution. For an answer, we can look back to the conception of a "moral right" which I sketched roughly along the lines of Mill's view. According to that theory, if we have shown that it is *morally required* to secure something for a person in a given society, we have already taken the first step in showing that the individual has a moral right to that thing. The second condition is that there must be an obligation to do something specific for a specific person. This second condition is obviously also met, since the welfare-maximizing system would identify all those individuals in a class to whom a certain income is due, and every one of them should be secured in it. So each specific person is identified, as a proper target for the distribution.

The third condition is that the recipient will be "hurt" or "deprived" if the donor has not done for him what ought to be done. Here again the condition appears to be met, for I suppose any loss of income—except to an already wealthy person—beyond what he might otherwise have had would count as a "deprivation." Finally, would the deprivation be "important"? Or is it something one should not feel ashamed about making a claim to? Here the answer seems to be: It depends on the disparity between the ideal and what one is actually getting, and how poorly off one is. We can probably agree that how much income one gets, at the bottom end, is pretty important. So it looks as if, given that the optimal distribution of income is morally required, we should opt for the view that the income one would get by application of the optimal system is at least normally one's moral right.

Is such an income a right, everything considered, or only a prima facie right? There is no reason why it should not be said to be only prima facie, since to say this is only to say that it must stand aside if more morally urgent considerations require it. I have already suggested that following the economically optimal plan might not be morally required, all things considered, in view of possible unfavorable effects of the system on freedom. If there were an atomic war, it is believable that the right to the optimal distribution must stand aside. It is conceivable that there might be some conflict between this right and the means necessary to end racial discrimination. And so on. So let us conclude that the right to a utility-maximizing level of income is prima facie only.

Utilitarianism and Some Details

At the outset I expressed some doubt whether reflection on utilitarianism would throw much light on the practical problems which baffle persons working on welfare legislation. But a clear, simple, conceptual framework like the utilitarian theory will have definite implications for these matters if any moral theory at all will do so. So let us look at some implications, encouraged by the thought that it is at least in the tradition of Plato for philosophers to make proposals about how practical affairs should be managed.

We shall use three simplifying assumptions as a framework within which to conduct our thinking. I shall not attempt to justify them (and the required justification would be different in each case), but I believe readers will be willing to grant them. The first is that we should think in terms of some program of universal medical service, since this would enable us to avoid some problems about who is to be entitled to "medicaid" and at what cost. Second, we must think in terms of a tax system in which "loopholes" have been removed. We do have a concept of income that is disposable for living, as distinct from expenses involved in obtaining that income. Deductions might be limited to legitimate business expenses, court-ordered child support, alimony, perhaps uninsured loss such as from fire or theft, and perhaps, in the public interest, charitable contributions. Third, I am supposing that somehow we can manage not to think about more than one tax-welfare system, specifically not about state-local taxes and welfare grants. I am supposing that, at least for our purposes, all this can be amalgamated.

There is also a further assumption, of a somewhat different kind, that we could make: Unless and until more scientific evidence to the contrary arrives, there is no reason grounded in utility for the tax-welfare system to treat males and females differently. Sex alone is not a reason for different treatment. If jobs outside the home are psychologically desirable for men, they are equally so for women; if a single male parent is expected, on grounds of public and personal benefit, to work as a condition for obtaining welfare assistance, a single female parent should equally be expected to work. It is conceivable that there are some physiological or psychological differences that make it utility-productive to treat the sexes differently, but as of the present no important differences are known (except that men cannot qualify for a pregnancy leave-of-absence). A tendency toward aggressiveness and superior ability at spatial visualization seem to be sex-linked, but these features are hardly relevant to the construction of a tax-welfare system.

Within the framework of these assumptions, what would be the main features of a tax-welfare system on which a utilitarian would insist?

(1.) The first thing is a guaranteed job for every adult who wants to work and will perform diligently in it. (If this is economically infeasible, at least a guaranteed job for everyone who would otherwise qualify for welfare payments.) To each job, of course, will be attached the income which the market provides, with whatever minimum wage restriction the optimal economic system (discussed above) would call for. It seems clear that in normal times a program of guaranteed jobs will involve some government-provided or government-subsidized jobs, and it is also clear that, in order to motivate persons to move to the private sector when possible, these jobs must pay less than the minimum wage in the private sector. A related desideratum is that, since it will optimize performance to have the best-qualified persons in the more demanding jobs, discrimination of all sorts—and especially on the basis of race, age, and sex—should be removed from the labor market (and the unions), and information and assistance should be given to facilitate placing persons in jobs where they can be used most effectively. Furthermore, there should be a training program available, so that all individuals can be prepared to perform useful work.

(2.) Before discussing the reasons for this requirement, let us look at its complement: a requirement that all able-bodied adults be *required* to work as a condition of receiving more than a subsistence income from welfare programs. Then the total income of members of an economic unit could be considered in reckoning whether, and how much, welfare assistance the economic unit is entitled to.[18]

There are several reasons for these proposals. The first is the extreme importance of a job for the psychological health and optimal development of every man and woman. We may concede that some jobs do not contribute much to psychological health or development, and one aim should be to make all jobs as meaningful (i.e., as challenging and interesting) as possible. It may be said that this is a good reason for making jobs available but not for making them a condition of qualifying for maximum support in a welfare program. It is true that there is a certain element of paternalism in the work requirement, in the thought that whereas a person might not take a job if he didn't need it for the income, he'd be better off if he did and later be glad that he had. But there is another reason, sufficient by itself: We cannot afford to provide modestly good incomes for the underprivileged without a work requirement (there are, probably, just too many who would elect to go fishing). The nation is economically able to provide a merely subsistence income for all who are prepared to live on that income in return for the privilege of leisure.

(3.) Over and above the job program there should be provision for a

subsistence level of support for persons able, but unwilling, to work; and for those who meet the work requirement or those who are unable to do so for reasons of health, disability, or age, there would be a supplemental assistance program, up to the level of the "optimal" income-distribution system discussed above. Such a program could be administered by the Internal Revenue Service through a negative income tax. The program would require some changes from the present arrangements, because, for instance, these supplemental assistance payments presumably would be made at least once a month, with only a final settlement at the end of the year. There would also have to be some job insurance program to provide temporary relief for unemployment. The negative income "tax" schedule would be so set as to make up the difference between the total work income of an economic unit and the level set by the optimal income system, whatever that might be. (The system, we should note, would provide work or assistance for single persons and childless married couples.) In this program, food stamps would disappear.

Since the above payments have to be covered by someone, income tax rates would go up, beginning at the point at which, on the optimal system, assistance payments would cease. But they would not go up in such a way as to remove incentive for performing well in one's job, for preparing one's self to move into more demanding jobs, or for moving into jobs where consumer demand calls for more personnel. We can hardly keep higher tax rates from having some effect on incentive—our present tax system already removes some incentive—but the tax would not remove incentives to a serious degree.

Let us look now at two problems of "equity" which currently concern persons working in the welfare program.

HORIZONTAL EQUITY

We have seen that a utilitarian is not concerned with matters of fairness or equity, as such, including horizontal equity in the sense of functionally equal support for similar situations. But he is interested in what comes to the same thing under a different description—in welfare-maximizing regulations, or "best buys." Thus he will advocate, as far as feasible, local variations in supplemental assistance payments based on the relative cost-of-living figures: Otherwise persons in low-cost communities will be funded for luxuries (less preferred items) which persons in high-cost communities cannot afford, so that the real benefit from the total expenditure would be less than it would otherwise be. (It might be argued, however, that it is a consumer good to live in a high-cost community, and that a system of equal payments leaves the individual the option of moving to a low-cost community if his preferences are to spend his income for other things than living in a certain place. Whether local variations in supplemental assistance payments will really optimize welfare, especially when administrative complexities are taken into account, is a matter for further research.)

Again, the utilitarian will advocate larger payments to the blind and handicapped, on the ground that enough is known of their utility curves (as compared with those of the average person) to make clear that an additional sum is needed for the marginal utility of their incomes to be equal to that of the average person receiving supplemental assistance. Further, the utilitarian will urge that payments be adjusted for the composition of the economic unit: say, a sizeable basic amount for up to two adults in the unit; a smaller sum for other adults in the same unit (but not so small as to make it worth their while to move into a separate unit); smaller sums for children, perhaps along the line of the Griffiths plan, declining after two (in the hope of discouraging persons from enlarging the family just to increase welfare payments—a practice which brings essentially unwanted children into the world). Obviously money is more efficiently expended in this way. If payments to economic units were equal, small families would be able to buy more luxury-type items whereas larger families would have to forego necessities.

VERTICAL EQUITY

The principle of vertical equity that appeals to persons concerned with welfare legislation is that welfare payments should not put a welfare family financially ahead of a nonwelfare family, and that they should not "unduly compress" the initial distance between the units. We need not here consider whether a utilitarian could or should support some utilitarian analog of the principle of vertical equity, because, apparently, the principle can in any case not be infringed by the utilitarian system of tax-welfare described so far.

There are three main points at which the principle is infringed under the present system. First, a family that barely qualifies for welfare support receives full rights to Medicaid, whereas a family that barely fails to qualify receives no Medicaid at all. Second, a family that barely qualifies receives child-care assistance, where one that barely fails to qualify does not. Finally, the schedule of assistance for those who qualify for welfare payments may place them financially ahead of those who wholly depend on wage income and barely do not qualify for welfare support. It is obvious that with a plan for universal medical service and for universal child care (or a system approximating this), the first two inequities would not occur. Moreover, a work-requirement would eliminate the third inequity; if a person does not work he will receive only a subsistence allotment, which will surely not place him ahead of those who do work. There will, of course, remain many inequalities; some people will be in interesting, high-paying jobs, for one reason or another. A utilitarian system will in effect reduce such disparities because of the high taxes on those who are well paid, but the utilitarian is not aiming to remove all inequalities in life. Perhaps he should; but if he should, then utilitarianism is to that extent a defective theory. The utilitarian will probably offer a practical defense of his position, against those sensitive to natural inequalities and other inequalities that arise out of them, by arguing that there is only so much a system of tax-welfare can be expected to do.

The principal question raised against such a system as I have sketched is whether it is not hopelessly expensive. The answer is no, since the welfare level at which negative income tax would begin is to be set at a point where the cost is not impossible. It is true that people in the upper income, even middle income, brackets would pay more taxes than they now do. They would not, however, pay so much tax that incentives would be significantly reduced. The level, as explained earlier, would be set at an optimal point, where the production of goods and services, taken with the distribution system, would leave total social *welfare* at a maximum. Those in higher income brackets may not rejoice at the prospect of higher taxes, but there are surely many who would happily give up something for the knowledge that no one in their society was in serious need. There is a question whether the provision of jobs on the scale suggested above is possible without significant changes in the economic organization of society; to the best of my knowledge, no one has yet proved that the provision of jobs would entail a revamped economy.

Changes in the welfare-support system in the United States in the past ten years, and the bills that have recently been presented to the Congress, suggest that the U. S. welfare system is moving slowly but steadily in the direction of the simple conception outlined above, although the system is certainly not here yet. The welfare support available varies greatly from one state to another; there is a complex system of different federal programs (Food Stamps, Medicaid, supplemental assistance to the disabled, etc.); there is a job program and the aim of encouraging work by training programs and by the schedule of welfare payments, but no work requirement; there are vertical inequities; and so on.

Is there anything the utilitarian can say about desirable changes in the system, and particularly about the assignment of priorities to the various objectives? He can say several things, although all of them are simply applications of the principle that the system should be changed in such a way as to maximize expectable welfare. The first is to increase the level of welfare benefits; welfare will be improved if the gap between the better-off and the worse-off is narrowed—and if this can be done without seriously disturbing incentives. Eligibility for assistance should be extended to all those who are willing to work but cannot find a job. It would be an obvious benefit to amalgamate state and federal programs and make the system uniform; but it is not obvious how to do so. It is not clear how to avoid the cost in utility of vertical inequities in the present system, which attempts to combine adequate support levels, incentive to work (by permitting supported individuals to keep most of their earnings even when so doing brings them above the poverty line), and no universal medical service. The cost is not vast, and the utilitarian will not worry about the inequity per se. But the problem is a good reason to change to a different system which does not have the problems.

Notes

1. The expectable net benefit is the sum of products of the utility of each consequence multiplied by its probability if the act is performed.

2. *Two Treatises of Government*, first published 1690. Second Treatise, Chap. 5, Sect. 26.

3. A. K. Sen, *On Economic Inequality*, 1973.

4. Variations in the degree to which these principles are incorporated into the system will have an impact on other objectives, such as administrative simplicity and maintenance of work incentives; thus the total impact of possible systems on the general utility will require comparing all these associated costs and benefits, but the procedure is at least clear in principle and does not rely on subjective intuitions about moral principles.

5. The requirement of importance may hold for all rights in society, civil or political; it is not so obvious that there are *no* rights which concern fairly trivial matters (for example, the right of the child to equal treatment from his parents) in some particular.

6. Suppose A has contracted with B to provide care for C, an elderly relative of B. Then we say that B has a right against A, that C be cared for. But, it might be asked, if C is the person who is harmed or deprived if the care is not forthcoming, ought we not to say that C is the right-holder? The correct answer for Mill to make, it would seem, is that B must be construed to be harmed by the failure to care for C; if it were not important to B that C be cared for, presumably he would not have paid A to provide care for C.

7. In some cases (such as the rights of a child in the family), there seem to be rights with which society should not concern itself, at least in the sense of providing legal protection. Perhaps Mill meant that society should concern itself with them only in seeing to it that sanctions are provided by public opinion or by conscience.

8. The last five sentences of the above paragraph arose out of conversation with Allan Gibbard.

9. J. S. Mill, *Principles of Political Economy*, 1848, p. 807.

10. *Ibid.*

11. *Ibid.*, p. 808.

12. *Ibid.*, p. 363.

13. Henry Sidgwick, *Principles of Political Economy*, 1883; *The Elements of Politics*, 1891. Both books had later editions.

14. *Elements of Politics*, p. 160.

15. This is the problem of vertical equity; see below.

16. I have discussed how such estimates may be made more fully in *A Theory of the Good and the Right*, 1979, chap. 16.

17. I have argued for this in the chapter referred to in the previous footnote.

18. Given this requirement, the question of child care arises. One possible solution is to make child care universally available, like medical service. This solution appears to be the only one which fully avoids problems of "vertical equity" (see below). Another possibility is that, if the government is prepared to pay a certain per-child sum for care (for, say, forty hours per week), this sum might be paid to any parent who prefers to provide care for his or her own children in place of taking a full-time job. On the other hand, having children is a consumer good, and an expensive one for somebody, and hence the parents should be prepared to shoulder part of the cost of child care in return for the benefits. (If they do not think there are benefits, they do not need to have the children.) Nor should they expect welfare support for an indefinite number of children (see below).

2

A Libertarian Perspective on Welfare

GEOFFREY BRENNAN
and DAVID FRIEDMAN

Introduction

In this paper, we attempt to articulate, and in some measure defend, a libertarian theory of income redistribution—of "welfare," in common parlance. The choice of the indefinite article here is crucial: It is by no means clear that all self-styled libertarians would agree with all the steps in our discussion—nor perhaps with the tentativeness of our conclusions. But we have, in large measure, been faithful to the spirit of mainstream libertarian thought as we see it in developing our argument. In this sense, what we offer *is* fairly described as a *"libertarian* theory."

The theory has three strands:

1. A position on the question of basic moral entitlements—that is, on what individuals should be recognized to "own";
2. A theory of what sorts of "gratuitous transfers" are desirable, given an initial definition of rights;
3. A theory of centralized as distinct from decentralized decision-processes (loosely, of political as opposed to market processes).

Each of these strands is an integral part of the fabric. Some natural-rights theorists would no doubt be content with the first strand—with the straight assertion that individuals have a moral right not to have their property transferred to others, however "deserving" the beneficiaries—and seek to dismiss welfare on such grounds. We do not do so for three reasons: first, because one of the historical foundations of the libertarian position is utilitarianism, and some, although probably not most, libertarians hold their libertarian position at least in part for utilitarian reasons;

second, because even natural-rights libertarians are more comfortable with their position if they believe that a "just" society is also, in a utilitarian sense, an attractive one; and third, because we believe that any defense of the libertarian position addressed to non-libertarians must make some concessions to the moral intuitions of its audience. We are thus prepared both to explain the libertarian stance from a "natural rights" perspective and to defend it from a utilitarian position, while recognizing that many libertarians would reject such a defense as unnecessary.

In what follows, we develop each strand in sequence and then discuss briefly some common criticisms of welfare familiar from the economics literature. The last section gives a brief summary and statement of conclusions.

The Libertarian Theory of Moral Entitlements

The point of departure for the libertarian is a theory (or perhaps a statement) of moral entitlements, both personal and proprietorial. The personal dimension springs naturally out of an individualistic view of humanity: Each individual is recognized to have an identity separate from others, and to have a "natural" freedom to *think* and to *act* when in isolation from those others. These freedoms are so natural that it may seem pointless to defend them on moral grounds. However, if we *imagine* their being violated, it seems intuitively clear that some moral harm would be done; on that basis, we might say that the right to think and, within a setting of total isolation, to act *are* moral entitlements. And it seems a relatively weak extension of this notion to assert that this latter entitlement also covers the case in which an individual acts so as to do no moral harm to another even though he does not act in total isolation.

Suppose we accept the moral entitlement of a man to himself in this sense, what follows? First, the right to "ownership" of oneself involves—must involve—the right not only to possess, but also the right to *use*, within the constraints set by the requirement that no one else is harmed. Within that bound at least, the right to the fruit of one's own labor is a natural consequence: Whatever one can produce *on one's own* one has a moral entitlement to. In a world with complex cooperative enterprise, this entitlement may not seem to take one very far—but it will, provided that the right of possession and use is extended to include the right of *alienation*. For once we allow the possibility that the individual may trade that which he has a right to (in this case his labor) for other things, provided only that any such "trades" are truly voluntary, then we also allow the prospect of complex cooperative production activities, in which each party has a legitimate right to that part of the output agreed to as the condition for his cooperation. If this is accepted, then it follows that the individual also has a right to that which he "purchases" with his income—including any accumulation of capital out of labor income. In this way, the notion that each individual has a moral entitlement to the fruit of his own labor, broadly defined, can be extrapolated as a natural moral consequence of his individuality.

To put the argument somewhat differently, the libertarian does not consider the world as a place in which bread falls from heaven, where the proper moral problem is one of dividing it, but as a place where individuals produce things of value—bake bread—and where each such thing thus appears not as common property, but as the property of a particular individual. The fundamental moral injunction is against harming the property (including the person) of another. Since individuals do not have property rights in other individuals, or in their relation with other individuals (absent explicit and voluntary contracts giving them such rights), the right not to be subject to aggression is not equivalent to the right not to be made worse off. A competitor, while he may lower the value of your property, does not "harm" it; indeed, he does not affect it at all. What he affects is your opportunity to sell it to someone else—and that opportunity is *not* itself property. Hence one can make a fairly sharp distinction between the aggressor, who injures you by violating your rights, and the non-aggressor, who "injures" you in the sense of making you worse off than if he did not exist, but does so only by affecting the way in which other individuals choose to use their property (for instance, by offering a competitive product at a lower price).

The derivation of moral entitlements to land and other natural assets is more strained. Richard Epstein has recently[1] attempted to derive such rights on the basis of the rule "first possession is the root of title," though his defense of that rule is ultimately consequential rather than via direct appeal to moral notions of ownership. John Locke avoids the problem essentially by assuming that, ab initio, such property is in excess supply, and no problems of ownership arise. For example, if land acquires value solely by the application of labor to improve it, and the supply of virgin scrub is initially limitless, then the issue of land ownership[2] can be partly, if not entirely, fudged. A more sophisticated version of this argument involves what Robert Nozick has called the "Lockean Proviso." If the alternative to private appropriation is that land be unowned, then I can be said to have injured you by appropriating the land only if my appropriation makes you worse off than if the land remained unowned. Since the institution of private property greatly increases the total productivity of the society, people will normally be better off than if all land remained unowned; according to Nozick's interpretation of Locke, land titles are conditional on this being the case. Thus, during a drought, a natural spring on private property may cease to be entirely private (since in the absence of privatization the spring would have been available to all), while a dug well does not (since if the land had remained common the well would never have been dug). It is important to realize that if the derivation of moral entitlements to one's own person is to be of much practical relevance, *some* "private" possession of land is crucial. If land is held collectively and if land is necessary for all production, then no purely bilateral contracts between parties for the purposes of production can be made without violating someone else's rights (i.e., the ownership rights of the other holders of the land). Only consensual contracts relating to the use of the land are legitimate.[3] For purely practical reasons, such consensual contracts are extremely difficult if not impossible to secure, so that appeal to them must whenever possible be avoided if the moral entitlements derived from personhood are to have much real value.

It should be noted that the failure of libertarian moral theorists to produce a completely satisfactory theory of ownership of land, while it implies uncertainty as to the exact status of property rights in land, does not in any way imply that the land belongs to "the people," "the state," or any other alternative claimant. To all such assertions the libertarian will reply that if the land was not produced by the individual, neither was it produced by the collectivity; the original individual claimant at least did *something* to create the value of the land (clearing scrub, for instance); the collective claimant did nothing at all. Insofar as the absence of a libertarian justification for ownership of land suggests anything, it is that land is unowned. It is this concept, that everyone has an equal right to use the land and that no one has the right to prevent others from using it, with which the Lockean Proviso, as described by Nozick, appears to deal.

One further point about this problem is its practical unimportance, at least in developed countries. As one of the authors has shown, total income from unproduced resources in the United States totals only a few percent of national income.[4] Hence the details of just how one acquires legitimate ownership of such property have only a small effect on the actual outcome.

Moral entitlements imply a set of moral obligations to recognize those entitlements on the part of all individuals. The obverse is not true. There exist "oughts" which do not imply, or derive from, moral entitlements. One ought not to lie, for example, but not because others have a right not to be lied to. One ought to be compassionate, but not because others have a right to compassion. In this sense, the libertarian position on moral entitlements does not purport to be complete—it is consistent with many different normative positions on questions which the theory of moral entitlements does not cover.

In a sense, the libertarian regards his obligation not to violate the rights of others as an obligation he owes to *them*, as distinguished from other sorts of "oughts" which are obligations that he owes to *himself*. Hence the violation of rights, to the libertarian, takes on a primacy among sins: If an act violates another's *rights*, it is morally reprehensible, whatever the desirability of the outcome. Consequences are secondary: Theft is theft, and hence wrong, even if the proceeds are used to endow a hospital or feed the poor. On this basis, Nozick describes these rights as "side constraints": The libertarian, whatever else his moral values, is contrained to act—if he seeks to act morally—so as not to violate any individual's moral entitlements.

It is important to emphasize at this point that the libertarian position is *not* equivalent to saying that one should act so as to minimize the total amount of rights violation that occurs. To steal a gun worth one hundred dollars is a violation of the owner's moral entitlements, and hence illegitimate, even if the thief's possession of the gun prevents a second thief from stealing two hundred dollars from the first thief. Nor does one have a moral *entitlement* to be protected by third parties from violations of one's rights by second parties. If A sees B stealing something from C, A may, or may not, be viewed as having a moral obligation to attempt to prevent B from violating C's rights—the libertarian position is silent on this. What is clear is that any such moral obligation (if indeed it is one) is, for the libertarian, qualitatively different from and less binding than B's obligation not to steal from C, or A's not to steal from either. In the context of welfare, this means that welfare payments, if they violate the legitimate rights of the taxpayers, cannot be legitimized by showing that the poor need the money in order to defend themselves against coercion by, say, private criminals.

Finally, it should be clear that the libertarian theory of moral entitlements is in no sense a theory based on "deserts." The rich do not have a moral entitlement to their larger incomes because they "*deserve*" more— any more than a beautiful woman has a moral right to the advantages of beauty because she *deserves* to be beautiful. The moral entitlement that the libertarian recognizes issues from the *legitimacy* of the possession, not from its "justice." In this sense, libertarianism is, in Nozick's terms, an entitlement ethic, not an "end-state" ethic. Consider a simple example. Suppose A and B agree to toss a coin to determine who should pay the other fifty dollars. It seems clear that, whatever the outcome, the winner is not entitled to his winnings because he *deserved* to win, any more than the loser deserved to lose. The winner is entitled to his winnings because he obtained them in a morally legitimate fashion—in this case, via a voluntary gamble. In much the same way, there is no presumption in libertarian theory that the poor are poor because they *deserve* to be: They may be seen as victims of bad fortune, bad health, low quality environment, or whatever; they may indeed be seen to be extremely deserving. But desert is inadequate justification for theft, and while violation of another's rights may deserve less condemnation if the violator is deserving and needy than under other circumstances, the poor do not acquire a moral *entitlement* to violate others' rights by virtue of how deserving they are.

All the foregoing discussion relates, of course, solely to the world of moral discourse. In order to translate that theory of *moral entitlements* into a *normative theory of legal entitlements*—that is, in order to go from the question of what individuals have a *moral* right to, to the question of what individuals *ought* to have a *legal* right to—requires an extra step, which libertarians generally have been reluctant to provide. This step is the provision of a purely positive theory of legal processes—a set of statements about how legal institutions operate and specifically about the extent to which the outcomes of legal processes are likely to be congruent with morally derived rules. It is clear, for example, that to the extent that legal outcomes are substantially arbitrary, or that the judiciary is corrupt or self-seeking in some other way, there may be limits on the extent to which one can expect moral entitlements and obligations to be enforced. Not all morally desirable acts ought rationally to be legislated: only those which one can expect the courts to enforce in a reasonably clear and even-handed way. One can conceive that, along such lines, a libertarian theory of legal entitlements might be devised which does not depend at all on the *moral primacy* of obligations not to violate others' rights, but rather on the judgment that these obligations are more amenable to legal embodiment than other moral obligations which are vague, subjective, or liable to distortion by legal processes. Traditionally this has not been the libertarian approach; the normative theory of legal entitlements has been derived more or less directly from libertarian beliefs on moral entitlements.

The foregoing discussion attempts to explicate the libertarian theory of rights. Three sorts of "defenses" of this theory can be mounted. The first—hardly a defense at all—depends on the self-evident nature of the moral truths propounded. The theory is seen as an attempt to articulate moral intuitions and is successful to the extent that it accords with the intuitive moral notions of the reader. The "natural rights" libertarians are essentially of this school: Nozick and Locke are examples.

The second is a rule-utilitarian defense. The libertarian position on legal rights is here justified on the grounds that is maximizes the possibilities for contract and hence makes available gains from trade that would otherwise be precluded. Here, the question at issue is not so much (if at all) one of moral entitlements, but rather one of how to define the bundle of rights so that transactions costs are minimized. With all rights well defined and assigned to individuals, a complex set of bilateral exchanges emerges, generating outcomes under which gains from trade are maximized— "optimal outcomes," in the terminology of mainstream economics. Variations on this defense are conceivable. One currently influential variant is to imagine individuals choosing among alternative definitions of rights, in ignorance of the identity of those to whom the rights so defined will accrue. If each individual chooses on the assumption that he is equally likely to "be" any of the different individuals in the society, this construction is equivalent to maximizing utility in the Von Neumann-Morgenstern sense. To the extent that those individuals seek to maximize expected returns, they will choose that set of rights which minimizes transactions costs; and to the extent one expects individuals to act in this way, the libertarian set of property rights could be justified on the basis of "constitutional consensus." More generally, utilitarian arguments of the sort discussed below can be combined with such an approach to justify libertarian conclusions. This sort of construction can, however, also be used to suggest *non-libertarian* legal rights, as it has been by Rawls, and would therefore be regarded by many libertarians as extremely hazardous.

A third sort of defense would likewise justify the libertarian set of property rights on the grounds of minimal transactions cost and (hence) of maximum choice, but would do so not because of standard economic efficiency notions but rather because of a desire to maximize individual freedom of choice per se. The Hayekian view seems closest to being of this type, although his defense of freedom of choice is in turn based on the judgment that from the unfettered "chaos" of individual choices, desirable social institutions and general human progress will and do emerge.

Libertarian Conception of Welfare Payments

Whatever the line of argument used to defend the libertarian position, it is clear that the position itself does not admit the moral *entitlement* of the claims of (potential) welfare recipients to the property of others. The first-line response to the question "What welfare receipts are legitimate within a libertarian theory?" is the single, simple answer: none! The legitimate role of government within the libertarian theory is at most the minimal one of protecting individuals' moral entitlements from both internal and external aggression and enforcing contracts entered into voluntarily. Since welfare recipients do not have rights to welfare, no redistributive activity through the agency of government can be justified.

It is, however, clear that there is nothing in the libertarian position which rules out the possibility of philanthropy. Indeed, it would be perfectly consistent for a libertarian to acknowledge a moral obligation on the part of all individuals to give to those less fortunate than themselves. It is simply that such a moral obligation does not involve a corresponding moral *entitlement* and hence should not involve any *legal* entitlement or obligation.

Of course, whether any such moral obligation is acknowledged or not, it seems quite clear that individuals do give things away and have a perfect moral right to do so. The motives from which such apparent philanthropy springs are obscure. Much which passes for "giving" may in fact be only one side of an implicit quid pro quo. The mother who gives to her child to "buy" peace and quiet; the husband who provides for his wife in return for domestic and uxorial services; the parents who provide for their children in return for support when they themselves are old—are examples. Perhaps even the "believer" who dispenses charity in this life in order to secure (better hopes of) salvation in the next fits this case. In many cases, however, considerations of motive are irrelevant: The "charity" at stake is direct and bilateral and can be organized and implemented directly through voluntary and decentralized processes.

The libertarian must, however, admit the *logical possibility* that this is not always so. There may exist a set of simultaneous contracts between all potential donors that will make each one better off, but which cannot be secured by voluntary action through decentralized processes. Suppose, for example, that there are many, identical, would-be donors who are concerned about the poor. Acting unilaterally, no one of them would make voluntary transfers to the poor because the value to each of a dollar's transfer is less than one dollar; however, acting together, all would make transfers because each donor need then contribute only the fraction $\frac{1}{d}$ of each dollar received by the recipients (where d is the number of donors). To be effective this arrangement must be mutually coercive. No donor can have the option of withdrawing, because each would rationally do so: Any one individual could have the benefit of seeing the poor made better off, without having to make his own contribution to costs. In other words, transfers to the poor become a "public good" to all potential donors—and as with other public goods, completely voluntary individual action will lead to under-investment in charitable activity. Some (perhaps all) potential donors will "free-ride" to some extent—perhaps to the point of making no transfers at all. As we know in such cases, there will exist some arrangement of transfers which if "imposed" by a collective institution *all* donors would prefer: If, somehow, all donors could be offered the choice of the purely voluntary outcome or an arrangement in which each contributed at a higher level on the understanding that all others would also do so, then there is some such latter arrangement which all would voluntarily choose. In such a situation there is thus a utilitarian—although not a natural rights—case for "involuntary" transfers.

There are then two conditions that must be met before any such case—even the conceptual case being considered here—can be made: First, the transfers must yield sufficient benefits to donors (as well as to recipients) to leave them better off; second, the transfers must involve public goods benefits as between donors. Can reasonably plausible settings in which both conditions hold be posited?

We have already mentioned the possibility of collective altruism. This possibility has been extensively analyzed in the economics literature under the slightly misleading rubric of "Pareto-optimal redistribution,"[5] and in any case is clear enough. Some slightly less obvious possibilities have also been discussed and perhaps deserve mention. We categorize them according to possible donor motive.

THE INSURANCE MOTIVE

This possibility first gained currency in the economics literature under the aegis of Buchanan and Tullock,[6] and is a line of reasoning that has in a different guise been exploited by Rawls. Essentially, the argument is that risk-averse individuals may support redistribution to the poor not from any concern over the poor but because the future is uncertain and each recognizes the chance that he may be poor sometime in that future. Clearly, one does not need the extreme form of uncertainty embodied in the Rawlsian veil-of-ignorance experiment to get a flavor of the Rawlsian distributional result. And it is clear that the necessary "free-rider" elements apply here, since each "donor" would gain if all other taxpayers contributed to transfers while he did not.

On its own, however, the argument here seems extremely weak, since it depends on the superiority from the donors' viewpoint of the transfer solution as compared with market insurance facilities. Arguments based on adverse selection problems might be mounted[7] for government intervention in private insurance markets, but even if such arguments were valid, it would still be far from clear that redistribution programs would be the most efficient alternative.

THE SELF-PROTECTION MOTIVE

It is commonly argued by proponents of welfare payments that such payments reduce the likelihood of civil unrest and revolution. Elements of such an argument can be found in Plato's *Laws*. To the extent that this is so, donor taxpayers could be seen as benefiting from transfers to the poor: If a set of bribes can be arranged that will keep potential revolutionaries inactive, thereby protecting the initial set of property rights, then donors may gain. Here again there is a public good, hence a utilitarian argument for welfare.

However, it should be emphasized that the payment of such bribes is only one of a number of means of dealing with potential revolutionaries, and is not obviously the most efficient. Our colleague Gordon Tullock, who has a somewhat morbid interest in these things, assures us that history is fairly much on the side of the rack, the firing squad, and Siberia. There is considerable evidence that he may be right. Furthermore, it is by no means clear that the poor represent the primary threat. Revolutions and coups, bloody and otherwise, more commonly involve a rearrangement of power among the upper echelons than a confrontation of income groups.[8] One ought to note, in any case, that if the poor *are* itching for revolution, transfers to them have the unhappy ambiguity of increasing their *capacity* to wage war as well as reducing their incentive to do so.

* * *

None of these possibilities on its own seems particularly plausible, or likely to justify much in the way of welfare payments. Taken *together*, they may take those libertarians who base their position on utilitarian arguments a little way toward a conceptual case for public redistribution—though not far. It seems clear that the main burden of proof must fall on the possibility of "collective" altruism. In this connection, it is perhaps worth restating that philanthropy of the type in which the donor receives satisfaction from the *act of giving* rather than from the improvement in the well-being of the recipient, whatever the source, does not fit the relevant requirements. Giving for the sake of giving is purely private, unless there are other altruists who also benefit from the improvement in the recipient's well-being.

Furthermore, it seems reasonable to suggest that where individuals are altruistically motivated, problems of "free-riding" are less likely to be intense. We would expect, and in large measure observe, the emergence of purely voluntary organizations which secure cooperative charity without the intervention of the coercive state. One can imagine non-members of such organizations benefiting in some ways from the organizations' activities, perhaps for the non-altruistic reasons we have already discussed, but on balance, it does not appear that the voluntary non-political solution would be likely to involve free-riding on an enormous scale. In this sense, the utilitarian case for political provision of charity seems very much weaker than the case for political provision of defense or law and order.

We have so far ignored one of the oldest and most powerful of the utilitarian arguments for increased equality of income. Each of us observes, in his own life, that income has declining marginal value. I receive more pleasure from an additional dollar when my income is three thousand dollars than when it is thirty thousand. While one cannot prove that this must be so, one can make a plausible argument by considering the simple case where my total utility is the sum of terms each of which presents the utility of consuming a single good; since I maximize my total utility, subject to the constraint of a given income, by consuming those goods with the highest ratio of utility to cost, it follows that as my income rises I find myself consuming, at the margin, goods with a lower and lower utility per dollar.

Even if we accept that each individual faces declining marginal utility of income, it does not follow that one man with an income of thirty thousand dollars a year receives less pleasure from an additional dollar than a different man with an income of three thousand; since they are different people they may have quite different utility functions. One might even argue, in the case of earned incomes, that it is precisely the person who, at any given income level, gets great pleasure from each additional dollar who will choose to work hard and so end up with a large income, while it is the ascetic with no use for money who chooses to be philosophically rather than gainfully employed. This argument becomes less persuasive where the income is not earned, and even in the case of earned income most of us, despite any philosophical qualms about interpersonal utility comparisons, are convinced that a dollar is worth a good deal more to a pauper than to a millionaire.

If one accepts the idea that the declining marginal utility of income applies on an interpersonal basis, it follows that the costless transfer of one dollar from a rich man to a poor man results in a net gain of utility; the rich man is injured less than the poor man is benefited. This argument, explicit or implicit, is at the heart of much of the support for welfare payments and similar programs.

It is perhaps worth noting that this argument is not an argument on the basis of "deserts" any more than the natural theory of rights is. Where one individual is a more efficient "machine" for the conversion of money into utility than another with identical income, utilitarian principles require a redistribution from the more miserable to the less miserable individual rather than vice versa. An argument on the basis of desert would presumably require redistribution from the happy to the most miserable, independently of the impact on total utility.

Both this Benthamite "aggregate utility" argument and the "contract" sorts of arguments suggested earlier provide a prime facie utilitarian argument in favor of public welfare. They do not, however, establish any argument on strict libertarian grounds for governmental transfers of income. To the extent that such transfers are involuntary, they would violate the rights of those whose money was taken without consent. If the transfers are voluntary, then the government has no advantage over private charitable organizations in arranging them.

What the arguments do provide is a reason why a utilitarian might reject the libertarian position; in order to answer this line of reasoning—in order to make libertarianism plausible from a utilitarian perspective—we must go on to look at some practical arguments that suggest that a system of compulsory transfers might have consequences that a utilitarian would find highly undesirable. In doing this we are, in a sense, filling out the argument that we sketched earlier, when we suggested that the existence of clearly defined and transferable property rights was desirable from a utilitarian point of view. The next two sections are devoted to this exercise.

Conceptual Possibilities versus Political Performance

Even supposing that we allowed the conceptual possibility of a public welfare program—a set of transfers—that was desirable from a utilitarian perspective, no case for government provision of welfare would necessarily be established. In order to make this extra step, it would need to be shown that the pattern of distribution which would actually emerge if government were to be assigned the responsibility for redistribution would be a desirable one. This is, of course, quite a general point, essentially independent of the particular view taken on desirable redistribution and of whether that view reflects libertarian, utilitarian, or other underpinnings. It simply happens to be a fact that libertarians tend, more than most, to include within the ambit of their discussion the inadequacies and peculiarities of political institutions.

The general issue at stake here is the domain of appropriate normative discourse. What is it, after all, that is being normatively evaluated? Much of the discussion of what we might loosely term "distributional ethics" proceeds as if the relevant domain were the set of all conceivable *distributions*, as if there were a pie of given size to be divided up, and the issue at stake was that of how the pie "ought to be divided." Now, the pie analogy may itself be inappropriate for a number of reasons—perhaps because, as the libertarian would emphasize, there are in fact a lot of little pies, and the conceptual issue is whether I can legitimately steal part of your pie. But suppose for the purposes of argument the single pie analogy is accepted. In what sense does the normative issue become simply one of how the pie ought to be divided? Surely it is relevant to ask how we are to ensure that the normatively determined shares will prevail. If, for example, the pie is given to the lion to carve up, what is to prevent him from taking the lion's share? If the division is to be determined by majority rule, what is to prevent some majority from splitting it among them and leaving none for the rest? If we posit plausible institutional settings within which the pie is to be divided, and make plausible behavioral assumptions about the actors in our little drama (by which we would seek explicitly to preclude the possibility that those actors will behave solely in accordance with the philosopher's independently derived moral norms), the crucial question is not how the pie ought to be divided, but rather which institutional setting for determining its division is likely to be best. To the extent that the alternative institutions are to be evaluated in terms of the division of income to which they give rise (rather than, for example, the division of decision-making power under which they are chosen), then the question of which "distributions of income" are best remains relevant. But the purely positive matter of what distributions emerge from what institutions is also fundamental, and must be elevated to a central role in any serious discussion of the questions at issue here.

Consider, for example, the simple statement: "the government ought to secure an equitable distribution of income." As a disembodied normative statement of the way in which governments *ought* to behave if they could, this is probably unexceptionable. But it is apparent that such a statement, at least as a logical precursor of distributional policy, is composed of two quite separate statements:

1. The government ought to be assigned the power to make transfers, and
2. The government, once assigned this power, ought to pursue the goal of equity.

The framework on which this second statement is predicated clearly presumes a notion of government institutionally akin to the Platonic philosopher-king—what has come to be called in economics the "benevolent despot" model of government. The "government" must have the *power* to set the distribution of income *dictatorially*, and it must have the inclination to be swayed by the mental calisthenics of the moral philosopher.

It is, however, clear enough that this is not an accurate description of political institutions as we know them. Political outcomes emerge as the equilibria of complex social interactions, in which various actors have varying degrees of power and all operate within the constraints set by the rules of the political game—periodic elections; universal suffrage; majority rule on the floor of the House; party politics; lobbying activity; bureaucratic discretion and so on. That these political processes are not yet fully understood by those who study them (public-choice scholars, sociologists, political scientists, or whatever) hardly bears. We can still agree as to the nature of what is being studied. We can still acknowledge that whatever outcomes emerge are not the result of a single decision which any single person (or mystic entity such as "the people") makes—that they emerge from the putting together of a whole range of individual decisions, in the making of which each actor is pursuing his own interest, defined broadly so as to include his own perception of morality to the extent that that weighs in determining his political behavior. Those who believe that this process has some automatic tendency to produce the "right" outcome ought to note that for almost two hundred years expert (economic) opinion has agreed almost unanimously on the desirability of free trade, and that throughout that period the United States has never been without tariffs.

One of the unfortunate implications of the approach which the "benevolent despot" model suggests appears to be a preference for dictatorial systems of government, in which the moral elite might hold sway. For questions concerning desirable distributions are really of the form: "What ought I do if I were dictator?" And the reason for asking a question of this type must either be that it *is* the practically relevant question—that the moral advisor believes political processes to be dictatorial *in fact*—or that it *ought to be* the practically relevant question. It is difficult to see any justification for either. It seems quite clear that governments are *not* unconstrained dictatorships, and equally that a normative case for unconstrained dictatorship would be hard to muster.[9] In fact, history is replete with examples of dictatorship—even ones in which moral considerations did weigh heavily—and experience suggests that they are often enough far from benign.

Consequently, if we posit that governments *are in fact* dictatorial—that electoral constraints, political competition, and the rest of the democratic panoply are mere show—then it is doubtful whether we would wish to assign governments the power to make transfers at all. If it were possible to constrain the exercise of dictatorial government by constitutional rules, it seems quite likely that the domain of government spending would be restricted to an extremely narrow range of activities—mostly "public goods" in the strict technical sense. To assign to government the constitutional power to make transfers could be predicted to lead to a highly capricious set of redistributions which almost no one would wish to justify normatively.

Yet if we instead consider political institutions as they actually are—or seem to be—we need to ask whether the situation is so very different. Will unfettered majority rule, electoral competition, lobbying, vote-trading on the floor of the House, bureaucratic discretion and the like, generate distributional outcomes that seem likely to be superior, on *any* normative grounds, to those that would emerge under a libertarian regime with the minimal state? Attempts have been made to answer this question analytically by examining the distributional outcomes in simple abstract models of majoritarian democracy. Generally, such models indicate that substantial redistributions will occur in the political process, but the direction of such transfers (at least in any single "election") is indeterminate. To be sure, the ultimate effect *may* be distribution-condensing: If the distributional effect of public spending is genuinely random and the distribution of benefits is reasonably widely spread, and if all such spending is financed out of taxes that are roughly proportional to income, the net effect over a sequence of elections may be to reduce disparities in income *on average*. But the effect overall is that of a rather chaotic lottery, in which some of the poor are made rather poorer and some of the rich much richer. And it is certainly not true in this setting that the higher the level of government activity the more equal the income distribution: On the contrary, the level of government spending that minimizes the variance of the income distribution may be remarkably small. Yet majority democratic processes do not necessarily have inbuilt restrictions that would keep the level of government activity within these bounds.

Defenders of public redistribution will no doubt point to the empirical record—to the existence of substantial welfare programs in most democratic states, and to statistics which purport to show the effects of government taxes and transfers on the share of income going, say, to the lowest and highest deciles. It is worth emphasizing, however, that it is the distributional effects of the whole *range* of government activity, including tariffs, zoning laws, regulations of all sorts, and non-welfare spending, that is at issue here. And it needs to be pointed out that the interpretation of statistical pictures is fraught with difficulties: The total impact of government activity on all incomes and prices is almost surely unmeasurable, and the simplistic partial view of this that the available statistics supply can be extremely misleading. In addition, most such analyses fail to distinguish between current and lifetime income—they thus treat a program such as Social Security, which takes money from a man when he is young and returns it to him when he is old, as "equalizing" incomes, even if in fact it tends, on average, to transfer money from the poor (in terms of lifetime income) to the rich.

The major thrust of this section is to pose the question: "Is 'equitable' redistribution via political process feasible?" If not, then it seems to follow that the state should not be assigned power to make transfers. At the very least, it ought to be acknowledged that what is relevant to the domain of normative discourse here is the comparison of alternative "institutions." For the libertarian, once the question is posed as an exercise in "comparative institutional analysis," the inadequacies of the political mechanism become only too conspicuous. Even if a conceptual case for welfare could be mounted within the libertarian framework the possibility of achieving the desired results via political processes as we know them seems ludicrously remote.

The Costs of Redistribution

Even if a system of governmental income transfers reduces inequality, a utilitarian judgment of such a system must depend in part on its costs; if making us more equal means making all of us poor, it is unlikely to be desirable in terms of any of the arguments for transfers which we have discussed. We must therefore ask what the costs of a government that has the power to make such transfers are likely to be. Many of these costs are of a sort which also apply to the existence of private charity; analytically, the difference is that in the private case, since virtually all costs fall on either the donor or the recipient, both of whom are voluntary participants, we can be reasonably sure that transfers will not occur unless they lead to net benefits. One can nonetheless argue that the existence of charitable feelings might in some cases have bad consequences similar to the consequences of governmental "charity."

The arguments here are of two types—an older argument that can be summarized under the rubric of "incentive questions," and a newer and less familiar argument, related to what is called "rent-seeking." Both are "consequential" arguments of a utilitarian type. The "incentive" argument begins with the observation that any systematic charity must implicitly categorize people according to whether they "qualify" as recipients or not—and equally, as to whether they are possible donors. Any such system of categories automatically creates incentives for people to alter their behavior so as to fit the recipient category and/or avoid the donor category. In the case of a tax-transfer system based on income level, for example, individuals have an incentive to reduce their nominal incomes, by shifting income into non-taxable forms, or by choosing more pleasant but less well-paid jobs, or by simply working less hard. This involves the substitution of less productive activities for more productive, or of lower valued activities (leisure) for more highly valued (the goods that income will buy). There is a net loss to all members of the community. In the limit, these losses can obliterate virtually all output. If, for example, all incomes were to be *equalized* via the tax-transfer process, then each individual would recognize that whether he worked or not would have negligible effect on his own income. Incentives to work, save, take risks, and so on would be virtually removed. We would either have to rely on individuals' moral sensibilities and social pressures to induce people to work, or some system of compulsory work with police supervision would have to be instituted.

Attempts have been made to assess empirically the incentive effects of the tax-transfer system based on adjustments in hours of work. The *average* loss per dollar of income transferred tends to be fairly modest, but the *marginal* loss (i.e., the loss consequent on transferring an extra dollar) turns out to be very substantial. Even so, the empirics do not pick up the effects of the tax-transfer system on retirement choices, occupational choice, risk-taking, and so on, which on the face of it seem likely to be considerably more significant.

The second sort of argument, based on "rent-seeking," relies on a different aspect of redistribution. Given that there are sums of money to be obtained from government (or charitable organizations), individuals will spend resources to get that money—not only by attempting to have themselves categorized into predetermined classes (the "incentives" point we have already examined) but also by attempting to determine (by influence, persuasion and possibly bribe) the classes themselves. This aspect of behavior, which has only recently begun to be analyzed system-atically, is known as "rent-seeking." In a world in which distributions are determined by favor or by bureaucratic discretion, or where influence and/or persuasion and/or bribery are activities with (possibly) high returns, we would expect resources to be devoted to those ("rent-seeking") activities. Medieval courts were run on such principles. One economist has estimated the cost to two countries (India and Turkey) of rent-seeking connected with one type of governmental activity (import permits) to be on the order of 10 percent of national income.[10] And it is clear that political lobbying has begun to reach very substantial proportions in the United States as well. The farmers' tractorcade in Washington is as much a cost of government subsidy programs as is the misallocation caused when excessive resources are drawn into the farming sector in response to rural subsidies. Once government (or any other body) gets itself into the business of distributing largesse, it invites the expenditure of resources by individuals in attempts to obtain that largesse—expenditures which may be at least as large in toto as the largesse itself.

It is said that in India and Africa, where begging is a well-ordered industry, parents will deliberately break their children's limbs and other-wise deform them so as to equip them better for a successful begging career. The end result can be a more grotesque set of beggars, no one of which is more successful than all would have been if all parents had been more squeamish. This excess of deformity is surely a social cost of the system, no less than the excess of beggars.

It is, to be sure, difficult to assess the magnitude of such rent-seeking (though attempts have been made in some simple cases, with staggering results). But they are to be taken into account in the determination of both government welfare activities and private charitable behavior. And it is clear that, in the eyes of some at least, these rent-seeking and incentive costs are sufficient to limit severely the desirability of charity of any type—private or public. Even if one is swayed by the utilitarian/ contractarian arguments in favor of transfers (whether voluntary or involuntary) one might nevertheless decide on balance that redistribution is undesirable—that one's compassionate instincts should be subjugated to avoid the incentive and "rent-seeking" effects of redistributional activity.

Summary

This paper has sought to offer, in obedience to its title, a libertarian perspective on welfare. This "perspective" has two aspects. The first involves a statement of the libertarian theory of "natural rights," and a speculation as to the implications of such a system of rights for (purely voluntary) transfers. The libertarian theory admits, in its strict form, no role at all for coercive government activity, in the area of redistribution or elsewhere. The second aspect of our argument involves an attempt to sketch a defense of the libertarian theory of rights from a utilitarian base. This second aspect has two strands: first, a theory of "political failure" that sketches some of the problems associated with redistribution through majoritarian democratic processes; second, two arguments as to why any departure from the income structure implied by libertarian rights may be extremely costly.

Even if the line of reasoning developed here is rejected, there is, we believe, one aspect of it that represents a challenge to all welfare proponents of whatever persuasion. This is the requirement that any purely ethical theory of distribution must ultimately be lodged in a theory of the institutions through which the distributional ethics are to be realized. The only domain of normative discourse that can be genuinely satisfactory in a policy setting is the domain of alternative (and feasible) institutions. The set of *conceivable distributions* does not represent an appropriate domain of discourse for anything other than the most remote and idle ethical speculation. When the limitations of the political process as a redistributive device are fairly faced, the pure "market distribution" may appear the least bad of the available alternatives.

Notes

1. In a set of lectures given at a recent Liberty Fund conference on "Liberty, Property and Justice" held in Blacksburg, July 1979. Elements of his argument can be found in his "Nuisance Law: Corrective Justice and Its Utilitarian Constraints," *Journal of Legal Studies* VIII (Jan. 1979): 49–102 and "The Next Generation of Legal Scholarship?" *Stanford Law Review* 30, no. 3 (Feb. 1978): 635–657.

2. Henceforth, we will use the term "land" to include all naturally occurring assets not ultimately derived solely from application labor input.

3. Note that this "common pool" problem does not emerge if land is held to be owned by the "king," or by some ruling elite; only if it is "owned" by all individuals in common.

4. David Friedman, *The Machinery of Freedom* (New Rochelle: Arlington House, 1978), pp. xiv, xv.

5. See, for example, Harold Hochman and James Rodgers, "Pareto Optimal Redistribution," *American Economic Review*, Sept. 1969; Dennis Mueller and George von Furstenberg, "The Pareto Optimal Approach to Redistribution," *American Economic Review*, Sept. 1971; and Geoffrey Brennan, "Pareto Optimal Redistribution: A Perspective," *Finanzarchiv*, no. 2 (1975).

6. See "The Calculus of Consent," Ann Arbor, 1962, ch. 13.

7. Along the lines of G. Ackerloff, "The Market for Lemons," *Quarterly Journal of Economics* LXXXIX (Aug. 1970): 488–500.

8. Free-rider problems emerge in organizing revolutionary movements, which make it unlikely that large amorphous groups will seek power by might. See Gordon Tullock, "The Paradox of Revolution," *Public Choice*, 1971, and Geoffrey Brennan, "Pareto Optimal Redistribution: The Non-Altruistic Dimension," *Public Choice*, Spring 1973.

9. Not least because answering the question "What *ought* I do if I were dictator?" will, for all except the least self-perceptive, admit quite different answers from the question "How *would* I behave?"

10. Ann Krueger, "The Political Economy of the Rent Seeking Society," *AER* LXIV: 291–303. For a more general discussion of constraints on transfers, see David Friedman, "Many, Few, One: Social Harmony and the Shrunken Choice Set," *AER*, March 1980, 225–32.

3

Paternalism and Welfare Policy

GERALD DWORKIN

Introduction

I shall present in this paper a number of conceptual and normative issues that are related to the concept of paternalism. I shall first consider the question as a purely philosophical one and then discuss the aspects of paternalism that arise in the context of income maintenance programs. By conceptual issues I mean ones that are connected with the definition and analysis of various concepts. Thus, if paternalism is connected with the concept of liberty we need an understanding of the concept of liberty and of what types of actions constitute interferences with liberty. If justifications for paternalism make reference to the incompetence of individuals or defects in their rationality then we have to understand the meanings of such notions.

On the other hand, in discussions of paternalism one may find a statement such as:

Neither one person, nor any number of persons, is warranted in saying to another human creature of ripe years, that he shall not do with his life for his own benefit what he chooses to do with it. [1]

Such statements make claims about the legitimacy or illegitimacy, the justification or lack of justification, the goodness or badness of paternalistic interventions. One might go further and develop a theory which would give reasons why paternalism was (was not) justifiable and in which circumstances. These are examples of normative investigations, investigations concerning the rightness or wrongness of paternalism.

43

There are assertions of still another kind that arise in discussions of paternalism—empirical claims. Given an understanding of ideas such as freedom and choice one can make claims about the empirical relationship between certain forms of delivery of income and the amount of freedom granted the recipient.

To give cash is to grant a degree of consumer choice. To provide commodities, on the other hand, channels the use of public funds more directly towards socially desired ends.[2]

I shall consider such claims to the extent that they are relevant to conceptual or normative issues.

Paternalism and Related Concepts

Historically the issue of paternalism has arisen with respect to the limits of state action, i.e., the question of under what circumstances the state is justified in limiting the liberty of its citizens. Therefore most analyses of paternalism have been tied to the use of coercion, in particular the use of legal sanctions against proscribed conduct. Let us call this the concept of *legal* paternalism. As I have defined this concept it is

interference with a person's liberty of action justified by reasons referring exclusively to the welfare, good, happiness, needs, interests, or values of the person whose liberty is restricted.[3]

Paternalistic measures are defined by the reasons or justification for the action, not by the action itself. One and the same restriction on liberty might be paternalistic if justified in one way and non-paternalistic if justified in another. One might forbid smoking because of the danger to the person who smokes (paternalistic) or because of the annoyance and danger to those around him (non-paternalistic).

Almost any piece of legislation is justified by several different reasons. Even if a piece of legislation was originally introduced for paternalistic reasons, as was the case for 19th-century abortion legislation, it may be possible for advocates of the statute to justify it without appealing to the original paternalistic motives. Therefore, it will be difficult to argue that any particular social welfare measure is paternalistic per se. One has to focus on the reasons that are actually given in defense of the measure or on the most plausible justification that can be given, and argue that these are fundamentally paternalistic in character.

The following are some examples of legislation which can reasonably be considered paternalistic.

1. Laws requiring motorcyclists to wear safety helmets.

2. Laws forbidding persons to swim at a public beach when lifeguards are not on duty.
3. Laws forbidding the sale of soft drinks containing cyclamates.
4. Laws forbidding the sale of laetrile.
5. Laws requiring individuals to spend a specific portion of their income on the purchase of retirement annuities (Social Security).

In addition to laws which attach criminal penalties to certain types of action there are laws, rules, regulations, which make it difficult or impossible for people to do what they wish, and which are justified on paternalistic grounds.

1. Regulation of the types of contracts that will be upheld by the courts. Thus, minors are not able to enter into various financial contracts.
2. Requirement for the ill to have "medically necessary" blood transfusions even in violation of their religious beliefs.
3. Civil commitment of the mentally ill on the grounds that they are likely to harm themselves.

Within the category of legal paternalism one can distinguish between *strong* and *weak* paternalism, and *pure* and *impure* paternalism. Strong paternalism justifies interference in terms of promoting the good of the person. Weak paternalism justifies interference in terms of preventing harm to the person being restricted. Thus laws against heroin are usually justified in terms of preventing the person from harming himself (weak paternalism). Compulsory education laws are usually justified in terms of promoting the good of the individual (strong paternalism).

In the case of pure paternalism, the class of persons whose liberty is being restricted is identical with the class of persons whose welfare is being promoted. An example would be laws against suicide. In the case of impure paternalism, the class of persons whose liberty is restricted would be larger than the class of persons whose interests are being protected. Forbidding the manufacture of cigarettes restricts the liberty of manufacturers who may not be themselves smokers.

It would be a mistake to argue that in the case of impure paternalism we are simply preventing some from harming others and hence not really acting paternalistically. For the crucial difference between these cases and others is that the harm is always such that it could be avoided easily if those harmed so chose. The incurring of the harm requires the willing cooperation of the victim. Hence the frequently used phrase "victimless crimes."

Clearly the concept of paternalism extends beyond the idea of legal paternalism. Not all paternalistic acts are acts of the state. Parents may restrict the liberty of their children, wives of their husbands, employers of their employees. Further, not all paternalistic acts involve interference with liberty. The doctor who lies to her patient about his illness or who transfuses blood to an unconscious patient, the employer who provides company housing for his employees, the teacher who refuses to let a student take a heavier course load, may all be acting paternalistically. What is common to these situations is that one person acts in the belief that such action is to another person's benefit in spite of the fact that he has reason to believe the person being helped would not approve of such action if asked explicitly.

It is this type of paternalism, which may but need not involve liberty-restriction, which is most relevant for the discussion of income maintenance programs. The use of vouchers or the provision of specific commodities may be considered paternalistic, but they do not involve the use of coercion.

Since paternalism involves acting in opposition to, or at least indifference to, the preferences of others, justifications usually involve a claim that the preferences concerned are in some way faulty or incompetent. Hence some understanding of the ways in which competence can be faulty is required to understand the normative arguments. I shall list some of the chief factors which impair the ability of individuals to make fully rational decisions and therefore provide the background against which claims for the legitimacy of paternalism arise.

IGNORANCE

In Mill's *On Liberty* he gives an example of when it would be legitimate to interfere with someone for his own good. It is the case of a man about to cross a bridge which he does not realize has been washed away. What justifies the interference is the man's ignorance of the actual consequences of his actions. He takes himself to be doing one thing (walking across a bridge) when he is actually doing something else (walking across a washed-out bridge). What makes the case an easy one is that all one has to do is inform him of the true situation to change his conduct. But, in some circumstances, there might not be time to do this, or one might not speak his language, and in such cases one might have to prevent him from acting. The justification for compulsory education laws rests on the similar argument that children are unlikely to know or appreciate the extent to which their future welfare depends on acquiring certain skills and abilities.

COMPULSION

One argument for making certain drugs illegal is the adverse effect they have on the freedom of the individual. Addiction makes it difficult or impossible for the user to retain his freedom of choice concerning the drug. I am not interested in whether the argument is a good one. It is an illustration of the use of the concept of compulsion to argue diminished competence. The compulsion can be internal, as in the idea of psychological compulsion, or it can be external, such as social pressures operating to tempt or coerce the individual. In either case the choices he makes or the preferences he expresses are not fully reflective of *him* and hence, it is argued, paternalistic measures are justified.

WEAKNESS OF THE WILL

Consider a person who knows all the facts about the probabilities of being injured in an automobile accident—the types and gravity of the various injuries, the reduction in probability and severity of injuries that results from wearing seat belts. Yet he never puts seat belts on when he rides in a car. It is not that he believes the inconvenience outweighs the possible benefits. He admits what he is doing is not rational. He just does it anyway. One might say that his beliefs do not connect in the appropriate fashion with his action. This defect of the will, first discussed by the Greeks, is called by philosophers "weakness of the will."

EMOTIONAL STRESS

People sometimes make serious decisions—in terms of their effect on future welfare—under conditions of great stress. Suicide is, perhaps, the best example of this. Moments of great loss or anxiety are the most likely to produce self-destructive impulses. Other environmental contingencies such as severe and long-lasting pain may cloud the individual's judgment. Because, as we say, the individual didn't know what he was doing his actions are again thought of as not fully his.

DIMINISHED RATIONALITY

I am using this as a blanket term to cover all the ways in which a person's thought processes may be distorted because of mental defects. Character defects, neuroses, personality disorders, psychoses, mental retardation, lack of impulse control, inability to defer gratification, all affect the ability of the individual to make rational decisions. I also use the term to include temporary or permanent states of unconsciousness. Thus a person in a coma would be an extreme case of diminished rationality. Individuals may suffer diminished rationality over the entire range of their actions (as in the coma case) or over a limited range (such as financial decisions). Their incompetence may be temporary or permanent. They may have never experienced rationality (severely retarded infants) or they may have lost it late in life (senility). All these factors will be relevant to assessing the kind and scope of paternalistic measures thought legitimate.

In all of these cases of diminished competence it can be argued that there is a gap between what a person wants and what is in his interests. And arguments against paternalism, such as Mill's, typically rely on claims about an individual's being a better judge of his own interests than any other person could be.

Clearly the question of what is in a person's interests is not the same as what he wants. If the questions were the same, then to say that a person wants something, but it is not in his interest to get it, would be meaningless, which it clearly is not. Nevertheless, there is some connection between a person's interests and the satisfaction of his wants or desires. As a rough approximation we may say that something is in a person's interests if it increases the likelihood that his long-range or settled or fully informed desires will be satisfied. We make a distinction between a person's present wants and what he would want if he were fully informed or fully rational. This, then, connects with the earlier remarks about incompetence, for in all such cases it can be argued that what the person wants is not what he needs or what is in his (best) interests. This leads us now to the normative issues concerning paternalism.

Justifications for Paternalism

I am going to consider a spectrum of views on the justification of paternalism. As far as I know nobody has held either of the extreme points on the spectrum, i.e., that paternalism is never justified or that it is always legitimate to act paternalistically. The strongest anti-paternalistic view is that of John Stuart Mill, who argued that legal paternalism is never justified with respect to any rational adult. His argument was utilitarian—appealing to the adverse consequences for human welfare of allowing society or the state to interfere with people for their own good. He believed that we either cannot advance the interests of individuals by compulsion, or that the attempt to do so always involves evils which outweigh the good done. His main reason for believing this is that he thought that the individual is the best judge of his own interests.

With respect to his own feelings and circumstances, the most ordinary man or woman has means of knowledge immeasurably surpassing those that can be possessed by anyone else.[4]

Therefore, balancing the good against the bad consequences of paternalism, Mill concluded that

Mankind are greater gainers by suffering each other to live as seems good to themselves, than by compelling each other to live as seems good to the rest.[5]

Several things should be noted about this argument. First, it is not clear to what extent Mill's premise about individuals' being the best judge of their own interests is an empirical or conceptual one. While it might seem, at first glance, to be a purely contingent question of who knows what is best for another, Mill had certain philosophical views about the inferences involved in trying to ascertain the contents of another person's mind which made it a necessary truth that I know more about my mental states than any other person can. Of course, even if it were true that I am the best judge of what I want or desire, it would not follow for that reason that I am the best judge of what I need or what is in my best interests.

Second, it does not follow from the fact that Mill held a strongly anti-paternalistic view with respect to government coercion that he must be anti-paternalistic in other areas. Perhaps doctors are better able to identify the interests of their patients than legislators the interests of their constituents.

Third, it is odd that a consequentialist argument should lead to an absolute ban of paternalism. For it is always possible that in a particular case the good consequences of interference outweigh the bad, and hence on consequentialist grounds justify paternalism. At most, one would seem to get a presumption against such interferences which could only be overruled by presenting good evidence that the case before one differs from the usual pattern.

There is, however, an argument stressed by Sartorius and others that in the absence of a criterion for distinguishing cases where the good consequences outweigh the bad, and in view of the strong presumption against paternalism, we are better off adopting an absolute ban: The losses attached to such a ban are outweighed by the losses involved in trying to pick out the small number of cases in which paternalism "works."[6]

There is a strongly anti-paternalistic view which does not rely on the consequences for human happiness being one way rather than another. This is the view that individuals have an absolute right to liberty which may not be infringed unless an individual violates or threatens to violate the rights of others. On this view a person may do (or permit another to do) anything to himself unless he has some obligation to a third party not to do so. The root idea underlying this view is the conception of persons as autonomous, as planning and leading their own lives. That these are important values and that paternalistic measures seem to infringe them cannot be denied. The crucial normative issue is whether these values are in some sense supreme, and whether there are justifications for paternalism that are consistent with, perhaps even supportive of, these very values.

A relatively weak claim for paternalism, i.e., one which justifies a minimal amount of such interference, is argued for by Feinberg in his article "Legal Paternalism."[7] His claim is that paternalism is justified to prevent self-regarding harmful conduct only if the conduct is substantially non-voluntary or (on a temporary basis) if needed to determine whether the conduct is voluntary or not. The advantage of such a justification is that it can be claimed that no violation of the agent's autonomy exists since his actions are already non-autonomous.

Some might consider the position too minimal in that it would not allow laws requiring motorcyclists to wear helmets, or the banning of cyclamates, or not enforcing contracts by which individuals sell themselves into slavery. None of these can reasonably be regarded as non-voluntary actions. A stronger argument which did justify the above laws could be couched in terms of preserving the individual's autonomy in the future. Such a position justifies intervening even when the agent is acting voluntarily now. But the view only allows a limited set of reasons as sufficient to justify paternalism, reasons which refer to the preservation of autonomy. Thus individuals would be prevented from selling themselves into slavery not because they are (necessarily) acting involuntarily now, but because such a decision destroys all future autonomy of the person.

One problem with this view is that unless there are some bounds put on the concept of autonomy every ultra-risky action could be forbidden. Mountain climbers, parachutists, stock car drivers are all risking life and limb, and hence, it would appear, their future autonomy. One way of limiting this line of reasoning would be the utilitarian argument that a person's happiness depends on his conception of himself, which might include being a risk-taking individual. Another way of drawing the line would be in terms of what limits on risks to their autonomy rational individuals would consent to.

According to this mode of argument paternalistic interventions are not justified by a balance of good versus bad consequences, nor by guaranteeing autonomy, nor simply on the grounds that the person is not acting fully voluntarily. All of these may be relevant factors which enter into the arguments for justifying paternalism but they enter in a special way. They enter as premises of an argument for what persons would agree to under certain ideal conditions. Different theories will specify the ideal conditions in different ways—rationality, knowledge, concern for their own prudential interests, etc.—but the form of the theory remains the same. The basic idea is that we are all aware of various irrational inclinations, of the possibility of accidents which render us unable to make reasonable decisions, of the possibility of ignorance of various kinds, of the force of temptation. It is therefore rational for us under certain conditions to protect ourselves against these contingencies by taking out a "social insurance" policy. We authorize others, in advance, to act on our behalf under certain specific circumstances.

It is a necessary condition, on this view, that the individual toward whom we are acting paternalistically will approve our decision, given the development or restoration of his rational powers, but this condition is not, by itself, sufficient because there is always the possibility of manipulating people's preferences so that they come to approve what was done to them. Hypothetical consent must play a role in this theory. With respect to legal paternalism the argument must be either that such consent would be unanimous or, in the event of less than unanimity, the administrative costs of working out special arrangements to limit the liberty of just those who would agree are very high, the interests to be protected, very important, and the limitation of liberty of those who would not agree, relatively minor.

At the other end of the spectrum is the purely consequentialist view. Paternalism is justified if and only if the harm to the individual that is probably prevented is greater than the total harm caused by acting against the person's wishes. One might add to this some notion of universalization. This justification attributes no special weight or value to the autonomy of individuals. Autonomy enters into the calculation only as one particular factor which affects the goodness or badness of the consequences. To the extent that people value autonomy interference with it will diminish happiness, but autonomy is granted no independent value. No intrinsic good is attached to being able to make one's own decisions even if they are, in some sense, mistaken.

Paternalism and Welfare

Having discussed in relatively abstract terms the conceptual and normative issues I shall indicate in this concluding section some of the current areas in welfare policy where questions of paternalism arise. This is not meant to be an exhaustive account, but rather illustrative of how the general philosophical issue arises in practical contexts.

CASH VERSUS IN-KIND TRANSFERS

If individuals need aid in order to meet a need for, say, adequate housing, there are at least three different ways of meeting that need. They can be provided with generalized purchasing power (cash or a line of credit) and then allowed to purchase the housing they need. They can be provided with the housing directly through a public housing program. They can be given vouchers which are valid only for the purchase of housing. More generally, people can be given financial aid in the form of cash, in-kind transfers, or vouchers. The argument in favor of non-cash aid is usually paternalistic (although it need not be). While cash grants give the individual the widest range of freedom, in-kind or voucher programs limit the individual's purchases to those goods which it is thought desirable for him to have, and which it is also thought he might not purchase on his own.

To give cash is to grant a degree of consumer choice. To provide commodities, on the other hand, channels the use of public funds more directly towards socially desired ends. Vouchers lie in between.[8]

The reasons why it is claimed that individuals might not purchase certain goods or services are varied. The individual may not desire the good. The individual may not know that he needs it. The individual may need and desire it but be subject to temptation to purchase other less-needed goods. These conditons correspond to the various defects of competence discussed earlier. The assumption behind in-kind aid is that individuals and families may be incompetent to make certain decisions and that in-kind aid or vouchers are a relatively non-coercive way for a government to influence them to make the kinds of decisions they would make if they were in fact able to maximize their own welfare. The argument in favor of vouchers rather than in-kind aid is that they insure the desired purchase that it is thought ought to be made but preserve a wider range of choice for the consumer. They eliminate the need for the government to provide as well as pay for the goods and services, and, it is argued, lead to greater efficiency though competition among various producers and suppliers.

The normative questions here concern the value of freedom of choice when weighed against welfare. Are more choices always preferable to fewer? Is the government entitled to determine how its aid will be used? If individuals have a right, say, to a minimum income, then is restricting the way that income can be spent illegitimate? How should the value of efficiency enter into this issue? There are important empirical questions about the kind of life various options lead to. Compare the lives of three individuals, one who receives surplus food, one who receives food stamps, and one who receives cash. A comparison of the relative quantity and quality of contact with bureaucrats would be illuminating.

It is useful to point out how one might justify an in-kind distribution over a cash payment on non-paternalistic grounds. For example, a society might wish to promote an equalization of, say, medical care, while allowing inequality in the distribution of other goods and services. To do this they must provide vouchers or in-kind distribution of medical care and not allow individuals to purchase such care with "regular" money.

INCOME AND SERVICE

In recent years there has been a move to break the line between the provision of income and the use of social services. The NASW policy statement claims:

Service, when offered within the context of eligibility investigation, tends to become a condition for obtaining financial assistance. This undermines the concept of assistance as a right and . . . interferes . . . with self-determination in seeking and accepting service. There is no reason to assume that financial need, in itself, necessarily calls for the provision of social services.[9]

Those who favor tying assistance to services usually do so for paternalistic reasons.

The underlying assumption of the service strategy is that the poor need assistance because, unlike the rest of the population, they are unable to make the relevant choices by themselves. The underlying assumption of the income strategy is, on the contrary, that what the poor really want is to make their own choices as they see fit. It is based on the notions that the poor are not so very different from the rest of us: they only have less money.[10]

There are conceptual and normative issues that could usefully be explored with respect to this matter. Is placing a condition, e.g., the use of social services, on the granting of financial aid a restriction of liberty? Is it a form of coercion? Does it make a difference with respect to whether we are interfering with liberty or not if the aid is thought of as something to which one has a right? Is it relevant morally whether the poor are poor *because* they cannot make the appropriate choice or are poor and *therefore* cannot make the relevant choices? Is the tying of services to the granting of aid less legitimate if the grant is something to which the recipient is entitled as a matter of right?

There are also complex factual matters to be settled. Are there classes of people who can be reached only by tying service referrals to income maintenance programs? Richard Titmuss gives some interesting data on the prevention of blindness in the aged. From 1948–62 the incidence of blindness caused by cataract declined 54 percent among those aged sixty to sixty-nine in England. This was mainly due to elderly people getting earlier preventive care. The important point, in this connection, is that most of the referrals did not come from doctors, but from the National Assistance Board.[11]

SOCIAL SECURITY

The final area in which paternalism is clearly present is the existence of compulsory state pension schemes. Though not an income support policy in the usual sense, these might be thought of as transfer payments from the young to the old. Is a person's liberty infringed when he is forced to save a part of his income for future use? He may not desire to do this and so the interference is against his wishes. The usual justification for this measure is that individuals might discount their future welfare in such a fashion that they would not provide adequately for their future.

One very interesting philosophical issue that arises in this area is the question of personal identity over time, and how this connects with the idea of a rational life plan. We know that our tastes and preferences change over time and any life plan must make provision for such changes while we retain our sense of self-identity. One interesting theoretical issue is whether a person who ignores his own future prudential interests is irrational. If the satisfactions of one's future self are as important as those of one's present self, then one is acting irrationally by discounting the future in favor of the present. Hence, one might get an argument for compulsory protection of one's future selves that is similar to the argument for the compulsory education of children.

One might also want to consider a non-paternalistic argument for such compulsory insurance schemes. It is all very well in principle to let individuals not save for the future as long as the consequences fall on them, and they do not expect help from us later. But this ignores the psychological strain put on the rest of us when we view a destitute individual and have to resist aiding him lest this totally undermine the willingness of others to defer consumption for later uses. On this line of reasoning we are really protecting ourselves and therefore not acting paternalistically. This argument remains essentially individualist in nature. It tries to show that what appears to be self-regarding conduct impinges on others' interest. But there are also a set of considerations which is less liberal and more communitarian in nature. We seek to protect others, not just to avoid hardship for ourselves, but simply because we *care* about them. A society may adopt various forms of paternalism as a way of expressing such concerns. That such concerns may lead to tyranny is clear. But a society without such mechanisms may not be worth living in.[12]

Conclusion

My tone in the last section has been tentative. I have raised questions but not provided answers. I have suggested which issues need to be explored but have not provided solutions. This is not because I hold some general view about philosophers refraining from giving concrete advice about substantive problems. I have given such advice in the past and shall continue to do so in the future.[13] But the area of welfare policy is one in which an empirically grounded knowledge of the effects (intended and unintended) of policy decisions is essential for deciding what policy to adopt. Too often in the past policies designed to help the poor or the ill have had their main effect on the income of professionals who administer and provide service under such programs. Therefore in the absence of such detailed knowledge I cannot decide whether, say, food-stamps or cash are more efficient, or more just, or more freedom-maximizing. Nor can I estimate which has a greater impact on the autonomy of the individual.

All that one can say with confidence is that paternalism by its very nature interferes with the autonomy of the individual, that autonomy is an important value for individuals, and that therefore paternalistic measures call for justification. The rest of the story lies in the details.

Notes

1. J.S. Mill, *On Liberty* (Fontana Library, 1962), p. 134.

2. J. Axinn and H. Levin, *Social Welfare* (New York: Harper & Row, 1975), p. 286.

3. G. Dworkin, "Paternalism," *The Monist* 56, no. 1:65.

4. Mill, p. 207.

5. *Ibid.*, p. 138.

6. R. Sartorius, *Individual Conduct and Social Norms* (Wordsworth, 1975).

7. J. Feinberg, "Legal Paternalism," *Canadian Journal of Philosophy*, Spring 1971.

8. Axinn and Levin.

9. National Association of Social Workers Policy Statement on Separation of Social Services and Income Security Programs, June 29, 1976.

10. L. Coser, "What do the Poor Need? (Money)," *Dissent*, October 1971, p. 91.

11. Cf. R. Titmuss, *Commitment to Welfare* (New York: Pantheon, 1968), pp. 70–71.

12. Conrad Johnson stimulated my thoughts on this topic.

13. N. J. Block and G. Dworkin, "IQ, Heritability and Inequality," *Philosophy and Public Affairs*, Part I, Summer 1975; Part II, Fall 1974; G. Dworkin, "Can Convicts Consent to Castration?" *Hastings Center Report*, October 1975.

4

Federal-State Relations and Income Support Policy

THOMAS A. AULT

Issues concerning the proper role of government in providing for citizens' welfare needs, and of appropriate functions of each level of government in a multi-level federalist system, go to the heart of any debate on the design of income support programs. Underlying different perspectives on what direction reform of existing programs should take are fundamentally different views pertaining to basic individual rights, the role of government generally, and the role of the central government in a federalist system. This paper will survey briefly the intergovernmental aspects of the current welfare system, touching on their historical roots and patterns of change. In subsequent sections, the paper will examine two broad intergovernmental issues which consistently dominate policy debates on income support policy: the proper role of the national government in setting welfare policies and administering the benefits, and its role in financing welfare benefits.

Existing Welfare Programs: An Intergovernmental Overview

Currently many different government programs affect the incomes of the low-income population. A person's well-being depends not only on earnings from employment and private savings and investment, but also on the interaction of often arbitrary rules governing eligibility and benefits over at least fifteen different government programs administered by numerous agencies, some federal, some state, some county. Three-fourths of total expenditures in these so-called "income security" programs are not even welfare benefits, but rather social insurance: Social Security, Unemployment Insurance, Medicare and Workmen's Compensation are the largest of these. Only about one-quarter of total expenditures derive from the traditional welfare programs wherein the receipt of program benefits is conditioned on family income and assets. But it is on these welfare programs that this paper will focus: an appropriate narrowing of consideration since it is the proliferation and complexity (and other characteristics) of these programs that have inspired frequent attempts at "welfare reform."

There is great diversity in current welfare programs in the roles played by various levels of government and in the basic eligibility requirements. Only one program, Food Stamps, offers a basic federal entitlement to all persons who are financially eligible. All other federal welfare programs are more limited in coverage. Supplemental Security Income (SSI) is available only to low-income aged, blind, and disabled persons. Aid to Families with Dependent Children (AFDC) gives benefits only to low-income children and their caretaker relatives in family units deprived of parental support due to death, incapacity, absence from the home (divorce, separation, desertion), and (in twenty-four states) the unemployment of the parent. Other welfare programs include the Earned Income Tax Credit (EITC), state and county General Assistance programs (GA), Veterans' Pensions, Medicaid, and Housing Assistance.

Answers to three questions underline the intergovernmental complexity that confounds these programs. Who sets program rules? Who administers the benefits? Who pays for the benefits?

Aid to Families with Dependent Children (AFDC) and *Medicaid*, the largest welfare programs, are grant-in-aid programs in which all levels of government—federal, state and local—participate in financing and in setting benefit and eligibility policies. State and local governments administer AFDC and Medicaid with very minimal federal oversight. Since their inception, these programs have been essentially state programs—with only limited, but growing, federal conditions. Note that the federal government is assisting states, not individuals, in these programs.

Food Stamps, as mentioned, is a federal entitlement program for individuals in which the federal government determines policy and pays the full cost of benefits, in the form of food coupons. The program, however, is administered by state and local governments.

Supplemental Security Income (SSI), serving the aged, blind, and disabled, is also a federal entitlement program for individuals, with largely optional state supplements.[1] The basic SSI program is all federal: policymaking, financing, and administration. State supplements may be state-administered, as in twenty-six states, in which case the state is totally free to set policy, or federally administered (seventeen states), in which case policy, except for benefit levels, must conform with federal policy in the basic entitlement program. In both cases, the supplements are financed

Table 4.1 *Current Income Assistance (Means-tested) Programs*

Program	Date enacted	Locus of Government Responsibilities			Coverage	Program Statistics (1978)[a]		
		Policymaking	Financing	Administration		Recipients (millions)	State/Local cost (billions)	Federal cost (billions)
General assistance	N.A.	State/Local	State/Local	State/Local	Varies	0.9	1.2	0.0
Veterans' pensions	1933	Federal	Federal	Federal	Veterans, dependents, survivors	2.3[b]	0.0	3.3
Aid to families with dependent children	1935	Fed./St.	Fed./St. or Fed./St./Loc.	State or Local	Families with parent incapacitated, absent or (in 27 states) unemployed	10.7	4.6	5.9
Housing assistance	1937	Fed./Loc.	Federal	Local	Families, singles, elderly, disabled	3.2	0.0	3.6
Food stamps	1964	Federal	Federal	State or Local	Low-income households	16.0	0.0	5.5
Medicaid	1965	Fed./St.	Fed./St. or Fed./St./Loc.	State or Local	AFDC/SSI recipients; medically needy	22.8	7.9	10.1
Earned income tax credit	1975	Federal	Federal	Federal	Low-wage families with children	6.3	0.0	1.2
Supplemental security income Basic federal program	1972	Federal	Federal	Federal	Aged, blind, disabled individuals	4.2	1.6	4.8
State supplements Fed. Administered		Fed./St.	State	Federal				
State Administered		State	State	State				
Total							15.3	34.4
Total (Federal/State/Local)								49.7

[a] Data for recipients give average monthly caseloads. Expenditure data are for the fiscal year. Many recipients receive two or more kinds of aid. An unduplicated count of recipients is not available.
[b] 3.5 million including dependents and survivors.

entirely by the states (except for special federal payments to three states, a continuation of "hold harmless payments" designed to protect states from cost increases during a transition period when the SSI program was implemented in 1974; the hold harmless payments gradually would have disappeared were it not for an indirect consequence of subsequent legislation).

General Assistance (GA) is determined, administered, and financed by state and local governments with no federal role. State or local GA programs fill the coverage gaps left by AFDC and SSI.

(Table 4.1 summarizes the major intergovernmental features of these programs and shows expenditure and recipient levels for a recent year.)

Clearly, current welfare programs lack a consistent rationale structuring federal, state and local roles. While policymaking (eligibility rules and benefit levels) is shared in many welfare programs, the federal government pays most of the bills—70 percent considering just the welfare programs, 80 percent considering the total income security system. Welfare programs continue to be administered mostly by state and county governments just as they were prior to 1935, when the first federal welfare programs were enacted. In fact, despite the steadily enlarging administrative role assumed by federal and state governments, in 1976 over 40 percent of all recipients of all public assistance were in county-administered programs, lingering evidence of the county-poor-law origin of public assistance.

The crazy-quilt pattern of intergovernmental relationships is both symptomatic and causative of many problems characteristic of the current welfare system. Intergovernmental complexity inhibits rational policymaking and effective, efficient administration. It also creates tension among the levels of government, often straining the cooperative federalism which is so essential to effective social welfare policy in this country. For example, tension emanates from the division of policy control. Policymaking by one level of government can require increased financial contributions of another, constitutionally independent level of government.[2] Yet another problem is delegated administration. Delegating administration to another level of government, whether a state to federal delegation as in federally administered SSI state supplements or a federal to state one as in the totally federally financed but locally administered Food Stamp program, often means that policies are not administered as desired, with the non-administering level usually lacking effective leverage over the administering one.[3] Finally, splitting functions weakens management accountability; administrators do not bear the full cost of mistakes.

Demands for Reform

The abundance of different programs with their idiosyncratic eligibility rules and intergovernmental chaos is but one source of the recurring efforts to reform welfare. In fact, those who most ardently seek to reform—usually federalize—welfare are probably much less concerned with program fragmentation and complexity than they are with a host of other problems. Welfare advocates want to eliminate what they perceive to be excessive administrative discretion and inequities in benefit levels and program coverage across states. Most advocates believe that these goals can be achieved best by complete federalization, including federal administration, of welfare. State and local governments, on the other hand, generally push for greatly increased federal financial contributions with a constant or diminished federal role in policymaking and administration. What dynamics underlie these positions?

STATE AND LOCAL ADMINISTRATIVE DISCRETION

Joel Handler asserts that the administrative characteristics of welfare programs are determined by the amount of behavioral control that society deems necessary for various beneficiary groups.[4] Handler believes that state and local officials and the body politic desire local administrative control over programs giving benefits to those whose poverty might be (at least partially) voluntary. Thus there is a coincidence of federal administration with routinized administration, usually of benefits to those whose poverty is assumed to be beyond their control. And there is a coincidence of state and local administration with highly discretionary, subjective rules. SSI, for example, which pays benefits to aged, blind, and disabled persons, is federally administered by Social Security district offices in a routine, largely non-discretionary manner. Most conditions attendant to the receipt of assistance were removed by the SSI legislation.[5] On the other hand, AFDC—paying benefits mostly to children who are illegitimate or whose parent (usually father) has deserted the family—is administered by states or counties with considerable administrative variation across (and even within) states.[6] Caseworkers often exercise substantial discretion in determining eligibility. And assistance is conditioned on recipients' compliance with a number of (mostly federal) requirements: registration and satisfactory participation in the work incentive program (WIN), assignment of child support and alimony rights to the state, cooperation with the state's efforts to obtain support payments from absent parents, submission to detailed budgeting and expenditure scrutinizing procedures in some states, and so on.

Why is welfare administration routinized for some categories of the poor and highly discretionary for others? Legislators' and administrators' apparent need to control more closely the behavior of certain recipients appears to relate directly to a concern that for some of the poor their condition of poverty might be voluntary. When one cannot devise a set of clear-cut criteria for separating the voluntary poor from the genuinely needy, decisions must be made, it is argued, on an individual case basis. Routinized administration is considered undesirable since it would necessarily cause unwanted hardship if a too restrictive rule were applied, or would provide assistance to those who ought to support themselves if a more generous rule were applied.[7]

INTERSTATE VARIATION IN WELFARE BENEFITS

The wide geographic variation in states' AFDC benefit levels and eligibility policies elicits perhaps the most widespread criticism among welfare advocates. In 1979, benefits (AFDC plus Food Stamps) for a mother and three children ranged from $3540 in Mississippi to over $6500 in Vermont and New York (and also in Alaska and Hawaii where the cost of living is significantly higher). The large range in benefits is not due to a few extreme states: Benefits exceeded $6000 in ten states and were less than $4000 in seven states (see Table 4.2). Welfare benefits for a mother and father, one of whom is unemployed, and two children varied from $2191 a year (Food Stamps only) in twenty-four states to over $6500 in Vermont and New York.[8]

UNEVEN DISTRIBUTION OF FEDERAL WELFARE SPENDING AND OF WELFARE TAX BURDEN

In 1978, monthly federal spending for each AFDC recipient varied from $68 in Idaho to $13 in Mississippi, a ratio of over five to one (see Table 4.3). In the Medicaid program, monthly federal spending for each recipient varied from $161 in Minnesota to zero in Arizona, which does not participate in Medicaid. (The comparisons exclude Alaska.)[9] Such large variations in average federal spending per recipient in the country's two largest welfare programs derive from the grant-in-aid nature of these programs. States decide whether to have the programs (as noted, Arizona still does not have a Medicaid program), what the benefit levels and detailed eligibility rules will be, and how the program will be administered. The federal government merely matches total state expenditures in the programs according to a statutory formula based on per capita income (so that poorer states receive higher federal matching rates). Thus, wide variations in state and local welfare spending cause wide variation in federal spending (the variation in federal matching rates reduces only a small portion of the total variation). In stark contrast, the Food Stamp program, a universally available federal income guarantee with nationally uniform benefit levels (except Alaska and Hawaii), shows much less variation: from $19 monthly per recipient in Michigan and Wisconsin to $32 monthly in Florida, Nevada and West Virginia (excluding Alaska and Hawaii)—a ratio of less than two to one (the ratio would be even less were it not for the fact that Michigan and Wisconsin's high AFDC benefits are counted as income in Food Stamps and thus reduce Food Stamp benefits paid in those states (Table 4.3).

Table 4.2 Maximum Benefit Levels for a Family of Four in 1979
(Poverty Level for Family of Four = $7,160[a])

State	AFDC	Food stamps	Total	Total as percent of poverty level	Has AFDC-unemployed father
Hawaii[a]	$6552	$1332	$7884	96	*
Vermont	5724	816	6540	91	*
New York	5712	816	6528	91	*
Michigan	5640	840	6480	91	*
Wisconsin	5496	888	6384	89	*
Washington	5268	948	6216	87	*
Oregon	5124	996	6120	85	*
Minnesota	5088	1008	6096	85	*
Connecticut	5100	996	6096	85	*
California	5076	1008	6084	85	*
Massachusetts	4752	1104	5856	82	*
Iowa	4740	1104	5844	82	*
Alaska[a]	5400	1896	7296	82	
New Jersey	4488	1188	5676	79	*
Utah	4488	1188	5676	79	*
North Dakota	4440	1200	5640	79	
Nebraska	4440	1200	5640	79	*
Idaho	4392	1212	5604	78	
Pennsylvania	4320	1236	5556	78	*
Rhode Island	4308	1236	5544	77	*
New Hampshire	4152	1284	5436	76	
South Dakota	4080	1308	5388	75	
Illinois	3996	1332	5328	74	*
Montana	3972	1344	5316	74	*
Maine	3768	1404	5172	72	
Dist. of Columbia	3768	1404	5172	72	*
Oklahoma	3708	1416	5124	72	
Colorado	3684	1428	5112	71	*
Kansas	3672	1428	5100	71	*
Wyoming	3660	1428	5088	71	
Ohio	3492	1488	4980	70	*
Delaware	3444	1500	4944	69	*
Virginia	3408	1512	4920	69	
Nevada	3312	1536	4848	68	
Indiana	3300	1536	4836	68	
Maryland	3204	1572	4776	67	*
Missouri	3072	1608	4680	65	*
West Virginia	2988	1632	4620	65	*
Kentucky	2820	1680	4500	63	
New Mexico	2748	1740	4452	62	
Arizona	2544	1764	4308	60	
North Carolina	2400	1812	4212	59	
Florida	2352	1824	4176	58	
Arkansas	2256	1860	4116	57	
Louisiana	2064	1908	3972	55	
Alabama	1776	2004	3780	53	
Georgia	1776	2004	3780	53	
Tennessee	1776	2004	3780	53	
Texas	1680	2028	3708	52	
South Carolina	1488	2088	3576	50	
Mississippi	1440	2100	3540	49	

[a]Because of a higher cost of living, the poverty line is higher for Alaska and Hawaii.

*Table 4.3   Total Monthly Spending Per Recipient for the Five
Largest Welfare Programs: Fiscal Year 1978*

State	Medicaid Total	Medicaid Federal share	AFDC Total	AFDC Federal share	SSI Total	SSI Federal share	Food stamps	General assistance
Alabama	$100	$ 77	$ 37	$ 27	$ 96	$ 94	$28	$ 98
Alaska	789	507	341	171	123	115	46	0
Arizona	0	0	49	23	120	119	31	123
Arkansas	126	97	47	34	92	92	27	0
California	140	72	107	53	178	70	22	34
Colorado	156	90	76	41	100	82	29	88
Connecticut	170	85	99	49	111	90	22	42
Delaware	148	81	74	37	105	98	26	0
Dist. of Columbia	163	83	81	41	130	128	24	155
Florida	107	60	49	28	113	113	32	0
Georgia	134	89	40	26	101	101	28	42
Hawaii	141	71	119	59	138	101	31	145
Idaho	139	83	107	68	101	90	27	0
Illinois	121	60	80	40	120	109	27	123
Indiana	203	116	63	36	98	98	27	0
Iowa	180	95	97	50	90	87	24	0
Kansas	158	74	81	42	92	92	23	114
Kentucky	94	67	57	40	110	106	28	0
Louisiana	126	91	39	27	108	108	29	62
Maine	138	105	76	53	89	75	27	25
Maryland	147	96	69	34	115	114	29	107
Massachusetts	134	74	106	55	142	61	22	137
Michigan	179	101	106	53	141	96	19	163
Minnesota	267	161	112	62	89	88	25	119
Mississippi	89	77	16	13	103	103	28	11
Missouri	98	58	57	34	96	92	27	61
Montana	215	126	67	41	108	100	29	40
Nebraska	197	106	90	48	92	86	23	0
Nevada	216	115	66	33	114	85	32	0
New Hampshire	186	121	84	53	98	98	27	53
New Jersey	135	72	87	43	127	104	27	121
New Mexico	110	83	43	31	111	111	30	97
New York	257	118	120	60	151	100	22	156
North Carolina	137	91	58	39	101	99	26	25
North Dakota	214	116	96	49	94	94	27	39
Ohio	139	86	71	39	113	113	29	80
Oklahoma	226	151	69	45	98	97	21	13
Oregon	169	99	103	59	99	96	26	72
Pennsylvania	254	122	91	50	132	101	24	139
Rhode Island	182	104	95	54	110	82	22	102
South Carolina	111	84	30	23	101	101	28	48
South Dakota	202	127	70	44	91	90	25	22
Tennessee	112	85	38	26	101	101	30	0
Texas	167	109	33	23	94	94	28	0
Utah	197	147	90	62	104	104	23	120
Vermont	161	111	95	64	122	84	24	0
Virginia	152	85	69	39	98	98	25	85
Washington	141	74	108	55	132	101	25	140
West Virginia	89	63	67	47	117	117	32	9
Wisconsin	210	130	108	63	123	61	19	86
Wyoming	240	114	79	42	96	96	27	36
Total	157	87	83	45	124	94	26	127

The state and local share of AFDC payments places a highly variable tax burden on state and local taxpayers. Using a frequently applied measure of tax capacity, the state and local tax burden of AFDC in New York State is almost three times the national average, while in Texas it is less than one-fifth of the national figure (Table 4.4).[10] This means that the relative tax burden is fifteen times greater in New York than in Texas. As with the interstate variation in benefit levels, these two states are not isolated extremes. For thirteen states, the tax burden is less than one-half of the national average, while for ten states, it is more than one and a half times the national average (implying that the tax burden in the latter states is at least three times greater than in the former states).

On the other hand, the states in which AFDC creates the heaviest state and local tax burden tend to be the big winners from the perspective of flow of federal funds. The net flow of federal funds for a state equals federal program expenditures going into the state minus the state's share of total federal tax dollars required to finance the program. For example, in 1975 the total federal cost of the AFDC program was about $5 billion. New York State's share of the $5 billion of federal tax dollars required to finance the program was about $483 million, almost 10 percent of the total federal cost of the program. But New York State received over $708 million in federal AFDC funds, making the state a net winner of about $225 million. Similarly, other states where AFDC requires heavy state and local taxes are net winners in the flow of federal funds:

California	$+119.7 million
Illinois	+ 43.5 million
Massachusetts	+ 66.4 million
Michigan	+119.4 million
Pennsylvania	+ 61.3 million

From the net federal funds perspective, the big losers are the states with low AFDC benefit levels—and this includes many of the poorest states based on per capita income or the tax capacity index.

Alabama	$− 13.5 million
Florida	−129.6 million
Mississippi	− 5.0 million
North Carolina	− 14.2 million
Tennessee	− 14.2 million
Texas	−177.7 million
Virginia	− 33.4 million

The point is clear. To leverage federal funds, a state must want to set benefit levels sufficiently high and be able to raise the requisite state matching funds. States unable or unwilling to do this, or states with a

Table 4.4   Relative State and Local Tax Burden of AFDC, by State (National
Average Tax Burden = 100)

State	Relative tax burden	State	Relative tax burden
Alabama	33.0	Montana	39.1
Alaska	84.9	Nebraska	48.4
Arizona	42.6	Nevada	36.5
Arkansas	51.9	New Hampshire	76.3
California	203.8	New Jersey	165.9
Colorado	86.7	New. Mexico	52.9
Connecticut	126.9	New York	289.9
Delaware	99.6	North Carolina	52.9
District of	352.2	North Dakota	46.5
Columbia		Ohio	114.3
Florida	19.2	Oklahoma	50.8
Georgia	53.3	Oregon	126.9
Hawaii	201.7	Pennsylvania	158.3
Idaho	51.7	Rhode Island	177.0
Illinois	189.5	South Carolina	31.8
Indiana	57.3	South Dakota	64.3
Iowa	89.2	Tennessee	42.5
Kansas	74.5	Texas	18.3
Kentucky	72.5	Utah	64.4
Louisiana	44.1	Vermont	132.2
Maine	121.8	Virginia	82.1
Maryland	113.1	Washington	139.5
Massachusetts	265.6	West Virginia	56.0
Michigan	241.8	Wisconsin	121.8
Minnesota	114.6	Wyoming	20.1
Mississippi	21.9		
Missouri	78.0		

relatively small low income population, will necessarily subsidize the high
benefit "welfare states" given current financing arrangements.

Trends of Change in the Federal Role

Criticisms like these generate pressures for the federal government to
reform the welfare system. Advocates of reform generally want to broaden
coverage and provide a nationally uniform minimum benefit, reduce large
interstate and intergroup benefit differentials, rationalize financing, and
simplify administration. Reform proposals usually would achieve these

objectives by means of a substantial increase in the federal role: a "guaranteed" minimum income (perhaps through a job) wholly or largely financed by the federal government, federally mandated eligibility rules, and, sometimes, a federal take-over of welfare administration.

Proposals with this thrust are not inconsistent with trends of the 1960s and 1970s. Indeed, the federal income assistance role increased steadily in these periods, in several ways. New programs were enacted: Medicaid; AFDC coverage for families with unemployed fathers; Food Stamps, the first federal welfare entitlement with universal coverage and nationally uniform benefits; SSI, a federally financed and administered income guarantee for the aged, blind and disabled; the Earned Income Tax Credit, a refundable tax credit for low income families with children. In fiscal year 1980, the federal government will spend about $27 billion on these new programs. The federal financial role increased substantially due to the new programs and to greatly liberalized matching rules for AFDC. A largely closed-ended AFDC grant formula was made open-ended. In 1960, the federal government financed 50 percent of all welfare benefits; by fiscal year 1980, this will have grown to over 70 percent. The federal policy presence grew with the fiscal infusion. In AFDC, for example, the federal government mandated work requirements and work refusal penalties, work incentive disregards, work and training programs, a new child support enforcement program, and a review of the adequacy of need standards (but without requiring states to raise payment levels). The federal role in administration entered a new phase with enactment of the first federally administered welfare program (SSI) and with new federal requirements to regulate how states administer AFDC and Medicaid: quality control programs with incentives and sanctions to improve payment accuracy, required use of social security numbers as recipient identifiers, required implementation of computerized matches, child support enforcement procedures, application processing deadlines, fair hearing requirements, and so on.

The tremendous growth in the federal role in social welfare programs and the persistent urging on the part of many for further federalization (welfare reform, national health insurance, workers' compensation) raise serious questions concerning the appropriate federal role. Given a federal structure of government, what is the function of the central government and of the states in meeting the social welfare needs of the citizenry? Certainly the philosophy of the Constitution would assign primary responsibility for social welfare to state and local governments. Such was the historical alignment of responsibility until the strong response of the federal government during the Great Depression. Even the New Deal programs, however, maintained primary responsibility for welfare programs with state and local governments. The new federal assistance programs were established as grant-in-aid programs to provide financial assistance to *states* rather than to individuals. Federal requirements were minimal. Not until the 1960s and 1970s did the Congress enact the first federal programs (Food Stamps and SSI) directly entitling individuals to benefits.

The New Deal welfare programs were sound in their adoption of a grant-in-aid approach to federal assistance. Good democratic reasons argue for diffusing power and for having vigorous state and local governments that keep power close to the people. Grants-in-aid provide a means for furthering central government objectives while retaining much of the power and autonomy of state and local governments. No doubt this accounts for the great popularity of grant-in-aid programs: There are now several hundred federal grant-in-aid programs.

What Is the Appropriate Federal Role in Welfare?

Many of the objectives long sought by welfare reform advocates could be attained either by adding new federal requirements to the current grant-in-aid programs or by abolishing these programs and creating in their stead a new federal entitlement program.[12] For example, supposing that the reform objectives were to establish a national minimum benefit and national eligibility rules and to improve federal financing, then the alternative approaches might be:

1. *Grant-in-aid:* Change AFDC grant-in-aid rules to require states, as a condition of receiving any federal matching funds, to pay a certain minimum benefit and to adopt federal eligibility rules. Increase federal matching rates to cover the increased expenditures, and possibly to provide state and local fiscal relief as well.

2. *Federal entitlement:* Eliminate the AFDC grant-in-aid program and replace it with a basic federal benefit, mostly if not entirely federally financed. States would be free to supplement the federal benefit; supplements could be subsidized partially by federal matching. The proposal could provide for federal administration, but not necessarily; possibly states would be given a choice. The proposal probably would consolidate separate categorical programs (AFDC, Food Stamps, possibly Housing Assistance) into one universal cash assistance program.

Under the first approach, the grant-in-aid structure of AFDC is maintained, but the conditions which states must meet to qualify for the grants are changed. Federal statute would specify national minimum benefit levels and national eligibility criteria (treatment of income and assets, composition of assistance units, work requirements, benefit reduction rates, and so on). To qualify for federal matching, state AFDC programs would have to meet the new statutory requirements.

The magnitude of these changes should not be minimized. The new federal requirements might be extensive and detailed, possibly greatly reducing state discretion and program options compared to current law.[13]

But since the grant-in-aid structure is kept, AFDC programs would remain essentially state programs—they would be more tightly constrained by federal requirements if they were to be eligible for federal matching funds, but they would remain state programs. Recipients' entitlement claims would be against state governments, not the federal government.

The federal entitlement approach is quite different. It is modeled after the SSI concept of a federal statutory entitlement to a minimum income, regardless of state of residence, to be administered and funded by the federal government.[14] Central to this concept is the transfer of responsibility to provide a basic level of income support from the states to the federal government. The federal government would be assisting individuals directly rather than contributing financially to state programs that assist individuals. In the grant-in-aid approach, by tightly specifying the conditions under which the federal government will contribute financially to state welfare programs, the federal government would be acting to establish powerful incentives for the states to provide a minimally adequate level. In the federal entitlement approach, the federal government itself becomes the provider of a minimally adequate level of income. Recipients' claims of entitlement would be against the federal government. This is a subtle, but, I believe, extremely important distinction.

This distinction underlies a substantially different role for the federal government under the two approaches. When the federal government is the grantor of an entitlement, it must specify every detail pertaining to the conditions under which the claim to the entitlement is valid. When a state is the grantor, this obligation falls upon the state rather than the federal government. It follows, therefore, that in the grant-in-aid approach, the federal government can specify constraints important to national policy goals, like benefit adequacy and work incentives, and leave the detailed specifications to state and local discretion. The federal role is smaller. Which of these alternatives is to be preferred?

FEDERAL ENTITLEMENT

First, let us consider arguments in support of the federal entitlement approach. Given a federal entitlement program, the federal government has clear authority and responsibility for making all program policy. The issuance of policies to implement all aspects of the program would be assured. There would be no conflicts of interpretation with state and local governments. Contrast this with the grant-in-aid approach. What is the federal government to do if a state fails to comply with one of the statutory conditions attached to receipt of the grant? It would have the legal authority to deny all federal matching funds to the state, but this would obviously be counterproductive. For this reason, a similar provision in AFDC has not been used in forty years. Unless the federal government develops new enforcement techniques, obtaining state compliance with federal policy mandates could be a major problem under the grant-in-aid approach, just as it frequently has been in the current AFDC program.

Closely related to the issue of policy control is the issue of administrative control. Very strong arguments can be made that a federally administered entitlement program would be more equitably, uniformly, and efficiently administered nationwide than would the grant-in-aid alternative. A major objective of most welfare reform proposals is to assure a minimum income to all families (either through cash assistance or a job). The most effective and certain way for the federal government to assure that this guarantee is fairly and adequately provided in every jurisdiction is to provide it directly. The federal government would have limited control over administrative procedures and outcomes if program administration were delegated to the states, as it would be under the grant-in-aid approach. And, as noted earlier, AFDC administration is highly variable from place to place. How would this situation be changed if the reform legislation merely added a few requirements to the present grant-in-aid structure?

The federal entitlement approach would minimize intergovernmental conflicts by eliminating shared responsibility for program functions. The federal government would set policy, administer, and finance the basic national benefit, while the states would be free to do the same, at their option, through state supplements. In contrast, the grant-in-aid approach would perpetuate the splitting of responsibility that has led to so many problems in the current system. For example, the federal government would pay most of the benefit costs while the states would specify the detailed rules and administer the payments. In all of this, the states would have little incentive to keep cost down. Payment accuracy and administrative efficiency could become serious problems.

In summary, a federally administered entitlement program offers the best chances for fully achieving the most frequently cited objectives of welfare reform: improved adequacy, equity, and administrative efficiency. Faced with local administration, shared policy responsibility, and a federal government largely powerless to deal with recalcitrant state and local jurisdictions, there is serious reason to question the extent to which the grant-in-aid alternative would achieve the reform objectives. Full realization of any of these objectives ultimately would depend on the states.

GRANTS-IN-AID

Now let us consider arguments from the perspective of the grant-in-aid approach. First, is it not true that whatever arguments can be made in support of a right to a minimum income can be made equally well on behalf of rights to minimally decent health care and education? Moreover, is there any reason not to believe that the federal government also might be able to provide these rights more equitably and efficiently (from a national perspective) than state and local governments? Arguments of this nature to support federalization of one or another state and local government activity can be applied to a large number of national concerns. In the limit, such reasoning could lead to the creation of a powerful central government with state and local governments left without domain and largely power-less. We may ask what meaning should be attached to federalism in this modern era given innumerable developments impossible to envision when our federalist system was created. But one point seems clear: The raison d'etre of the theory of federalism was to decentralize and diffuse the power of the central government. Vigorous state and local governments were considered essential to the production of basic liberties.[15]

Of course, total emasculation of state and local governments now seems an unlikely development in this country. Probably the federalization of one program would undermine our basic libertarian rights very little, if at all. But the power of the federal government already has increased dramatically in this century. And major institutional changes of this nature tend to become accepted over time, perhaps becoming the norm and the justification for an accelerating round of changes. Certainly this line of reasoning argues for placing a heavy burden of justification on proposals urging further federalization of previously state and local functions.

Second, good arguments other than libertarian ones can be made for keeping the social welfare function in the province of state and local governments insofar as practicable. For example, programs of public welfare may enjoy greater public support if they build on people's sense of community, their sense of responsibility to care for people "close" to them. This is consistent with what seems like the proper hierarchical ordering of responsibility to provide for people's well-being, beginning with oneself and family and progressing to local and state government and finally to the central government. Also, programs designed and adminis-tered locally can better reflect community preferences. This, too, can strengthen public support for welfare programs.[16]

In our federalist system, state and local governments are responsible for planning for the full complement of public needs necessary to support communities: management of the local economy, police and fire protec-tion, public education, maintenance of roads and public facilities, public welfare, etc. Since these local government functions are greatly interdepen-dent, a breakdown in one area can be caused by or lead to a breakdown in another. From a systems perspective, then, one can argue that relieving local government of its responsibilities in one particular area is an unwise action that could lead to inefficiencies or problems elsewhere. For exam-ple, applying this argument to welfare programs, one might hypothesize that local governments are most likely to address some of the causes of poverty (for example, inadequate education and training, discrimination, poor housing, benefits that are too high given prevailing wages) if they retain substantial responsibility for welfare programs. Also, since state and local governments are responsible for managing their economies, welfare programs are more likely to be responsive to changes in local economic conditions if they are administered locally. This could mean such things as an early warning to administrators that the local economy is faltering and that public assistance workloads will rise, or an aggressive job referral program when the economy is strong and a less active program when the local job market is not very promising.[17]

Another argument in favor of keeping local control over welfare programs relates to a basic taxpayer dilemma. Taxpayers do not want public money supporting those who could reasonably be expected to support themselves, but neither do they want to ignore those genuinely in need of help. As discussed earlier, the possibility that the poverty of some might be voluntary is a primary reason why the public has been unwilling to routinize welfare administration for certain categories of the poor. When there is no public consensus on a set of clear-cut criteria for separating the voluntary poor from the genuinely needy, substantial administrative discretion is necessary to allow individualized decisions. Further, beyond maintaining case-by-case administrative discretion, there seems to be a desire to maintain state/local political control over welfare programs serving these questionable poor. As Joel Handler observes,

Providing relief to people who may or may not be considered voluntarily poor has always provided several moral conflicts. Without belaboring the issue, the working taxpayer finds it intolerable to pay public funds to support idleness . . . , but he also cannot inflict too much hardship, since the inevitable sufferers are guiltless children of blameworthy parents. These moral conflicts and dilemmas are felt most keenly by those who live in daily contact with the reality—the working taxpayers in the communities and the neighborhoods. At the local level, the taxpayers distrust the state officials, and the state and local people distrust the federal government. The anguish caused by supporting the questionable poor is not felt that strongly in the legislative halls, and certainly not in the professional bureaucracies. There is great distrust and lack of confidence in the federal government to be sufficiently sensitive to local needs and interests for these intensely felt problems.[18]

On the other hand, there are problems with giving administrators discretion, and particularly so in a welfare program where many in the client population already are discouraged and devoid of self-esteem. Discretion can be easily used in a manipulative, paternalistic manner, thereby further undermining self-respect. In fact, arguments for substantial discretion in welfare administration derive from a view that welfare is more charity than a right. These arguments in effect assert a donor's prerogative to determine that a person is involuntarily poor before granting assistance. Yet another problem with discretion is its invitation to abuse—and there are plenty of examples of abuse in the history of welfare administration.[19]

A final argument for reforming welfare in a manner that retains the grant-in-aid structure and, with it, certain state and local flexibility is that many of the welfare policy dilemmas have no analytically superior solutions. Designing welfare programs requires balancing conflicting desiderata: benefit adequacy versus work incentives; work incentives versus target efficiency; adequacy and work incentives versus costs and caseloads; coherence, control and administrative efficiency versus tailoring assistance to meet individual needs; and so on. While empirical data and rational thought can lead to constraints that narrow the choices, these processes cannot point to uniquely optimal solutions. So why impose one solution nationwide, particularly since the single option chosen might well be quite suboptimal in certain local areas? Certainly the lack of a unique superior solution is a strong argument for allowing local preferences to tailor welfare programs best to meet local needs.

GRANT-IN-AID OR FEDERAL ENTITLEMENT? A SUMMARY APPRAISAL

We have considered arguments for a totally dominant federal role, as in the federal entitlement approach, and arguments for a grant-in-aid approach that allows the federal government to establish basic policy constraints but that preserves substantial state and local flexibility to tailor programs to local needs. What are the relative strengths of these arguments as we search for a preferred approach? Can arguments for one of the choices be shown to be based on more fundamental values? I do not think so, though I am not qualified to speak as a moral philosopher. Advocates of a federal entitlement program can argue that all persons have a basic positive right to a minimal well-being, that the central government has the responsibility to assure this and other basic rights, that (at least some) state and local governments have failed to provide this right fully and fairly to all their citizens, and, therefore, that the federal government should directly provide a minimal income to all persons not able so to provide for themselves (note that this argument does not presume the form of the guarantee: It could be either a guaranteed job or a guaranteed cash support or some combination). On the other hand, advocates of maintaining the grant-in-aid structure can argue that a minimal level of income is only one aspect of citizens' rights to a minimal well-being, that maintaining the social welfare of persons and communities is the proper responsibility of state and local governments, that moral concern for vigorously maintaining our most basic liberties should dominate any rights people have to a guaranteed minimal existence, that this dominant moral concern requires limits on the scope of the central government, and, therefore, that the central government should not move to take over every state and local function not perfectly executed by these governments, even if people's rights to a minimally adequate existence are suffering to some (not intolerable) extent.

An important issue to consider here is whether the federal government would be treating its citizens inequitably were it to take note of the unequal treatment of low-income persons in the various states, but to take no action to eliminate the inequalities. The arguments developed by Conrad Johnson elsewhere in this volume bear usefully on this issue. Johnson argues that the demands of equity must be considered with respect to a reference group and that in the case of the social distribution of welfare benefits, the appropriate reference group is given by the social arrangements, especially the political organization.

If society is organized as a loose federation of substantially autonomous sub-communities, each having a government with authority to provide for the welfare needs of its citizens, so that the powers of the federal government are restricted to other things (e.g., defense), then the requirements of equity focus on inequalities and inconsistencies in the treatment of citizens within each sub-community, but not, primarily, across sub-communities. On the other hand, if society is organized in such a way as to give a strong central government the power to oversee the provision of welfare benefits, then equitable considerations tend to be extended across the community.[20]

Johnson further notes the importance of the distribution of power and authority in the society. A government's failure to eliminate inequalities does not constitute inequitable treatment if the government lacks either the power or the authority to do so. If a government lets inequalities stand out of respect for the limits of its own authority, then the failure to act does not imply approval of the unequal treatment. Johnson writes that "the establishment of a federal budget for the purpose of financing welfare benefits does not necessarily involve any provision for federal authority over the ways in which individual sub-communities distribute the relevant services among their members."[21] Finally, recognizing the possibility that the institutional arrangements used to define the scope of equity may themselves be flawed, Johnson argues that it would be setting the standard too high to expect them to be beyond moral reproach of any kind. Rather, "existing social arrangements defining the structure of authority must be above grave moral criticism. So long as existing arrangements are tolerable, they, and not any hypothetical ideal arrangements, are to be used for purposes of distributing benefits and for finding the reference group(s) by means of which the equity of those distributions is to be judged."[22]

Under the structure of the current grant-in-aid system, the federal government does not have the authority to distribute welfare benefits to individuals. Rather, it makes federal matching payments for the expenditures of state and local governments disbursed according to benefit levels and program options that those governments elect. Thus, intrastate and interstate differences in these welfare programs are arguably not inequities that the federal government can address without exceeding the present limits of its authority. Nor has the current grant-in-aid system been shown to be subject to grave moral weaknesses sufficient to compel its elimination and replacement with a federal entitlement program. In short, the argument that welfare programs must be federalized to eliminate inequities has been stretched too far. The case for moving to a federal entitlement program must be made on other grounds.

Considering the totality of arguments for the grant-in-aid versus the federal entitlement approaches, I believe that those favoring the grant-in-aid approach are more compelling. Arguments for a federal entitlement program are mainly ones of increased accountability, efficiency, and equal treatment across states. As persuasive as these are viewed within their own narrow perspective, they ignore the division of governmental responsibility in our federalist system and the importance of diffused governmental power for maintaining fundamental liberties. Accountability, efficiency, and equalization of services arguments can be made in support of federalizing most any social welfare activity. A substantial burden of proof is necessary for federalization arguments to become absolutely compelling: proof that state and local governments are seriously violating persons' welfare rights and that federal takeover of the function is the only solution. Such proof is lacking in the case for federalization of cash assistance programs. While a demonstrated need exists for a more active federal role in setting and enforcing constraints like minimum benefit levels and broader coverage, this mandate does not require federal takeover of all policymaking and certainly not federalized administration. Accretions to the central government's power should be accomplished in small steps with a heavy burden of justification of the need for each increment.

Federal-State Roles in Financing Welfare Programs

The federal government has assumed a large and growing role in financing the country's welfare expenditures. Much of the political pressure for welfare reform derives from a desire to relieve even further the financial burden of welfare on state and local governments. While many people would question a dominant federal role in welfare policymaking or administration, few challenge the proposition that the federal financial role should grow.[23]

I believe that the arguments for a dominant federal role in financing welfare programs are considerably more compelling than are arguments for a dominant federal policymaking or administrative role. First, many federal grant programs have successfully provided incentives for state and local governments to increase expenditures. Grants lower the relative prices of specific expenditures or increase the income available to local governments (or both) and thereby encourage expenditures. As noted earlier, grants allow central governments to pursue national policy goals by stimulating particular types of state and local spending rather than by increasing direct federal expenditures. Applied to welfare programs, grants have allowed the federal government to further redistribution objectives without enacting federal entitlement programs.[24]

A second argument for federal financing recognizes that all of the benefits of local welfare expenditures are not captured within the community making the expenditure. Welfare recipients in one community use their grants to buy goods produced in another. Recipients move, or decide not to move, from one community to another. These situations argue for one community to subsidize (partially) another community's welfare cost—or, for the federal government to do so acting as the community's agent.[25]

Probably the most compelling justifications for federal financing of welfare is the set of arguments based on the advantages of the federal tax base compared to state and local tax bases. The federal tax base is large, relatively immune from behavioral responses to progressive taxation, and able to withstand the falling revenues of a recession. State and local governments, on the other hand, have considerably fewer resources on which to draw and are less able to rely on progressive taxes. If the excess of taxes paid over benefits received becomes too large for any business or income group, an incentive is created for that group to relocate to a community offering a more favorable return on tax dollars. This constraint forces local governments to raise revenues by relying more on the "benefits received" approach than on "ability to pay." Obviously, this implies an inherent limit on the amount of redistribution that is possible drawing only on local tax bases. Thus, as many writers have observed, there is good reason for local governments to be concerned primarily with the economic prosperity of local citizens and businesses and to rely more on regressive taxes; and for the central government to address whatever distributional anomalies result. These arguments justify central government actions to distribute income from one individual or community to another.[26]

Finally, during a recession, transfer expenditures rise as revenues fall. Since state and local governments have a severely limited capacity to deficit finance, a recession could force them to cut welfare benefits or raise taxes. Either action could deepen the effect of the recession. The federal government can address this problem either by permanently financing most of the cost of transfer payments or by increasing intergovernmental grants when the unemployment rate is high (e.g., CETA countercyclical public service employment).

Of course, many of these arguments for substantial federal financing of welfare expenditures can be turned around to argue against such a federal role. For example, to discourage income redistribution, one would favor limiting the federal financial role to force greater reliance on state and local tax bases. Assuming local administration of welfare, a large contribution should be maintained to provide an incentive for prudent administration. Finally, increases in federal funding inevitably increase the federal role in policymaking and administration and may ultimately create pressures for further federalization.

Notes

1. State supplements are not optional in two respects. First, states are required to preserve the benefits of those who were receiving benefits under the predecessor state programs in effect when SSI was implemented. (Currently, less than 50,000 beneficiaries nationally receive these mandatory supplements.) Second, in 1976 Congress passed an amendment prohibiting states from lowering supplement levels. Thus, although states can freely decide the level of state supplements—and whether to supplement at all—once that level is set, the 1976 amendment precludes states from making any downward adjustment. (To be precise, the amendment contains an exception whereby a state can lower supplement levels so long as aggregate state expenditures on supplements are not reduced. Thus, benefit levels could be reduced if the caseload were growing.)

2. For example, since AFDC is an open-ended grant program, federal expenditures are influenced substantially by state program and administrative policies. Even if a state were to set its benefit levels at twice the poverty line, the federal government (meaning, of course, taxpayers in all of the other states) would be required to subsidize the totality of payments made. Federal policy decisions can have a similar effect on state expenditures. For example, the Social Security Act requires the Secretary of HEW to define what shall constitute unemployment in determining eligibility in the AFDC Unemployed Fathers program. A restrictive definition will mean lower welfare expenditures in a state without a General Assistance program, relative to what expenditures would be under a more liberal definition. States like California and New York with sizable General Assistance caseloads, however, would prefer a more liberal definition in order to receive federal matching for what otherwise are fully state-financed General Assistance cases.

3. For example, HEW lacks effective tools for getting recalcitrant states to comply with federal requirements in AFDC and Medicaid. The only sanctioning procedure at HEW's disposal is to hold a compliance hearing, and if a state is found out of compliance, to cut off all federal funds in the program. This is a weapon of overkill and is almost never employed—the last time was over thirty years ago. Sometimes when the compliance process is initiated (or threatened), compromises are negotiated. Usually, however, when a state has a major issue at stake, HEW is forced to relent and state preferences prevail. Viewed within the philosophy of the grant-in-aid approach and the history of these programs, this is not surprising. Similarly, states are even more powerless in affecting the policies of the Social Security Administration regarding federal administration of SSI supplements.

4. Joel Handler, "Federal-State Interests in Welfare Administration," *Issues in Welfare Administration: Intergovernmental Relationships*, Studies in Public Welfare, Paper No. 5 (Part 2) (Washington, D.C.: Subcommittee on Fiscal Policy, Joint Economic Committee, Congress of the United States, March 12, 1973), pp. 9–11.

5. Supplemental Security Income (SSI) provides a guaranteed annual income to poor aged, blind, and disabled persons with few conditions (principally an assets test that can be viewed as part of the means test). SSI is federally administered and is a matter of right. There are no liens against estates (even though over 20 percent of SSI recipients own their homes) and no demands that grown children contribute to the support of their needy parents, features that had existed in the predecessor grant-in-aid programs.

6. Recent studies show that there continues to be substantial variation in almost every important feature of AFDC administration: accessibility and ease of the application process (caseworker attitude and helpfulness, number of visits and amount of paperwork required to complete an application, etc.), administration of work requirements, use of investigative procedures, administration of child support enforcement, and so on. Local discretion in AFDC administration can be used to keep down costs and caseloads. See, for example, Booz, Allen, and Hamilton, *Comprehensive Study of AFDC Administration and Management*, Contract performed for the Department of Health, Education and Welfare, Social Security Administration (Washington, D.C.: Booz, Allen and Hamilton, 1977). See also Frances Fox Piven and Richard A. Cloward, *Regulating the Poor: The Functions of Public Welfare* (Vintage Books Edition; New York: Vintage Books, Random House, 1971).

7. Joel Handler, "Federal-State Issues in Welfare Administration," pp. 9–11.

8. In twenty-four states, poor families with an unemployed father were eligible only for Food Stamp benefits since AFDC coverage of families with an unemployed father present in the home is a state option. Benefit levels for 1979, as shown in Table 4.2, are taken from U.S. Department of Health, Education and Welfare, *President Carter's Proposal for Welfare Reform*, Detailed Fact Sheet Accompanying Work and Training Opportunities Act of 1979 and the Social Welfare Reform Amendments of 1979 (Washington, D.C.: U.S. Department of Health, Education, and Welfare, May 23, 1979), p. 24.

9. Table 4.3 was computed by the author using expenditure and caseload data for each program.

10. The Advisory Commission on Intergovernmental Relations (ACIR) has conducted extensive research on measuring the comparative fiscal capacity of state and local governments. The ACIR developed an approach known as the "representative tax system." The representative tax system defines the tax capacity of a state and its local governments as the amount of revenue they could raise (relative to other state-local governments) if all fifty state-local tax systems applied identical tax rates (the national averages) to their respective tax bases. All commonly used tax bases are considered by the representative tax system: general sales, individual income, corporate income, property, estates, licenses, natural resources, etc. The state and local tax burden imposed by AFDC, as shown in Table 4.4, was computed using actual state and local AFDC expenditures in 1975 and each state's potential tax yield under the ACIR representative tax system. The potential tax yield was taken from U.S. Department of Health, Education and Welfare, *Tax Wealth in Fifty States* (Washington, D.C.: The National Institute of Education, U.S. Department of Health, Education and Welfare, 1978), pp. 12–13.

11. Data on net fiscal flows was taken from Martin Holmer, "Welfare Reform and Fiscal Relief" (Unpublished welfare reform planning paper written for the Office of the Assistant Secretary for Planning and Evaluation, U.S. Department of Health, Education and Welfare, May 1977).

12. Indeed, President Carter's 1977 welfare reform proposal, the Program for Better Jobs and Income, adopted the latter approach; the president's more modest 1979 reform proposal, the Social Welfare Reform Amendments of 1979, adopted the former.

13. The alternative of maintaining the grant-in-aid structure and reducing federal requirements—possibly going all the way to a no-strings block grant—is discussed later.

14. Some federal entitlement proposals, for example, President Carter's 1977 Program for Better Jobs and Income, included an option for state administration. If a state were to retain program administration, however, it would be acting as an agent of the federal government. For this reason, state administrative procedures would be highly prescribed by federal regulations.

15. For an interesting discussion of federalism, see Paul E. Peterson, "Federalism and the Great Society: Political Perspectives on Poverty Research" (Unpublished paper prepared for the Committee on Evaluation of Poverty Research, National Research Council, Assembly of Behavioral and Social Sciences, National Academy of Sciences, Washington, D.C., October 1978).

16. These arguments are not meant to apply to the issue of how welfare programs should be financed. A state or local government may need and want more extensive welfare programs than its tax base can comfortably support—without raising taxes to the point of driving out higher income families and businesses, for example. The question of proper financial arrangements is addressed later in the paper.

17. Of course, when the local economy falters, causing an increase in welfare caseloads and costs, local tax revenues are likely also to be falling due to the weak economy. This constitutes a very strong argument for financial assistance from outside the local community. See discussion that follows regarding the appropriate financial role of the federal government.

18. Handler, "Federal-State Issues in Welfare Administration," p. 10.

19. See, for example, Piven and Cloward, *Regulating the Poor.*

20. Conrad Johnson, "Equity: Its Scope and Relation to Other Objectives," Chapter 3, this volume, p. 131.

21. *Ibid.*, p. 132.

22. *Ibid.*, pp. 133-4.

23. Those arguing for a smaller federal financial role do so principally on two grounds: (a) fiscal austerity and a belief that the largeness of the federal tax base will lead to greater and unjustified welfare spending; and (b) a belief that a larger federal financial role will lead inevitably to a greater federal presence in policymaking and administration, possibly culminating in complete federalization.

24. For an excellent review of the literature examining the effect of federal grants on state and local expenditures, see Edward M. Gramlich, "Intergovernmental Grants: A Review of the Empirical Literature" (Paper presented at International Seminar on Public Economics Conference, Berlin, January 1976).

25. *Ibid.* p. 3.

26. *Ibid.* pp. 3–4. See also Peterson, "Federalism and the Great Society: Political Perspectives on Poverty Research," pp. 26–28 and Richard A. Musgrave, *The Theory of Public Finance: A Study in Public Economy* (New York: McGraw-Hill Book Company, 1959), pp. 3–27, 61–115, and 160–184.

PART TWO

Specific Objectives and Priority Problems

Introduction

In recent decades, a number of specific objectives of income support policy have come to be widely recognized and accepted. These objectives, however, are subject to differing interpretations when used as the basis for policy formulation. There is also substantial disagreement, particularly in the debate between conservatives and liberals, regarding which objectives should have priority over others. Moreover, it is a widely understood fact that there are inherent conflicts among these recognized objectives that seriously stand in the way of any attempt to maximize them simultaneously.

Among the most important of these widely accepted objectives are the following:

Adequacy. An income support program should be designed so that every recipient receives income sufficient to meet minimum needs, however defined.

Equity. Two different conceptions of equity are recognized in income support policy planning: "Horizontal" equity is the principle that those in similar circumstances be treated similarly, leaving open the question of what factors are relevant in determining what is to count as similar circumstances. "Vertical" equity, on the other hand, requires that people in different positions in the income distribution be treated differently by virtue of their different positions.

Work incentives. Income support programs should encourage employment by those able to work. In addition to requirements that employable recipients seek employment and take suitable jobs if available, employed recipients should be permitted to retain a portion of their earnings as an incentive to work.

Target efficiency. Income support programs should be planned so as to meet the needs of precisely those who are the most destitute.

Family stability. Policies and benefit structures should encourage families to remain intact and should avoid possible incentives toward family break-up, such as more generous treatment of families where the husband and father is absent than where he is present.

The papers in this section are all concerned with problems about these objectives from one or more of the following perspectives: Key concepts such as horizontal and vertical equity are analyzed and characterized; the role of these concepts in policy formulation and evaluation is explored and critically appraised; and arguments in support of one or more objective as having a claim to priority are presented. The objectives under discussion, for the most part, are equity—both vertical and horizontal, adequacy, and family stability. Throughout the essays, however, the objective of work incentives plays an important role in the analysis and appraisals presented.

The papers by Jodie Allen and David Lindeman, though quite different in their respective emphases, are in one important respect complementary. Each paper underlines a particular goal of equity: Allen's, that of *vertical* equity; Lindeman's, that of *horizontal* equity. Stated in an abstract way, the goals of vertical and horizontal equity are unexceptionable; some philosophers have even thought of them as requirements of reason itself. Vertical and horizontal equity become more controversial principles when we begin to fill them in by giving an account of the characteristics that make situations different or similar.

For Allen, vertical equity requires both that those in greater need should benefit more than those in lesser need, and that tax and transfer policies should not be such as to reverse the position of persons in the resulting income distribution or unduly compress the distribution. As she notes, these principles tell us something "fairly specific" about how to treat differently situated people and about what makes their situations different. The principal subject matter of Allen's paper is the application of these principles to program designs in the fields of cash income support, medical care, day care for children, food stamps, and the jobs program. A central problem which emerges in Allen's discussion is that of providing goods and services to program recipients in amounts which may seem unfair to self-supporting persons outside the program, or which may deter efforts to become or remain self-supporting. Allen identifies a wide variety of possible solutions to the problem. Each has its own merits, but certain drawbacks as well.

In his discussion of horizontal equity, Lindeman makes fundamental use of the proposition that "those with equivalent needs should receive equal benefits." This prescription is the contrary of the principles of vertical equity offered by Jodie Allen. Her position is that income differentials prior to the receipt of income support should not be unduly compressed as the result of receiving support payments. Under Lindeman's criterion, however, two families with equivalent needs would receive the same net income irrespective of any prior differences in income levels. Depending upon which of these policy alternatives is chosen, recipients of income support would receive differing amounts of benefits.

Lindeman's paper identifies and analyzes the most serious breaches of horizontal equity in our existing system—exclusion from most programs of some groups of needy individuals; more favored treatment of some groups over others (e.g., the aged over families with children); and geographical inequities in benefit levels. He proposes some guidelines for future policy decisions to alleviate these problems, including a rethinking of the categorical distinctions on which the present system is based.

Conrad Johnson's paper, "Equity: Its Scope and Its Relation to Other

Objectives," addresses the problem of conflicting objectives from the viewpoint of getting a clear understanding of what conflicts there really are, and of their importance in the formulation of income support policy. In pursuing this strategy, he selects a number of illustrative examples for detailed examination. In each instance, he shows that an apparent breach of equity is not a genuine breach, or that the problem is less important than appears at first glance. For example, one widely criticized feature of the present system is inequality among states in the levels of benefits paid in Aid to Families with Dependent Children. Such inequalities are not necessarily instances of inequity, according to Johnson's analysis. When the question of equity is relativized to different reference groups (in this instance, the citizens of individual states), the inequality in benefits between them is not necessarily an instance of inequity. The argument for this conclusion is based on an analogy from social arrangements for the care of children. Whatever group—family, extended family, community—has responsibility for care of children, the responsibility for equitable treatment does not extend beyond the range of that group. The moral demands of equity hold in the first instance within these reference groups but not among them.

In his paper on "Conflicting Objectives and the Priorities Problem," Norman Daniels is principally concerned with arguments in support of adequacy of benefits over the claims of vertical equity and work incentives. When priority is given to the latter objectives, he notes, the effect is likely to be one of holding benefit levels below wage levels of the worst-off (or nearly worst-off) employed workers. (Policies that have this effect have been under heated debate for more than a century under the name of "less eligibility.") When benefits are determined on this basis, factors extraneous to the living requirements of the recipients control the upper limits of benefit levels.

Daniels's analysis reveals the existence of some complications in attempting to assign priorities to these objectives that do not appear at first glance. He identifies two factors which need to be taken into account:

(1.) How much change in basic social arrangements is being contemplated in discussing the priority problem, i.e., how much do we take to be fixed, and how much revision is to be considered? For those who take the income support system to be only the means of making minor corrections in social institutions, the answers to priority questions will be different from those given by persons who see income support in the context of far-reaching changes in distribution of economic goods. Thus the question of conflicting objectives is seen to be many problems, depending on the assumptions being made.

(2.) In any consideration of moral principles as a basis for resolving the priorities problem, we must also take into account our estimate of general social compliance with ideal norms of social justice. (Daniels calls this the "Context of Compliance.") The moral grounds for assigning priorities to those objectives will be different in a context of full compliance with ideal norms than in one of extensive non-compliance. When these two factors are taken together, Daniels shows, further complications arise. His own position is that adequacy of benefits has the strongest claim to priority in the existing "context of compliance."

Martha Phillips's paper on "Family Impact of Income Support Programs" examines in detail the numerous ways in which income support policies may affect—favorably or unfavorably—the stability of families that receive income support benefits. She identifies and discusses six aspects of family life on which program policies could conceivably have an important impact: (1) preventing family break-up; (2) repairing "broken families"; (3) discouraging illegitimacy; (4) discouraging childbearing; (5) securing support from absent parents; and (6) encouraging mothers in female-headed families to work. Phillips argues that income support policies should concentrate primarily on providing economic support to those in need. Efforts to formulate policies intended to stabilize and strengthen family life, she argues, are unlikely to succeed, or will be unacceptable to the general public. Moreover, in some instances, at least, these efforts will be incompatible with goals of adequacy and equity. Concern for family stability can best be expressed, she concludes, in vigilant observation of income support programs for the purpose of identifying and correcting any policies which cause significantly negative effects on family structure and functioning.

In her article, "The Economic Support of 'Fatherless' Children," Barbara R. Bergmann examines the respective roles of public agency and absent fathers in supporting children in one-parent, female-headed homes. Her initial premise is that the traditional family pattern of adult male support of children is breaking down, and that in consequence new institutional provisions need to be worked out for the economic support of these one-parent families. More specifically, (1) to what extent can absent fathers be expected and required to support their children, and (2) what support can be and should be expected from the employment of the mothers?

The problem of support, Bergmann points out, is serious: One out of three fatherless families fell below the poverty line in 1977. Only an estimated 5 to 10 percent of the income received by these families comes from support payments. Ought fathers to be absolved from responsibility? Bergmann argues that mothers should not be required to carry the entire burden, and that absent fathers should bear substantial responsibility. She argues for a standard formula in which the absent father would contribute one-half of the costs of family life. The government should, she asserts, supply the following: high quality child care, cash payments where parental support is not possible, and a mandatory public system of support payment collection, preferably on the model of the withholding tax.

PV

5

The Concept of Vertical Equity and Its Application to Social Program Design

JODIE T. ALLEN

Introduction

The concept of "vertical equity," while not a formal construct in traditional systems of justification, has come into wide use in recent years as a guiding principle in the design and evaluation of a variety of social programs intended to affect the distribution of income. More honored, perhaps, in the breach than in the observance, the concept has nonetheless exerted considerable influence on the design of the plethora of income-tested cash and in-kind programs aimed, inaugurated, or expanded in the late 1960s and early 1970s with the intent of improving the general social and economic well-being of lower income persons or increasing their consumption of certain "merit" goods.

What is fair in the distribution of access to goods and services in a society has been the subject of millennia of debate and it would be presumptuous for this pragmatic practitioner of policy formulation, and sometime observer of the social and political scenes, to attempt to provide a thoroughgoing analysis of ethical concepts with respect to income redistribution, much less a definitive statement of preferred norms.

This paper will, however, attempt a tentative definition of the concept of vertical equity in the form of several heuristic principles for the development of social programs which might be said to accord with both prevailing notions of fairness and overall notions of social utility.

The remainder of the paper will address the application of the vertical equity concept, as defined, in the design and operation of several tax and transfer programs, noting in particular: where the concept has come in conflict with other policy objectives (welfare programs); where the concept has been ignored with unsettling results (medical assistance and day care programs); where the concept has been implicit in the basic design of a program but inadvertently violated in the construction of program details (food stamps); and where the concept is particularly difficult to apply, as in the provision of relatively indivisible benefits such as jobs and housing.

Lastly, some possible remedies for these problems are suggested together with some cautionary observations on the potential for increased conflict between prevailing notions of redistributional equity and the continuation of recent trends in the development of social programs in the United States.

What Do We Mean By Vertical Equity?

The notion of equity is obviously central to the design of government transfers programs, that is, those programs whose primary or sole purpose is to alter the distribution of income and wealth in society by bestowing benefits on one class of citizens and levying taxes on another to finance them.[1] There are, to be sure, sound practical justifications for such redistribution. On the positive side, there is the stimulation of economic growth; on the negative, the avoidance of social unrest. Some, such as James Tobin, would argue that no further justifications are either required or attainable.[2] But whether one sides with the moral absolutists or seeks such utilitarian origins for prevailing ethics, it seems clear that the question of fairness is central to the justification of redistribution programs.

Getting down to cases with respect to what constitutes equity in the design of such programs is, of course, another matter. In theory, equity requires that we give each person his "due." In practice, the lack of agreement on what constitutes just deserts may reduce the precept to a tautology. At the very least, however, there can be little argument with the notion that whatever it is we are redistributing, equal benefits should be given to persons who are "equally situated" as measured by some criteria deemed relevant to the purpose of the distribution. In the parlance of income redistribution, this has come to be known as the principle of "horizontal equity." While there may be a great deal of controversy as to what constitutes "equal situation" in any particular application, there is widespread acceptance of the horizontal equity principle of equal treatment for equal persons.

Horizontal equity is, however, a rather weak precept as a guide to program design. All it tells us is that whatever is given should be given equally to equals. No guidance is provided as to what might constitute an appropriate level of benefit for award. Perhaps that is why there is far less agreement with respect to the companion concept of "vertical equity," which, by telling us how we should treat people who are "unequal" in some measurable respect, implies that there is some appropriate amount of redistribution or at least some limiting conditions.

Redistribution programs have as their purpose the alteration of the "pre-program" distribution of income in a society.[3] The very existence of such programs implies some societal discontent with the pre-program distribution, at least with respect to the program's "reference group(s)," i.e., its intended beneficiaries. At the least, then, it seems equitable that those most in "need," however defined for the purposes of the program, should end up—after the program benefits have been distributed and the taxes to finance them collected—better off when compared to their less "needy" fellow citizens than before.

The economist's theory of declining marginal utility of expenditures provides further utilitarian support for this notion, since, ignoring side effects for the moment, aggregate societal happiness can be increased by providing additional consumption for the most needy at the expense of curtailed consumption by the more affluent.

But how far does equity require us to go in this direction? At one extreme is the egalitarian view that equity in government programs ultimately requires *equality of outcome*. In the case of government redistribution programs this would imply equality of post-tax, post-transfer income with compelling circumstances, such as the maintenance of incentives for work and saving, required to justify any residual post-program differences. Given that, at the least, innate differences in ability and the workings of chance will inevitably produce considerable differences in first-round income in a market economy, such a requirement for equality of outcome inevitably requires considerable inequality in treatment by government programs.

John Rawls provides a theoretical justification for the egalitarian position by envisaging an intitial social contract in which members of a forming society decide on a subsequent distribution of income and assets without knowing what their own future position in that distribution (this being revealed later) will be.[4] He concludes that, to borrow a phrase from the game theorists, people would pursue the "mini-max" strategy[5] of choosing an equal distribution of income.

It is noteworthy, however, that in a recent colloquium of distinguished social scientists and political observers of varying political persuasions, none found the Rawlsian concept persuasive.[6] Virtually all agreed, on either ethical or utilitarian grounds or both, that some amount of redistribution was desirable to achieve at least a minimum universal level of subsistence, but even the most ardent advocate of economic equality among the discussants, Arthur Okun, stopped short of thoroughgoing egalitarianism, albeit primarily on pragmatic grounds.[7]

Perhaps of greater relevance for the non-elitist is that even the most casual empiricism will confirm that the egalitarian notion of what is fair does not accord at all with popular notions on the subject. Attitudinal surveys, legislative histories, and existing statutes provide us with a remarkably consistent and considerably different view of prevailing norms. This is not to suggest that ethical principles should be determined by the rule of the current majority, even if it is a substantial one. One might argue, however, that a concept of vertical equity which flies so clearly in the face of public and historical preferences will have little relevance as a working guide to policy formulation in the area of income redistribution.

Explicit redistributional programs such as welfare consistently score very low in the public esteem. (A typical finding is that of a Harris poll of August 1977 in which only 24 percent of the public thought it would be a "very serious loss" if the federal government cut welfare spending by a third[8].) Despite their redistributional inefficiency, "universal," i.e., non-needs-tested programs such as Social Security and Unemployment Insurance garner far greater public support and far larger shares of the public dollar. And despite the obviously greater redistributional efficiency of the progressive income tax over regressive or proportional forms of taxation such as payroll and consumption taxes, income taxation is out-classed only by the rapidly escalating property tax in unpopularity, while the highly regressive Social Security tax and the mildly regressive sales tax appear as the popular favorites.[9]

In an interesting review of popular attitudes toward equality, Everett Ladd finds a long and consistent historical antipathy among Americans to the concept of *equality of result*. Surveys of working class opinion have astoundingly low assessments of the "proper" level of taxation for those with very high incomes (10 percent!) and there is widespread support, even among minorities and "activist" groups, for the notion that it is fair to reward persons not only for additional efforts but for special talents or education which have allowed them to enter more lucrative occupations.[10]

Should we then conclude that American notions of equity are best embodied by Herbert Spencer's *Social Statics?* Clearly not. On the one hand, as Ladd observes, Americans have shown an equally strong and stable commitment to the objective of equal opportunity and willingness to spend public dollars for its achievement. There is strong and consistent popular support for the notion that the government should insure that all Americans have the opportunity to earn a decent living.[11] And even in the wake of the "Proposition 13" tax revolt, a recent Roper poll found strong popular support for direct public job creation to assure the opportunity to earn a basic living particularly among priority groups such as family breadwinners and the disadvantaged.[12]

It must also be observed that, whatever our popularly expressed misgivings in this regard, we live in a society that has witnessed a 135 percent increase in the real value of transfer program benefits over the last decade to an expenditure level equal to 10 percent of the gross national product.[13]

However begrudgingly, our ideas of equity have shifted in the direction of the egalitarian—but with strongly stated reservations. Or perhaps it is the other way around. In general in America we view what is given as equitable but we have come to harbor sufficiently strong doubts about certain aspects of the status quo to cause us to feel that direct intervention in the distribution of income and resources is morally justified if the results of such intervention do not come into conflict with even more basic notions of equity as requiring *equality of treatment* rather than equality of outcome.[14]

In the face of these contradictory and shifting guidelines, what might serve as ethical guidelines at least for the moment?

A Working Definition of the Vertical Equity Concept

Faced with these conflicting signals from theoreticians, politicians, and the body politic, policymakers and analysts have had, nonetheless, to develop a working approach to the definition of vertical equity in the design of tax and transfer programs. While no rigorous definition of the limiting principles is possible or perhaps even useful, I believe that one can describe a set of heuristic principles to guide policymakers in the design of redistributive programs which are congruent (or at least not in outright conflict) with prevailing notions of what is fair in our society. For convenience, in further discussion I shall group these principles under the heading "vertical equity," realizing that such a formulation may not be accepted by either the thoroughgoing egalitarian or the ardent advocate of the status quo, or be of universal applicability in other societies or times in which dissatisfaction with the pre-program distribution of income is more acute.

The first of these principles is that noted earlier. In a program whose purpose is to redistribute access to money, goods, or services for the purpose of reducing inequality in the satisfaction of basic needs, those in greater need should benefit more than those in lesser need. Note, however, that, at least in the case of cash transfers, this rule does not necessarily require that the direct distribution be proportional to pre-transfer need but simply that the net effect on incomes after both transfers and taxation are accounted for be progressive, i.e., "pro-poor" in effect. Thus one might distribute a fixed benefit but achieve redistribution through progressive taxation to finance benefits.[15]

The second principle specifies a limiting condition on the operation of the first. The constraint is this: *Given a distribution of income, the effect of tax or transfer policies should not be such as to reverse the position of persons in the resulting income distribution.* That is to say, if Person *A* (or an aggregation of persons commonly regarded as an economic unit, such as a family) has a "private income" (including earnings, rents, dividends, and other property income) of, say, $10,000 and Person B has a private income of $8,000, the taxes levied on Person A, less any governmental benefits, should not be so high as to cause his post-tax, post-benefit income to be less than the income of Person B after that income has similarly been reduced by taxes and augmented by benefits. In other words, "rank order" must be preserved.

The third principle applies an additional, more ambiguous constraint. Not only should the positions of persons not be reversed, but the distance between them in the distribution should not be "unduly" compressed. The last principle is the standard "exceptions" clause which allows deviations from the preceding rules in the case of compelling circumstances. In particular, persons deemed to be different from others by virtue of some special need or quality may be preferred to others not in their reference group.

Vertical equity thus tells us something fairly specific about how to treat people who are "unequal" as measured by some factors deemed to be relevant. As noted earlier, its companion concept, "horizontal equity," by contrast, tells us how to treat people who are "equal" and simply stipulates that persons in "equivalent circumstances" be treated equally by government policies. Together these tenets would appear to reduce considerably the latitude of government action in altering the distribution of income whether by intent or indirection.

The tenets, however, give rise to a host of ancillary problems of both measurement and concept. These, in turn, allow ample room for interpretation in program design. What is an "economic unit?" A nuclear family? Everyone who lives together? Defining an economic unit as the basis for taxation or transfer eligibility may in itself give rise to problems of both vertical and horizontal equity. For example, inequities are produced if a person receives less favored treatment in a program by virtue of a particular living arrangement and that loss is not fully compensated by the benefits of that living arrangement as compared to the status of those receiving preferential program treatment. How should we value government benefits? Benefits in kind (government-provided goods and services or earmarked subsidies) may not—for a variety of reasons, including artificially inflated pricing induced by the subsidy itself—be valued at cost by the beneficiary. Even cash transfers may have their net benefits reduced by "transaction" costs—stigma, inconvenience, loss of privacy—associated with their receipt. In this latter regard it is important to note that the method of distribution may be as important as the amount distributed.

And, of course, the tenets themselves are hardly unambiguous guides to action. What are the "compelling circumstances" which justify exception? What is "undue" compression? What are "equivalent circumstances" and do these differ according to the particular purpose of a government program?

Finally, there is the most basic of questions. Why do we care about vertical equity at all? And how much do we care when the concept comes into conflict with the achievement of important social goals or other competing concepts?

Practical Bases for the Vertical Equity Concept

Before turning to the problems of practical application of the vertical equity concept, as defined, it is important to note that it has strong utilitarian underpinnings. The most obvious is that the preservation of vertical equity, as I have defined it, is tantamount to the preservation of incentives for work effort and saving—at least to the extent that, in a non-coercive society, financial gain is taken to be the surest and most stable source of motivation for productive work effort. In simplest terms the mechanics of this effect are straightforward (although understanding of the phenomenon, even after ten years or so of active "welfare reform" debate, is remarkably limited, not only among the public but among the ranks of those in direct position to affect such matters). If you give benefits to some people and none (or a reduced amount) to others, you reduce the intitial difference between their net income positions. When you tax some people but not others (or some people relatively more) to pay for these benefits (assuming they are not being financed by some friendly foreign power), you further reduce the dispersion of income positions, particularly if the taxed class is not also among the beneficiary population. At the extreme the net effect of differential tax and transfer policy may be to eliminate income differentials altogether.

Translating these actions into effects on work effort is somewhat more complicated. Economists predict three effects on work effort, two of which operate to reduce it. The first is the "transfer income effect" associated with the provision of a benefit other than in return for an equal amount of goods and services. If a government subsidy makes it possible to sustain (or increase) a given level of consumption with a reduced (or the same) amount of earned income, then the incentive to maintain (or increase) the current level of earnings is reduced.

The second work-reducing effect is the so-called "compensated substitution effect" associated with the reduction of benefits, and/or increase in taxation, as private income increases. If, in an income-tested program, benefits are reduced as a function of income from other sources, that rate of benefit reduction acts as an effective "tax" on income. For example, if a welfare program provides a basic income benefit of $5,000 to a family with no other income, but offsets that benefit dollar for dollar by the amount of income from other sources, then the family with $5,000 of earnings is no better off than a family with no earnings. Over the range of zero to $5,000 a family thus faces an effective "tax rate" of 100 percent, i.e., the government takes back a dollar for every additional dollar they earn. If the benefit is reduced by only fifty cents for each dollar of private income, the tax rate is 50 percent. The effect is thus the same as in a direct tax program. These benefit reduction rates reduce the effective wage rate received by a person (for example, a marginal tax of 50 percent reduces the net return of an hourly wage of $4 to $2). In so doing they lower the "opportunity cost" of an additional hour of leisure. That is, the net loss in income associated with reducing work effort may be considerably reduced and, ceteris paribus, one would expect some substitution of leisure for work effort to be induced.

The third effect, which works in the opposite direction, is the "tax income effect." The imposition of a high tax or benefit reduction rate means that, at any level of private income other than zero, a person's disposable income will be lower than it would otherwise have been. This in turn may stimulate additional work effort if the desire for increased consumption or saving is sufficient to offset the work-reducing effects of the transfer income itself (if such is present) and the tax-induced reduction in net wages.

The strength of these incentives and their net effect on persons in different income and life cycle circumstances are, of course, empirical questions. Several major field experiments have been launched to measure the impact of transfer programs on the work effort of prime age adults in families. The largest and most reliable of the experiments, the Seattle-Denver Experiment, recently produced the following findings. Cash transfer programs of the size and design most frequently discussed in political debate do reduce work effort and those reductions can be related to both the level of benefits and the magnitude of the benefit reduction rate. However, with a relatively low income guarantee (about 75 percent of the poverty line) and a combined tax rate from all sources (positive taxes plus benefit reduction rates) of 50 percent, these reductions can be held to tolerable levels (about 10 percent for husbands, 26 percent for wives, and 7 percent for female heads of families).[16]

It is noteworthy that as the result of the concomitant receipt of benefits from the variety of cash and in-kind transfer programs now operating in the United States and the associated cumulation of their benefit reduction rates, many low-income persons now face considerably weaker incentives for work than those cited above. From this perspective, policymakers who seek to liberalize or extend income-tested benefits may find themselves with considerably less "wiggle room" than they might like.[17]

But I would emphasize again my belief that the justification of vertical equity as I have defined it does not depend solely on the desire, indeed, necessity, for maintaining work effort at least among most of our able-bodied citizenry. The concept also recommends itself to most people as simple "fairness." Perhaps this commonplace perception, like many other ethical principles, is simply a rationalization of a basic societal need, in this case the obvious desirability of encouraging productive work, saving, risktaking, and innovation. But it is worth noting that the destruction of the Nixon administration's Family Assistance Plan for welfare reform was completed by Congressional unveiling, at the instigation of the then Senator from Delaware, John Williams, of the host of vertical inequities which that plan either created or left unremedied, and that that distinction was based not only, or even not so much, on expected reductions in work effort (since such had not then been quantified) as on the popular and Congressional feeling that the whole system wasn't fair. Ask any ghetto youth if it is fair for someone whose family is on welfare to get a special benefit—say free medical care or a job—that someone who isn't on welfare but is just barely making it can't get, and you may be surprised at the vehemence of his reaction.

Applying the Concept to Program Design

In the end, vertical equity is a question of getting down to cases. In the remainder of my discussion I will focus on the application of the notion of vertical equity in several tax and transfer programs, noting in particular: where the concept has been explicitly addressed in the design of programs but the results come in sharp conflict with other policy preferences (welfare programs); where the concept has been totally ignored with unsettling results (medical assistance and day care); where application of the concept has been implicit in the design of a program but failure to make it explicit has led to unintended results (food stamps); and where the concept is particularly difficult to apply, as in the provision of valuable benefits which are relatively indivisible or, at least, practically divisible only into discrete amounts of considerable size (subsidized jobs and housing).

One preliminary caveat is in order. It is possible that when several transfer programs are operating simultaneously, their net effect may be to cancel out each other's deficiencies so that the multiple redistributive impact is vertically equitable while the singular pattern is not. To the extent that large general public expenditures, such as education, differentially favor the better-off, or are at best proportional to income, the redistributive impact of governmental programs may also be considerably muted. However, as several studies have demonstrated,[18] the design of transfer programs in the United States is generally such that their deficiencies in design tend to compound rather than compensate over the income ranges in which they operate. It is thus instructive to consider the individual program features that produce this cumulative effect.

WELFARE PROGRAMS

The welfare application is the most obvious. I have already reviewed the mechanics of the typical welfare program with a basic guarantee for those with no other income and a benefit reduction rate that offsets the net benefit payable by some percentage of income from other sources. Vertical equity didn't play much of a role in the early design of welfare programs for three reasons: Benefits were generally restricted to classes of the poor assumed to have limited, if any, labor market potential (the aged, disabled, and husbandless women with children); benefits were generally low relative to prevailing wages; and preferential treatment of these groups compared to low-income families was justified on the grounds of the exceptional and certainly unavoidable circumstances in which they found themselves. All of these justifications for violation of the vertical equity principle have come under increasing attack, at least as they apply to the female-headed family group and even to some of the borderline disabled. Welfare and related benefits have risen relative to the wages available to many of the working poor. As more and more women, including those with small children, enter the labor force, the irrelevance of work incentives for welfare mothers has become increasingly questionable; and pressures have mounted for the extension of benefits to working poor and near-poor two-parent families, many of whom find themselves paying taxes to support benefits to persons whose disposable incomes may be higher than their own.

But introducing "vertical equity" into welfare programs is easier said than done. One way would be to reduce the basic guarantee given to those with no other income. You won't find many votes in Congress for that. The other is to reduce the benefit reduction rate so that benefits are tapered off gradually over higher income ranges and income compression at the lower end of the distribution is reduced. The problem with this solution is that it extends benefit coverage to persons higher in the income distribution. This, in turn, increases not only transfers costs, but caseloads as well, two equally unpopular political phenomena. Furthermore, within the ineluctable confines of a budget constraint, extending coverage to new classes of the poor means fewer dollars available for "fiscal relief" to most governors and a few well-known mayors, which, as anyone of passing familiarity with welfare knows, is the only really strong force behind current movements for welfare reform. If actions of the House Special Subcommittee on Welfare Reform last year are any guide, fiscal relief can beat vertical equity hands down any time as a guiding principle to the Congress.[19]

MEDICAID

Public policy has produced even more flagrant violations of the vertical equity concept in the case of in-kind or earmarked transfers such as medical assistance and day care. In these cases the outcome is perhaps more understandable since the transfer of income is less explicit, although, if the benefits provided have, in fact, any real value to the recipients, the redistributional impacts are every bit as real as in the case of cash transfers. The founding fathers of Medicaid (persuaded mostly by inattention that all they were doing was federalizing modest, locally controlled programs of direct medical vendor payments for welfare recipients) launched in 1965 what was to become a $20 billion program of first-dollar medical coverage for a substantial portion of the low-income population as well as certain categories of needy persons not on welfare. The results of unleashing so generous a subsidy of demand into a market characterized by limited supply and near monopolistic provider control (side by side with the even more expensive but less comprehensive Medicare program for the aged and disabled) were predictable. Both prices and utilization rose dramatically so that by 1978 the average insurance value of Medicaid was estimated at $840 per person for all covered recipients, including the aged and disabled poor, and at $462 per person, or $1,850 for a four-person family with children, a relatively healthy group.

Medicaid violates vertical equity on two scores. First, there is the infamous "notch" caused by the fact that while full coverage is extended to all eligibles, eligibility is, in general, restricted to persons who are also eligible for welfare. If earnings on other income increase even one dollar beyond the eligibility limit for welfare, the former eligible thus abruptly loses a benefit worth on the average some $1,850 to his or her family.[21] Family A with income slightly above the welfare limit can thus end up having a lower total effective income, i.e., less purchasing power, than Family B, with income, including welfare, as much as $1,800 less, if Medicaid coverage is of equal potential value to both families.[22]

But there is an even more serious equity problem implicit in the Medicaid design. This problem is that, at least in states providing broad-gauge Medicaid coverage, welfare recipients are assured a level of medical care beyond the financial reach of all but the most affluent. In dramatic but not unlikely terms, we may find the policeman's wife waiting in line at the local clinic while the welfare mother meets her prearranged appointment with a Park Avenue specialist.

DAY CARE

Day care presents the same problem. Since day-care standards are set, by and large, by day-care advocates, it is not surprising to find that the sort of day care which meets federal standards—and which federal day-care planners prefer to subsidize—is very expensive. The going estimate for high quality day care is now about $200 per month per child, or $2,400 a year for one child and $4,800 for two.[23] Again a situation is produced in which, apart from the very affluent, only the most "needy" mothers who receive full or near full subsidies can "afford" to purchase a presumably valuable commodity. Sliding scale fee schedules, which require progressively higher contributions as user income increases, can help to avoid an out and out "notch" over some income range by tapering net benefits gradually. But unless we are prepared to extend partial subsidization to the very high income levels at which a family could afford to pay the full freight itself, a net income reversal is unavoidable at the point at which subsidy eligibility is terminated. Again, one should remember that the income levels at which eligibility for day-care subsidization is likely to be lost are in the range over which welfare and medical assistance benefits are also lost while income and payroll tax liabilities mount. Thus the total magnitude of the income reversal encountered as earnings increase over a one or two thousand dollar range may be very substantial. And there are other potential losses as well.

FOOD STAMPS

At first glance the Food Stamp program may appear to be a model of equitable program design, and, indeed, it is perhaps our most thoughtfully designed income maintenance program. In the original Food Stamp program design, benefits were tapered gradually as income increased by requiring participants to pay progressively higher amounts for a fixed "coupon allotment" determined on the basis of family size. In general, participants were required to pay 30 percent of net income for their stamps after deductions were made for certain other classes of expenditure judged to be essential.

Viewed by itself, the Food Stamp program appears a model of both horizontal and vertical equity (if we ignore the problem of cumulation of benefits and their associated benefit reduction rates for multiple program beneficiaries). All of the poor, not just preferred classes, are eligible, and basic benefits are adjusted for household size and other living arrangements. Benefits are tapered gradually and at a reasonably modest rate. Apart from some peculiarities in the benefit schedule addressed by the recent amendments, there are no explicit benefit notches. But even the Food Stamp program has harbored its own vertical inequities. The first of these is a violation—unintended to be sure, but flagrant nonetheless—of the first "law" of vertical equity, i.e., that net benefits should be proportional to need. In a laudable attempt to provide "equity" in the individual case, policymakers in the Department of Agriculture over a number of years introduced a series of deductible expenses into the computation of net income for the purpose of determining purchasing requirements. The purpose, of course, was to be sure that participants had enough money left to buy their stamps after they had made payments for housing, clothing, medical care, school expenses, day care, and other worthy goods and services. The net effect of these "itemized deductions" was to achieve a distribution of Food Stamp benefits which was at best proportional and, over some parts of the covered income ranges, even regressive. The origins of this unintended outcome are not hard to find. Few of the poorest recipients could afford to buy many of the deductible items. As a result they ended up paying close to the nominal 30 percent of income purchase rate. More affluent participants could afford far larger purchases of deductible items so that in many cases their net incomes, after deductions, were actually lower, and their net benefits correspondingly higher than their more needy fellow participants.[24] Recently enacted amendments to the Food Stamp law will remedy this inequity by instituting a standard deduction and sharply limiting itemized deductions.

The Food Stamp program, however, continues to harbor an implicit notch, albeit one of scant magnitude compared to those implicit in Medicaid and day care programs. Again, the problem arises from inattention by the program's designers and supporters to the role of the program as a redistributor of income. Such inattention, if it was not unintentional, was at least understandable. Wrapped in the banner of nutrition, an income maintenance program can flourish. Viewed as an explicit device for income distribution it is likely to die on the Congressional cutting-room floor. Again, the problem is that when you define redistribution in terms of a substantive objective such as adequate nutrition or housing or medical care, the basic "guarantee" or package of benefits decided upon is likely to bear scant relationship to what families considerably higher in the income distribution than the presumed target population are able to afford on their own.

Shortly after data from the most recent Bureau of Labor Statistics Consumer Expenditure Survey was released I made a simple comparison which suggests that this may be the case. In 1975 the Food Stamp coupon allotment for a family of four was $162 a month. Adjusting for price differences between 1975 and the time of the survey (1972–3), we find that a family of four with a then median income of $13,500 spent only $8 a month more on food at home (including various items not purchaseable with Food Stamps) than the amount guaranteed under the program for the very lowest income person. Judged by a standard of *adequacy* this achievement is highly commendable. But again the keepers of vertical equity might interject a sour note. One might accept a complete compression of the bottom half of the income distribution with respect to food consumption (which is what a coupon allotment set close or equal to the median level of food consumption amounts to). But can one then justify phasing out the subsidy anywhere in the income distribution below the income level at which a rational consumer would be willing and able to sustain such consumption on his own? To do so clearly produces a "notch" with respect to food consumption. One may counter with the argument that while increases in income can in those circumstances clearly lead to reduced food consumption, total utility is still increased since the family could, presumably, still choose to purchase the full coupon allotment in food. Still, there is something questionable about subsidizing a higher level of food consumption at the lowest income levels than substantial numbers of higher income families are willing to purchase on their own.

On the other hand, Congress is understandably queasy about extending eligibility for the high transaction cost Food Stamp program to half the population. And there is also the palpable absurdity of subsidizing food consumption to average citizens in the best fed country in the world.

Eliminating the purchase requirement will reduce this problem since, except at the very lowest income levels where full benefits will be paid, participating families may now choose to divert some income, previously earmarked for food, to other purposes they deem more essential. Short of "cashing out" the program altogether, the only complete solution is to abandon exogenous standards of nutritional adequacy (which are, in any case, rarely realized in the consumption patterns of participants or, indeed, of most Americans)[25] and adopt a relativistic basis for determining coupon allotments. In this approach Congress would decide, on some practical grounds, what constitutes a reasonable income limit for Food Stamp eligibility. The coupon allotment would then be set equal to whatever amount families at the eligibility limit are observed to spend on average for covered food items. In this fashion, while families would not choose to increase their consumption of food as income approaches the eligibility limit, they would not, at least, tend to reduce food consumption when the limit is passed.

JOB PROGRAMS

A final problem in designing "vertically equitable" social programs is that, in some types of in-kind programs, the benefit provided is relatively indivisible, so that adjusting benefits in smooth inverse relation to income is difficult if not impossible. Public Service Employment (PSE) is such a case. Giving someone a job is a benefit worth several thousand dollars (at least if the person would otherwise have been unemployed, as is presumably the usual case in a PSE program). If you wish to target eligibility for such jobs on the most needy, an obvious method is to establish an income limit for eligibility. The problem with such a rule is that it creates an inevitable net income "notch." A family with income even one dollar below the limit receives a benefit, that is, a job, worth several thousand dollars. A family with income one dollar above the limit receives nothing.[26]

The jobs component of the administration's Program for Better Jobs and Income (welfare reform) attempts to avoid these difficulties by using two rationing devices which I, as their author, think are an efficient and equitable compromise. The first is that jobs are restricted to one per family and that job must be taken by the family's sole or "principal" earner. The principal earner is the adult in the family who, with exceptions with respect to current availability for work, in the last six months either worked the longest hours or earned the most.[27] The second restriction is that wages in the subsidized jobs are set at or close to the minimum wage so that they will not compete heavily with most jobs in the regular public and private economy. If we can assume a normal desire for income maximization on the part of potential applicants, these two rules together effectively restrict participation to the relatively small number of families whose best earner could otherwise not find a steady job paying even the relatively modest wage offered by the program.

The vertical equity implications of this rule are worth examining in some detail. Essentially we have eliminated the earnings distribution for families below the program wage. No principal earners need earn less unless they prefer to do so (in which case we can assume they are experiencing more than commensurate non-monetary returns for their choice). This compression, however, is tolerable because it is caused by *increases* rather than by decreases of the returns to work effort. And we have not created a "notch" at least with respect to primary earners. Those who were earning more before the program are still better off than those who were not. The existence of a secondary earner in a participating family with previously lower earnings can, of course, cause participating Family *A* to have post-program earnings higher than another Family *B* with initially higher earnings. But in this case justification for the outcome can be found in the fact that the reason for the more favorable final income position of Family *A* is the greater work effort of the additional earner relative to Family *B*. If, as we have observed, an essential basis of the concept of vertical equity is the notion of reward for "merit," in this case work effort, this outcome cannot be said to be inconsistent, per se, with the principle.[28]

Possible Solutions to the Vertical Equity Problem

The success of efforts to cope with the problem of vertical equity in the design of tax and transfer programs has not been assisted by the fragmentation of program responsibility among numerous Congressional committees and governmental agencies, nor by a certain lack of candor in addressing the redistribution potential of in-kind or earmarked transfers. Nonetheless, policymakers and analysts have attempted a variety of direct or indirect solutions. We have noted the latest attempt in the design of the welfare reform job component.

In other in-kind programs, such as day care, housing or medical assistance, the introduction of benefit vouchers, the value of which could be determined on a sliding income scale, has been suggested as a method of rationing scarce resources, introducing some element of consumer sovereignty and thereby, it is hoped, exerting some restraint on both service quality and price. One problem with such solutions is that the markets into which the subsidized consumer is sent forth, armed with his voucher and perhaps a modest amount of informational assistance, are typically characterized by shortage of supply and dominated by providers who can, all too easily, capture the net value of the voucher by the simple device of raising prices. Another problem is that while a sliding scale may avoid an out and out "notch," it does so at the price of cumulating benefit reduction rates over a larger range of the income distribution.

Another, time-honored method of redistributing scarce resources is through "trickle down." In the housing field this has meant the process whereby government subsidy of new housing construction has upgraded the housing quality of middle-income consumers and thereby released somewhat older or inferior housing for occupancy by lower-income residents who can, in turn, vacate inferior stock. In the manpower area, the closest analogy is "creaming," whereby scarce resources for training and other types of manpower upgrading have been focused on those who can benefit most readily from them. The jobs vacated by these upgraded workers can then presumably be taken by less skilled workers who may then become next in line for assistance.

Another way of skirting the problem is to continue to erect special categories of persons whose preferential treatment is justified by reference to conditions of particular merit or "no-fault" disadvantage such as age, disability, or failure of normal expectations. One problem with this approach is that there are few such circumstances which command universal recognition of merit. Another is that constructing such preferential categories may inadvertently provide incentives for people to adjust their behavior or circumstances so as to meet the qualifying conditions. As noted earlier, suspicions of this sort have long been harbored with respect to the growing members of fatherless families and even, in more recent years, have emerged with respect to the sudden upsurge in the numbers of those qualifying as disabled under the liberalized Social Security Disability and Supplemental Security Income programs. As James Tobin has suggested, it may well be that "the opportunities for innocuous and fair categorical discrimination are quite limited."[29]

Such rationing devices can be justified as efficient methods of maximizing total returns to investment. Compared to the alternative of "leap frogging" the most disadvantaged over many others who are only slightly better off, they may also be judged more equitable, at least by the standard discussed here. The major problem with the trickle-down approach may be that it is not connotative of the sort of swashbuckling commitment to solving the problems of the poor which gladdens the heart of political speechwriters.

A more ambitious remedy is to "universalize" subsidies for social services and merit goods, that is, to provide them free to everyone. This is the approach which has been taken in the highly developed "socialist" countries of Western Europe, although not without some recent signs of social and economic strain. The negative features of this approach are restriction of consumer choice, both with respect to the subsidized good and to alternative consumption choices as well, pressure on prices and supply, and, of course, substantial increases in the tax burden. While universal programs cause even greater overall compression of the income distribution, they are considerably less likely than income-tested programs to lead to income reversals. The pressures they exert on the supply of subsidized goods and services may, however, reduce the net benefits per dollar of expenditure relative to more restricted programs.

A last and perhaps, in the long run, most promising remedy is indirect intervention to equalize the "prefisc" distribution of income by equalizing access to earned and property income.

Conclusions

In searching among these remedies, or alternatively, deciding to dismiss the problem as the least among possible evils, we are clearly in need of some ethical guidelines. As Robert Lampman observed, even several years ago, we are fast approaching the point where we cannot continue our enthusiasm for the social program designs of the sixties and, at the same time, pay lip service to the principle of vertical equity and the concern for work incentives that it implies.[30]

Even the federal income tax, long a model of "notchless" perfection and careful attention to marginal incentives, is under severe strain as pressure mounts to incorporate within its structure special subsidies for day care, low earnings, private-school tuition, and the like, or to offset the regressive effect of other governmental policies, such as natural-gas deregulation, which may raise the price of essential commodities. To the extent that these "tax expenditures" confer special benefits on "disadvantaged" groups of taxpayers, are phased out over some range of income, or require the raising of marginal rates to finance them, questions of vertical equity arise.

How much compression in the income distribution can we tolerate? Judged on empirical grounds the answer may be quite a lot, if the success of in-kind programs in institutionalizing income reversals is any guide. One way of justifying departures from vertical equity, then, is the notion of restoring someone to parity of circumstance. Essentially, this is a decision that an income reversal is not really such if the benefit conferred does nothing more than compensate for "extraordinary" disadvantage such as that caused by illness or the death of a breadwinner.

But once we go down this road, as we have noticed, it is not easy to stop. The liberal tradition of policymaking in America is such that, as Nelson McClung has wisely observed, program designers and advocates feel that they have not done their job unless, at least for the target population, "there is no demand unmet at a zero price." Combine that proclivity with the trend toward "entitlement" based eligibility[31], and a squeeze on the unsubsidized consumer seems inevitable. To the economist, the immediate question is, can we afford the economic and social costs of this result? To the philosopher, the question is, can we justify it?

Notes

1. Virtually all government expenditure and tax programs affect the distribution of income in one way or another. This paper, however, will focus on those programs whose primary purpose is simply to transfer income (or access to merit goods such as food, shelter, or medical care) directly from one group to another on a basis other than the purchase of goods and services. Note, however, that part or all of the beneficiary class of a transfer may also be and often is included in the larger donor class which finances the program.

2. James Tobin, "Considerations Regarding Taxation and Inequality," *Income Redistribution*, Colin Campbell, ed. (Washington, D.C.: American Enterprise Institute, 1977).

3. In theory, there exists a "pre-fisc" distribution of income against which the redistributive effects of all government tax, transfer, and expenditure programs should be measured. In practice, the permeation of all aspects of the modern economy by direct and indirect governmental expenditures greatly complicates the measurement of the redistributional impacts of government policy. Most analysis is thus limited to measuring the marginal impact of each redistribution program, and in a woeful number of cases even the revenue raising side of a transfer program is ignored. For a discussion of these and related issues, see Tax Foundation, Inc., *Tax Burdens and Benefits of Government Expenditures by Income Class, 1961 and 1975* (New York: Tax Foundation, Inc., 1967); I. Gillespie, "Effects of Public Expenditures on the Distribution of Income," in R. Musgrave, ed., *Essays in Fiscal Federalism* (Washington, D.C.: The Brookings Institution, 1965); R. Musgrave and P. Musgrave, *Public Finance in Theory and Practice* (New York: McGraw-Hill, 1973); and M. Reynolds and E. Smolensky, "The Post Fisc Distribution: 1961 and 1970 Compared," Discussion Paper No. 191–74 (Madison, Wisconsin: Institute for Research on Poverty, 1974).

4. John Rawls, *A Theory of Justice* (Cambridge: Harvard University Press, 1971), Chapter 4.

5. That is, they will avoid risk by minimizing their maximum possible loss.

6. Colin Campbell, ed., *Income Redistribution* (Washington, D.C.: American Enterprise Institute, 1977).

7. Arthur M. Okun, "Further Thoughts on Equality and Efficiency," *Income Distribution*, pp. 13–33.

8. E. J. Dionne, Jr., "The Politics of Jobs," *Public Opinion*, Vol. 1, March/April 1978.

9. "The Tax Revolt," *Public Opinion*, July/August 1978, p. 29.

10. Everett C. Ladd, Jr., "Traditional Values Regnant," *Public Opinion*, March/April 1978.

11. A *New York Times/CBS* opinion poll found that between 70 percent and 80 percent of respondents from both ends of the political spectrum supported the notion that "the government ought to see to it that every one who wants a job can get one." (Adam Clymen, " 'Conservatives' Share 'Liberal' View," *New York Times*, January 22, 1978).

12. Albert H. Cantril and Susan Davis Cantril, *Unemployment, Government and the American People: A National Opinion Survey* (Washington: Public Research, 1978). 47 percent of respondents favored an unconditional government job guarantee, while only 20 percent of respondents thought that the government should not provide jobs to any population group.

13. Joseph A. Pechman, ed., *Setting National Priorities: The 1978 Budget* (Washington: Brookings Institution, 1977), p. 252.

14. A venerable summation of the American attitude might be Aristotle's notion of distributive justice as requiring that "awards should be 'according to merit'; for all men agree that what is just in distribution must be according to merit in some sense, though they do not all specify the same sort of merit." With respect to the distribution of public goods, proportionality is to be the guiding rule "for the justice which distributes common possessions is always in accordance with . . . proportion . . ." (*Nicomachean Ethics*, Bk V: Ch. 3(A)). There is also rectificatory justice which may seek to amend the outcome of private transactions in which one party is unfairly disadvantaged, a principle readily extended to support the notion of government redistributional activities. But Aristotle's approach seems to come closer to reflecting public views with respect to the presumptions to be established in

the process. That is, that, apart from proportionate distributions of common goods, the case must be made for governmental intervention to alter the distribution of income produced by the private transactions of citizens. The burden of proof thus lies with those who would redistribute income rather than the reverse.

15. The situation is trickier in the case of benefits in kind such as medical care or other very expensive benefits. In this case even a pro-poor distribution of benefits might actually produce a regressive net effect if the form or level of taxation required to finance the benefits were such as to lead to net losses of disposable income among the needy.

16. U.S. Department of Health, Education and Welfare *Summary Report: Seattle-Denver Income Maintenance Experiment Midexperimental Labor Supply Results and a Generalization to the National Population*, February 1978, Table 4, p. 19. Note, however, that more generous plans produce, as expected, considerably larger responses. The duration of the guarantee also affects the expected response. For example, the average reductions in hours worked across all experimental plans for families enrolled in a five- rather than a three-year experimental plan were 13 percent for husbands, 20 percent for wives, and 17 percent for female heads of families. Also note that the plan parameters cited here are considerably more moderate than those currently operative in welfare programs in all but the most penurious states.

17. For an excellent analysis of the cumulative benefit and tax problem and the resulting limitations on transfer policy reform, see Henry Aaron, *Why is Welfare So Hard to Reform?*, Studies in Social Economics (Washington, D.C.: The Brookings Institution, 1973).

18. See for example, Aaron (1973) and Joint Economic Committee, Subcommittee on Fiscal Policy, *Studies in Public Welfare*, especially Paper Nos. 1 and 4 (Washington, D.C., 1972).

19. The cumulative impact of the various provisions of the bill as it emerged from the Committee in January 1978 is to impose an 85 percent marginal tax rate on most working poor families, with possible examples of cumulative rates over 100 percent in certain circumstances.

20. The source of all the estimates cited in this and the following paragraphs is Raymond Uhalde, Jodie Allen, and Harold Beebout, *Analysis of Current Income Maintenance Programs and Budget Alternatives, Fiscal Years 1976, 1978 and 1982*, Report submitted to the Congressional Budget Office by Mathematica Policy Research, Inc. (Washington, D.C., 1977), especially p. 131 and p. 220.

21. Medically needy coverage in some states mitigates this notch somewhat by providing partial coverage to persons who are "categorically" but not income eligible (i.e., they have incomes above the welfare eligibility cutoff but they fall into one of the categories of persons eligible for welfare—aged, disabled, single-parent families with children, or, in some states, families with unemployed fathers.) Under these provisions recipients must "spend down" their income on medical expenses to the income eligibility limit before receiving compensation for additional medical expenses. The "notch" is thus replaced by a 100 percent tax on income over a range determined by the experienced level of medical expense.

22. Whether Medicaid coverage is valued by recipients at its full cost to the government is debatable, particularly given allegations of widespread provider abuse. But there is ample testimonial and anecdotal evidence that Medicaid coverage is highly valued by recipients and envied by non-recipients and that its potential loss may exert a definite effect on work effort decisions affecting welfare eligibility.

23. In 1974 a study done by HEW for the Senate Finance Committee estimated the cost of high quality day care at $193 a month. (U.S. Senate Committee on Finance, *Child Care Data and Related Materials*, October 1974). The "National Day Care Supply Center Study," currently being sponsored by HEW, found in its preliminary report that the average cost of "comprehensive child care" in federally supported centers was $2,100, with many centers reporting substantially higher costs.

24. For a more complete discussion of the equity issue in Food Stamp program design, see Jodie T. Allen, *Options for Improving the Equity and Efficiency of Benefit Determination Procedures for the Food Stamp Program*, U.S. Department of Agriculture, Food and Nutrition Service, Publication No. FNS-143 (Washington, D.C.: 1975).

25. For a description of the currently employed food plan, see U.S. Department of Agriculture, Agriculture Research Service, *The Thrifty Food Plan* (Washington, D.C., 1975). For a critique of the nutritional efficacy of the program, see Kenneth W. Clarkson, *Food Stamps and Nutrition* (Washington, D.C.: The American Enterprise Institute for Public Policy Research, 1975).

26. Some tapering of benefits might be produced by varying hours of work, but such variations greatly compound the already substantial problems of creating useful work situations suitable to the skills of eligible applicants.

27. For a more complete description of the jobs component of the administration's welfare reform package, see "An Employment Approach to Welfare Reform: The Program for Better Jobs and Income," in U.S. Department of Labor, *Employment and Training Report of the President*, 1978.

28. Of course everyone does not agree with this analysis. For example, see Nancy M. Gordon's critique and the author's rebuttal in "Women's Roles and Welfare Reform," *Challenge*, January/February 1978.

29. Tobin, "Considerations Regarding Taxation and Inequality," p. 127.

30. See Robert J. Lampman, "Scaling Welfare Benefits to Income: An Idea That Is Being Overworked," *Policy Analysis* I, no. 1 (1975): 1–10.

31. Entitlement-based programs assure benefits to all who meet the established eligibility criteria (typically family size and income) as distinguished from "needs based" limited service programs in which benefits are rationed to those among the eligible who are deemed most in need as determined by some additional criteria.

6

The Concept of Horizontal Equity and Its Application to Social Program Design

DAVID LINDEMAN

Introduction

No issue, except perhaps concern about the integrity and efficiency of welfare administration, has dominated the welfare reform debate more than the issue of "horizontal equity." A persistent indictment of the welfare system is that it treats needy people unequally, that some groups are treated better than others despite equal need.

This paper will explore the proposition of horizontal equity—that individuals equally situated should be treated equally—primarily in the context of the existing means-tested programs and proposals to change them. In the first section, we discuss some basic issues related to the basic formulation: whether categorization of the needy violates the concept of horizontal equity; how to measure well-being; and the extent to which the beneficiary's own sense of satisfaction should figure into the calculation of well-being. In the second section, we explore more fully the traditional bases of the current system and the leading critique of the last two decades. The next two sections discuss two acute issues in the present policy debate. The last section puts forward a way to view the roles played by means-tested assistance and some suggestions from that point of view on how to alter current law.

Horizontal Equity—What Does It Mean?

The phrase "horizontal equity" derives ultimately from the notion that "equals should be treated equally, unequals should be treated unequally." In the welfare policy debate, this moral imperative is often translated into the policy prescription that those with equivalent needs should receive equal benefits. Of course, this policy prescription is not as simple as it first appears. For example, these various complexities arise when one tries to implement the policy: (1.) A household composed of five people has greater need than a household composed of three people. (2.) There exist geographical variations in the cost of goods and services: A nationwide money standard will mask these variations, overcompensating some and depriving others. (3.) The economic well-being of certain household units is inherently less than others: The disabled individual incurs greater costs than the non-disabled individual; the single-parent family incurs costs (and lost leisure) that the two-parent family does not; religious beliefs may impose costs on some households not generally borne by those of the majority faith (e.g., the costs of keeping kosher in a locality without a large Jewish community). (4.) Need must be measured over a certain time period and the choice of a week, a month, or a year as the controlling interval has important consequences.

Obviously, the determination of "equal need" is not an easy one. Further, in discussing this matter of horizontal equity two levels of analysis often are mingled: (1) how the population should be divided into groups; and (2) how persons within these groups should be treated.

On the first level, the public debate concerns the rights and wrongs of the preferential treatment afforded certain groups (for example, the aged) compared to other groups (for example, young single people and young married couples without children). As we shall discuss later, society categorizes the low-income population; it declares that, despite similar income and resources, individuals are sufficiently dissimilar according to other criteria that they should be grouped into a set of (more or less) mutually exclusive categories. These dissimilarities arise from our collective judgment about the ability of a particular low-income individual to hold his or her own in the labor market. While clearly there are exceptions within any one group—the vigorously capable septagenarian, for instance—we make the judgment that most of the time people within a preferred category lack the means to earn a requisite income under reasonable conditions. Neither the transfer system as a whole, nor the welfare system as a component, is "unfair" merely because there exist categories within it. Questions can arise, however, about the assignment of particular individuals to one group instead of another, and as to whether there are so many exceptions within the categories so as to invalidate them.

On the second level of analysis, society debates how particular individuals within categories should be treated. In effect this is a debate concerning the measure of "well-being" of individuals within particular categories.

These two debates are not easily separated, for an analysis of at least some of our current categories may be translated into an analysis of the comparative well-being of individuals across categories. For example, many infirm aged and disabled persons incur certain abnormal expenses. That being the case, it may be argued that we construct our categories to be preferentially generous to the aged and disabled not only because we do not expect such individuals to work for their livelihood, but also because we see that individuals in this class incur expenses that, if not compensated, would leave them with less disposable income than the non-aged or non-disabled. Similarly, the argument can be made that single-parent families, regardless of their position on the income continuum, have fewer household resources than two-parent households with the same gross income.

Intrinsic to the question of discerning comparable well-being is the issue of the extent to which differences within the population that flow from individual choice should be recognized. For example, should the desire for leisure of some portion of the population be satisfied at the expense of the rest of the population? Although a subset of the population prefers a large amount of leisure, the general society will not willingly finance that preference. (In fact, very few may desire a condition of completely subsidized leisure; arguably almost all individuals eventually prefer a condition of "useful activity" with the nexus of human contacts the work place entails. Rather than expending efforts to reorient those few who prefer total leisure, it might be more cost-effective for the society to subsidize the preference. But, for a variety of reasons, each of which would involve considerable discussion, society is very unlikely to embrace such a policy.)

The issue of interpersonal differences in preferences also shows up in the comparison of the relative treatment given two-parent and single-parent families. Unlike being aged, the status of being a single parent is in many cases a voluntary status. If this status also entails some extra costs, what claim do individuals in that class have against others in the society that those additional costs be offset? A more obvious manifestation of the issue is the recurring debate in welfare policy concerning the extent to which recipients' consumption patterns should be constrained, if at all, through in-kind benefits and vendor payments. It may be argued that too much emphasis on the preferences of the donors (taxpayers) results in an unfair constraint on the divergent preferences within the recipient population. While many of these problems can be avoided by reliance on "objective" measures—such as a simple formula that uses only gross income and household size—we should recognize that such measures implicitly contain choices about difficult questions of social policy. As is often the case in public policy, however, the society may end up choosing this kind of measure, for it is the alternative which almost all competing groups and viewpoints hold as their second-best position.

Traditional Policy and Its Critique

Traditional welfare policy understood these dilemmas, though the language in which that policy was expressed perhaps differed from the language of contemporary economists and moral philosophers. Geographic variations in living costs were handled in the manner most natural to American federalism—the states were left to prescribe different needs standards which (especially for reasons of housing costs) varied within the several states. In many states, the needs standard in any particular case was constructed by the caseworker's adding together particular "needs" from a list. Cases with earned income were given (since 1962) further individual attention by means of itemized work expenses—the caseworker having the ability to recognize, among other things, the special costs incurred by some in the production of income (e.g., the handicapped individual with extraordinary transportation costs commuting to work). A compromise was implicitly made between immediate and longer-term temporal measures of need: The "current" month was used as the measure of available income, but heavy reliance was placed on an assets test to screen out those whose income might be temporarily low, but whose economic well-being over a longer time period was deemed sufficient.

More fundamental than these benefit-calculation rules was the decision to divide the population into demographic categories. The social consensus concerning distributive justice has long reflected a judgment that certain events or conditions are (in general) involuntary and deserving of our collective sympathy. Age, widowhood, and physical impediment are the conditions least disputed. Matters become more debatable when the conditions are unemployment or "single-parentness" (at least for reasons other than the breadwinner's death or incapacity). Within the general category of disability or incapacity subtle distinctions can be made, and are made, among various types of physical and mental impairments.

Underlying this complicated categorization is a pessimistic, or at least not very optimistic, view of human nature. Much of labor being tedious and low-paying, many, given the opportunity, will opt out of the economic system and subsist on the generosity of others. Thus, sympathy and a sense of self-preservation combine in a decision that society's collective charity should concentrate on those situations which are deemed involuntary. Indeed, the argument can be taken one step further. If we accept as inevitable that assistance will be extended to the old, the disabled, widows, orphans, and the unemployed, then society should require that its more fortunate members contribute toward the benefits that they will receive if they should require such assistance. From this logic arises "social insurance," collectively enforced prudence which further legitimizes the receipt of benefits upon the occasion of one of these involuntary conditions.

This overall view of the transfer system is still held by most people;

however, there have been and continue to be critics. In general there exist two camps of criticism. One group holds that the structure is fundamentally sound, but there exist gaps (the more liberal view) or excesses (the more conservative view) that need correction. Examples of this critique may be found all the way back to the origins of the present structure of the American welfare state. The more "radical" critique comes essentially from economists who have put forward the "Negative Income Tax" (NIT) (or its intellectual cousin the "Refundable Tax Credit" or the "Credit Income Tax") as an alternative system. To what exactly the NIT is an alternative is often unclear. At the most extreme, the NIT or Credit Income Tax is put forward as an alternative to the entire transfer system—the social insurance programs as well as means-tested programs—and as integral to a substantial reform of the tax code. Less ambitious are proposals that put forward the NIT model as an alternative to the means-tested programs, most especially federal participation in those programs.

This NIT critique gained adherents partly as a remedy to what were increasingly seen as *inequities*—not just inadequacies or excesses—in the present welfare system. The variations in payment levels among the states were found hard to justify on grounds other than local distributional preference. (For example, in the Aid to Families with Dependent Children program, Texas, a relatively rich state, pays only $140 per month to a family of four with no other income, while Oregon, a state of comparable wealth, pays $411 per month in its program. The low-payment level of $120 per month in Mississippi is easier to understand, for Mississippi is a relatively poor state. But note that Maine, also a very poor state, pays $349 per month.) Similar variations in computational rules have little apparent logic; for example, Louisiana treats family income far more generously than Georgia, despite roughly equivalent payment levels and state per capita income. Why, the argument goes, should these differences in treatment exist, especially given the heavy financial contribution made by the federal government? Further, that contribution comes from federal taxes falling upon all citizens, regardless of their location, in an equal manner in proportion to their income. If the federal levy is uniform, should not the federal benefits share that uniformity?

Furthermore, the traditional welfare system excluded certain groups, especially two-parent families headed by able-bodied breadwinners. This exclusion has in recent years eroded with the introduction into the AFDC program of the Unemployed Parent (or Father) option (AFDC-U), the Food Stamp program, and the Earned Income Tax Credit. (Further, such families are likely to be covered by Unemployment Insurance.) But despite these recent expansions at the federal level, and despite additional compensating steps taken solely on the initiative of some states, the two-parent family is still treated less generously than the single-parent. This disparity not only exists when the two-parent family has no other income, but also when the family has earnings equivalent to those of a single-parent family. At the extreme a two-parent family will be paying taxes while a neighboring single-parent family with gross earnings that exceed those of the two-parent family is still receiving welfare benefits as an earnings supplement. Negative income tax proponents often argue that this reversal is fundamentally unfair.

Finally, NIT advocates occasionally have pointed to the inequities resulting from the very short accounting periods in current welfare. Need for welfare assistance is typically measured on a monthly basis. (Supposedly, the basis is the "current" month, but because of verification requirements, the usual measure is the month just passed.) Where a family's income fluctuates during the course of a year it might receive welfare during several months. In contrast, a neighboring family, with exactly the same annual income, but earned at a steady rate just above welfare's monthly eligibility ceiling, would receive no assistance whatsoever. Should not the "need for assistance" be measured on the same temporal dimension as the "ability to pay," namely yearly income?

In the next two sections we will explore two of the more acute problems of horizontal equity faced when trying to apply the NIT model to welfare reform: how to treat the single-parent versus the two-parent family, and what to do about the accounting period.

Single-parent versus Two-parent

The most common criticism of the welfare system is that it treats the two-parent (or "intact") family less generously than the single-parent (or "dependent") family. As is often the case, rhetoric has lagged behind reality on this matter. The difference is no longer between something for the single-parent family and nothing for the two-parent family. The growth and maturation of the Food Stamp program and the Earned Income Tax Credit have transmuted the issue. These are federal entitlement programs with no variation in benefit levels across states and which pay their benefits in either cash (the EITC) or coupons that are tantamount to cash (Food Stamps). We are now left with the perceived inequity of something less for the two-parent family and something more for the single-parent family.

Over the same period that Food Stamps and the EITC have moved to equalize the position for the two-parent family, the introduction in 1969 of the earnings disregard (the so-called "30 and one-third") into AFDC went in the other direction, favoring low-income single-parent families relative to two-parent families with equal earnings. Thus, the earnings disregard, along with a separate disregard for work expenses, allows the single-parent family with earnings as high as $17,000 to receive AFDC as a supplement to their other sources of income. In contrast, supplementation for two-parent families cut off at $9,100 (Food Stamps) and $10,000 (the EITC).

There exist then two vantage points from which to judge the relative equity position of two-parent and single-parent families: namely, the situation at the guarantee level when the family has no other means of support but government transfers, and the situation along different points of the earnings continuum until government benefits, as supplementation to earnings, cease.

The first of these situations—what we might call the *income support* function of government transfers—is what has drawn most attention in the debate concerning the equity of the welfare system. The state, acting on behalf of society, will safeguard a destitute single-parent family at anywhere between 50 percent and 90 percent of the poverty level. In contrast, the destitute two-parent family might be asked instead to survive at a guarantee level around 30 percent of the poverty level. Of course, such circumstances are rare: The incidence of Unemployment Insurance among two-parent families is high, and the populous industrial states invariably have picked up the AFDC-U option to back up their UI programs. Nonetheless, UI coverage is by no means universal and often has low replacement rates, and AFDC-U contains several restrictions that limit eligibility and discourage participation. Thus, there can and do exist situations in which the two-parent family is expected to survive on much less than the single-parent family. The reason for the distinction lies in history and the expectations around which the transfer system was created. When we started to construct the welfare state in the 1930s, the phenomenon of single-parentness was small and, correctly or not, was thought to result almost solely from widowhood. Thus, helping the single-parent population through welfare was seen as advantaging only a small subset of the total population—a group, widows and their children, whose plight instinctively draws sympathy and invites charity. For the rest, a robust full-employment economy, perhaps abetted with public works and public service jobs, would provide sufficient and adequate income opportunities.

Were the single-parent population still small and its status, on the whole, indisputably involuntary, and were we better able to engineer full employment on a consistent basis, there would exist no substantial grounds on which to indict the transfer system as inequitable. Given that this is not the case, however, should we continue to allow the single-parent family to receive a guarantee that exceeds that extended to the two-parent family? Virtually every welfare reform effort of the past decade has answered that question in the affirmative. Every proposal has permitted, encouraged, or mandated that the states supplement the prescribed national minimum with higher benefits for the single-parent population. A permissive posture can be justified on grounds that it would be proper for the federal government to override state preferences to be more generous to certain groups. Nonetheless, the involvement of federal money and/or federal dictates calls into question whether, as a matter of national policy, guarantees for single-parent families should be more generous than those extended to two-parent families. Another way of posing the question is: Can the implicit or explicit "two-tier" nature of past and present welfare reform proposals be justified on equity grounds?

The underlying dilemma here is the conflict between providing adequate assistance in cases of genuinely involuntary unemployment and actually encouraging unemployment by overadequate assistance. Should we view this dilemma differently with respect to two-parent families than we do with respect to single-parent families? The answer to this question turns on the ability and desirability of single parents' working, which raises the issue of the social consensus regarding women and their participation in the labor force. While AFDC eligibility is framed in terms of single-parent status, the reality, of course, is that those single-parent families are overwhelming female-headed. Do we expect a woman in those circumstances to work? Originally the answer was no. But as the nature of the caseload changed from widows to women who are divorced, separated, deserted, or who have children out of wedlock, there was a parallel shift in expectations about their place in the work force. One cause for the shift is the belief that the "dependency cycle" can be broken only if "welfare children" perceive that work is an important part of life, that society respects you and you respect yourself only when you play some role in the economic organism. Thus, the emphasis on work requirements in AFDC has often gone hand in hand with a parallel emphasis on social services, employment counseling and training, and (in some cases) sheltered work environments.

In addition to this rehabilitation ethic in AFDC one senses in recent years a deeper force at work, namely women's liberation and the marked increase of women at all income levels in all segments of the national economy. As those who finance welfare, the amorphous mass termed the middle class, are themselves increasingly two earner couples and separated, working, single parents, their views inevitably change about AFDC mothers working. The logic takes hold that "if I must work to provide for myself, then 'they' ought to work as well." Rightly or wrongly, social policy follows not only from an objective analysis of the group needing help, but also from a projection about their own condition by those providing that help.

There exist two possible solutions to this issue of equity between two-parent and single-parent households. The first is the simpler. If our concern about work effort is sufficiently dominant to dictate certain constraints placed on assistance to "expected-to-work" two-parent household heads, then exactly the same constraints should bind "expected-to-work" single-parent household heads. Exactly where the "expected-to-work" line gets drawn for single-parent heads depends largely on social attitudes concerning child rearing and social views concerning the availability of "adequate" day care. But once that line is drawn (e.g., only children below the age of six exempt the single-parent) there exists a strong case that single-parent and two-parent household heads should be treated alike for purposes of a work requirement and the guarantee extended during periods of unemployment.

A less obvious solution would be to allow the single-parent guarantee to be larger than that given to two-parent families but to compensate in the benefit reduction rate. To explain this second solution an example may be helpful. Assume that our "maximum" guarantee for the two-parent family is approximately $5,400, and further assume that we reduce that amount by fifty cents for each dollar of earnings. When earnings are equal to $6,000 (the minimum wage full-time), the family will be 55 percent better off than when its head was unemployed. Now, we could achieve a parallel result for the single-parent family by giving it the same guarantee and reduction rate that we gave the two-parent family. We can also achieve a parallel result by extending to the single-parent family a larger guarantee—say $7,200—and then reducing that amount at the rate of thirty-five cents for each dollar of earnings. That combination will also yield a 55 percent return to the decision to take a minimum wage job. This latter solution has two significant consequences. First, while the return to work would be the same, the extra height in the guarantee will independently lessen the single parent's willingness to work, causing us (assuming we are serious about work effort) to rely more heavily on negative reinforcements (work test sanctions). The second is that the "breakeven" (the place on the earnings continuum where benefits cease) for the single-parent family would be $20,600. Compare that breakeven to the $10,800 breakeven for the two-parent family.

We see, therefore, that the question of differential treatment for the single-parent household has consequences beyond the guarantee. As a matter of policy, do we expect to be more generous to single-parent families in what we give as *income supplementation* across the earnings continuum? In one respect, the question almost answers itself. If we expect single parents to work, a necessary precondition to their working is that they purchase (or the government provides) child care. Once that unique expense is taken into account, the condition of two-parent and single-parent families, in terms of net disposable income, may be equalized. But beyond the problem of child care, there are, many argue, other costs to being a single-parent.[1] It is obvious that two adults living together constitute an economic unit in which outside labor and household chores can be shared so as to give each a reasonable amount of leisure. The single adult, especially with children, either must forego some leisure or purchase another's services in order to accomplish the same amount of outside and home production. While difficult to separate from the issue of child care expenses, these special "costs" of single-parentness arguably deserve separate recognition. In other words, even after child-care expenses have been compensated, the single-parent's income should be measurably higher than that of the two-parent family with the same earnings in order that it may purchase the necessary services and/or be compensated for the cost leisure.

Taken to its extreme, this argument could imply "welfare" phase-out levels as high as $25,000 to $30,000, depending how much were deemed necessary for "adequate" child care and the value placed on the lost leisure. Such eligibility ceilings go far beyond any conventional view of the welfare system. Were we to extend differential assistance to single-parent families to such levels, it is probable that we would not do so through explicit welfare benefits.

We could take the problem of child-care reimbursement out of the standard welfare calculus and put it into a separate program, perhaps relying on the tax system. It is possible that we might expand the Earned Income Tax Credit so that it is somewhat more generous for single-parent "head of household" filers than for the "married joint" filer, and in that connection move those two filing statuses to a common tax schedule, thus lowering the relative tax burden now borne by head of household filers. In contrast, however, a review of these actual and proposed changes in AFDC since the early 1960s indicates that we are slowly moving to treat so-called "expected-to-work" single-parent household heads the same as two-parent household heads for purposes of the welfare guarantee and any work requirement. In other words, from the perspective of *income support* we are moving to a position of strict equality, but from the perspective of *income supplementation* we will continue to extend a more generous treatment to the single-parent family in order to equalize its condition in terms of net disposable income. Nonetheless, even with respect to income supplementation, it is probable that society will impose at some point along the earnings continuum (probably around medium income) a standard of equity measured in *gross* income terms. In other words, at some point society is likely to make the judgment that, regardless of your special characteristics, you now have sufficient income that you will be treated no differently from those without those characteristics. This imposition of a gross income standard grows out of a basic social assessment discussed earlier—how voluntary is the condition which occasions the transfer. It suffices to observe that there often exists, to a greater or lesser degree, mutual agreement leading to a separation or divorce. Each case of a single parent with a child borne out of wedlock has its unique volitional or involitional quality. In cases of death or desertion, the parent left with the children in no way contributed to his or her condition.

Unless we are willing to engage in a probing assessment of how voluntary or involuntary each single parent's situation is, we are forced ultimately to make a judgment about the class as a whole. As previously indicated, we tend to suspend any inquiry into the volitional quality of the condition so long as earnings remain roughly below medium income. Below this point we worry more about net disposable income. Above that point, I sense that we switch criteria, weighing more heavily the often voluntary quality of single parentness, and measuring equity and the need for assistance in terms of gross income. Unfortunately, as practitioners of tax and transfer policy know too well, there is no easy way to dovetail these two perspectives in a manner that does not lead to confiscatory tax rates on earnings over some range in the earnings continuum. The problem appears inescapable and the only question is where best to place that confiscatory rate. The alternative is to advantage all single-parent families, regardless of their incomes, relative to all two-parent families. This I believe the society will not do, especially as the condition of being a single parent becomes more widespread.

Accounting Periods

Another perplexing issue in the welfare reform debate has been the length of the so-called "accounting period," i.e., the time over which the need for assistance is measured. Society has always recognized that a household's income of the particular moment does not necessarily reflect its total well-being. An example may help clarify this dilemma. A typical family might have earnings at a per annum rate of $15,000 (approximately twice the poverty level and roughly four-fifths of medium income) and have accumulated no more in assets than a house, an auto, personal and household effects, and a very modest amount in cash. Were the family's income to fall to the per annum rate of $7,500, under current Food Stamp rules, including exclusions from assets, the family would be eligible for that program. Were the family's income to fall to zero, the family might also be eligible for AFDC-U. At year's end, the family's annual income could fall between the two rates and still be above the normal eligibility ceiling. If the family had nine months at the $15,000 rate and three months at the $7,500 rate, its annual income would equal $13,125, well above the $9,100 limit prescribed in Food Stamps. Do we want such a family to be eligible to participate in a welfare program for those three relatively low-income months? Put another way, why should this hypothetical family be eligible for assistance while a like family with exactly the same assets and annual income, but earned in twelve equal monthly installments of $1,095, would never be eligible for assistance? The current program structure, it may be argued, not only treats like families unequally, it encourages them to hold assets in excludable forms and it overly rewards those with irregular income patterns.

For NIT proponents the solution to the accounting period issue is to measure income over some relatively long period of time such as a calendar year. Just as we do not assess one's ability to pay solely on income in the last month of the year, we should not assess need solely on the current month's circumstances. Further, with a longer accounting period and an imputation of an income flow from a family's total wealth, there is no need for a distinct assets test with its attendant and inequitable exclusions, stigma, and perverse incentives.

In the Credit Income Tax variant, the tax and transfer systems become so comingled that a family may elect its credit in a refundable form on a monthly basis at any time during the year. Because a CIT also has a linear marginal tax rate from the first dollar and probably would rest upon mandatory withholding at that rate from all income at every possible source (e.g., savings accounts as well as employers), the correct "reduction" in the refundable credit automatically takes place without having to go through a separate income-testing mechanism. (Without discussing the details, it might be possible to run a CIT with a non-linear tax rate if all other parameters were the same. The tax rate schedule probably could not contain more than three brackets.)

We are a long way from adopting an NIT or CIT as a full or partial substitute for the current transfer system. Nonetheless, that perspective shows signs of causing us to rethink certain aspects of the present program structure. The proposition put forward in recent welfare reform proposals for a long retrospective accounting period, averaging past income by one of several formulas, has failed to acquire acceptance beyond the narrow confines of some professional income-maintenance analysts. The notion did provoke considerable debate and the Congress is now studying the feasibility of "recouping" benefits, after the fact, from households that had high annual incomes, but which drew welfare benefits for some limited period within the year. A variant of this approach is to include some or all of a household's welfare benefits in the income tax base. The decision last year to include unemployment insurance in the tax base may be seen as a precursor. These after-the-fact methods of adjustment contain some potentially fatal defects in the form of work disincentives and the discouragement of certain forms of family formation. To counter these flaws we might have to create a structure of exceptions and special rules, the end result of which could be so complicated as to frustrate the entire endeavor.

The third program innovation of the past decade, the EITC, dealt with the accounting-period criterion by adopting the tax system's calendar year, thereby eliminating the need for a separate assets test. Recently Congress provided that the EITC will be paid out as part of the withholding system instead of a single lump sum at year's end. This intrayear disbursement perforce will result in some overpayments among those with fluctuating incomes and causes, therefore, the need to reconcile with those households at year's end. Fortunately, in most such cases the tax system's de facto overwithholding in the higher income months will offset the EITC overpayments in the lower income months.

Guidelines for Future Policy

The debate in the past decade over welfare reform has revealed that we hold ambivalent attitudes about this ethical norm of horizontal equity. As Conrad Johnson has pointed out in his article, equity measured in a geographical sense depends upon how we define the relevant "community." In the American federal system that is not always easy, for while the nation as a whole is the most relevant tax base for income distribution and is an interdependent economic community, we are reluctant to deed all aspects of welfare policy over to the federal government. A strong residual sense persists that only on the local level can there exist both the social sympathy and the individualized scrutiny into the reasons behind the request for aid that many believe ought to underlie welfare administration. Similarly, while concern for equity, target efficiency, and administrative burden have caused us increasingly to move to uniform income definitions (e.g., a standard work expense deduction) and to flat or consolidated benefit levels in existing programs, we recreate that complexity anew through the proliferation of new entitlements. While we enact ever more stringent work requirements with respect to single-parent households, we nonetheless continue to treat them far more generously in the welfare system, a distinction that belies the stated principle that we expect single-parent household heads to work as much as we do household heads in a two-parent family. More generally, though the SSI program is a substantial advance in redressing previous inequities in our treatment of the aged and disabled, we nonetheless, as James Rotherham points out, perpetuate in the structure of the entire transfer system a differential treatment against those who made out least well in the employment system. What follows are three suggestions that may help sort out some of our contrary policies in the welfare area.

First, we should understand that we tend to constantly shift between two measures of well-being. On the one hand, we purport to measure well-being in terms of gross income—households with the same gross income should pay equal taxes and receive equal transfers. On the other hand, for incentive or other reasons, we depart from that measure and define special income definitions for particular groups, the single-parent and disabled populations being the leading examples. In departing from the measure of gross income, we should first ask whether the adjustment being sought makes sense across the income distribution, at least across the bottom half of the distribution. The question is necessary, for the introduction of such an adjustment is likely (absent an arbitrary cut-off or "notch") to extend benefits into the earnings continuum well beyond conventional notions of poverty or near-poverty. Once into those income ranges we have to step back and ask whether this is a result we wanted. Should two-parent households, or able-bodied households, be paying taxes to help sustain neighbors who have equivalent gross incomes? Unless the distinguishing demographic characteristic brings with it an inevitable, measurable, and highly noticeable expense—such as child care in the case of single-parent households, or special transportation and other special work-related expenses in the case of the disabled—the measure of gross income ought to dominate. We lack any other touchstone which can give us a measure of equal treatment, however imperfect. If that basic criterion of equity is not met, then it really does not matter how refined our measures of well-being are within particular sub-categories. Further, when we begin to adjust for the lost leisure associated with the single-parent status, we necessarily enter into a contentious area, in which opinions are predicated on judgments about how volitional the status is and the possible effects of the lifestyle on social cohesion.

Second, we should recognize that the welfare system, along with portions of the social insurance system, can be divided into two basic income brackets. The bottom bracket consists of those program elements which support a household when, for reasons of unemployment, desertion, death, or disability, the adults either have no earnings or those earnings are quite small and infrequent. In contrast, the top bracket consists of those program elements which supplement a household's income when at least one adult is working full time at the minimum wage. By enlarging the EITC and making the child-care tax credit refundable, we can slowly eliminate the need for either AFDC or Food Stamps in the top bracket. By shifting exclusively to the tax system's annual accounting period in the top bracket, we also eliminate the need for an asset test on benefits paid in this portion of the earnings continuum, and we substantially increase the overall equity and target efficiency of the transfer system.

Assistance in the bottom bracket may be seen as income support to those whom we do not expect to work, either for a short period while engaged in job search or job training, or for longer periods because of a condition such as a work-impairing disability or responsibility for the care of a very young child. In order to be responsive to these circumstances, the program or programs that work within the bottom bracket must have short accounting periods. To compensate for the potential inequities occasioned by those short accounting periods, we can take two steps. Admittance to the means-tested programs in this bottom bracket should be conditional on a reasonable liquid assets test with an imputation to income from the value of the major exclusions from the assets test, principally the home. In addition, benefits paid under these programs should be included in the income tax base. These measures would militate against the capricious nature of the current structure which irrationally favors those with certain kinds of wealth holdings and income patterns.

Third, we should recognize that the bottom bracket contains within it a set of distinctions that are outmoded. (This does not mean that all categorical distinctions should be avoided; rather that the present structure should be revised to reflect changed social conditions and expectations.) Persuasive arguments have been made elsewhere in this volume about the social necessity and moral correctness of conditioning transfers, or public charity, to a greater or lesser degree, on a work requirement, at least in the absence of showing that such requirements will be used to extract labor under intolerable conditions or to channel a particular group into less desirable areas of labor. Except in the cases where young children are present in the household and provided that adequate day care is available, society, through the way work requirements have been rewritten over the past two decades, has increasingly made the judgment that able-bodied single-parent household heads, except under limited circumstances, have no greater claim to non-conditional income support than two-parent household heads. Thus, if guarantee levels and/or replacement rates must be kept within certain bounds to preserve minimal work incentives, that policy should apply equally to "expected-to-work" single-parent household heads as to two-parent household heads. (An obvious exception to this policy is the case where the child in a single-parent household is very young.)

By the same token, we should recognize that AFDC-U, or some such means-tested program, is in reality the poor man's unemployment benefits program. Given that fact, and given the fact that we have no certain knowledge as to who pays the unemployment insurance payroll tax (specific employees, all labor, consumers, holders of capital, or some combination) similar rules concerning the length of benefits should apply in both programs, including the circumstances under which we leave the unemployed individual no choice but to accept public employment (assuming there is a public jobs program available as a last resort).

The past two decades have been a constant give and take between two schools of thought in welfare reform—those who want comprehensive reform along the lines of an NIT or a CIT, and those who argue for more traditional reform using existing program structures. In the typical fashion of such social debates neither school prevailed, but both contributed to the development and implementation of some very significant changes in the structure of welfare. As Henry Aaron writes, we are close to the end of this round of legislative activity. If the most recent proposal of public service jobs and relatively modest changes in AFDC succeeds, the country's income transfer system no longer will have any serious gaps and deficiencies. We can only hope that this initiative passes and that we can put behind us these last glaring inequities. Having done so, it is then time to realign existing expenditures within the current set of institutional arrangements to reflect the new realities of the system we have created and the different populations which it serves. In doing so, we not only have to disenthrall ourselves from the traditional categorical distinctions and specific methods of means-testing, we also must abandon the chimaera that there exists a simple and single program structure that will satisfy all objectives in a fully equitable manner.

Notes

1. Clair Vickery is a leading exponent of this view. See, for example, "The True Poor: A New Look at Poverty," *Journal of Human Resources*, Winter 1977. The issue has been debated in the tax literature for two or more decades, particularly with respect to two spouse households. In some households both spouses work, and in others only one spouse works. Should the tax burden be the same when such households have the same money income regardless of the total number of hours in labor force used to produce that money income?

2. For an extensive analysis of this subject, see Morgan et al., *Five Thousand American Families—Patterns of Economic Progress*, Survey Research Center, Institute for Social Research, The University of Michigan.

7

Equity: Its Scope and Its Relation to Other Objectives

CONRAD JOHNSON

Preliminaries

The design of new welfare programs, or the reform of existing ones, raises very serious questions about what the objectives of such changes should be. And beyond the task of delineating what these objectives are is an equally serious set of problems having to do with ranking objectives in case of conflict. Indeed, the position we are to take when our goals conflict is usually the more important question; for it is much easier to get rational agreement on a list of (perhaps conflicting) goals than it is to get rational agreement on such questions as how *much*, if any, of one is to be sacrificed in the pursuit of another. If a welfare program could be devised that would be inexpensive, simple to administer, fully equitable, and wholly adequate in its provision of benefits to precisely those who need them, while at the same time encouraging people to work when they can, there would be relatively little disagreement about its desirability. But when some pair of these virtues is such that both cannot be maximized in the same system, we are confronted with a problem of the kind that is recurrent, and indeed, constant, in the formation of policy.

There are several distinguishable ways in which philosophical reflection can be of help in addressing the problems about conflicting objectives. One would be to give a survey of the various positions philosophers have taken either on the general questions about conflict,[1] or on priority rules that have been designed to solve particular conflicts.[2] In this paper there will be occasional reference to the positions philosophers have taken on general questions or on particular priority rules, but no general survey. I think that, especially in the case of such strong priority rules as Rawls's notion of *lexical* priority,[3] it is only moderately interesting to describe the notion and to point to its possible use in ordering principles or goals. The idea becomes compellingly interesting only when convincing arguments for a particular lexical priority are given. Since I do not find any of Rawls's arguments for various lexical priorities fully convincing,[4] and since an inquiry into the subject would take us far too deeply into Rawls's theory and the voluminous comment that has been made on it, I do not address the issue head on. In any case, even if we do adopt Rawls's ideas about priorities, much needs to be done to see just where and how those ideas would apply to the problems of welfare reform.

There is a second way in which philosophical reflection can make the problems of conflicting objectives somewhat more tractable. By getting a clearer understanding of each of a set of objectives, we will be in a better position to see when that objective really does come into conflict with another, and when the conflict is, as it were, a pseudo-conflict, or, at least, not nearly as important a conflict as we thought. I attempt to provide some examples of this in the present paper. One example is the introduction of the idea of a *reference group* for purposes of explaining limits on the scope of equitable considerations. Thus I will maintain that not all disparities between the level of welfare benefits provided in one community (or state) and those provided in another constitute *inequities*; when they do and when they do not is a very interesting and extremely important philosophical question. Another part of the discussion in this paper concerns a second kind of limit on the scope of equitable considerations. Principles, rules, and policies governing the distribution of burdens and benefits operate at different levels: At one extreme are fundamental principles governing the overall distribution of, say, income among various segments of the populace and basic policies of furthering economic growth and productivity. Descending to the more specific levels, there are rules (whether legal or moral) that together determine that one particular named individual is to receive such-and-such a specific amount, while another is to receive some other specified amount. In applying principles of equity, it is important to understand that equitable considerations arise in different ways at different levels, and the requirements of equity become specific at the level of specific rules. These distinctions are important in understanding the extent to which distribution in accordance with some dimension such as amount of work done is governed by considerations of equity. Thus if equity requires that the working poor should enjoy a greater gross income (i.e., income support plus wages) than the non-working poor, we will also need to know *how much* more they should be able to enjoy and whether equity gives an answer to this question, or if we must turn elsewhere for a resolution. Distinctions of level are useful in understanding the circumstances in which constraints of equity pre-exist a decision, will be created by it, or can be bypassed by that decision.

Some additional remarks should help to place my treatment of equity within a more general framework. Two pairs of concepts appear often in the literature: *horizontal equity* is contrasted with *vertical equity*; *formal* principles of justice are distinguished from *material* principles.

In discussions of equity in the design of systems of taxation or programs for the provision of goods and services, including income support and welfare benefits, a distinction is usually made between questions of horizontal equity and vertical equity.[5] *Horizontal equity* is the principle that people in equal positions should be treated equally.[6] One frequently mentioned example of a horizontal inequity in the current operation of welfare programs is the considerable variation there is from state to state in the levels of benefits provided and the standards of eligibility for benefits.[7] *Vertical equity* requires that those in different positions should be treated differently.[8] A typical example of what vertical equity requires is that the degree of income assistance should vary with the degree of need and that those who earn and/or save more should end up with a greater total income.[9] An often-cited example of a vertical inequity is the situation in which a woman works and earns money but ends up with no more, and perhaps less, than another who does not work, but who has access to a federally subsidized home and who draws untaxed AFDC benefits.[10] The notions of horizontal and vertical equity derive primarily from the literature of economics; they are not usually to be found in philosophers' discussions of justice and equity. In my discussion of the problems of equity, I will make no essential use of the distinction, though it will be possible to employ it to categorize most of the examples I use.

In recent philosophical discussions of justice, a distinction is often made between *formal* and *material* principles of justice.[11] The principle that similarly situated persons are to be treated in the same way is a formal principle because it leaves wholly unspecified which features make two persons' situations similar and which make them dissimilar. Some, like Frankena and Perelman, hold that such a formal principle is a rule of reason, holding not just for conduct, but for scientific investigation as well. A principle that distribution of some good is to be made in direct proportion to need, or to merit, or to amount of time worked, or in accordance with some amalgam of these factors, would be a *material* principle. The economist's notion of horizontal equity seems to correspond fairly closely to the notion of a formal principle; vertical equity, since it is usually stated in connection with a particular conception of the relevant dimension(s) in accordance with which the distribution should vary, is a material principle. In other cases, the idea of vertical equity seems also to be a formal principle, requiring that genuinely different cases be given different treatment. As Richard Musgrave puts it, "The requirements of horizontal and vertical equity are but different sides of the same coin."[12]

One way of approaching questions of equity would be to focus on various material principles in an attempt to construct an adequate account of equity in the distribution of burdens and benefits. Thus one might attempt to argue that the amount of time worked corresponds to, or reveals, one's individual merit, and that, for that reason, those who work ought to receive more than those who do not. Or one might argue that the distribution of benefits ought to vary in accordance with need, or in accordance with variations in some other dimension. The following discussion of equity will not proceed along these lines. The main reason for this is that questions such as the extent to which people should be rewarded for the work they do cannot be given a very fixed and determinate answer apart from a framework both of established social goals and of fairly rich empirical data about the consequences of distributing in accordance with the material principle in question. To take an example, arguments about the extent to which people should be rewarded for the work they do quite appropriately develop into arguments about whether there is a need for work of this particular kind (i.e., whether it is of some social value, and if so, how much) and whether it is necessary to provide an incentive for this kind of work. It is a mistake, though a tempting one, to argue in a priori fashion for material principles which, though they are rather deeply engrained in our everyday thinking, are not fundamental principles. This is not to say that rational decisions about the adoption of material principles in a particular well-defined context are unimportant or unavailable; it is only to say that they do not yield well to abstract and general methods, nor, usually, are they appropriately decided in the philosopher's study. I shall return to this point concerning fundamental as opposed to subordinate norms later in the paper. The primary purpose of this paper is to shed some light on the nature of the requirements of equity: the scope of equity; the occasions of its conflict with other objectives of welfare programs; and the circumstances in which equity properly takes priority over other objectives.

One familiar and much discussed conflict of objectives arises in the attempt to provide an adequate level of income support in a way that will still provide incentives to work, will minimize costs of the program, and will be equitable. For if a benefit recipient is permitted to keep all earned income without a reduction in benefits, then there is inequitable treatment of those who did not start out on the program vis-a-vis those who did; if a benefit recipient is not permitted to keep all earned income, and such income is "taxed" at an especially steep rate, then the incentive to get work and become self-supporting is very much diminished.[13] Another much discussed conflict arises in the following way: If, for reasons of simplification and equity nationwide, the same level of benefits is to be provided for all who are in similar circumstances, then either the overall costs of the program will increase dramatically or benefit levels will have to be quite low and, indeed, substantially *reduced* from their present levels in some states.[14]

A Problem of Scope: The Relativity of Equity to a Reference Group

Not every inequality (say, in the levels of benefits to similarly circumstanced people) from community to community constitutes an inequity. Another way of putting this point is that not every program designed to reduce such inequalities will, other things being the same, serve to reduce the total of inequities in the world. There are many quite different reasons for this, but I want to consider just a few that will help, in the process, to illuminate the idea of equity, what it requires, and the circumstances under which the demands of equity come into conflict with other desirable goals.

We can see the issues a bit more clearly if we turn to a kind of situation that is quite removed from a government's provision of welfare benefits, but is still close enough to be instructive. Consider a society in which the institution of the family is in good repair and, indeed, flourishes: With only rare exceptions, each person belongs to a full and intact family unit. There are, of course, very substantial differences between families with respect to their wealth; but no family enjoys so much wealth that it could, by dividing up that wealth, provide for the needs of all in that society. If families[15] are to be equitable in distributing resources, is it necessary that each should consider the needs of *all* persons in society, whether or not they are members of the family in question? Equity, and equal treatment generally, does not require that the head of a family distribute that family's resources equally among, say, all children, even if not doing so would result in significant inequalities for the children of different families. That this is so can best be seen if we imagine what would happen if the head of some *one* family were to decide to distribute that family's resources (originally earmarked for its children) to children generally. The result would be a gross deficiency in the support given to children of that family; indeed, it would be an inequitable deficiency. Each family must give its members (in this case, its children) primary consideration. Equity requires that each family head give equal consideration to the members of that family, but this equal consideration does not extend across family boundaries.

If we ask why it is that equitable treatment in this case is an intrafamily, but not interfamily, matter, several things can be said. First, this relativity to the family is due, in important part, to social arrangements and conventions that could well have been otherwise. There remain many different arrangements by which functions of child care provision could be carried out. One is the familiar institution of the family. Another is an arrangement whereby all children are provided for by the state. Still another would be an arrangement in which society is divided up into small communities, larger than families yet smaller than the entire society, and the children in each community are provided for by that community, acting as a kind of corporate entity. In the second, the demands of equity would extend across the whole society: If the state provided more for some children than for others, and did this without systematic good reason, there would be an inequity. In the last, the demands of equity would extend across communities, but not across the entire society. Consequently, significant disparities in the support provided by different communities would not constitute inequities in anything like the same sense that they would if a centralized authority were responsible for distributing goods for the entire society. Now, to say that equitable treatment is relative to a reference group, and that what this group is depends in large part on social arrangements that could be otherwise is not at all to say that these social arrangements are entirely arbitrary; nor is it to say that we cannot subject these arrangements to moral criticism, and even less is it to say that we are left with no way of making a rational choice among alternative social arrangements. One of the reasons why it may become necessary and important for the state to take over (and indeed, in some cases, be organized for) the function of providing for the needs of certain of society's members is precisely that the old institutions, for various reasons, fail: Perhaps not everyone has a family;[16] or perhaps the inequalities in family wealth, and consequently in the extent to which they can provide for their members, become grotesquely exaggerated. But given an institutional arrangement that allocates responsibility in a certain way for providing for people's needs, and given that it works tolerably well and is not open to grave moral criticism, the demands of equity apply to those persons and institutions that have the responsibilities for distribution, and the inequalities that raise questions of equity are those that arise within the groups for which those persons and institutions have responsibility.

But again, why is it that such a fundamental moral requirement as that of equitable treatment should extend only over a particular group as defined by social arrangements? Is it not the case that all human beings, merely by virtue of the fact that they are persons, are to be respected? The answer to these questions touches interestingly on other moral considerations that are especially pertinent to the debates about the state's role in providing welfare benefits. It is surely true that to ignore the demands of equity is to deny some persons the respect that, as persons, they deserve. For a parent consciously to deny one child the same concern and attention that a sibling gets, and to do this for no good reason, is to treat the former as less important, as not having the same worth as a human being. A child that perceives this inequity may come to view him- or herself as being less important; thus the child may come to have diminished self-respect. But if a parent does not provide some other person's children with the same concern and attention, that does not show the same failure to respect human worth; not, at least, unless that parent is understood to have the responsibility to care for those children as well. In short, if I reasonably understand that A's and B's welfare are entrusted to my care, and that C's welfare is some other person's concern, I do not show any less respect for C's human worth by not paying attention to C's welfare. And if C understands that his welfare is not my responsibility, but belongs to someone else, then C has no reason to think of my lack of attention as showing any diminished respect for his worth as a human being.[17]

Let us turn now to the case of the social distribution of welfare benefits, or of income assistance. Though surely some of the characteristic marks of the parent-child relationship, notably love, do not mark the relationship between government and citizen, the demands of equity are in much the same way relative to the social arrangements that allocate responsibilities for providing benefits.[18] But how do we determine what these social arrangements are so that we can then determine how the requirements of equity are divided up? This is obviously a complex question, but we can isolate several of the most important factors. One such factor is the political organization of the society. If society is organized as a loose federation of substantially autonomous sub-communities, each having a government with authority to provide for the welfare needs of its citizens, so that the powers of the federal government are restricted to other things (e.g., defense), then the requirements of equity focus on inequalities and inconsistencies in the treatment of citizens within each sub-community, but not, primarily, *across* sub-communities. On the other hand, if society is organized in such a way as to give a strong central government the power to oversee the provision of welfare benefits, then equitable considerations tend to be extended across the entire community.[19] A central reason why the actual political organization of society is so important in determining the groups across which the equity principle extends is that, given such a division of responsibility, each authority can pay primary attention to comparisons within its community without this implying any differential assessment of the worth or importance of citizens. In this, there is similarity to the case of parents providing for their children.

Another factor bearing on the extension of the principle of equity is the fiscal arrangements made for financing the provision of welfare benefits. A federal authority to tax and to allocate to sub-communities for the purpose of financing welfare benefits naturally brings with it the demand, as part of the principle of equity, that sub-communities be treated equally in the allocation of monies.[20] It is instructive to consider why this is so. Recall the way in which equitable treatment is linked to the idea of the equal worth of human beings: If the welfare of both A and B is in my care, and I allow a significant difference in the benefits they receive without any good reason for the difference, I do not manifest equal respect for their human worth. Quite clearly, the kinds of relationship that are covered by the expression "in my care" are many: I might simply find myself in the position of having to distribute things between A and B; or I might explicitly agree to take A and B into my care. The relationship between government and citizen is, to be sure, much more complex than this. Usually there is no *one* individual in government who has the authority and power either to create or eliminate unjustified inequalities among citizens, and if there is moral culpability (for failures to eliminate these inequalities), it is collective rather than individual. But the simple model will carry us some distance in understanding the circumstances under which governmental acceptance of inequalities becomes inequitable treatment. My failure to eliminate an unjustified inequality in the level of benefits received by A and B does not constitute inequitable treatment either if I do not have the *power* to eliminate the inequality or if I do not have the *authority* to do so. (Let us suppose that the social arrangements for allocating authority are, on the whole, just and not open to serious moral criticism.) The case of the family again serves as an illustration of how authority may be lacking: It is no inequitable treatment of anyone if I fail to take away from some other parent's child in order to give more to mine, though there may be a considerable inequality between them, and one for which no systematic good reason can be given. Similarly, it is no inequitable treatment in my dealing with the needs of two persons if I give all the benefits to the one who is near me and none to the person who is beyond my reach on a faraway island. In such a case I do not have the power to avoid the inequality.

In the relationship between government and citizens, either of these— lack of power or lack of authority—can operate to limit the scope of equity. If an organ of government fails, due to the lack of one of these, to eliminate an inequality that would otherwise be an inequity, its failure cannot reasonably be taken to show a lack of equal respect for persons. The main idea here is that *(1)* an individual or organ of government cannot be expected to go beyond its power in eliminating inequalities (philosophers sometimes capture this bit of wisdom in the apothegm that "ought implies can"); and *(2)* the failure of an individual or organ of government to eliminate an inequality, where that failure is due to its respect for the limits of its own authority, manifests no lack of respect for persons; for we are supposing that the structure of authority is itself generally just, and so that it is in some sense (which we cannot explore here) justifiable to all.

The establishment of a federal budget for the purpose of financing welfare benefits does not necessarily involve any provision for federal authority over the ways in which individual sub-communities distribute the relevant services among their members. "Federal control" and "federalization" are terms that can mean many different things. But where both the authority and power are present, there is a deep and pervasive reason why it becomes increasingly *proper* for the central budgetary authority to examine the ways in which individual members of the sub-communities are being treated, and even to make intercommunity comparisons of the ways similarly circumstanced individuals are treated.[21] Thus intercommunity differences, once not the subject of scrutiny because there was no authority and power to carry out this scrutiny, now require a good justification if they are to be equitable. Knowingly to allow such differences without any good reason is to take the attitude that some citizens matter less than others; that they do not deserve equal consideration. Similarly, if each person has a right to some subsistence level of benefits (suppose that this is a right that human beings have whether or not it has been provided for by statute), then pressure is appropriately exerted on a sub-community that fails to provide these benefits to its members. This is a kind of governmental application of a simple moral precept: If someone's rights are being violated, and by a simple failure to play a role essential to carrying out the violations you could help to bring about respect for those rights, you should do so.[22]

Before ending the discussion of the relativity of equity to a reference group, there is another issue that must be given attention if serious misunderstandings are not to arise. I have said that the scope of equity depends in large part on institutional arrangements. Now, it is obvious that institutional arrangements that allocate power and authority are themselves not always the best, and are sometimes open to the most serious moral criticism. One objection that might be raised against the foregoing account is that we often quite properly demand that institutions be changed or newly brought into existence precisely in order to eliminate inequities, or to bring about some other desirable result. It might be objected that, in order to proceed with the idea that the scope of equity depends on institutional arrangements, we must know that those institutions themselves are above reproach, and this is rarely, if ever, the case. There are many moral criticisms that can be raised against existing structures of authority and power: They may distribute benefits inefficiently; encourage uses of power that are demeaning to citizens; result in great inequalities in benefits for which no good reason can be given.[23] The answer to this objection is that existing social arrangements defining the structure of authority must be above grave moral criticism, but it would be setting the standard too high to expect them to be beyond moral reproach of any kind. To see this, suppose that social arrangements divide society into autonomous sub-communities, governed respectively by A, B, and C. Benefits are distributed within each community by its governing authority. Suppose that, though this arrangement works fairly well and is not seriously flawed, the *ideal* arrangement would be to combine the sub-communities into one under a single central organ having authority to distribute benefits. So long as existing arrangements are tolerable, they, and not any hypothetical ideal arrangements, are to be used for purposes of distributing benefits and for finding the reference group(s) by means of which the equity of those distributions is to be judged. To use the ideal (but not existing) arrangements for either of these purposes would be far worse than to adhere to the existing ones. For there are typically many different hypothetical arrangements that are equally ideal, and even if not, individual judgments may conflict about what the ideal is. Thus for individuals to act and make judgments in accordance with their own conception of the ideal is to make coordination around any particular plan difficult to bring about and maintain. This argument loses strength, however, in proportion to the evils of existing arrangements. The evils of a collapse of coordination may in some cases be slight compared to the evils of existing institutions.

Equity versus Community Preferences

The preferences of a community or political subdivision, as expressed through a majoritarian process, should be given weight in the formation of public policies and legislation and, in particular, in the design of income support programs. In a system that aims at being democratic, this seems a terribly obvious thing to say. But there are important limitations, both constitutional and moral, on the weight that is to be given to community preferences. Thus, for example, the decision of a majority seriously to restrict permissible modes of dress or religious practices would not, and should not, be honored. Restrictions on the operation of the majoritarian principle typically appear in the form of rights, the recognition of which we can build into our political and legal system, and our moral thinking, at various levels. For example, if we accept a theory of justice like that of Rawls, then its fundamental principles place constraints on the range of acceptable constitutions; a given constitution places contraints on the range of acceptable legislation; a given piece of legislation may place constraints on the acceptable range of administrative policies, and so on. Thus a constitution that violates fundamental principles of justice would not be made acceptable simply because it was wanted by an overwhelming majority; and an unconstitutional piece of legislation is no less invalid because it is favored by a huge majority. The Rawlsian principles of justice establish in this way rights and constraints of a very general kind. A constitution and subsequent legislation establish more specific rights and constraints.

Now, the requirements of equity, when their scope is properly understood, take priority over the preferences of the community. In this way, equity can be thought of as putting a rather strong constraint on the authority of community preferences. The idea that there are legitimate constraints on community preferences is deeply entrenched in the liberal political philosophy of thinkers as different as Locke and Mill, Hayek and Rawls; it has been given a utilitarian foundation, as in Mill and Hayek, and a contractarian foundation, as in Rawls. That citizens should be treated equitably even though a majority may prefer an inequitable alternative is again an idea that has been argued for in many different ways by philosophers as diverse as Rousseau, Kant, Hayek, and Rawls. I shall not recapitulate any of these arguments here, nor present a new one. In this paper I simply take as starting points two ideas that have been central in liberal political thought: (1) that there are moral constraints on the authority of community preferences; and (2) that one of these constraints is that of equity. Now, if, in the formulation of an income support program, one small group is for no good reason provided with none or with a lower level of benefits than another group, even though it is similarly circumstanced, that inequity is not justified by the fact that to eliminate it would make the program cost more, and the majority would prefer not to bear those costs. Deliberately to provide for or allow inconsistent or anomalous treatment of one segment of the community cannot be morally justified by pointing to the preferences, or slightly greater satisfaction, or somewhat reduced burdens, of the majority. But the priority of equity to community preferences must be carefully understood in light of the scope of equitable considerations. First, there is the fact, already discussed, that comparisons for purposes of equity are in an important way relative to a reference group. A significant intercommunity inequality does not, merely because it is an inequality, automatically constitute an inequity, though through a political (or administrative, or fiscal) unification of several communities into one, that inequality may become an inequity as well. Given that equity does not extend across two communities, the moral restrictions on setting a level of benefit higher or lower than those of another community are not as severe, and there is correspondingly more room to yield to community preferences.[24]

There is another point about the scope of equitable considerations that is both of general interest and helpful in understanding the extent to which equity places limits on the implementation of community preferences. Equity is in large part what Brian Barry calls an *interstitial principle*.[25] Typical problems of equity occur *within* a framework of general social policies and principles and the particular rules established for implementing those policies and principles. That is to say, *given* particular goals, principles, and rules, problems of equity occur when there are inconsistencies and anomalies in the rules, or in their application. In these cases, spotting inequities requires mainly a sharp eye for inconsistency. One does not always have to argue about the abstract principles and goals themselves; neither is it necessary to introduce new abstract principles into the system; instead, inconsistencies are to be ironed out using those policies and principles as given. This is not to say that issues of equity do not arise at the more fundamental levels; it is only to say that many problems of equity do not go that deep. Now, for example, assume that we start out with it as given that those who work more should receive more gross income; that this is important because it is wrong that people should get no reward for working; and, in addition, it is thought that it will increase social efficiency if people have an incentive to enter into productive work. Now suppose that, to implement these ideas, a program is adopted which has as a consequence that recipients under the program who are working receive more than non-recipients who are working. Given the operating policies and principles, this is an inconsistency that is an inequity unless some further policy justifies it: If the ideas of incentive and of enjoying the fruits of one's labor govern, how is this difference to be explained? Perhaps some good rationale can be given; but it would seem insufficient simply to point to the adventitious fact that some people just happened to start out on the program while others did not. But while equity makes quite specific demands in a case like this, calling for elimination of this inconsistency in treatment, it may be quite silent on such a question as: *How much* more gross income should those who work have over those who do not work? This is not (necessarily) any question at all about consistency, for the ideas of work-incentive and of possessing the fruits of one's labor tell only that those who work should get more; they do not necessarily tell how much more. Indeed, the determination of this might properly be left largely to community preferences. This is yet another example of the way in which the principle of equity goes into operation *after* the larger social choices—such as those of political, fiscal, and administrative structure, and of large and abstract social values—have been made.

Another example may help to clarify the point, as well as to relate equity to community preferences. Suppose that we adopt the idea that income support programs are to be designed so that those who work harder are to receive more. The operation of this policy would not *necessarily* create any inequities. It is possible to imagine a small community in which there are moderate variations in the amount that people work, and no significant variations in any other respect: a community, say, of three-person families all of whose members have roughly the same needs. But suppose now that in the community there are bachelors whose work is equal to that of the heads of large families.[26] Adhering to the single formula "equal gross income for equal work," there would be an inequity *if* we take as one of our social goals that it is the needs of individual persons that must be provided for by our income policies. Given this social goal, a presumption would be raised against the results of applying the pure work formula in such cases. But notice that, in constructing a combined formula taking account of need and of work, a considerable variation in the relative weights given to need and work is possible. Further, the principle of equity does not single out one of these as the only equitable one. Once a particular formula is chosen, however, *it* can be used, in many cases, to point out new inequities: "You are treating X according to this formula, but not Y. What is the rationale?" Notice also that, in picking this combined formula from those in the broad range of acceptability,[27] all sorts of considerations having little to do with equity, or even with fairness, play an important role. Thus available resources, administrative efficiency, the economic value of an incentive to work, and even community preferences, have a proper role to play. Once the formula is chosen, however, equity goes into operation again, but this time with more specific demands.

Now, just as many problems of equity arise only after the large social choices have been made, so it is true that some problems of equity can be simply bypassed by making choices at a higher and more all-encompassing level. Indeed, it is a mistake to suppose that we can always hammer away at the problem of determining whether and how much a person is to be rewarded for work (as opposed to need) by straining our commonsense ideas of merit and need, for we may quickly strain those ideas to the breaking point without decisive results. First, when left at the level of commonsense intuitions, questions about the extent to which merit (whether this means ability, effort, achievement, or moral desert) or need should govern distributions tend to be hopelessly vague and indeterminate, as do their answers. In deciding whether A merits more than B, or needs more, we tend to be reduced to the trading of scattered and conflicting intuitions.[28] To the extent that we seek to give an *argument* for our intuitions, we must go beyond them and speak in other terms, such as the way in which distribution in accordance with some material principle will further some end or be congruent with some more fundamental principle.[29] The most substantial and convincing discussions of distribution in accordance with merit, for example, proceed in this way.[30] A second, and perhaps more basic, reason for moving to a more fundamental level than our commonsense notions of the role of merit and need is that the relative weights to be given to the commonsense notions of merit and need is properly made to vary with social and economic conditions. There is no a priori answer to the question how they are to be weighted.[31] In a time when the provision of an incentive to work is of paramount importance and virtually everyone is capable of some amount of work, both legislation and moral thinking might be well justified in stressing reward for productive work over attention to need. In other times, the reverse emphasis might be appropriate.

The Analogy of Equal Protection Theory

From the discussion so far, many will recognize at once the similarities between the requirements of equity, when conceived in this way, and the theory of equal protection review in Constitutional law. These similarities can be put to use in trying to understand when and to what extent the requirements of equity have priority over other social goals. Thus a central problem of equity is the determination of when a set of particular rules operates in an inequitable way to give benefits or impose burdens on some while not treating others in an equal way. Yet, clearly, some classifications for the purpose of providing different levels of benefit are appropriate and are quite consistent with equity. For example, those who are in serious need of income assistance (by an appropriate measure of need) should be provided with more than those who need less; those who work and save should have more gross income than those who do not, and so on. A difference in benefit level, or in gross income, does not, in general, amount to an inequity if a systematic and good rationale can be provided for making such a classification with its associated difference. (What constitutes a *good* rationale is itself a deep question; but there is considerable philosophical agreement that a good rationale in such a setting must be one that is in principle acceptable to all, or acceptable to all rational persons who take an impartial point of view, or acceptable to all parties in a Rawlsian original position, etc.) Not all classifications or differences of this kind are supported by a systematic good rationale, and I explore some of the reasons for this further on.

Now, the similarity to the theory of equal protection review in Constitutional law lies in the following. In the review of legislative classifications to determine whether they are consistent with equal protection requirements, a distinction is made between the classifications themselves (appearing in particular legislative rules) and the purposes, goals, etc., that they are designed to implement. A classification, of course, *fits* the legislative purpose more or less well: The classification may be *over*-inclusive in the sense that some persons or items are included that do not further the purpose in question; or it may be *under*-inclusive in not including some whose inclusion would further the purpose in question; or the classification can be both over-inclusive and under-inclusive. If it is neither of these, there is a perfect fit. Of course, in the design of legislation, as in the design of any set of particular rules, it would be expecting too much of legislative designers that they provide in every case a perfect fit between classification and purpose. Whether equal protection requires a very nearly perfect fit or that there simply be a rational basis for the classification depends upon the classification, and on whether there is a fundamental interest involved, such as voting rights or the right to travel. If either the classification is "suspect" (classification by race being the paradigm case), or fundamental interests are involved, then a strict test is applied: There must be a very tight fit between classification and legislative purpose, and the purpose must be to advance a valid state interest. If neither a suspect classification nor a fundamental interest is involved, then it is necessary and sufficient for acceptability that the classification have some rational basis.[32]

Now, it is obvious that income assistance and related programs providing benefits to the poor employ rules and classifications that fit the purposes of the programs with varying degrees of precision. Using the equal protection model, we can see what in general to look for in deciding whether differential treatment is an inequity, and if so, whether its elimination should have a high priority that would justify significant sacrifices elsewhere, such as in administrative efficiency, or in incurring greater costs of individualization. Differential treatment (whether this is due to classifications or to unforeseen inconsistencies in the operation of a set of rules) would require a very strong justification where it touches on fundamental individual *rights*. If a set of rules has the effect of limiting, or adversely affecting, some in the enjoyment of their rights, then the justification must be especially strong. In addition, the adverse effect must be no more or less than is required by the justification. For example, suppose a set of rules operates to make a distinction between female- and male-headed families, providing benefits to the former that the latter do not receive. If there are adverse effects on the rights of family members, as perhaps in the provisions for minimum health care or education for children, then it would not be a sufficient justification for *this* particular distinction that male-headed families are *generally* less needy than female-headed families. Rules allowing more detailed individualization would be necessary, even at greater cost of administration. On the other hand, minor differences in the level of cash assistance provided to similarly circumstanced families would be justifiable if this difference were an inevitable result of rules designed to reduce administrative complexity, and any revision of the rules eliminating the differential support would be much more inefficient to administer. Note that one important difference between the explained standards of equal protection review and the case of equity is that the former are linked to specific classifications and the purposes behind those classifications. Problems of equity, on the other hand, arise *both* from explicitly formulated classifications (with their associated purposes) *and* from unintended and unforeseen differential treatment that so commonly creeps into any set of programs or rules that develops in hodge-podge inconsistency.

Some Remarks on Coherence and Control

An HEW briefing paper states as one of the objectives of income security programs and policies that they "should work in harmony as a result of deliberate planning and foresight, and should be subject to overall policy and budget control in both the executive and legislative branches of government."[33] There are certainly some strong reasons, primarily of efficiency, for coherence and control. Dramatically different levels of benefits in different communities, for example, can serve to encourage migration from one community to another, and this can make program costs intolerably large in some communities.[34] And, to the extent that there is an easily available option of moving where benefits are larger, the work-incentive effect of limited benefits may be reduced. Further, coherence and control can help to avoid the situation in which individual states or communities are encouraged to fiscal irresponsibility by allowing them to vote for services, only a fraction of whose costs they will be required to pay.[35] We can see more clearly some of the ways in which the pursuit of coherence and control can in some cases create additional requirements of equity and in other cases helps to avoid or eliminate problems of equity.

The objective of treating people equitably is related to the objective of coherence and control in somewhat complicated ways. Here my remarks must be sketchy. First, there is a very important fundamental fact: Inequities tend to be pervasive when programs and reforms are adopted piecemeal and in haphazard ways. The reason for this is that problems of equity are so typically due to unforeseen differences of treatment— differences which, precisely because unforeseen, are especially likely to be unjustified and unjustifiable. For example, one program provides benefits to all in category A; another program is adopted in order to provide benefits to all in category B; but, unbeknownst to the designers of the second program, there is a substantial number of people belonging to both categories A and B. The result is an especially high level of benefit to members of this joint category, and the difference has no good reason in favor of it; indeed, there is a moral presumption against it. Foresight and planning with an eye to coherence and the whole can minimize this source of inequities.

Given a welter of existing programs, coherence often can be achieved only by sweeping them aside and adopting new measures from a macro point of view. Disregarding for a moment the expectations that the old programs may have fostered, the adoption of a coherent set of programs from a macro point of view has the advantage of avoiding a number of problems of equity by, as it were, moving to a level above them. Thus if a partial program continues to exist, and reform is made on a piecemeal basis, the familiar problems of equity arise: If X, who is covered by this existing program, receives such-and-such level of support, then why not Y, who is in similar circumstances? But if the macro point of view is adopted, and a coherent set of new programs taken as the goal, decisions about the level of support become open to a much greater extent, and so long as decided-upon levels of support are consistent, decisions about how high they are can take place on a more general level of social policy.

The adoption of the macro point of view, precisely because it involves the making of larger social decisions, may for that reason arouse more controversy than piecemeal attempts to make reforms on grounds of equity. There are several reasons for this. One is the familiar conservative counsel of caution about making sweeping social changes in pursuit of overall rationality.[36] The social structure is too complicated and contains too many delicately interlocking parts to be subjected to large-scale tampering. A second reason is that the macro point of view, since it does open up large-scale questions of social goals and policy, raises deeper questions about which ideals of social justice and conceptions of the good society are correct. As already suggested, questions of equity are in large part interstitial, being confined to ironing out inconsistencies and anomalies in sets of specific rules that have already been adopted to implement social goals that themselves have already been adopted. Confining criticisms of social institutions to criticisms of their inequities *can* be a way of confining criticism to their special detail.[37]

Finally, achieving coherence and control does in one respect bring with it more stringent demands of equity. This can be seen if we reflect again on the way in which equity is relative to a reference group. Political and fiscal subdivision make it possible for sub-communities to be the reference groups for purposes of equity, and this means that intercommunity inequalities are less likely to run afoul of the principle of equity. The more centralized oversight and control, however, the more it is that differences in treatment of similarly circumstanced people in different communities become the responsibility of those with central authority.

Notes

1. For example: whether conflicts between goals, between principles and policies, etc., are an inevitable feature of the moral landscape; whether, in cases of conflict, we have no recourse but to appeal to intuition; whether priority rules can be devised to reduce our reliance on intuition; whether the choices that we make in establishing trade-offs between two fundamental values can be rational in view of the fact that these choices are, by hypothesis, not made by appeal to any further, more fundamental principle; and so on.

2. The best-known recent philosophical attempt in this direction is provided by John Rawls in *A Theory of Justice* (Cambridge, Mass.: Harvard University Press, 1971). There he employs the idea of a relation of *lexical priority* as holding between principles, or between maximization goals under the same principle. A principle P has lexical priority over P' if and only if *no* sacrifice (however small) of the requirements of P is justified by *any* gain (however large) in satisfying the requirements of P'. (See pp. 40–45.) Rawls holds that his first principle, requiring that each person have an equal right to the most extensive basic liberty compatible with a similar liberty for others, has lexical priority to the second principle, which requires that social and economic inequalities are to be arranged so that they are both reasonably expected to be to everyone's advantage, and are attached to positions and offices open to all (Section 11). Rawls provides the bulk of his argument for the priority of liberty in section 82 of his book. In addition, the interpretation of the notion of "everyone's advantage" (in the second principle) that Rawls favors is one that gives lexical priority to maximizing the expectations (i.e., the life prospects viewed from the social station) of the worst-off representative individual. (See pp. 75–83.)

3. See note 2.

4. For a survey and discussion of some of the problems, see Joel Feinberg, "Rawls and Intuitionism" in *Reading Rawls*, ed. Norman Daniels (New York: Basic Books, 1974), p. 108.

5. See, for example, Richard Musgrave, *The Theory of Public Finance* (New York: McGraw-Hill, 1959), p. 160.

6. *Ibid.* See also HEW Paper #2, "The Income Security System: Purposes, Criteria, and Choices," p. 4.

7. See Lester M. Salamon, *Toward Income Opportunity: Current Thinking on Welfare Reform* (Institute of Policy Sciences and Public Affairs of Duke University & The Ford Foundation, 1977), p. 55; Bradley Schiller, *The Economics of Poverty and Discrimination* (Englewood Cliffs, N.J.: Prentice-Hall, 1976), p. 173.

8. Musgrave, p. 160.

9. HEW Paper #2 (note 6), p. 4.

10. I draw this example from Salamon, p. 61.

11. See Chaim Perelman, *The Idea of Justice and the Problem of Argument* (London: Routledge & Kegan Paul, 1963); William Frankena, "The Concept of Social Justice" in *Social Justice*, ed. Richard B. Brandt (Englewood Cliffs, N.J.: Prentice-Hall, 1973), p. 100.

12. Musgrave, p. 160.

13. See Salamon, ch. 2; Schiller, ch. 12.

14. Perhaps the most famous attempt to move in the direction of simplification and nationwide equity was that of the Nixon administration's Family Assistance Program. See Salamon, pp. 137–148. Nixon, in a television address on August 8, 1969, said that the very different benefit levels in different states were "wrong; no child is 'worth' more in one state than in another state." (quoted in Daniel P. Moynihan, *The Politics of a Guaranteed Income: The Nixon Administration and the Family Assistance Plan* (New York: Random House, 1973), p. 221.

15. We can, if needed, imagine that each family is headed by one person whose responsibility it is to make decisions about the distribution of resources.

16. Among the prominent figures in the history of political and social philosophy, Hegel saw more clearly than most the main ways in which the development of what he called "civil society" (*bürgerliche Gesellschaft*) "tears the individual from his family ties, estranges the members of the family from one another, and recognizes them as self-subsistent persons. . . . Thus the individual becomes a son of civil society which has as many claims upon him as he

has rights against it." (*The Philosophy of Right*, trans. T.M. Knox (New York: Oxford University Press, 1952), § 238.)

17. One recent writer argues that school expenditures that are unequal on an interdistrict basis are wrong partly because they tend to damage the moral development of children within those districts (and perhaps other districts, if they know about the inequality): "Development of the capacity to understand the moral equality of people, and to ignore morally arbitrary differences, is hindered by inequalities in expenditure that children naturally perceive as differential assessments of basic moral worth." (David A. J. Richards, *The Moral Criticism of Law* (Belmont, Calif.: Dickenson Publishing Co., 1977), p. 152). Now Richards's statement, as it stands, may be roughly true. But surely, whether a person (and, indeed, a child, unless children inveterately make mistakes about these things) perceives such inequalities as a differential *assessment* of *moral worth* must depend in large part on (a) whether the inequality is perceived as resulting from anyone's action or anyone's assessment of anything; and (b) whether such assessment as is made is any assessment of moral worth at all.

18. It is worth noting that Rawls's theory of justice leaves conspicuously undiscussed the question: to what group (a state, the nation, the world community) are the principles of justice to apply? If Rawls's principles apply to nations separately, then the distribution of wealth and liberties that they require will be very different from what they would require if they applied to the entire world community, or included all rational beings on another planet. What is more important than a flat answer to this question (which might be given in a word) is a plausible rationale for that answer. This omission in Rawls's theory is discussed in: Brian Barry, *The Liberal Theory of Justice* (Oxford: The Clarendon Press, 1973), ch. 12; T. M. Scanlon, "Rawls's Theory of Justice," *Reading Rawls*, ed. N. Daniels (New York: Basic Books, 1974), pp. 202–203; Charles Beitz, "Justice and International Relations," *Philosophy & Public Affairs*, Summer 1975, p. 360; Conrad Johnson, "Actual-v. (Rawlsian) Hypothetical-Consent," *Philosophical Studies* 28 (1975): 41.

19. The writings of F. A. Hayek, in addition to their more familiar stress on the importance of liberty and the dangers of centralized management of the economy, show an acute awareness of the fact that an increased centralization of services brings with it increased moral requirements on that authority responsible for the provision of those services. See, for example, *The Road to Serfdom* (Chicago: University of Chicago Press, 1944), ch. 8.

20. Of course, it will most likely bring with it the *political pressure* to allocate on an equal basis. My point here is that such political pressure would then be based on the solid foundation of the familiar principle of equity.

21. As I am about to explain, then, the extension of central control, either fiscal or political, is, to a significant extent, quite literally self-justifying. But note that this does *not* mean that it is always right or desirable that all political and fiscal authority be centralized. On the contrary, there may be powerful reasons for avoiding such centralization, and the increased moral demands that such centralization involves can be avoided by avoiding, as much as possible, the first steps into the circle.

22. An additional comment on the existence of rights may be appropriate here. First, there is what I would call the *emergent* (and, correspondingly, *evaporating*) character of some rights. This can perhaps best be seen in the following. A very central category of rights is those that involve a correlative duty on the part of some other person(s). Thus if I have a right to be provided with $150 per month income support, then some person(s) and/or organization(s) have the duty to provide me with that $150. Now consider the following example. A small child is drowning in shallow water. An able-bodied adult is the only person nearby, and could easily save the child with no risk to himself. It is plausible to maintain that the child has a (moral, if not also legal) *right* to that help on that occasion, and the correlative duty falls on the adult. But though our duties to our fellow human beings may indeed require us to make sacrifices for them, and sometimes significant ones, we do not have a *duty* to make heroic sacrifices. If saving the child would have involved enormous risks to the adult, there would not have been any duty to save the child, and thus no correlative right. However, suppose that there is a group of adults standing nearby, and, though any individual acting alone could not save the child without enormous risks, by their *coordinated* action they could

save the child with no more than negligible risk to anyone. Does the child have a right to the help? Yes, *provided* the group has some combination of leadership, training, organization, or is in such other circumstances as to make its coordinated action possible. When the requisite number of people come on the scene, and the requisite elements enabling coordination are present, there is an *emergent collective duty* and, correlatively, an emergent right. But when such number of elements are missing, so is the duty, and so is the right. Of course, such a very general and vague duty as to "do what we reasonably can" exists quite apart from the adventitious facts of number of people, resources, social organization, etc. But *specific* duties and rights quite often emerge and evaporate in the way explained.

23. One such good reason *might* be the preservation of a degree of autonomy of the states in a federal system in order to prevent abuses of power at the federal level. Note that this would be an issue concerning the justifiability of institutional arrangements—a kind of macro-question—and not one concerning the justifiability of any administrator's decisions within that system.

24. Of course, there are other constraints. Setting a benefit lower than another community does may violate no one's right to equitable and fair treatment, but if all have a right to a certain minimum, and the reduction in question goes below that minimum, then community preferences are by themselves insufficient to justify the reduction.

25. *Political Argument* (London: Routledge & Kegan Paul, 1965), pp. 152–155.

26. This example parallels one of Perelman's *(The Idea of Justice,* p. 33).

27. Broad considerations of fairness and equity can play a role in setting the vague boundaries on this range of acceptability, too. Thus it would be unfair to those who have a hard time finding work (because of general unemployment) to place too much stress on work as opposed to need.

28. For some of the difficulties, see John Hospers, *Human Conduct* (New York: Harcourt, Brace & World, 1961), pp. 433–451.

29. This is the crux of much of the dispute between utilitarians and intuitionists, particularly in British moral philosophy in the nineteenth century. My claim here is a somewhat weakened echo of John Stuart Mill's, who said, "I might go much further and say that to all those *a priori* moralists who deem it necessary to argue at all, utilitarian arguments are indispensable." *Utilitarianism* (Indianapolis: Bobbs-Merrill, 1957), p. 6.

30. See, as a case in point, F.A. Hayek's argument against the principle of reward according to merit and in favor of the principle of reward according to achievement as valued by a free market. *The Constitution of Liberty* (London: Routledge & Kegan Paul, 1960), pp. 93–97.

31. Rawls too stresses the subordinate place of commonsense norms: "Moreover, it is essential to keep in mind the subordinate place of commonsense norms. Doing this is sometimes difficult because they are familiar from everyday life and therefore they are likely to have a prominence in our thinking that their derivative status does not justify." Rawls, *Theory of Justice*, p. 307.

32. The *locus classicus* for these ideas is J. Tussman and J. ten Broek, "The Equal Protection of the Laws," *Cal. L. Rev.* 37 (1949): 341. For other presentations, see Owen M. Fiss, "Groups and the Equal Protection Clause," *Philosophy & Public Affairs*, Winter 1976, p. 107; see also Richards, *Moral Criticism of Law*, pp. 138–140, and more recently, *American Constitutional Law*, by Laurence H. Tribe (Mineola, N.Y.: The Foundation Press, Inc., 1978), Chapter 16.

33. HEW Paper #2 (note 6), p.5.

34. If we focus on the different burdens borne by the citizens of different communities, and if we suppose that there is a central organ that could coordinate programs and eliminate these differences, then the differences do constitute an inequity.

35. This kind of case is discussed by Musgrave, *Theory of Public Finance*, p. 182. A parallel to the inefficiency resulting from migration in search of greater welfare benefits is the inefficient allocation of resources and location of industries due to different levels of taxation. (See p. 160.) Musgrave recognizes, however, that this, and possibly other inefficiences, may be a (presumably acceptable) cost of political subdivision.

36. See, for example, Michael Oakeshott, "Rationalism in Politics" and "Political Education," *Rationalism in Politics* (London: Methuen, 1962). See also Hayek, *The Road to Serfdom.* Hayek is not, of course, a conservative in anything like the same sense that Oakeshott is. Moynihan (*Politics of Guaranteed Income*, pp. 144–146) makes the point that conservatives were very cautious about the Family Assistance Program partly because they believed no one knew what its consequences would be.

37. See Barry, *Liberal Theory of Justice*, pp. 152–155.

8

Conflicting Objectives and the Priorities Problem[1]

NORMAN DANIELS

Some Remarks on Strategy

Welfare planners, reformers, and critics alike face a "priorities" problem whose form is somewhat alien to the philosopher. They must debate priorities among a long list of conflicting "objectives"—all of which are taken to be goals and desiderata of the welfare system[2]. Thus the objectives of providing adequate benefit levels for those in need and of minimizing work disincentives for those receiving benefits are seen to conflict in the existing system and in many proposals for reforming it. Vertical and horizontal equity objectives are seen to conflict with adequacy objectives, work incentive objectives, or target efficiency objectives. When such objectives conflict, which should take priority?

The philosopher approaching this question is made to feel uneasy, as if in the presence of something unfamiliar and slightly threatening. He is not used to handling objectives, let alone determining priorities among them. They are like strange, unanalyzed rocks, forming a conceptual moonscape. Indeed, it is not clear they are all of a kind at all. Some have the clear glint of moral fiber. Others, plain efficiency in rock, have that compact structure economists find so beautiful. Still others are streaked with the sedimentary layering of administrative dross. And some have an impossible quality about them, like the stubborn insubstantiality of prejudice and ideology. Still, the word from mission control is to toss all these objectives into the scales and *weigh* them, as if there were a moral force that could induce an ordering among them in the way gravity induces an ordering among otherwise unanalyzed moonrocks.

147

Some philosophers would clearly be more comfortable if they could map this moonscape onto more familiar terrain. Suppose each welfare objective could be beamed through a Moral Approximator. This device can formulate the moral principles that might be thought to govern social institutions were the corresponding objectives embodied in them. Even allowing for scatter, leading to generality and vagueness, the Approximator might uncover such principles or maxims as these: (1) People with equal levels of need should receive equal benefits; (2) People with unequal levels of need should be treated differently; (3) People with greater needs are entitled to greater welfare resources than people with lesser needs; (4) Transfers that provide work incentives are (morally) preferable to transfers that do not; (5) Transfers should not reverse income rank orderings (e.g., between recipients and ineligible non-recipients); and so on. In these principles, we can see the moral image of such objectives as horizontal and vertical equity, adequacy of benefit levels, work incentives, and what has been called "fairness."[3] Now the philosopher can raise the question about priorities in a language he may find more familiar: "What are the priorities among these principles?"[4]

This question about the priorities of principles is itself plausibly transformed into a question about how we might reason in favor of a particular ordering. Specifically, we might hope that our welfare principles or maxims and their ordering might be deducible from some more general moral theory. For example, utilitarianism, with its one super-principle, might, for a given set of conditions, produce a specific ordering of the "rule-of-thumb" welfare maxims or principles.[5] Similarly, a theory containing more than one basic principle, like Rawls's justice as fairness, might impose an ordering on our maxims. Either alternative would reveal what I shall call a *non-intuitionist* structure in our moral reasoning.[6] In contrast, we might find that our welfare principles or maxims are not derivable from any more general set of ordered principles. This *intuitionist* outcome does not bar our forming moral *judgments* about how to proceed in cases of conflict in particular cases. Rather, all it means is that the *justification* for such moral judgments does not derive from some general ordering of more basic principles.

It is worth noting that the labels "intuitionist" and "non-intuitionist" do not commit us to a view of the *foundations* of moral reasoning. After all, nothing has been said about what justifies accepting either type of non-intuitionist account. Rather, I have here only labeled a distinction in the structure of moral reasoning about (at least some) particular cases: Either it does or does not reduce to reasoning from principles with a general ordering to them. If all that could be said about the justification of utilitarianism or Rawls's ordered principles is that we all happen to believe them true—indeed, we intuit their truth and the order among them—then there would be little to distinguish the justificatory status of what I have called intuitionist and non-intuitionist structures (even assuming compara-ble consensus on particular cases in the non-intuitionist case).[7]

The strategy of seeing whether plausible welfare priorities are derivable from standard non-intuitionist theories seems attractive. It could provide systematic reasons, rooted in broader theoretical issues, for favoring one set of priorities over another. It could even reveal something about the relative strengths and weaknesses of the different moral theories. And even if it failed to yield priorities for certain principles or objectives, it might tell us something about *why* we fail to get a theoretically illuminating ordering. Unfortunately this path is not all roses. Even aside from thorny questions about the acceptability of these general theories, and even aside from the sensitivity any derivation of priorities has to empirical claims about social conditions, serious obstacles block its easy pursuit. Moreover, these obstacles involve important questions about the clarity of our priority question.

In the second section I argue that the priorities problem is not a determinate one unless we specify two features of the context in which it arises. First, we must determine whether or not we can significantly alter fundamental institutions of the society. That is, we must know what the "framework" for the question is. Second, we must specify, for any given framework, whether or not the institutions comply with acceptable principles of justice. That is, we must make explicit the "context of compliance." Only when the priorities question is made determinate in these ways is it possible to assess specific claims and arguments about the ordering of welfare objectives.

In the third section I consider an argument that fairness or vertical equity considerations prohibit reversing income order through welfare transfers. The argument, if successful, would impose a strong constraint on the adequacy of benefit levels. I suggest that once we specify frameworks and contexts of compliance, the burden of proof shifts against this priority argument. In the last section I examine two questions underlying debate about the relative importance of work incentives and adequacy of benefit levels. First, what social and economic institutions affect willingness to work and create conditions under which we can hold people responsible for failure to work? And second, when, if ever, is it just to treat the wage levels of the worst-off workers as a ceiling on adequacy of benefit levels? Answers to these substantive questions again depend on specifying frameworks and contexts of compliance. So it is to these notions I now turn.

"Frameworks" and "Contexts of Compliance": Ambiguity in the Priorities Question

The priority question is unclear for two distinct but interacting reasons. First, it is unclear because it does not specify a relevant framework within which the question is posed. Yet, with regard to different frameworks, answers to the priorities question, even from within the same general moral theory, may differ. Second, it is unclear because it does not specify a context of compliance: With regard to a specific framework, does the priorities question arise in a context in which appropriate standards of justice and morality are generally complied with, or are we quite far from compliance? Each of these notions, frameworks and contexts of compliance, needs further comment.

Consider frameworks first. A framework is determined by how much of the basic fundamental political, social, and economic institutions we take to be fixed and how much we allow to be revised in the social system under question. The more major changes of fundamental institutions we allow, the more *basic* the framework.[8] Suppose our task is to design a set of basic social and economic institutions that yields a just income distribution, and we are free to alter such things as property rights, control over the means of production, institutions that affect job opportunity, and so on. Then our framework is a fairly basic one and our priorities question becomes, "What kinds of priorities among principles of distributive justice should we adopt in designing income transfer mechanisms?" (Of course, this question may not yet be within a most basic framework since it presupposes incomes differentiated by job.) But we might also formulate a framework that holds much less up for revision. Suppose we accept as a given the basic economic and social structures within the United States (though we might allow many minor changes of detail in them). Suppose, further, we assume these institutions resistant or immune to change. We might refrain from asking any question about the justice of these basic arrangements and instead frame the question, "What are the moral priorities among objectives (or principles) for a welfare system having a limited role in adjusting income levels for a relatively special class of people in the U.S. economy?" Indeed, we might imagine this question to have slightly different frameworks if asked by a legislator and an administrator: Each might be willing to take somewhat different features of the system as fixed.

The general problem that arises, once we note the possibility of different frameworks, is that "the priorities question" is really different questions which have different answers. Consider, for example, a general moral theory like Rawls's, that places constraints on the kinds of inequalities that can emerge through the operation of basic social and economic institutions.[9] It may seem to put adequacy considerations above various other objectives when we take the framework to be the justice of basic institutions.[10] The same theory may give quite different answers (or none at all) if it is addressed to the priorities among principles that are appropriate to less basic administrative or legislative frameworks. For example, efficiency or merit considerations might emerge as having greater importance once the more basic framework and its considerations of equality are held fixed. This distinction among types of frameworks may provide us with one way to understand Conrad Johnson's claim that equity is an interstitial notion:[11] It can be interstitial within a less basic framework while at the same time be a central constitutive notion in a more basic framework.

The distinction among frameworks is quite general and can arise within the context of any general moral theory. It is clearly relevant to Rawls's theory, since he invokes distinct stages in the choice and implementation of principles of justice.[12] In such a stage theory, we might imagine that priorities among principles in less basic frameworks may differ from priorities at more basic stages, providing the less basic principles do not alter basic structures in ways that violate more basic principles. Frameworks are important within a utilitarian approach as well. For example, we might imagine asking, "Taking certain social and economic institutions as given, which principles or maxims governing welfare reform produce a social order that maximizes goodness?" The ordering of principles of equality, merit, and efficiency within this less basic framework might be different from the ordering that holds in a more basic framework.

If I am right, a selection of frameworks is presupposed in asking the priorities question. We do not face one priorities question, but many. But then, it is easy to see why there is a general obstacle to implementing the promising strategy I outlined earlier. The same general theories may give different priorities for questions raised in different frameworks.

Unfortunately, there is yet another confounding factor blocking pursuit of that strategy. Much recent work in general moral theory, especially theory of justice, is concerned with what can be called *ideal* or full-compliance theory. In Rawls's construction, contractors select principles they can live with on the assumption the principles will generally be complied with. On comparable utilitarian constructions, rules for regulating the social system are adopted because they would tend to maximize goodness were there general compliance with them. Such ideal theories can be used, so it is argued, to criticize existing institutions and to point us in the direction of better alternatives. Still, general theories throw notoriously little light on two critical issues. What is the most effective strategy for moving from noncompliance to compliance contexts? What deviations from ideal principles are permissible in the pursuit of compliance? The first is generally dismissed as a problem in political science. The latter receives scant discussion, e.g., as the issue of "dirty hands."

Notice, however, what happens when we put the distinction among frameworks together with worries about compliance. In making the distinction about frameworks, I have supposed we could step back from questions about the priorities that govern basic structures and ask about the proper ordering of principles for less basic frameworks. Nevertheless, a general moral theory can throw light on priorities for principles in less basic frameworks *provided we assume compliance* with appropriate principles of justice for the more basic frameworks. If we cannot assume such compliance, it is hard to see how we can begin to evaluate priorities for less basic frameworks. Under compliance assumptions, we assume the principles for less basic frameworks are constrained not to determine more basic principles. In the absence of compliance, we lack even this constraint.

How do we then evaluate priorities for principles for less basic frameworks? We might aim for the principles that would be ideal were compliance with more basic principles already in effect. Such an approach might, on some views, have its justification in its value for moral education. The principles would provide us with a living example of the ideal. An alternative approach might lead us to seek priorities for principles which have the effect of moving the whole distribution toward a more just one, that is, toward a distribution that would better comply with the requirements of more basic principles.

Each suggestion faces objections. The former seems insensitive to the deeper injustices that exist and risks degenerating into a somewhat hypocritical moral scrupulosity. Suppose, for example, someone thought that distribution in general should be meritarian, that is, that shares of social goods should be proportional to effort expended (or some other measure of merit). To insist that such a meritarian principle be involved in the welfare system when it is not complied with in general risks the charge of misplaced scruples. The alternative approach, however, may involve trying to use the welfare system to rectify inequities that only more basic changes in the social system can correct. That is, it involves implicitly—and maybe illicitly—shifting frameworks.

The worries I have raised about frameworks and contexts of compliance do, of course, muddy the waters, at least with regard to the promising strategy I outlined earlier. But I have not raised these worries just to point out ambiguities that may underlie the priorities question in the abstract and which thus pose hypothetical, theoretical difficulties. I raise them because they point to ambiguities that pervade the *actual* search for priorities in welfare reform. For example, some see the welfare system as a relatively *special* and *minor correction* to institutions which generate acceptable inequalities. Others construe the welfare system—or proposals for reforming it—as part of a general income transfer system which *constitutes* an acceptable redistribution of social goods. Accompanying this divergence there are differences both in the frameworks within which the priorities question is being raised and in the estimates of compliance of the system as a whole with basic principles of justice. What this suggests is that some of what appears to be straightforward moral disagreement about appropriate priorities for principles governing the welfare system may be disguised disagreement about the framework and context of compliance surrounding the priorities question. To be sure, there may well be more basic moral disagreement underlying this divergence about frameworks and contexts of compliance, but it is likely in turn that some of the disagreement is traceable to differences in social theory. We shall see one form this may take in what follows.

I turn now to consider specific arguments for priorities among central welfare objectives. The distinctions I have made concerning frameworks and contexts of compliance will prove essential to evaluation of these arguments.

Vertical Equity, Merit, and Adequacy

Key discussions of welfare reform have suggested that the central conflict of objectives is between adequacy of benefit levels, on the one hand, and, on the other, maintenance of work incentives and various horizontal and vertical equity considerations. Of course, a thorough discussion of adequacy considerations would require clarification of the many conceptual and measurement problems surrounding the notion of need. Here I will ignore these issues. Indeed, though I use the notion "adequate benefits," I provide no careful definition of it, nor estimate what it means operationally or in dollars. I do have, however, some guiding intuitions. I believe that benefit levels that leave a family unit at or slightly below poverty levels are of questionable adequacy. They may prevent the most extreme deprivation, but they do very little to provide a family with a structure of opportunities that makes it possible to improve prospects for family members significantly. These intuitions bear on the form the conflict between adequacy levels and other objectives usually takes. Arguments based on these other objectives end up pushing benefit levels below a de facto ceiling which consists of the income levels of the worst-off (or near worst-off) employed workers. At this point, of course, the issues about frameworks and contexts of compliance become critical.

I begin with some arguments based on claims about vertical equity. These arguments have just the kind of de facto ceiling effect I am concerned with. But first it will be necessary to say something about the notion of vertical equity as it is used in the context of the welfare debate. David Lindeman has noted that the notions of vertical and horizontal equity incorporate different clauses of the Aristotelian formal principle of justice, "treat equals equally, unequals unequally."[13] But to make the formal principle have any content at all, it is necessary to specify the *relevant characteristics* by reference to which "equals" and "unequals" are to be identified as such. Thus, we must know if we are talking about equals with regard to need, work status, marital status, and so on. Moreover, to make the formal principle have a content anything like what we recognize in the welfare context as horizontal and vertical equity, the relevant characteristics must be incorporated into supplementary distributive principles. For example, "People with equal needs should receive proportionally greater benefits," and so on. In the welfare context, neither horizontal nor vertical equity is just a formal notion. Each carries with it, explicitly or implicitly, substantive distributive principles and a specification of the relevant characteristics for determining equality or inequality of cases.[14]

Jodie Allen has articulated four principles she thinks capture a working notion of vertical equity for welfare contexts:[15]

1. Those in greater need should benefit more than those in lesser need.
2. Post-tax, post-benefit *income rank ordering* should match pre-tax, pre-benefit rank ordering.
3. Tax and benefit policies should not "unduly" compress pre-tax, pre-benefit *distances* between incomes in the rank ordering.
4. Compelling circumstances may allow deviations from 1–3.

There is an internal structure here. Principles (2.) and (3.) constrain the appeal to needs considerations in (1.). *Only if* we preserve income rank order and income distances are we allowed to distribute benefits proportionally to needs. Needs-based considerations are not allowed to cut across the initial income ordering. In effect, the needs-based principle of distribution is restricted in applicability to those persons who fall *within* a given income group on the initial rank ordering, presumably within groups on its lower end. The force of Allen's principles is to compel us to say it is a *violation of equity considerations* to permit concern for the adequacy of benefit levels to reverse any pre-tax, pre-benefit income ordering.

Construed as an explication of our actual, working concept of vertical equity, the analysis faces serious problems. First, throughout our income transfer system as a whole, there is no sanctity to pre-tax income rank orderings of the sort embodied in principles *(2.)* and *(3.)*. Various tax provisions at both federal and state levels, some based on need (like medical deductions and exemptions for dependents, age, and handicaps), others based on type of income source, lead to reversals of pre- and post-tax income orderings. Allen might suggest, in defense against this point, that principles *(2.)* and *(3.)* are features of our notion of vertical equity *as restricted to welfare transfers*. She might claim support by pointing to the resentment many in lower income groups feel toward welfare transfers they see as too generous.[16]

But this defense already points to the second problem facing treating Allen's notion of vertical equity as a description of our actual notion. Some features of our existing welfare program lead to just the sorts of income reversals barred by principles *(2.)* and *(3.)*. To be sure, some people challenge these reversals on grounds of vertical equity, which may be what underlies Allen's claim she is explicating a notion dominant in the field. But there is serious question how universal or dominant the notion is, since others find no violation of vertical equity considerations in at least some of these income order reversals. Indeed, many would argue that a key problem with our whole income redistribution system is that it does *not* produce *enough* income reordering in response to differences in needs.

Perhaps, then, Allen's principles constitute a proposal about how we *ought to* employ vertical equity considerations in the welfare context. As such, it forces us to assess the justifications for the principles and their priorities. Allen suggests that both considerations of utility and considerations of fairness support her analysis.[17]

The utilitarian justification depends on showing that preservation of income rank ordering and distances between income ranks both act to constrain work disincentives, and that, in turn, these work incentives help maximize utility. I shall return later to consider both utilitarian and non-utilitarian arguments in favor of giving priority to work incentives over adequacy of benefits. Suffice it to note here that Allen builds these arguments into the very notion of vertical equity. Vertical equity emerges, on this view, as not one objective but three, for it is a notion with *three* central components: a needs-based component, with low priority; a utilitarian component (work incentives), with high priority; and a meritarian or fairness component, also with high priority. Some of the conflict between Allen's arguments from vertical equity and other arguments based on vertical equity derive from differences in the concept of vertical equity itself. For example, some may take vertical equity in the welfare context to consist primarily of Allen's principle *(1.)* (with qualifications). Then, conflicts between vertical equity and adequacy considerations might evaporate, though both might conflict with other objectives. On such a view, Allen accomplishes the appearance of an equity argument against income order reversals only because she has conflated other notions with issues of equity. I am not here interested in this jurisdictional dispute about the scope of the notion of vertical equity. On either view, what will ultimately count is the weighting of these different considerations, presumably in the light of more general distributive theory.

I return, then, to what may be the most interesting suggestion in Allen's analysis, namely that support for the heavy weighting given to principles *(2.)* and *(3.)* comes from considerations of fairness. The thrust of Allen's claim seems to be that it is *unfair* for the welfare system to reverse any income rank ordering or to collapse unduly any income distances. Now, it is important to note that the "unfairness" here does not derive from straightforward libertarian considerations. Allen does not challenge the legitimacy of an income redistribution system on the grounds that it automatically violates the liberty and liberty-based entitlements of all persons being taxed for welfare purposes. Allen challenges *only* those transfers that alter rank order or unduly collapse income inequalities. Allen says little to back up this claim about fairness. Indeed, she suggests it may be just "a rationalization of a basic social need" (encouraging productive work); still, it is at least perceived as a matter of fairness.[18] In any case, it is interesting to inquire what general moral views might make the claim plausible. Such inquiry requires, however, that we specify a *framework* in accordance with our earlier discussion.

To begin with, consider a very basic framework, one in which we can reorder basic institutions to comply with the following meritarian principle of distributive justice: Absolute levels of reward aside, income rank ordering should reflect the desert or merit of the income earner.[19] Different notions of merit might be subscribed to here, such as "reward according to contribution to society (as measured market value of one's work)" or "reward according to effort expended (calories?)" or "reward according to a combination of ability plus effort." So meritarian social orders might differ in their rank orderings. But for any such meritarian order to be realized, a broad range of facts about basic social and economic institutions must be fixed: facts about the structure of opportunities, including access to jobs, facts about the availability of jobs, and facts about the process through which income levels are determined. At best, of course, these meritarian principles and the social orders that correspond to them form only a fragment of a full theory of justice; but let us leave aside this qualification. Of course, we could debate the acceptability of such meritarian principles as basic principles of justice. A promising start in such a debate might be based on Rawls's views in *A Theory of Justice*. But this debate is not our task here and I would like, instead, to point to some problems with Allen's principles, leaving aside questions about the acceptability of the meritarian basic principle.

Suppose we construe Allen's principles *(2.)* and *(3.)* as an attempt to extend, still within a basic framework, the general meritarian principle to welfare contexts. We might think we needed principles for welfare, even within a meritarian social order, because we still must make allowances to meet the needs of those people who are legitimately *excused* from being held accountable to meritarian reward considerations: The excusing conditions would reflect special problems they face. But if the population to whom Allen's equity principles are to apply is that part of the population which it makes no sense to hold responsible for their inability to meet their needs, then it is hard to see why it is so important not to reverse income rank orderings in order to guarantee them adequate benefit levels. Perhaps for those who fare badly because they merit little, principles *(2.)* and *(3.)* might be thought appropriate. But for those who are excused from merit considerations, and for whom we have some concern that their needs be met, adhering to these principles seems a misplaced scrupulosity, if not an outright inconsistency. Once we remember that in our society the great majority of those on welfare are not able-bodied adults capable of working, this objection to Allen's principles looms more important.

Let us shift to a less basic framework, one that holds many features of basic social and economic institutions in the United States relatively fixed.

We might first ask, in seeking principles for this less basic framework, whether the United States's system is in general compliance with meritarian general principles. Do we live in a system in which, on the whole, pre-tax, pre-benefit income rank order and income distances comply with some basic meritarian principles? Answering this question would involve us in considerable social theory. We would need to see if conformance to such a meritarian principle gives us the best explanatory account of why we have the income ordering and distances we have. My own best guess is that we do not live in anything like such an order, but I cannot argue for the conclusion here. For the sake of argument, assume that I am right. Someone might still argue for Allen's principles in this non-basic framework by urging that we seek principles that *would* best fit were compliance to obtain (ignoring my previous argument). But this is to urge that we hold to meritarian restrictions on need satisfaction for welfare recipients even though we admit we fail to comply with such restrictions elsewhere in the system. Unless it could be shown that so applying these welfare principles really moves us directly closer to overall compliance— rather than toward a heartless exception to non-compliance—or unless it could be shown that these principles are indirectly important because they provide us with a model of the moral ideal we can learn from—rather than a model of moral hypocrisy—then the case for the priority of principles *(2)* and *(3)* falls well short of being convincing.

Before turning to the matter of work incentives, it might be worth summarizing what I have been arguing, at least to clarify the structure and scope of my remarks. I have construed Allen's principles of vertical equity as implying that it is unfair to interfere with income order in the name of adequacy of benefit levels. I have sought to sketch a general moral view, actually a principle, which might be thought to lend weight to Allen's principles, if any view does. But the meritarian view does not so directly support Allen's principles as might be thought, neither within basic nor non-basic frameworks. Since I also argued that Allen's principles do not capture our actual views of vertical equity, and since I have undercut what I take to be the most plausible way of trying to justify them, the burden of proof seems to shift onto those who, on grounds of fairness, would give low priority to adequacy considerations.

Work Incentives and Adequacy

Some of the most vigorous discussion of conflicting objectives focuses on the relationship between work incentives and adequacy of benefit levels.[20] I have already noted Allen's attempt to incorporate a worry about work incentives into the concept of vertical equity, through her principles *(2.)* and *(3.)*. But I want here to consider some of the issues surrounding work incentives in a broader context than that provided by Allen's strong claims about income ordering. In practice, giving priority to work incentives over adequacy takes the form of imposing a de facto ceiling on basic benefit levels, namely, a percentage of the income levels of very low-wage full-time workers. Not all income rank ordering is thus preserved, à la Allen, but one crucial ceiling does operate. If there are problems with such a ceiling, there will be even greater problems with Allen's proposal.

I would like to consider two sets of issues which are involved in granting priority to work incentives. The first concerns the social bases for willingness to work and the view that people have a responsibility to work. Clearly if work requirements and incentives are to be an important feature of welfare transfer systems, we must have a good understanding of what makes people want to work and the conditions under which they may be held responsible for failure to work. As we shall see, the attribution of responsibility to work requires a stance be taken on some basic questions of distributive justice. Second, if the form that the priority of work incentives takes is using the income levels of one group as a ceiling on the benefits granted others, then much will depend on the justice of the distribution that leads to the income level at the ceiling. To see these issues more clearly, I shall discuss both of them, in turn, in basic and non-basic frameworks.

Suppose we ask our priorities question in the context of a basic framework. That is, we can view basic social institutions as revisable, and our task is to select principles of justice to govern them. We can assume that some of the social support we view as welfare transfers would be necessary in a just social order. So our priorities question asks the relative importance of maintaining work incentives and adequate benefit levels, but in a context which allows fundamental alteration of many institutions.

In such a basic framework, we must ask some basic questions about work incentives. What factors affect the willingness to work? What is the importance of intrinsic rewards in work? How should we use a structure of extrinsic rewards to attract people into different kinds of work? What is the importance of control over the conditions and product of one's work? These are hard questions. Moreover, they interact. In conditions of fair equality of opportunity, one might expect extrinsic rewards would play a more important role in attracting people to burdensome jobs with few intrinsic rewards than to jobs with high levels of intrinsic reward. So the structure of opportunities open to people interacts significantly with what we usually take to be "incentives." My guess is that in social orders with fair equality of opportunity, extrinsic rewards would play a much diminished role from what they play in our society. But of course this is speculation. The important point is that in a basic framework, we are open to considering the many factors which affect willingness to work, and the role played by extrinsic incentives, such as those involved in welfare proposals, might be quite different.

These general considerations have implications for whom we hold responsible for the failure to work and how we hold them responsible. If a just arrangement of opportunities and general work incentives exists, then an individual's failure—or refusal—to work can be assessed in one way. But if an unjust arrangement of opportunities and incentives is itself part of the explanation for an individual's failure or refusal to work, then responsibility should be assessed in a different way. Consider the moral hazard that might be encouraged by providing high, adequate benefit levels to those in need of welfare assistance. Whom we hold responsible—and how we penalize them—for not working and opting instead for welfare depends on what other assumptions we are free to make about the actual work opportunities the people face and the more general institutional bases for work incentives in the society as a whole. Under some conditions, it might be proper to make adequate satisfaction of needs contingent on willingness to work—against a background of just institutions, we might come down quite hard on free-loaders. But under other conditions, what we view as "incentives" may function more like coercions, and we may be making the worst-off members of a society pay twice for their circumstances. The point I am making cuts across the fact that different general moral theories might disagree on what constitutes a just set of background conditions. All such theories must adjust their notions of responsibility and blameworthiness for failure to work in the light of what is known about the diverse conditions that contribute to willingness to work.

The second issue, the effect on adequacy of maintaining work incentives through a de facto ceiling, is also illuminated by the perspective of a basic framework. Some general theories of justice impose more serious constraints on inequalities than others. Indeed, some theories, e.g., certain versions of libertarianism, impose no such egalitarian constraints at all. Maintaining work incentives by imposing a ceiling on benefits set by the income of relatively low-paid workers will have different effects depending on what constraints the theory of justice imposes on how poor those low-paid workers can legitimately be. On more egalitarian theories, one might retain work incentives by keeping benefits below a ceiling, but that might not mean benefit levels were inadequate. Welfare recipients would be protected by the constraints on the well-being of the workers whose income forms the ceiling. On less egalitarian theories, adequacy may not be protected since the ceiling might already be low. Within a basic framework, one's task is to select principles of justice, and thus to debate the merits of one such distribution versus others.

Let us now shift frameworks to a non-basic one, taking as relatively fixed many central features of the U.S. social and economic system. In this framework, the issue of work incentives assumes a rather stark form. The relatively low wages of the poorest sectors of the working class act as a de facto ceiling on the adequacy of benefit levels. The rationale is that, if basic benefit packages are low relative to the income of full-time workers on low wage scales, then it is less likely that able-bodied workers will opt for welfare over work.[21] Our priorities question in this framework thus takes the form: "Should income levels of the low end of the working population be used as a ceiling on benefit levels in welfare transfers?"

I want to look at the issue of responsibility to work and the justification of ceilings again, in this less basic framework, but first, it is worth noting something about the form taken by arguments for the priority of work incentives. Specifically, arguments for work incentives need not be based on utilitarian considerations, as it is often thought. Consider two forms of argument often heard. The first takes as its premise the assumption that the overall welfare budget is relatively fixed. It infers that the main effect of work disincentives is to slice the welfare pie into smaller pieces, threatening the adequacy levels of those really in need. This argument could be raised on utilitarian grounds or on non-utilitarian grounds. So, too, there could be different grounds for raising another common argument. This one assumes the welfare budget is somewhat more elastic. The main effect of work disincentives would then be to increase the tax burden imposed on others. The bad effect might be the resulting economic disincentive for the employed, or the unfairness of the increased burden. Moreover, not only can non-utilitarian arguments be used to support giving priority to work incentives, it is not clear to me a thorough utilitarianism would end up supporting them, at least in the form they take in our less basic framework. But I leave the point unargued.

Instead, let us turn to the issue of responsibility for working. What view we take of assignments of responsibility to individuals who fail to work—or refuse to take available work—will depend on estimates of the context of compliance surrounding our less basic framework. Suppose someone—I include myself here—finds the existing structures of opportunity and incentives in the United States to fall far short of what would provide a reasonable foundation for promoting willingness to work. Then the assignment of responsibility—even blameworthiness—to those who fail to work seems highly problematic. It is certainly problematic when jobs are scarce or unavailable, and it remains problematic when available jobs are hard, burdensome, unrewarding, and often dead-end. In such a setting, justifying ceilings on adequacy levels on the grounds that people ought to be held responsible to work is an unsupportable move. If, however, one finds the U.S. system to be in compliance with a preferred theory of justice, but one that requires no such program of opportunities and incentives as I think necessary, then one might think the granting of priority to work incentives justifiable. To resolve the dispute, of course, would require debating the fundamental questions between these theories.

We must again estimate the context of compliance in order to take up the issue of constraints on adequacy levels imposed by wage ceilings. Do the inequalities in income levels in the United States, including the levels of the worst-off employed workers, constitute a just array of inequalities? Are the income levels of workers who constitute the de facto ceiling on benefit levels in compliance with basic principles of just distribution?

No doubt some would argue that the basic social and economic institutions in the United States are just. They might, for example, support a general theory which provided no constraints on inequalities other than those that result from the market and the U.S. tax structure. Assuming proponents of these theories would also judge the structure of opportunities and incentives underlying willingness to work to be just, they would comfortably ascribe responsibility and blame for certain failures to work. Against the background of such a judgment of compliance, it might then be argued that work incentives be given priority through de facto ceilings. Of course, even this judgment must be qualified by assuming certain empirical conditions obtain. Among them would be *(a)* the availability of jobs for those to whom the incentives are to appeal, *(b)* the effectiveness of such incentives as a motivation for work (which partly depends on the kind of work available); and *(c)* the possibility of aiming incentives at the right population without penalizing unduly children or other dependents. It is an important and interesting feature of our moral situation that there is considerable disagreement about whether such empirical conditions obtain, even aside from basic judgments about the justice of the system as a whole.

Others, however, are hard pressed to provide justification rooted in general moral theory for the kinds of inequalities in income, wealth, power, opportunity, and ability to exercise liberty that we find in the United States. I find myself among them. In particular, many feel it is not just those eligible for welfare who suffer injustice in this system, but also large segments of the employed working class who live under burdens of inadequate income, opportunity, power, and liberty. Against the background of this judgment of non-compliance with acceptable principles of justice, holding adequacy levels under the ceiling of already inadequate income levels seems to be compounding injustice with injustice. The worst-off suffer doubly—both for their predicament and the predicament of others.

Once this judgment about non-compliance is made, the temptation is to answer the priorities question from a somewhat different perspective. One route is to urge expanding the welfare transfer system into a more broadly redistributive system. Adequacy might then be achieved without risking work disincentives by providing a transfer of benefits to a broader segment of the working class. This solution involves an implicit shifting of the framework to a somewhat more basic one. It is also recognizable as the strategy pushed by those who seek to use the tax transfer system in a more broadly redistributive way.

Another route, one that stays within the less basic framework, is to urge provision of adequate benefit levels, even if doing so means risking significant work disincentives. The justification for this solution might be that we do not in this way penalize those in need of welfare for the presence of still other injustices in the system. Moreover, the affirmation of a principle of distribution based on need might be thought to have long-term positive effects on moral education and the likelihood of political change. It might be worth noting that even those who view the welfare system as primarily cooptive, for example, as a dampening influence on class struggle, might nevertheless be concerned to secure adequate benefit levels for reasons such as those sighted.

What emerges, then, is a special case of a general possibility noted earlier. In a context of *non-compliance* with a moral theory that places great weight on work incentives and responsibility to work, we may be led to deemphasize work incentives in favor of other concerns. And we may be led to do so by considerations from within the very theory in question.

My discussion has not touched on many of the other conflicts in objectives the welfare literature has raised. Thus I have said nothing about some of the kinds of the horizontal and vertical equity considerations that conflict with efforts both to downplay and to emphasize work incentives. My general inclination is to think some of these inequities tolerable if they are part of a reasonable program to eliminate more fundamental injustices in the system. Perhaps this outlook is compatible with Conrad Johnson's suggestion, already noted, that we view some of these inequities as "interstitial" and assess their importance by standards we elsewhere use in the context of "equal protection theory." Moreover, I have said nothing about related issues, like the "notch" problem, primarily because I think these problems can be reduced in significance through a more unified and "rationalized" welfare system.[22] In these ways my discussion is incomplete.

I have, however, concentrated on what I take to be a central source of difficulty with the debate about priorities. The discussion is often divorced from more general and fundamental inquiries into the justice of the system within which the welfare structures exist. And, there is too much inclination to treat the question as one that arises within a framework that allows little to be altered but welfare policy itself. Adopting such a stance is *itself* a moral decision. Within such a truncated view of the problem, there may be little philosophy has to offer. If philosophy is to play an illuminating role in public policy debate, it cannot be restricted to the casuistic task of rationalizing a least worst alternative.

Notes

1. I thank Hugo Adam Bedau, Peter G. Brown, Josh Cohen, Conrad Johnson, and Paul Vernier for helpful discussion of some of the ideas in this paper. Research for this paper was partly funded through National Center for Health Services Research Grant No. R01 HS 03097–01 and through a Tufts Sabbatical Leave, 1978–79.

2. Cf. Michael C. Barth, George J. Cargano, and John L. Palmer, *Toward an Effective Income Support System: Problems, Prospects and Choices*, Institute for Research on Poverty, University of Wisconsin-Madison, 1974, pp. 39–42; see also HEW, "The Income Security System: Purposes, Criteria and Choices," 1977, pp. 3–8.

3. The worry about maxim (5) and its relation to fairness is expressed in Jodie T. Allen, "The Concept of Vertical Equity and Its Application to Social Program Design," Chapter 5, this volume.

4. Actually, the translation of the priorities problem from "objectives" to "principles" only has the appearance of simplifying it. To order these principles, we must turn to general moral theory. But we might just as well try to order our concerns for different "objectives" we have in cooperative social systems by appeal to general moral and political theory, e.g., the theory of justice. So it is less the form and more just the language of the priorities problem that is unfamiliar to the philosopher.

5. The issue is even clearer for an "ideal moral code" type of utilitarianism, e.g., of the sort Brandt develops in *A Theory of the Good and the Right* (New York: Oxford, 1979).

6. The label is used this way in John Rawls, *A Theory of Justice* (Cambridge, Mass.: Harvard University Press, 1971).

7. Of course, that is not all that can be said about their justificatory status. See, e.g., my "Wide Reflective Equilibrium and Theory Acceptance in Ethics," *Journal of Philosophy* LXXVI, No. 5 (May 1979): 256–282; also my "Reflective Equilibrium and Archimedean Points," *Canadian Journal of Philosophy* X, No. 1 (March 1980): 83–103.

8. For discussion of what institutions are here viewed as fundamental, see John Rawls, "The Basic Structure as Subject," *American Philosophical Quarterly* 14, no. 2 (April 1977): 159–165; see also, Hugo Adam Bedau, "Social Justice and Social Institutions," *Midwest Studies in Philosophy* III (1978): 159–175.

9. Cf. Rawls's Second Principle: "Social and economic inequalities are to be arranged so that they are both: (a) to the greatest benefit of the least advantaged consistent with the just savings principle, and (b) attached to offices and positions open to all under conditions of fair equality of opportunity. *A Theory of Justice*, p. 30.

10. Interesting questions arise, incidentally, about the applicability of Rawls's theory to welfare and health issues. Cf. Frank Michelman, "Constitutional Welfare Rights and *A Theory of Justice*" in Norman Daniels, ed., *Reading Rawls* (New York: Basic Books, 1976), pp. 319–347. For a discussion of the applicability of the theory to related issues about need satisfaction in the health care domain, see my "Rights to Health Care: Programmatic Worries," *Journal of Medicine and Philosophy* 4, no. 2 (June 1979): 174–191; and "Health Care Needs and Distributive Justice" (unpublished).

11. Conrad Johnson, "Equity: Its Scope and Its Relation to Other Objectives," Chapter 7, this volume.

12. Rawls, *A Theory of Justice*, Section 31.

13. Cf. David Lindeman, "The Concept of Horizontal Equity and Its Application to Social Program Design," Chapter 6, this volume.

14. Here I disagree, at least for the context of welfare discussions, with Conrad Johnson's suggestion that horizontal equity is a formal notion whereas vertical equity is a material (or substantive) notion. Cf. Johnson, "Equity: Its Scope and Its Relation to Other Objectives," Chapter 7, this volume. Jodie Allen seems to agree with Johnson; see "The Concept of Vertical Equity," Chapter 5, this volume.

15. Allen, "The Concept of Vertical Equity," Chapter 5, this volume.

16. We must be careful in inferring what "principle" lies behind this resentment. Much of it is based on misperception of welfare benefit levels by those not on them—often fed by

racist and anti-poor portrayals in the media and by demagogic pointing to scapegoats by politicians.

17. See Chapter 5, this volume.

18. Allen, "Concept of Vertical Equity," Chapter 5, this volume.

19. Here I use the notions interchangeably, but see my "Merit and Meritocracy," *Philosophy and Public Affairs* 7, no. 3 (Spring 1978): 206–223, for caution on this looseness and for discussion of related issues about the role of merit considerations in distributive justice.

20. Cf. Barth, et al., *Toward an Effective Income Support System*, Ch. 3 and 4; also, Henry J. Aaron, *Why is Welfare So Hard to Reform?* (Washington, D.C.: Brookings Institute, 1973), ch. 4, 5.

21. There is some empirical evidence to support the view that the size of the basic benefit package is the main determinant of work disincentives. Some of the same evidence indicates, however, relatively minor disincentive effects in general, especially for able-bodied heads of households. More sizeable effects show up for part-time "supplementary" work. Cf. Leonard Goodwin, *Do the Poor Want to Work?* (Washington, D.C.: Brookings Institute, 1972.) Also see the chapters in Henry Aaron and Barth, et al. noted in note 20.

22. E.g., some of the force of Henry Aaron's proposals is in this direction. Cf. *Why is Welfare So Hard to Reform?*, ch. 6.

9

Favorable Family Impact as an Objective of Income Support Policy

MARTHA H. PHILLIPS

The United States has never articulated an explicit family policy despite its intense preoccupation with symptoms of stress in the institution of family life. Public policies nevertheless have innumerable implicit impacts on families, influencing decisions to marry or separate, to have children, or not, to expand or contract household membership, and to provide materially and emotionally for family members.

Because family life is a nearly universal experience, policymakers and their constitutents frequently believe "they know a good one when they see it." Consequently, policy has frequently been based more on blind instinct, common sense, and good intentions than on hard data and clear objectives in many family-related areas. Unfortunately, recognizing a "good family" and prescribing a rational, consistent, and explicit family policy, even within the context of a single income transfer program such as the one providing Aid to Families with Dependent Children (AFDC) are two vastly different propositions.

Family impact analysis is particularly pertinent to the AFDC program. Participation in this program is precipitated primarily by changes in family status, and AFDC eligibility requirements and benefit schedules often appear to influence the decisions recipients make about family structure and functions. AFDC is a principal program in the nation's public welfare system, and as such is the focal point of efforts to reform the welfare apparatus through either comprehensive or incremental steps.

In the following pages, the concept of family impact analysis will be explored in terms of the forty-year history of the AFDC program and through six specific family policy concerns frequently considered in conjunction with the existing program and with welfare reform initiatives: preventing family breakup, encouraging single parents to marry, discouraging illegitimate births, discouraging child-bearing by women who receive AFDC, encouraging fathers to pay child support, and requiring mothers to work. Each of these six policy concerns will be viewed from three perspectives. The empirical evidence will be reviewed regarding the extent to which incentives predispose recipient behavior in expected or unexpected directions under the AFDC program and, where relevant, under the recent income maintenance experiments. The desirability of using AFDC or other income maintenance schemes to change recipients' behavior with regard to each policy concern will be explored. The feasibility of achieving specific goals pertaining to each policy concern will be evaluated in terms of both probable political acceptance and likelihood of effectiveness in achieving desired results.

The conclusion drawn from this review of family policy concerns is that trying to get low-income people to conform to conventional family structures or financial support patterns ought not to be an explicit *objective* of income support programs. Family policy concerns are far more appropriately viewed as a *constraint* on existing or proposed income support programs. An income support program should be evaluated primarily on its fairness, equity, and adequacy. Only when unexpectedly large negative impacts on family structure or functioning occur should family impact concerns dictate the design of income support policies.

Family Impact

Family impact analysis as a technique is still in its infancy. Analysts are wrestling with such basic issues as "What is a family?" and "What is an impact?" Although measuring the impact of public policies on families can involve countless layers and angles of examination, it may be useful to divide family characteristics into at least four areas of particular public policy significance:

1. Structural elements: decisions regarding marital status (marriage, divorce, separation, desertion, cohabitation), children (having one's own, adoption, or foster care of someone else's children, abortion, sending one's children elsewhere), household composition (nuclear family, extended family, or "augmented" families which include nonrelatives), and reliance on and contact with kin living outside the household.

2. Economic functions: providing for basic material needs of family members.

3. Nurturing, health, and socializing functions: encouraging and supporting children's physical, intellectual, and emotional growth and development and providing all family members with psychological suste-

nance, opportunities for expressions of intimacy, and socialization into the wider community.

4. Coordinating and mediating functions: orchestrating and scheduling family activities, linking family members with services and benefits and programs in the "outside world."[1]

The impact of government programs on these family characteristics eludes easy definition. To the extent that programs make decisions more or less costly, or change non-financial incentives to promote certain behaviors regarding family status or functions, they can be deemed to have a family impact.[2] Relative family impact can be measured against several standards: behavior under proposed changes may be compared with behavior under the existing program, behavior under the existing program may be compared to behavior in the absence of any program, or behavior under proposed changes may be compared with behavior in the absence of any program. A program has an impact if it makes participants or potential participants *more or less* favorably disposed to act in certain ways or if it *increases or reduces* costs of various behavior; the concept of impact does not require eliminating *all* costs or incentives associated with specific decisions. Most behavior, however, is the more or less rational result of *many* incentives, motivations, perceptions, and pressures, acting in combination. Of course not all of the pressures or incentives affecting families are related to the program being examined, and non-program motivations frequently prevail. Often, incentives go unheeded because program recipients have scant knowledge of the options available to them. Thus, changing what appears to be the dominant program element having an undesirable impact may not result in any or very much change in behavior of program participants.

Even defining what constitutes a favorable or unfavorable family impact is confused by the fact that a particular policy or contemplated change may have uneven effects on various functional and structural aspects of family life. A few examples may make this clear. As will be discussed in succeeding pages, increasing families' ability to meet their economic support functions by increasing AFDC benefits may also greatly increase the rate of marital dissolution, an outcome which, all else being equal, is probably harmful to children. A strict AFDC work requirement may conflict with the ability of a welfare mother to fulfill the nurturing and coordinating roles although it may in the long run enhance her family's economic support capability.

Ideally, government programs should facilitate maintenance of stable, well-functioning family structures. In reality, it is more frequently the case that a program addresses just one of the functional or structural areas relating to family life, and changes in the affected area then trigger responses in the family's handling of other roles or structural arrangements. Unpleasant as it sometimes is even to contemplate the trade-offs, the mere existence of government programs affecting any aspect of family life means that value decisions have been made—either implicitly or explicitly. This would be true even in a fiscally unfettered welfare reform climate. The imposition of stern budgetary constraints on federal welfare policy make consideration of family impacts all the more necessary.

In such an examination of the different potential impacts of the AFDC program, it is helpful to remember that its primary function and first priority is to provide an economic safety net under eligible individuals and families, sufficient to enable them to meet basic human needs—food, clothing, and shelter. It is to be hoped that this economic function can be fulfilled in such a way as to minimize accompanying family impacts that are generally viewed as "negative," while building on those deemed to be "positive." But this may not always be the case, as in the example of the relationship between AFDC benefits and marital dissolution. Such trade-offs, however, seldom have to be made on an either-or basis, and it will usually be possible to structure income maintenance in such a way as to encourage generally favorable outcomes for the majority of affected families.[3]

The AFDC program has a number of elements that can be adjusted to achieve various family impacts: the level of welfare benefits in relation to the recipient's other income alternatives and the prevailing economic climate, the likelihood that individuals meeting various criteria will receive benefits, the rate at which taxes and benefit reductions offset earned income, eligibility rules (e.g., that the recipient must maintain a home for a dependent child), and definitions of assets and income. A number of family inpacts have been hypothesized regarding these elements in the current AFDC program:

1. The availability of AFDC to single but not to married mothers favors a decision to bear an illegitimate child rather than marry the child's father, particularly if he has doubtful breadwinning prospects.

2. Remarriage by an AFDC mother is discouraged, particularly if she is already receiving unreported assistance from the man, in addition to AFDC. But marriage between an unrelated man and woman already living together is encouraged to the extent that they are not required to forfeit AFDC benefits for the woman's child.

3. A decision by an unwed mother to move away from her parents' home and establish her own household is encouraged by the higher benefits she receives as the head of her own household than as her parents' dependent and by the extent to which these benefits offset the cost of achieving privacy.

4. A regular pattern of child support by absent fathers is discouraged by reducing AFDC benefits to the children by the amount of paternal payments, thereby eliminating any net positive benefit to the child.

5. Work registration requirements for adults when their children reach school age may be an incentive to bear or informally adopt another dependent child in order to maintain eligibility.

6. The program strongly encourages the birth of the first child, the presence of whom is required for AFDC eligibility.

7. The addition of subsequent children to the family is somewhat encouraged since benefits for these children reduce the cost of their upbringing, even though such costs are not entirely eliminated.

8. Smaller living units or living alone is encouraged rather than large family or non-relative groups to the extent that the differential between the costs of maintaining single and multi-person households is narrowed.

9. Resource-sharing among related or unrelated individuals would, if reported, reduce benefits and is therefore discouraged.

10. Including non-poor individuals in the living unit is discouraged since their income and assets would reduce benefits or entirely eliminate eligibility for members of the unit.

11. Extended family arrangements for the support of children are recognized to several degrees of kin relationship and encourage informal adoption of children by relatives.

12. The availability of benefits at adequate levels encourages husbandless mothers to keep their children with them and stay home to care for them while they are young.

Growth of Federal Welfare Benefits for Families

This long list of often anti-marriage and pro-natal incentives is the result of four decades of incremental decisions shaping the AFDC program. The federal welfare program began in 1936 as a public assistance model based on the exchange of involuntary helplessness for public support.[4] Subsequently, attempts were made to impose prevailing moral standards and norms on AFDC recipients and to curb the phenomenal increase in numbers of dependents.

The program originated almost as an afterthought to the controversial old-age assistance legislation. Its aim was to help economically distressed widows with young children keep their families together during the tough Depression days when destitute women had few alternatives and when fewer than half managed to keep their children with them.[5] It was obvious that any federal funds provided them, however meager, would have a beneficial impact. It was equally clear that their husbands' deaths, which caused their plight, were beyond their control and not of their choosing.

In these early years, 1936 through the end of World War II, the Aid to Dependent Children (ADC) program enjoyed warm political support. Congress even increased federal matching in 1939 to encourage greater state participation. Benefits were paid on behalf of dependent children, but not for their mothers or other caretakers, and children at first almost always entered the rolls because of their fathers' deaths. In 1943, however, for the first time more children were entitled to ADC because of their fathers' absence than because of their fathers' death.

By 1950, absence of the father as a cause of ADC dependency was so prevalent that the possibility of negative family impact first showed up on the legislative record. The Director of the Bureau of Public Assistance testified before the Senate Finance Committee that

requiring that a parent be absent from the home before his children can receive assistance places a kind of financial premium on a broken home and exerts an influence exactly opposed to the purpose of the whole aid-to-dependent-children program; namely to keep families together.[6]

In 1956, Senator John Kennedy unsuccessfully offered an amendment to include needy children of the unemployed, even though the father remained at home, arguing that

when the father becomes unemployed, the family cannot receive aid to dependent children unless the father deserts. The federal law thus puts a premium on desertion. I believe this is immoral and unsound.[7]

Five years later, as President, Kennedy repeated these arguments partly in response to extreme and prolonged poverty in Appalachia. HEW Secretary Ribicoff testified before the Ways and Means Committee that

there is no reason why a hungry child of an unemployed father should not be fed as well as a child in other unfortunate circumstances. . . . What we are trying to do with ADC is keep families together. Certainly we should not, as a society, so conduct our programs as to discourage a family grouping or to encourage a parent to leave the home in order for his children to receive aid in their basic needs.[8]

These arguments prevailed at last, and the program of aid to dependent children of two-parent families with unemployed fathers began in May 1961, available at state option. In 1962, the title of the program was changed to Aid to Families with Dependent Children (AFDC), and the Unemployed Fathers (UF) program was extended to 1967.

By 1967, the Unemployed Fathers (UF) program was drawn tightly enough to negate its pro-family aspects. Eligibility for unemployment compensation, even in inadequate amounts, precluded UF assistance. The requirement of recent and substantial workforce participation often excluded young fathers and the hard-core unemployed, and was presumably an attempt to separate the deserving from the underserving. UF programs were established primarily in industrial states which had already assisted this population. Attempts in 1967 to make UF mandatory for all states failed, despite arguments that the lack of the program encouraged family breakup. Today, although some thirty states participate, more than three-quarters of UF families live in just seven states. Job search, training, and registration requirements have kept rolls under 200,000 families nationwide even in times of high unemployment.

The concern over family-splitting incentives that led to the establishment of the UF program also contributed to the creation of the social services adjunct to welfare benefits in 1956. These services, designed to avoid and reduce welfare dependency, were intended to help meet the official ADC goals of maintaining and strengthening family life and helping parents and relatives of needy children attain maximum self-support and personal independence consistent with the maintenance of continuing parental care and protection.

Accompanying the concern about family stability evidenced in the UF and social services programs was a crosscurrent of requirements and practices intended to force AFDC families into conformance with prevailing moral standards and norms. In 1950, a legal requirement was added to the Social Security Act that law enforcement officials be notified of desertions so that attempts could be made to locate the father and obtain child support.

Administratively, the "man in the house" rule was used by nineteen states and the District of Columbia to enforce moral standards on AFDC recipients—and, not incidentally, to limit caseloads—before it was outlawed by the Supreme Court in 1968. The existence of a "substitute father," whether or not he actually contributed to the support of the children of the woman with whom he cohabited, was sufficient to deny AFDC to the woman and her children. Midnight raids to search for such substitute fathers further discouraged AFDC growth.

States attempted to deny aid to the families of illegitimate children. Louisiana stopped benefits for some 20,000 families whose homes were "unsuitable" because the dependent children had been born out of wedlock. The federal response in 1961 was to deny federal matching grants to states not assisting "unsuitable" homes unless other provisions were made to care for the children from these homes. To assist the states in making such provisions, federal payments were authorized for children placed in foster homes pursuant to court determination that the child's natural home environment was contrary to his or her best interests.

By 1967, surging AFDC enrollment and the transformation of the clientele had sharply altered the political climate surrounding the program from one of compassionate beneficence to one of indignant parsimony. The program had metamorphosed into an income transfer program benefitting primarily families deserted by their men and, in rising numbers, families where no husband had ever been present. The legislation enacted that year reflects these altered perceptions. States were required to furnish family planning services to adult welfare recipients and to establish procedures for determining the paternity of AFDC children, locating absent fathers, and collecting child support payments. A "freeze" was placed on the proportion of federal funding for children receiving benefits because of a parent's absence from the home, and although the freeze soon thawed, its enactment indicated increased concern over AFDC subsidization of growing rates of actual or apparent desertion. Work requirements for mothers were enacted as a further attempt to reduce dependency. Under the Work Incentive (WIN) program all recipients were required to register for jobs or training unless they were legally exempt for various reasons, one of which was being needed in the home by children under the age of six.

The juxtaposition of solicitude for family stability with steps to compel moral rectitude on the part of AFDC recipients continues today. In 1975, for example, Congress wrote a "runaway fathers" law to establish paternity and secure child support payments. In 1977, President Carter made "incentives . . . to keep families together" one of his goals for welfare reform.

Family policy concerns continue to generate debate over how AFDC and welfare reform incentives ought to be structured. Six of these concerns will be discussed in the following pages as they relate to family structure, and the economic, nurturing, and coordinating functions of families. Four of these concerns are primarily structural: keeping family units (husbands and wives) from splitting up, repairing "broken" families, discouraging poor people from having children out of wedlock, and discouraging poor people from having more children than they can support. The remaining two concerns are economic: encouraging fathers to assume support of their children and encouraging poor mothers to work and contribute to the support of their families.

Although the marriage, child-bearing, and work issues are the central family policy concerns of the AFDC program, they are not the only ones. Whether or not childless couples—who by many people's definition constitute families—or single childless individuals should be entitled to benefits if they are in circumstances comparable to those that entitle families with children to benefits is of special concern because of its equity and cost implications. How to treat households that take in nondependent relatives, how to treat two or more families living in a single household, and the age at which dependent children in welfare families should be considered self-sufficient are other such issues which raise perplexing questions of equity and family impact. These issues, however, are peripheral to the six major concerns discussed in the following pages.

PREVENTING FAMILY BREAKUP

The availability of AFDC benefits to one-parent families but seldom to two-parent families has long been presumed to encourage fathers to leave home in order to qualify their families for benefits. The empirical evidence (after discounting "statistical desertion") indicates only a slight causal relationship between the level of AFDC benefits available to women and rates of marital dissolution, but a significantly stronger relationship between the level of benefits available to two-parent families and their marital stability.

At least some AFDC-precipitated desertion is a statistical rather than real phenomenon. This "statistical desertion" occurs when the father claims to have left home but remains in the immediate vicinity, continues to act as a father to his children, and provides whatever financial support he can.[9] The family gets both AFDC and the father's support, making them better off than it would be under either AFDC or the husband's wages alone. For these families, the financial incentives even under a welfare program supporting two-parent families will still favor "statistical desertion" unless benefits for two-parent families exceed those for single-parent families to such an extent that they surpass amounts needed to insure that, allowing for economies of scale, relative equity based on need is preserved.

Permanent marital dissolution (as contrasted with "statistical desertion") has been assumed to be related to the impact of low incomes on increasing marital dissatisfaction through unfulfilled male breadwinner role expectations and the frustrations of trying to meet family needs with inadequate resources. It could therefore be expected that increasing the income available to two-parent, low-income families would reduce their rate of family breakup. This could be accomplished through increasing male wages, female wages, or welfare benefits. However, tending in an opposite direction to this "income effect" is the so-called "female independence effect," which occurs when wives, through their own earnings, welfare benefits, or other sources, have income alternatives to continued dependence on their husbands. To what extent the "independence effect" causes marital dissatisfaction which culminates in marital breakup or merely facilitates the termination of what has already become an unsatisfactory situation is not clear and must await further study. A better understanding of this effect is crucial to a responsible assessment of welfare program family impacts.

A number of studies in recent years examined the impact on marital status of earned income and benefits under the existing AFDC program.[10] There was some evidence that higher AFDC benefits, especially in relation to male earnings, were accompanied by a slightly higher rate of female-headed families, particularly for blacks. But these studies taken together led to the conclusion that the effects of AFDC on family dissolution are small and that allowing intact families to receive benefits "probably cannot be viewed as a major policy lever on family organization."[11]

Against this empirical background predicting neutral or slightly positive effects on family stability from an income transfer program providing benefits regardless of marital status, the initial findings of the federal income maintenance experiments were unexpected. When these experiments provided benefits to two-parent families with employed fathers, marital dissolution rates were substantially greater in the experimental group than in the control group not receiving benefits. In New Jersey, Seattle, and Denver, the families on the least generous support plans experienced the largest increases in marital breakup, doubling their dissolution rate, while those on high support levels maintained their previous dissolution rates or experienced slight reductions.[12]

Several factors other than the structure of benefit amounts and eligibility requirements have been suggested to explain the results of the income maintenance experiments on marital stability. Recipients probably had far better information than "ordinary" low-income individuals about the operation of the program and available options. This program did not carry the same stigma as a welfare program. Participants' knowledge that the experiment was only a few years' duration may have forced "now or never" decisions to dissolve unsatisfactory marriages.[13] It is also hypothesized that dissolution rates may have peaked in the early stages of the experiment and that under a permanent program dissolution rates would be lower.[14] But to the extent that these factors do not discount the results of the income maintenance experiments, welfare reform along the lines of the Carter administration proposal, i.e., relatively low benefit payments and eligibility for two-parent, low-income families, would result in *more* rather than *fewer* broken marriages.

The policy options suggested by these findings are discouraging. One explanation suggested for the high dissolution rates in the experiments is that the female independence effect operated more strongly in favor of dissolution than did the income effect in maintaining marriages. This may mean that regardless of desirability of structuring a welfare system that discourages dissolution, it may not be feasible to do so simply by altering benefit levels and eligibility requirements unless benefits for two-parent families are made so much higher than those for single-parent families that the income effect would dominate the independence factor. Doing this would not only violate equity principles but would be too expensive to be considered a realistic policy option in the current stringent fiscal climate. The draconian alternative of paring down the benefits for single-parent families relative to two-parent families moves away from rather than toward the priority goal of meeting basic human needs.

The importance of husbands' wages in encouraging marital stability offers an additional policy option.[15] Bishop argues that the income maintenance experiments may have increased marital dissolution because either husbands reduced their work efforts when receiving benefits or their low wages comprised such a small portion of family income compared to benefits that their male role performance was below par in the eyes of both husband and wife. He suggests that constructing a system that provides hidden benefits through (male) workers' paychecks would enhance the male breadwinner role performance and have a positive income effect without creating a female independence effect. He outlines a private-sector wage-subsidy device for providing income maintenance to married men which, although quite complicated administratively, has some precedent in the earned income tax credit.[16] (However, the earned income credit is available regardless of the worker's sex. It increases the earning power of women as well as men and thereby enhances the independence effect.) Confining such benefits to men would doubtless prove highly controversial and unconstitutional in an era of feminism and two-worker families. Limiting the benefit to the primary wage earner, as the Carter administration proposed for guaranteed jobs, avoids some of these problems but is nonetheless controversial from the feminist perspective.

In light of these overwhelming problems in structuring an income maintenance system which does not increase marital dissolution, one must decide whether this goal is worthy of such a stupendous effort. As far as public policy is concerned, this is primarily a question of the well-being of children affected by divorce and desertion. Although divorce, desertion, and marital stress occur with greater frequency at low income levels than high, marital instability is so pervasive throughout our society that about one-third of first marriages occurring in the 1970s are expected to dissolve. Even though remarriages usually occur, it is now estimated that four out of every ten children born in the 1970s will spend a part of their childhoods in one-parent families, usually with their mothers.[17] When the better-off segments of our society so frequently fail to achieve marital bliss, it may seem ill advised to place too high a priority on regularizing marital patterns among people eligible for welfare. Since it is difficult to specify the alternatives to divorce—which occasionally mean reconciliation and a happy household but often involve stress, anger, physical abuse, and an atmosphere destructive to children's well-being and nurturing—even a successful pro-marriage policy may not always achieve the desired favorable results.

The strongest evidence in favor of a pro-marriage policy is that two-parent families generally have higher incomes available for rearing their children than do one-parent families. The burdens of children from the lowest economic groups have been repeatedly chronicled—lower cognitive development, poor health and emotional and social damage.[18] However, these economic effects on children's well-being could be, at least in theory, largely remedied through income transfers, regardless of their parents' marital status. Therefore, on both counts—feasibility and desirability—the goal of achieving marital stability is difficult to defend as a top-priority welfare reform goal.

REPAIRING "BROKEN" FAMILIES

Encouraging single mothers to marry or remarry is implicit in many welfare reform agendas. However, empirical evidence indicates that the structure of the AFDC program appears to have at most a tangential impact on mothers' proclivity to (re)marry. The AFDC benefit structure does not coerce women into marriage; nor, since Supreme Court decisions in 1968 and 1970, does it penalize them either for marriage or cohabitation (as long as their mate is not the natural father of their children). Several studies indicate that availability and/or receipt of AFDC tends to reduce the probability of marriage for female family heads by about 2 percent over a five-to-seven-year period. Other non-AFDC factors such as the age and attractiveness of the woman as a potential marriage partner were more important in predicting remarriage rates.[19]

Given the relatively neutral impact of AFDC on (re)marriage decisions, it was not expected that the provision of benefits to one-and two-parent families under the income maintenance experiment would have much effect either. However, in the Seattle and Denver experiments, there were distinct ethnic group responses. Chicanos delayed remarriages, responding to the independence effect. Blacks increased marriage rates, responding to the "dowry" effect created by the continuation of benefits after marriage. White women exhibited no clear effect in either direction.[20] Thus, even allowing remarried mothers to enjoy higher family incomes than "still-married" mothers was not sufficient incentive to encourage (re)marriage in all ethnic groups.

Even though the structure of the welfare program appears to have at most a tangential impact on mothers' proclivity to (re)marry, this goal has still not been discarded. Some 85 percent of children receiving AFDC currently do so because their fathers are absent from home, 2.6 percent because their fathers are deceased. (Re)marriage of their mothers would indeed reduce this public burden. Marriage to a "good provider" may be the best economic ticket for their mothers as well, given the below-poverty-level AFDC benefits available in most states and the dim prospects most welfare mothers have of getting well-paying jobs.

The desirability of (re)marriage as a welfare goal can be legitimately questioned, however. The high incidence of female-headed families, currently comprising some 14 percent of all families, means that such family types are no longer deviant or unusual. The lack of a husband may not deprive a mother's children of the support or presence of an adult male since cohabitation is not penalized and since many "absent" fathers maintain contact with their children. However, if the mother of an illegitimate child marries the child's father, she would, under current law, lose her benefits and be worse off than before, especially if the father has been supporting and seeing his family "on the quiet," as is often the case. The quality of the relationship between the stepfather and stepchildren is at least as important as the financial outcome. "Having a man in the house is not always an unmixed blessing for the children," one observer noted.[21] The mother herself must also consider the trade-offs between the increased emotional and financial benefits likely to be associated with (re)marriage and the extra demands on her time and energy for household production.

Perhaps one reason why the goal of encouraging single mothers to marry or remarry is seldom articulated is that it is highly controversial politically. It is fine to urge married couples to stay married, but a public policy of persuading unwed mothers, divorcees, and widows to find husbands to support them has a calculating edge that does not make for good political soapbox oratory. Publicly espousing this goal may, indeed, release a furor. In 1977, a leaked executive branch memo advocated that

for families in which there are small children and only one parent . . . the incentives should be arranged so that individuals prefer the two-parent arrangements. The earnings at work should be sufficiently greater than the dole on welfare to encourage . . . women who are single parents to remarry.[22]

The immediate protests by the Women's Bureau, the Women's Lobby, the National Organization of Women, the National Welfare Rights Organization, and other groups indicated that they rejected marriage as a solution to the welfare dilemma.

As has been suggested, it may be possible in theory to make welfare benefits so low that welfare mothers would have no choice but to marry. However, such a benefit level would sharply conflict with the central goal of the welfare system—providing a level of economic support sufficient to meet basic needs—particularly for those families where the mother is unable to find a mate. Thus, neither the conceptual or political feasibility nor the desirability of getting welfare mothers to marry is demonstrable.

ILLEGITIMACY

Illegitimacy is often presumed, not illogically, to be an undesirable side effect of the welfare system. In 1973, 46 percent of AFDC families had at least one child born out of wedlock. Because many unwed parents cannot earn adequate incomes, 60 percent end up receiving AFDC at some time while 80 percent of the out-of-wedlock children not legitimized or adopted receive welfare. Welfare eligibility is conditioned on having a dependent child. AFDC reduces the cost of raising children. It offers to women pregnant out of wedlock an economic alternative to marriage. Case studies and interviews of young women with illegitimate children suggest that for some girls, setting up their own households supported by welfare seems like an improvement in their lives, giving them adult independence, recognition and autonomy, and an escape from unhappy homes. This option has a degree of economic utility as well for the girl who is a poor student, has dismal employment prospects, and whose child has been fathered by a youth unable to provide economic support.

The preponderance of available empirical evidence[23] seems to suggest that these apparent incentives associated with AFDC benefits and eligibility in reality have slight impact on illegitimacy rates, while other factors such as increased education, availability of contraception and abortion, and geographic region are the significant variables. This was particularly true of studies making gross comparisons of illegitimacy rates and state AFDC levels,[24] but studies which took into account other variables similarly found that AFDC levels were less significant than other factors.[25] Even an effort to trace the chain of events and decisions which culminate in an illegitimate birth failed to find any conclusive relationships between illegitimacy and AFDC programs.[26] AFDC factors were found to have nothing to do with whether a young woman became sexually active or pregnant. As to deciding whether to continue a pregnancy, and if proceeding, whether to marry and legitimize the birth, low AFDC benefits were linked to higher probabilities of abortion, which reduced the rates of either legitimizing marriages or illegitimate births. High AFDC acceptance rates were, contrary to expectations, linked to a significantly lower proportion of out-of-wedlock births. Even the availability of UF, which would give couples a means of support if the husband were unemployed, more strongly influenced abortion rates than marriage probabilities. Despite such meager evidence linking AFDC with illegitimacy, the theoretical incentives are so strong that analysts "are unwilling to reach a final conclusion that no such effect exists, and it is tempting to believe that their reluctance is justified."[27] Many policymakers concur.

Perhaps it is the desirability of avoiding out-of-wedlock births, particularly to poor women, that explains the persistence in seeking data to demonstrate that a welfare program could be structured to reduce illegitimacy rates. Not only do children born out of wedlock have higher rates of mortality and morbidity and an extremely high probability of ending up on welfare, but their families as well are disadvantaged by generally lower incomes, greater marital instability, lower educational attainment, and a larger eventual family size. Out-of-wedlock conceptions that force early marriage are related to a high incidence of later economic problems and divorce.[28]

The percentage of out-of-wedlock births has increased primarily because the total number of births has declined, but the number of illegitimate births—nearly half a million in 1976 out of 3.1 million total births—is not trivial considering the consequences of illegitimacy. The nonwhite population has a disproportionate 60 percent of out-of-wedlock births even though nonwhite babies comprise only 19 percent of all births. In 1980, more than 50 percent of nonwhite births were out of wedlock. Studies of family life in the black community suggest that although out-of-wedlock babies are loved and welcomed, their births are not consciously planned for or desired. Kin networks from both mothers' and fathers' families help care for and support the children, and more than two-thirds of the fathers of AFDC children in one study recognize their offspring.[29] While these strengths in family life in poor, black communities help families cope with the adverse effects of illegitimacy, it is doubtful that out-of-wedlock births have any favorable consequences outweighing those of legitimacy.

Thus, although there is general agreement that finding a way to discourage illegitimate births is desirable, there is nothing to indicate that the income maintenance system, no matter how organized, will achieve this effect. In the eighteen years since Louisiana cut off welfare benefits to homes rendered "unsuitable" by illegitimate births, it has gradually come to be realized that denying or curtailing benefits for this reason would make the outlook for illegitimate children and their mothers even bleaker than it is already, penalize the children for a status over which they have no control, and, possibly, punish the mother for not choosing abortion over illegitimacy. A more acceptable alternative might be the suggestion put forth in the 1977 hearings that "incentives for marriage prior to the conception of children and the subsequent assumption by fathers of their legal and economic responsibilities to their children" should be created.[30] One such incentive advocated was the provision of job training and opportunities for younger minority males who are at the family formation stage. This notion implies that couples expecting an out-of-wedlock birth usually consider marriage seriously. A study in New York City indicated, to the contrary, that for more than three-quarters of the sample's women who were pregnant out of wedlock, the relationship was either marked by so high a degree of tension as to justify separation, or the choice was not theirs to make. However, the fact that in 55 percent of the cases, benefits exceeded the man's income means that AFDC cannot be ruled out as a possible explanation.[31] The possibility of neutralizing pro-natal incentives by allowing childless single and married people to receive benefits was proposed in Carter's 1977 plan but was quickly dropped by Congress as too expensive.

In summary, reducing illegitimacy is an objective worth striving for but one which is probably beyond the reach of the welfare system. Indeed, it will probably continue to be the function of public welfare to provide an economic safety net for many of those suffering the consequences of illegitimacy, a fact which makes punitive measures unacceptable and renders positive incentives the only route to be explored. There is little cause to expect, however, that any welfare-related incentives will affect illegitimacy rates nearly as much as other factors outside the welfare system.

DISCOURAGING CHILDBEARING

The AFDC program is frequently alleged to encourage women not only to have the first child required for benefit eligibility but to bear subsequent children in order to increase benefit amounts. Although the average AFDC family has only two children, 36 percent have three or more and 10 percent have five or more, compared with 29 percent and 5 percent respectively in the general population of families with children. Examination of the AFDC program, however, indicates that it contains both positive and negative incentives for bearing children.

The principal negative incentive for bearing children is the gap between the amount of AFDC awarded on behalf of children born to recipient families and the cost of rearing those children. As the child grows older and more expensive, this gap increases. Total benefits for families in two-thirds of the states do not reach the amounts deemed sufficient to meet basic needs. Another negative incentive to child bearing is the reduction in the mother's chances of securing the employment that would enable her to escape welfare dependency. Generally, AFDC recipients indicate that they desire smaller families than do women not receiving welfare,[32] a recognition, perhaps, of these incentives against having more children.

The AFDC program appears to offer pro-natal incentives as well. For example, the disparity between how much people think is needed "just to get along" and how much they actually receive in benefits may constitute such a pro-natal incentive. Rainwater found that by popular consensus, a family of seven was seen as needing 46 percent more income than a family of two.[33] Nixon's welfare reform plan in 1971 would have given a seven-member family 250 percent more than a two-member family. Carter's 1977 proposal would have given a seven-member family $6,000, double the $3,000 for a two-member family.[34] The current AFDC benefit structure in most states allows between 100 and 250 percent more to eight-person families than to two-person families.[35] Despite the fact that the benefit amounts never exceed and often fall well below the basic needs standard, if, as Rainwater suggests, they are perceived by recipients to offer large families amounts sufficient to enable them to get along, they would constitute a pro-natal incentive. Several studies fail to demonstrate a clear relationship between the level of welfare benefits or income in the general population and fertility. However, there seems to be a positive relationship between the degree of certainty of receiving benefits and a woman's inclination to bear additional children[36] and between the family's income relative to its peers and the number of children they decide to have,[37] particularly as regards having four or more children. After an AFDC recipient has two or three children, the negative impact of additional children on her personal freedom and employability may be outweighed by the positive values associated with having children.

The arguments in favor of discouraging AFDC recipients from bearing additional children appear to outweigh the arguments against. Women receive AFDC because the children they already have cannot otherwise be adequately supported. The difficulties and drawbacks faced by children from low-income families have been noted above. Taxpayers who might willingly assist large families in need of public assistance because of changed circumstances might justifiably balk at subsidizing the increase in the size of recipient families. This would be particularly true of taxpayers who themselves might have postponed, limited, or forgone childbearing because of inadequate financial resources. Any "right" to have children which may exist would have to have been satisfied in order for a woman to be eligible for AFDC, and her inability to support her offspring would weigh heavily against any presumed right to bear still more children.

Despite these arguments, the income maintenance system does not lend itself to changing childbearing behavior of recipients. Non-program incentives for childbearing, discussed above, far outweigh the impact of welfare eligibility, benefits, or availability. Reducing benefits per additional child to the level where they would be perceived as clearly inadequate (such as by limiting filing units to three or four persons, not allowing filing unit sizes to increase after being entered on the rolls, or allowing progressively lower benefits for each additional child) would be neither politically acceptable nor in consonance with the concept of benefit adequacy. The severe fiscal constraints on income maintenance programs preclude any notion of positive incentives such as "bonuses" for not becoming pregnant during the course of the year, and in any event, it is doubtful that such a bonus scheme would have the desired impact. Requiring even mothers with very young children to work might reduce an inclination to have additional children, but such a requirement would conflict sharply with the nurturing functions of affected families.

The most feasible options for limiting the growth in family size appear to lie outside the structure of the income transfer system. The present controversiality of government subsidization of abortions eliminates that option for the foreseeable future. Perhaps the most effective and feasible approach is the one already being pursued—family planning services, which in 1973 were received by some 11 percent of all AFDC families.

In summary, although it may be desirable to discourage recipients of income maintenance from bearing additional children, it is difficult to establish that the AFDC program either encourages or discourages such increases in family size. The options for manipulating income maintenance program variables to discourage recipients from having additional children appear to be politically unacceptable or in conflict with the underlying goals of bolstering the family's economic and nurturing functions.

PATERNAL SUPPORT

Family economic functions are at the crux of the AFDC program. One of the most frequently discussed AFDC objectives is reducing the necessity for public assistance to families headed by women by getting absent fathers to support their children. Data reviewed and analyzed by Jones, Gordon, and Sawhill indicated that during the 1960s and early 1970s only one-fourth of AFDC mothers had child support orders, and another 6 percent had informal agreements. Amounts were in the range of $7 to $9 per week per child, but even at this low level, payment performance was poor. Only 45 percent of mothers with payment orders received regular payments (though not necessarily for the full amounts) according to one national survey; in the AFDC sample only 22 percent of the fathers were in full compliance and another 33 percent were in partial compliance. Roughly 40 percent of all divorced, separated, and single women never received financial assistance from the fathers of their children, and the 60 percent getting some support included many who received irregular, partial or short term payments. In a given year, only about 3 *percent* of all eligible female-headed families received enough child support or alimony alone to put them over the poverty level.

The reasons for this abysmal child support situation involved shortcomings of the legal system, the difficulty of establishing paternity, the unwillingness of some women to have any connection with the fathers, and the fathers' job stability and health. Interestingly, fathers' records in providing payments did not seem to be much affected by their total earnings or the ratio of support payments to those earnings.[38]

In response to this situation, the federal government decided to pursue aggressively the enforcement of fathers' child support obligations. Title IV-D of the Social Security Act, the so-called "runaway fathers program," became effective in July 1975. It provides federal funds to support state efforts to establish paternity, locate fathers, and secure their payments to mothers receiving AFDC and, on a voluntary basis, non-AFDC mothers. AFDC mothers must cooperate in establishing paternity and locating their children's fathers as a condition of receiving benefits. In fiscal 1979, $365 million was spent to collect $1.3 billion, 45 percent of which collections were on behalf of AFDC recipients. HEW reports that in fiscal 1978, paternity was established by the courts for 110,700 children; 1,142,000 absent parents were located; 315,700 support obligations were established; and the AFDC caseload dropped to its lowest level since August 1971. The Child Support Enforcement Program has been so well received that in July 1978, HEW Secretary Califano announced "Project Responsibility," the purpose of which was to double AFDC child support collections by the end of fiscal 1979. In short, this program has been both politically and substantively successful in increasing paternal child support payments.

A major reason for supporting vigorous pursuit of fathers' child support obligations has to do with the causes of AFDC dependency. When the program began, widowhood accounted for most cases; today it accounts for less than 4 percent. In contrast, fathers' absence from the home accounts for about 85 percent. Most often, children today receive AFDC because of their parents' marital instability and almost as many—one-third—are on the rolls because of illegitimacy. Eventually most single mothers marry or remarry, but many become dependent on welfare before their children are grown.

These statistics fly in the face of a generally held belief that *both* parents have a duty and obligation to support their children to the best of their ability and to rely on public assistance only if absolutely necessary. Krause observes that the public welfare system can support the children of shirking fathers only when there are few of them. But if illegitimate children and female-headed households become the predominant situation, as seems to be the case in several cities, our institutions will have to find alternatives or break under the weight of excessive responsibilities. It can be argued that we must return to enforcement of individual obligations if we are not willing to pay for public support of a large percentage of our children.[39]

Over the long term, there is the additional possibility that as the inevitability of paternal support becomes generally perceived, people will avoid having more children than they think they can support. Knowing that he has inescapable financial obligations to children he already has may make a man limit the number of children he has subsequently.[40] It is also possible that third-party enforcement and collection may secure greater compliance than depending on the ability of estranged and hostile ex-spouses to achieve voluntary compliance. Third-party intermediaries tend to neutralize the emotional factors involved in both giving and receiving support assistance.

Not everyone agrees, however, that paternal support obligations ought to be energetically enforced. It is argued that AFDC children will not only fail to receive increased support from vigorous enforcement, but that they may end up with less total income than before.[41] Welfare benefits are reduced dollar for dollar by child support payments, leaving the family with the same total income. But in many low-income communities, fathers provide occasional help, gifts, and emergency financial assistance which, not being reported, supplement rather than supplant the mother's welfare payment. Acknowledgment of paternity also opens the way for a child to participate in the frequently widespread kin network of mutual financial, emotional, and in-kind assistance. Blaydon and Stack argue that stringent welfare sanctions against low-income black fathers who are not contributing regularly to the support of their children may cause some fathers to deny paternity and thereby deny their children participation in their kin network as well.[42] It is also suggested that vigorous enforcement would drain resources from the father's current family, forcing this second family onto the public relief rolls and into such poverty that the father may desert the second family in order to make them eligible for AFDC. Requiring the mother's cooperation as a condition of receiving AFDC means forcing her to answer questions which many deem to be severe invasions of privacy, particularly given the nature of the questions that may be asked in order to establish paternity.

The child-support enforcement program has been opposed by fathers and their families who object to having paychecks, pensions, and other income garnisheed in order to pay child support to children from a prior union who are currently living with their remarried mothers in comfortable financial circumstances. In some of these situations, the father's second wife must go to work because support payments to the father's children from a previous marriage do not leave his current family with enough to live on. Some fathers object to the enforcement of child support orders as an invasion of privacy and a violation of their "rights" to establish new families free of encumbrances from the past.

There appear to be several policy options regarding fathers' child support, in addition to the federal program currently in force. Blaydon and Stack suggest that child support enforcement "is better done in a uniform and equitable way, with incentives as well as requirements for compliance." They seem to be suggesting that fathers' support payments should not be entirely offset by welfare reductions but should leave the family somewhat better off.[43] Permitting families to retain a portion of child support payments in addition to their AFDC benefits, however, would produce uneven results for families in otherwise similar circumstances, depending on whether they received child support and how much was paid. A related option—an administrative policy of "looking the other way" so that fathers could supplement AFDC benefits outside the system—similarly produces uneven and inequitable results. A universal child support system through a comprehensive income redistribution based on the tax structure or an entitlement program has been advocated many times in recent decades as an alternative to the present welfare system. Such an approach would ignore fathers' child support obligations in favor of reliance upon public support of children. Given the present political and fiscal constraints, such a massive revision of our economic and social structures is not foreseeable.

To sum up, there is no doubt that AFDC dependency could be significantly reduced through a vigorous enforcement of fathers' child support obligations. Such a program is being implemented and appears to be contributing to the hoped-for reduction of AFDC dependency. The extent of unfavorable side effects, such as denial of access to the fathers' kin or undue hardship for the fathers' current families, are unknown at this early stage of the program's operation. The fact of the program's existence and vigorous enforcement indicate its strong political and practical feasibility. Its enactment reflects the generally held belief that fathers have an obligation and duty to support their children and to rely on public assistance only if absolutely necessary. It also marks an overt decision to pursue private support of children and not to turn to a public and perhaps universal system of child support.

MATERNAL SUPPORT

Whether or not AFDC mothers should be required to work is the most recent family impact issue to emerge in the welfare reform debate. Unlike the matter of fathers' support, it is far from being resolved. One of the principal purposes behind establishment of AFDC was to permit mothers deprived of male support to remain home to care for their children. But this objective is out of harmony with several recent trends in the society. First, a majority of wives and mothers with children under age eighteen in the general population work outside the home, and many of them contribute income needed to keep their families above the poverty level. Second, the feminist movement has urged economic self-sufficiency for women, because so many fail consistently to receive adequate or any economic support from men. Third, the accelerated pace at which female-headed households are being formed is testing the limits of the welfare system. Finally, the dramatic increases in AFDC program costs during the late 1960s and early 1970s heightened efforts to limit government outlays for this purpose.

Adult AFDC recipients are required to register for work or training under the Work Incentive program. Women with children younger than age six may be exempted from this requirement. Some 47 percent of AFDC mothers in 1973 indicated that they were not participating in the work force for this reason. Only 14 percent of AFDC mothers worked outside the home; their income averaged $257 a month.

A number of family-impact arguments can be made in favor of the work requirement. First and foremost is the economic function of the family. One of every three female-headed families in 1976 had a poverty-level income despite receipt of AFDC. Of the 800,000 families headed by women living solely on AFDC, 94 percent were below the poverty level. Over 60 percent of those who supplemented their AFDC with earnings were also below the poverty level.[44] Advocates of requiring AFDC mothers to work contend that in the long run the favorable family outcomes will outweigh any negative consequences. A young woman or teenager with several small children and no husband can look forward only to a life of being ground down by the welfare system, inadequate income, and eventual unemployability years hence when her youngest children are grown if she does not find employment now. As one observer put it, "Few people seem to grasp how very isolated and harassed many AFDC mothers feel year after year, how little they know about how to improve their circumstances, and how ill prepared they are to support themselves eventually."[45] Feminists contend that considering the low remarriage rates for women with young children, AFDC mothers would do better for themselves and their children in the long run by sacrificing the present time/income benefits of AFDC in favor of gaining a foothold in the work force and a start toward self-sufficiency.[46]

Those who favor the mothers' work requirement minimize the impact on children. They point out that the negative effects of poverty on children have been well documented and increasing family income through mothers' work would probably alleviate many of these problems. Half of the nation's children under age eighteen have working mothers as do half of children under age six in female-headed families, without notably disastrous results. And having the mother at home is no insurance against problems: witness juvenile delinquency and emotional problems even in affluent, one-worker, suburban families.

What little reliable evidence there is on the impact of day care on children does not indicate any harmful effects. One study found no ill effects of "typical" as opposed to ideal day care on low-income infants.[47] A critical review of current research similarly concluded that although available research is limited in both quantity and depth, with several important unresearched or poorly researched issues, what empirical knowledge there is does not indicate any adverse consequences of good quality infant day care on maternal attachment and intellectual or social development.[48] This lukewarm approval is corroborated by the fact that hundreds of thousands of mothers at every income level willingly or reluctantly place their children in day care every year.

Finally, advocates of the work requirement for AFDC mothers point out that mothers' continuation in the work force throughout the childbearing years is rapidly increasing and that a great many new mothers return to work after only a short maternity leave. For many of these mothers, work is necessary to keep their families out of poverty. They resent seeing their tax dollars used for subsidization of other mothers' full-time homemaking and child-raising activities.

There are a number of arguments against requiring AFDC mothers to work. As a simple matter of economics, it is doubtful that the family will come out ahead financially, at least in the short run. Vickery contends that economists have, in general, overestimated the income of AFDC families with working mothers by ignoring the value of lost household production and by including reimbursement for working expenses as income. By her computations, if the family values the mother's services in the home other than child care at only $.85 an hour, the AFDC family is still better off with the mother staying at home rather than going into the work force at $3.00 an hour. Given the educational level, training, and work readiness of many welfare mothers, it is doubtful that they could command more than this $3.00 an hour initially, much less the $3.50 to $5.00 an hour Vickery calculates is needed to put the AFDC family above the poverty threshold.[49]

Opponents of the work requirements reject the tentative findings that day care is not harmful. They point out, correctly, that because "bad" day care has been hidden from officials and its existence steadfastly denied by its providers, the effects of "bad" care have never been systematically studied. Only a small percentage of children are served by organized centers while the rest disappear into a wide range of unregulated informal arrangements about which very little is known. It is sometimes suggested that the only way to be sure children are not being harmed is to provide indisputably good care—which often carries an extortionate and unrealistic price tag of $3,000 to $4,000 a year per child. Subsidizing such care for several children so their mother can earn $3.00 an hour is obviously out of the question. Some child development experts contend that only mothers themselves can provide mothering adequate to prevent psychological damage.[50]

The importance of the mother and homemaker was emphasized by witnesses at the 1977 hearings of the Welfare Reform Subcommittee who argued that mothers of older as well as younger children ought to be relieved of work requirements if their children have special needs because of handicaps or a "rough" neighborhood.[51] They emphasized the continuing need for mothers' home production when older children are present. Witnesses questioned the wisdom of requiring a woman to care for someone else's home and children for pay while receiving little credit for doing the same thing in her own home.[52] Another opponent observed that AFDC is an investment in children and as such is designed to keep mothers out of the labor force. She believes it is unrealistic to expect more poor mothers to take on a wage-earning role to support their children and simultaneously effectively discharge homemaking and mothering roles.[53]

Federal policy has flirted with this issue but has avoided a universal work requirement. The WIN program requires all AFDC recipients to register for work or training, but exempts people for several reasons, including being needed at home. The administration's 1977 welfare reform proposal included a work requirement for mothers whose youngest child was age six or older and required mothers of school-age children to work only part-time in order to be available when their children were out of school. Principal earners—mothers in single-parent families—were eligible for subsidized training or job opportunities. Both of these approaches compromise between those who want no work requirement at all and those who would prefer a more stringent requirement. They may, however, be as far as the government can go, given the prevailing controversy over the proper weight to place on the economic versus other family functions. In short, from the family impact perspective, there is not clear-cut guidance on this issue. The economic functions interact with the nurturing and coordinating functions, and weighing the balance probably must remain an individual, subjective process.

These family policy concerns lead to confusion and controversy. Changing family behavior in the economic "mainstream" as well as the cost of obtaining behavioral changes via an economic support system make it questionable which family goals the AFDC program should pursue, if any. If welfare policy were to put first priority on family goals, we would soon find that what little agreement was evident in previous debates would evaporate. A few examples demonstrate the difficulty in combining welfare and family policy objectives.

1. We may want to provide families with adequate resources to nurture their children, but we might well balk at doing so if it encourages poor people to have more children than they would have had otherwise.

2. We value stable marriages as the most appropriate combination of economic, emotional, and nurturing circumstances for raising children, but question whether women should be economic hostages to marriages that they would abandon—for profound or frivolous reasons—if they could financially afford to do so.

3. We understand a special obligation to make sure that the children who constitute the next generation are assured an upbringing that will enable them to be responsible, contributing citizens, but we resent being forced to subsidize children of "irresponsible" parents, particularly when many others are remaining voluntarily childless.

4. Abortion and forced marriage as alternatives to illegitimacy provoke near-violent controversy, but we are almost equally distressed at the possibility that welfare provides women who are pregnant out of wedlock with an alternative role as female heads of households and may thereby encourage them to favor this option.

5. We want parents to be economically responsible for their families, but we cannot decide whether mothers as well as fathers should be required to work or guaranteed work.

At the root of these conflicting values is the tension between the impact of welfare on the structural characteristics of families and its impact on the economic and nurturing functions of families. Income assistance programs are intended to bolster families' economic functions so they can better attend to their nurturing responsibilities. But economic intervention either facilitates or encourages a change in family structure.

The absence of a welfare policy that is overtly designed to include incentives strong enough to result in a conventional structure for most welfare families (i.e., the presence of a working father, a homemaker mother, and dependent children), is probably explained both by the fact that agreement on these structural objectives is only superficial and by the realization that the incentives would have to be very strong (costly) indeed to overcome the other forces that enter into the decisions individuals make about marriage, children, and work. The "conventional" family type comprises only about 15 percent of all families today in the United States, and the "typical family of four" makes up only about 7 percent. With so few families in the general population conforming to the traditional standard, there is little likelihood of requiring such conformance of welfare families. The plurality of styles and cultures in the United States further precludes imposing family structure requirements on welfare recipients (above and beyond the existing one that usually denies benefits to two-parent families). The strong incentives that would be necessary to achieve structural results would undoubtedly be controversial. For example, efforts to deny benefits to families with illegitimate children and to freeze the number of families with absent fathers eligible for federal-state matching funds were short-lived when it became evident that they had a punitive impact on the children involved. Pro-family incentives which offer extra benefits to families conforming to a legislated norm would be challenged as inequitable.

In the absence of agreement and/or willingness to pursue a "pro-family" policy (in terms of family structure), some have advocated that we try to keep the impact of welfare at least as neutral as possible. The idea would be to design a system that did not raise or lower the financial or non-financial costs of making decisions with regard to marriage, child-bearing, or child support. However, efforts to devise such a system with neutral *incentives* have run headlong into the interaction between economic assistance and family structural changes. Systems which give direct or tax-related benefits to individuals regardless of marital status enhance the "independence effect" which enables and perhaps causes women to leave their husbands. Any such system which includes benefits scaled to family size reduces the cost of raising children and can be said to have a pro-natal impact. The same is true for schemes which involve subsidizing families while children are dependent in return for a pay-back tax after the children are grown. The only policy option which is unquestionably neutral with regard to incentives affecting family structure is to have no welfare system at all. Only then would the financial and non-financial costs of making decisions with regard to marriage, children, household composition, and child support not be affected.

A second neutrality possibility exists, however. This would be to try to design a system which has little or no impact on behavioral *outcomes* even though the law and regulations appear to contain incentives toward certain structural or economic outcomes. Trying to describe what such an operationally neutral program might look like leads to the conclusion that the existing patchwork of benefits is as neutral in its outcome as any other approach. Some of this neutrality is achieved by keeping potential recipients in the dark about the availability of benefits and the certainty of receiving them. The lack of information results from different benefit structures and eligibility requirements from state to state and administrative and regulatory practices that are obscure, arcane, and frequently changing. This tends to neutralize incentives and target benefits, instead, on individuals who become eligible for welfare for reasons other than the fact that they were responding to welfare program incentives. The low level of benefits in many states—often far below the levels required for meeting even basic needs—helps to dampen the "independence effect" and the pro-natal incentives that would be implicit in adequate or generous benefit levels. The 1968 and 1970 Supreme Court decisions make welfare marriage-neutral for women. They can keep their present husbands and still receive benefits by merely signing affidavits that their husbands have left home, and they can take new husbands or boyfriends without losing benefits for their children. About the only prohibited option is letting the father publicly assume his role as head of the family. Possibly the sole area where the existing system may have an incentive effect is the subsidization of out-of-wedlock births which encourages pregnant women to choose this option over abortion or marriage, although conclusive evidence that this is so has yet to be found.

The very things that make the existing program neutral in its family structure impacts also make it a target for reformers' efforts—low benefits, varying treatment of different family types, lack of coverage of childless individuals and single people, sporadic and uneven availability of benefits, bureaucratic obstacles, and general lack of information to potential and actual recipients about how the system works. Any efforts to remedy these characteristics of the welfare system will have an impact on family-related behavior. These outcomes may, depending on one's view, be desirable or undesirable, but probably will be uneven, involving trade-offs between benefit levels, availability, and program information on the one hand and a slightly increased rate of marital dissolution and female-headed families on the other hand. These and other potential trade-offs ought not to be made in the dark. Potential family impacts of any proposed changes should be thoroughly considered and carefully monitored. To the extent that incentives regarding family structure and nurturing characteristics are altered by changing the income support system, these changes ought to be weighed seriously.

No clear guidelines can be offered in advance for deciding between different options, based on family structure and family function impacts. First, not only is it virtually impossible to reconcile the conflicting values regarding the importance of achieving specified family structures, but when these conflicts are ranged against economic variables, any remaining vestige of consensus disappears. We would prefer, for example, that the welfare system not leave poor people worse off than they would be in its absence. But weighing the degree of well-being on both the scales of family structure and economic considerations may produce different results. It is doubtful that the public policy process is capable of or should attempt to make the choice between the two. Marital instability, for instance, is frequently perceived negatively, and families that break up are seen as less well off than those that stay together. However, providing welfare to enable people without other income to escape from abusive marriages which seriously threaten the well-being of the adults and children involved generally receives sympathetic approval even though it means the dissolution of a marriage. But when welfare benefits also facilitate the light-hearted abandonment of a marriage on a frivolous impulse, stern public disapproval ensues, particularly if children are involved. Similar examples could be cited with regard to having children and meeting child support responsibilities.

Second, the public policy choices will seldom be "either-or" situations, but rather will be questions of more or less. Increasing benefit levels may also be accompanied by slightly higher divorce or childbirth rates. Stricter paternal-support enforcement may slightly increase the number of fathers denying paternity. Simply providing better information about how the system operates may affect the rates at which people make various decisions with regard to family structure. Most of the time, however, these family decisions will continue to belong to the private realm.

AFDC began as a limited, small program to help children of widows. But income support has grown to the point where "universal" income maintenance benefits are being considered which could affect a rather large segment of our diverse, pluralistic population. The highest priority ought to be placed on achieving an income support that is fair, equitable, and adequate, however those terms might be defined. Efforts to regularize family life through such a system are unlikely to be acceptable or to succeed and would probably be incompatible in many instances with the income support goals. Welfare reform, therefore, should concentrate on its principal function of providing economic support to individuals. This is not to say that as a society we will not continue to value families for many important reasons—including their unique capacity to function in economic, nurturing, and coordinating roles. The welfare system, therefore, should be vigilantly monitored for any changes that it might cause in family structure and functions. In the rare instances where existing or proposed policies are found to have unexpectedly large, negative consequences for significant numbers of recipient families, alternative policies will have to be sought. More frequently, it will be the case that existing or proposed welfare policies will have only a marginally negative impact on family structural stability, on the nurturing or coordinating functions. In such instances, it will probably be preferable as a matter of public policy to continue to give the highest priority to providing financial assistance in the most equitable and adequate manner feasible and to relegate family impact considerations to a position of secondary importance.

Notes

1. Family Impact Seminar, *Interim Report* (Washington, D.C.: Institute for Educational Leadership, The George Washington University, April 1978), pp. 36–44.

2. Maurice MacDonald and Isabel V. Sawhill, *Welfare Policy and the Family* (Washington, D.C.: The Urban Institute, September 29, 1977), pp. 4–5.

3. This paper is focusing on AFDC and proposed income support reforms. It is important to remember, however, that the system of "welfare" is considerably broader and includes a wide range of public and private social services designed to meet the needs of poor families. As will be discussed in later pages, income support alone is frequently an inadequate or insufficient tool for addressing the needs and problems of families. Family planning services, for example, appear to be a far more effective way to limit family size than a manipulation of the AFDC benefit schedule. Requiring mothers to work depends as much on the availability and adequacy of child care services as upon the requirements of the income maintenance system. A thorough review of the family impact of the welfare system in the United States would therefore require examination of these social service programs as well as other income maintenance programs such as food stamps, health insurance, housing programs, disability, unemployment, and old age insurance.

4. Gilbert Y. Steiner, *Social Insecurity* (Chicago: Rand McNally & Co., 1966), pp. 112–14.

5. Mary Joe Bane, *Here to Stay: American Families in the Twentieth Century* (New York: Basic Books, Inc., 1976), p. 13.

6. Margaret Malone, *Aid to Families with Dependent Children–Development of Program and Current Issues* (Washington, D.C.: Library of Congress Legislative Reference Service, Ed290, March 13, 1968), pp. 9–10.

7. *Ibid.*, p. 18.

8. *Ibid.*, p. 19.

9. U. S. Congress, Joint Economic Committee, *The Concept of Family in the Poor Black Community*, by Carol B. Stack and Herbert Semmel, Joint Committee Print, Study Paper 12, Part II (Washington, D.C.: Government Printing Office, 1973), pp. 275–305.

10. Marjorie Honig, "AFDC Income, Recipient Rates, and Family Dissolution," *Journal of Human Resources* IX, no. 3 (Summer 1974): 303–322; Joseph J. Minarik and Robert S. Goldfarb, "AFDC Income, Recipient Rates and Family Dissolution: A Comment," and Marjorie Honig, "A Reply," *Journal of Human Resources* XI, no. 2 (Spring 1976): 242–260; Heather L. Ross and Isabel V. Sawhill, *Time of Transition: The Growth of Families Headed by Women* (Washington, D.C.: The Urban Institute, 1975); Phillips Cutright and John Scanzoni, *Income Supplements and the American Family*, Joint Economic Committee Study Paper 12, Part I, pp. 54–89; and Stephen K. Mayo, "The Household Composition Effects of Income Transfer Programs," *Public Policy* (Summer 1976).

11. Ross and Sawhill, *Time of Transition*, p. 124.

12. U. S. Congress, House Committee on Agriculture, Committee on Education and Labor, Committee on Ways and Means, *Administration's Welfare Reform Proposal, Hearings*, before the Welfare Reform Subcommittee, House of Representatives, on H.R. 9030, 95th Congress, 1st Session, 1977, Part III, testimony of John Bishop, pp. 1207–21.

13. Bishop suggests, to the contrary, that a permanent program might have higher dissolution rates than a temporary one since families promised five-year benefits split up more frequently than those promised three-year benefits. *Ibid.*, pp. 1213–14.

14. Nancy Brandon Tuma, Michael T. Hannan, and Lyle P. Groeneveld, *Variation Over Time in the Impact of the Seattle and Denver Income Maintenance Experiments on the Making and Breaking of Marriages* (Menlo Park: Stanford Research Institute, Research Memorandum 43, February 1977).

15. Lee Rainwater, *Poverty, Living Standards, and Family Well-Being*, Joint Economic Committee Study Paper No. 12, Part II, pp. 209–216; Marc Fried and Ellen Fitzgerald, *Family and Community Life in the Working Class*, Joint Economic Committee Study Paper No. 12, Part II, pp. 332–38; MacDonald and Sawhill, *Welfare Policy*, p. 26.

16. U. S. Congress, *Welfare Reform Hearings*, testimony of John Bishop, 1222–37, 1245–82.

17. Kenneth Keniston and The Carnegie Council on Children, *All Our Children* (New York: Harcourt Brace Jovanovich, 1977), p. 4.

18. Advisory Committee on Child Development Assembly of Behavioral and Social Sciences, National Research Council, *Toward a National Policy for Children and Families* (Washington, D.C.: National Academy of Sciences, 1976), pp. 38–39.

19. MacDonald and Sawhill, *Welfare Policy*, p. 32.

20. Tuma, Hannan, and Groeneveld, *Variation Over Time of Income Experiments on Marriages*, pp. 19–24.

21. Andrew Billingsley, *Black Family Structure: Myths and Realities*, Joint Economic Committee Study Paper No. 12, Part II, p. 317.

22. U. S. Department of Labor, Office of the Assistant Secretary, *Memorandum for Secretary Marshall from Arnold Packer on Welfare Reform Briefings*, March 14, 1977.

23. An exception is the finding of Barbara S. Janowitz that for nonwhite younger women larger welfare payments are associated with higher illegitimacy rates. "The Impact of AFDC on Illegitimate Birth Rates," *Journal of Marriage and the Family*, August 1976, pp. 485–94.

24. Phillips Cutright, *Illegitimacy and Income Supplements*, Joint Economic Committee Study Paper No. 12, Part I, pp. 90–138.

25. Alan Fechter and Stuart Greenfield, *Welfare and Illegitimacy: An Economic Model and Some Preliminary Results* (Washington, D.C.: The Urban Institute, August 1973).

26. Kristin A. Moore and Steven B. Caldwell, *Out-of-Wedlock Pregnancy and Childbearing* (Washington, D.C.: The Urban Institute, September 1976), pp. 28–87.

27. Ross and Sawhill, *Time of Transition*, p. 109.

28. Moore and Caldwell, *Out-of-Wedlock Pregnancy*, p. 159.

29. Stack and Semmel, *Concept of Family*, p. 287.

30. U. S. Congress, *Welfare Reform Hearings*, testimony of Robert E. Mitchell, National Council on Family Relations, Vol. IV, p. 2574.

31. Blanche Bernstein and William Meezan, *The Impact of Welfare on Family Stability* (New York: Center for New York City Affairs, New School for Social Research, 1975), as discussed in Moore and Caldwell, *Out-of-Wedlock Pregnancy*, pp. 72–75. Barbara S. Janowitz found that while male unemployment rates were never found to have a significant impact on illegitimacy rates, male income had a consistently negative impact, suggesting that marriage is discouraged and illegitimacy encouraged when fathers lack adequate means of support. However, the holding of this effect even for older (aged 30–34) women who almost never married to legitimize a pregnancy led Janowitz to conclude that the negative impact of income on illegitimacy may stem more from a positive correlation of income and contraceptive knowledge than from income and illegitimacy.

32. Harriet Pressner and Linda Salsberg, "Public Assistance and Early Family Formation—Is There a Pronatalist Effect?" *Social Problems* 23, no. 2 (December 1975): 227, cited in Moore and Caldwell, *Out-of-Wedlock Pregnancy*, p. 77.

33. Rainwater, *Poverty, Living Standards, and Family Wellbeing*, pp. 235–239.

34. For a not-expected-to-work mother and her children.

35. As of July 1977.

36. C.R. Winegarden, "The Fertility of AFDC Women: An Econometric Analysis," *Journal of Economics and Business* 26, no. 3 (Spring 1974): 159–166.

37. Fred W. Reed, J. Richard Udry, and Maxine Ruppert, "Relative Income and Fertility: The Analysis of Individuals' Fertility in a Biracial Sample," *Journal of Marriage and the Family*, Nov. 1975, pp. 799–804; Stephen J. Bahr, Bruce A. Chadwick and Joseph H. Strauss, "The Effect of Relative Economic Status on Fertility," *Journal of Marriage and the Family*, May 1975, pp. 335–342.

38. Carol Adaire Jones, Nancy M. Gordon, and Isabel V. Sawhill, *Child Support Payments in the United States* (Washington, D.C.: The Urban Institute, Oct. 1976).

39. Harry D. Krause, *Child Welfare, Parental Responsibility, and the State*, Joint Economic

Committee Study Paper No. 12, Part II, pp. 255–274.

40. Wisconsin even went so far as to require a man with a legal obligation to support children from an earlier union to get court permission in order to remarry. Permission would be granted only if the man could prove that he had met all support obligations for previous children and that they were not likely to become public charges. The Wisconsin law was struck down by the Supreme Court on January 18, 1978, by an eight to one vote as being violative of 14th Amendment equal protection guarantees.

41. Colin C. Blaydon and Carol B. Stack, "Income Support Policies and the Family," *Daedalus*, Spring 1977, pp. 147–61; Stack and Semmel, *Concept of Family*, pp. 292–301.

42. Blaydon and Stack, "Income Support Policies and the Family," pp. 153–56.

43. *Ibid.*, p. 156.

44. Heather L. Ross, "Poverty, Women and Children Last," *Economic Independence for Women*, ed. by Jane Roberts Chapman (Sage Yearbooks, Vol. 1, 1976), pp. 137–44.

45. Winifred Bell, "AFDC: Symptom and Potential," *Jubilee for Our Times: A Practical Program for Income Equality*, ed. by Alvin L. Schorr (New York: Columbia University Press, 1977), p. 261.

46. Janet E. Harrell and Carl A. Ridley studied the relationships among employed mothers' work satisfaction and the quality of mother-child interaction and concluded that they were positively related to one another, a finding which suggests that the time/income trade-offs may not be as onerous as assumed. "Substitute Child Care, Maternal Employment and the Quality of Mother-Child Interaction," *Journal of Marriage and the Family*, August 1975, pp. 556–64.

47. Barbara Radloff, "Average Day Care: Harmful or Beneficial?," *Carnegie Quarterly* XXV, no. 3 (Summer 1977): 5–6.

48. Louise Silverstein, *A Critical Review of Current Research on Infant Day Care* (New York: Columbia University School of Social Work, 1977).

49. This does not imply that Vickery opposes work for welfare mothers; she merely illustrates the dubious initial financial benefits of doing so. Clair Vickery, "Economics and the Single-Mother Family," *Public Welfare*, Winter 1978, pp. 18–21.

50. Selma Fraiberg, *Every Child's Birthright: In Defense of Mothering* (New York: Basic Books, 1978).

51. U. S. Congress, *Welfare Reform Hearings*, testimony of Child Welfare League of America, Vol. IV, pp. 2232–57.

52. U. S. Congress, *Welfare Reform Hearings*, testimony of Robert E. Mitchell, National Council on Family Relations, Vol. IV, p. 2553.

53. Winifred Bell, "AFDC: Symptom and Potential," p. 263.

10

The Economic Support of "Fatherless" Children[1]

BARBARA R. BERGMANN

Most public welfare payments in the United States have always gone to families consisting of a divorced, separated, widowed, or single woman and her children. Currently, the extensive debate concerning welfare reform has gone on with relatively little direct attention being paid to the "basic welfare family"—the family with children but without a father present. In particular, there has been little systematic exploration of the various modes by which such a family group might be supported economically, and no comparison of the various modes of support with respect to adequacy, feasibility, and fairness. The issues on which the debate on welfare reform has thus far been focused—work incentives, forms of support, incentives for families to split up, ways to characterize trends in the distribution of income—are not, of course, entirely unrelated to the question of modes of support for the "basic welfare family" and the economically "fatherless" children it contains. Nevertheless, there are important issues more directly related to the support of "fatherless" children which do bear on welfare reform, and which have largely been ignored or skirted. This paper attempts to begin to address these questions more directly than has been done in the past.

The thesis we shall advance here is that the social and economic system which ensured a flow of economic resources from adult males to children and ensured that few children would be "fatherless" has been breaking down, and that the arrangements we now have for the economic care of "fatherless" children need basic reexamination. A support system which might have been tolerated at a time when "fatherless" children and their mothers were a small and outcast group is being strained by huge numbers and changing mores. More than one out of six children are currently living apart from their fathers, and more than one-third of these are in poverty. New institutional arrangements need to be created to handle the job of ensuring on a regular basis the channeling of income to single parents and their children. Considerable thought and discussion is needed concerning how such arrangements can be made just and adequate, and as to the source, nature, and size of the economic flows they will channel. In this paper, we shall attempt to discuss some of the outstanding issues concerning such institutional arrangements and give an outline of one possible system, which we shall claim has important virtues not offered under present arrangements.

One major question concerning the support of children which has been skirted in the debate on welfare reform and which we shall explore in this paper is the question of whether, how, and in what quantity economic resources can and ought to be extracted from the biological father for the support of a child with whom he does not live. A second and related question we shall deal with, which has had little explicit discussion even in the debate on "work incentives" for welfare recipients, is the question of how great a proportion of the economic resources used by the child who lives with its mother but not its father can and ought to be derived from the productive activity of its mother.

Factors Influencing the Form of Economic Support Systems for the Young

THE SOCIOBIOLOGY OF THE SUPPORT OF OFFSPRING

Many systems for economically supporting offspring are possible, and it is desirable for our purposes to avoid at the outset the assumption that any one system is the right or inevitable one. It is instructive to review in a cursory way the various modes which are possible, and the factors influential in establishing one or another mode of support. Humans are not the only species with this problem. The lower animals must also manage the feat of supporting their young, and we can learn about the determinants of behavior from seeing the solutions they have adopted under varying circumstances. As is well known, animal species vary widely with respect to the extent to which there is transmission to the young of goods and services produced by the activities of adults and with respect to the pattern of transmission.

In many species, no activity on the part of either parent contributes to the offspring after the male and female gametes are united; many water-born creatures follow this pattern. In a small number of cases, it is the male parent who assumes the major role in contributing to the offspring;

the best known case is that of the seahorse, in which the male takes on the task of incubating the eggs and shepherding the newborns, while the female parent stays entirely clear of this duty. In a larger number of cases, the female parent devotes considerable effort to the support of the offspring, with the male parent contributing little or nothing. Some species, notably birds, have evolved into a pattern whereby the male parent and the female parent both make extensive contributions in terms of time, effort, and attention to the raising of their young. Still another pattern is that of group or extended family contributions to support of offspring. Among wild dogs, both males and females of a pack will contribute food to the pack's young, without regard to parenthood.[2]

What seems to make the difference in the pattern which evolves is the number of young produced, the nature and extent of their needs, and the luxuriance of the environment in supplying such needs. Where the environment can supply the needs of enough of the young to guarantee species survival without the mediating effort of either parent, neither parent contributes goods or services. Where the environment is such that the efforts of only one parent are needed to supply adequate support for the offspring, and where that parent can do so with enough energy to spare for the economic activity which is necessary to keep *itself* alive for the requisite period, the other parent will not contribute. It is in the remaining cases, where the needs of the offspring are great, and where the efforts required to meet those needs could not be met by one parent without the danger of the premature death of that parent, that both parents and/or other relatives contribute.

In mammalian species, the female parent is obviously equipped to make the exclusive contribution of the offspring's first feedings, but a material contribution from the male parent or other group members may be forthcoming, depending on the species. Our closest animal relatives, the primates, would seem to fall into the pattern of maternal support for the youngest infants with little or no economic contribution from males.

Among humans, the physical needs of the young require greater time and effort to satisfy than among primates, especially in colder climates. Perhaps more importantly, the invention of tools and the elaboration and multiplication of consumer goods make possible a style and standard of life which in most environments has not been sustainable by a mother and children lacking important contributions from other adults. Among human societies, contributions from males to the sustenance of the young usually take the form of donated goods or money, and only rarely the direct provision of personal services by the male to the child. Despite this, substantial contributions from males is the general rule. There are exceptions: Among certain populations, males make no productive contribution at all; in these communities, men spend their lives in recreational activity, and adult men and children are entirely supported by the work of women. In other societies, males may do some work, but also spend large amounts of time in activities which have low value in terms of material production, but high value in terms of recreational content—such as hanging around the bazaar, big game hunting, or soldiering. One may question in these cases whether fathers make a productive contribution which exceeds their own consumption.

In most Western countries, the general rule has been a vigorous contribution to economic production on the part of all but the highest caste males. Substantial contributions from fathers (or father-substitutes such as relatives or the state) to the economic support of children has been necessary to the sustenance of life at anything above the barest physical subsistence. However, in the more advanced countries, economic progress may be bringing to an end the era in which substantial contributions of money or goods from males are necessary to the physical well-being of the young of humans. This theme will be developed below.

TRADITIONAL ATTITUDES AND PRACTICES CONCERNING THE
ECONOMIC SUPPORT OF CHILDREN

Social systems, at least in Western countries, have traditionally dealt with the problem of "fatherless" children by attempting to insure that as few of them as possible came into existence. The major mechanisms for doing so have been the institution of marriage, a taboo on sex for unmarried women, and disgrace and deprivation for women bearing children out of wedlock, and for the "illegitimate" children themselves. Marriage may be thought of as a mechanism for attaching a woman and her subsequently born children onto the entourage and/or property of a man, other than her father. It has traditionally conferred on a man certain rights—exclusive right to her obedience and her sexual and domestic services, and assurance of paternity. It is these rights which make it worthwhile for a man to concern himself with the upkeep of the "property" that produces these services. He does this through economic contributions to the sustenance of the wife and children to the extent that such contributions are traditional and are necessary and desirable from his point of view. This view of the institution of marriage puts a wife and children on a par with the land and animal flocks or slaves which a man may own, of which he also is motivated to take care for the sake of his own interest.

From another, but not necessarily conflicting, point of view, the institution of marriage has been thought of as having women and children as its major beneficiaries. Even in the absence of marriage, the argument runs, women would have children, either because it is in their nature to want sex and/or children, or because unmarried (and therefore unprotected) women would be raped, and thus forced to have children. If many or most women are going to have children anyway, the economic strain of child rearing is such that it becomes desirable that each woman attach to herself and her children a man who would make economic contributions to their sustenance. The disadvantages that a woman has traditionally suf-

THE ECONOMIC SUPPORT OF "FATHERLESS" CHILDREN

fered in marriage—more or less severe domination by the husband, a requirement (in the absence of servants) that she do all housework, a double standard with regard to sexual fidelity—can be viewed as the price she has had to pay for this support. Like any other price, it is influenced by "supply and demand." The "supply" consists of all the women desiring a permanent economic connection with a man. Both the number of such women and the terms on which they will be willing to live with a man affect the price paid by each woman. The price is also affected on the "demand" side—by the number of men who desire the exclusive sexual and personal services of a woman, and the terms on which the men are willing to obtain them.

Because of its concern with "fatherless" children, society has always, up to the present, at any rate, been deeply concerned with the economic and social consequences of the end of the marriage relationship. The extended family, where it still exists, takes up the economic burden of the widow and her children. If the extended family structure is strong, the system which minimizes "fatherless" children may even be consistent with easy divorce. ("I divorce thee, I divorce thee, I divorce thee," suffices to relieve a Moslem man of a wife.) Under such a system, the man may keep the children and send the woman back to her father or brothers. In the West, divorce has, until recently, been difficult and expensive, and thus most easily obtained by the rich. A divorce judgment involving a wealthy man would customarily be accompanied by a judgment for substantial child support and alimony, and his wealth would make the collection of the judgment relatively easy.

The taboo against premarital sex for women has served the dual purpose of restricting the supply of sex partners available to men (and therefore encouraging men to give economic support to women and children within marriage) and, of course, reducing the number of children who were without a father's support. Where a child was conceived outside of wedlock, vigorous and sometimes violent efforts were made to effect a wedding of the mother and the father before the birth. Where a "shotgun wedding" could not be performed, the disgrace to the woman was reflected back onto her parents, sometimes with results inimical to the economic welfare of the infant. The stern father showing the door to his daughter and her newly born illegitimate child has for some time been only a stock comedy figure, but long after parents ceased acting that way in such circumstances, the parents' chagrin and the community's disapproval surely must have served as a punishment to a woman who had had an illegitimate child. The avoidance of "punishment" of this sort may still motivate behavior in an appreciable part of the population, although the proportion seems to be diminishing.

To sum up, traditional social institutions and mores have had the effect of keeping a high proportion of children with and receiving economic support from adult males. It is obvious that some of the most important of the traditional habits and arrangements which past generations relied on to perform this function—a taboo on premarital sex for women, a stigma on illegitimate births, the all-but-undissoluable marriage of unequals, the extended family—no longer operate for considerable parts of the population in the West. In the United States it may well be true that they have ceased to operate for a majority of the population.

BIRTH CONTROL AND CHILD SUPPORT

We may speculate that one vital element in the decline of traditional institutions has been the development and ease of access to contraceptive devices and to safe and legal abortion. Contraception and abortion must surely have contributed importantly to the atrophy of the taboo against premarital sex for women, since their availability removes or at least reduces the chance that a woman will have to bear an extramarital child unwillingly as the result of any single act of sexual congress. We can further speculate that indulgence in premarital sex by more women reduces the incidence of marriage by reducing the incentive for a man to marry. ("Why should he buy the cow if he can get free milk?") A greater availability of unmarried female sexual partners may also increase the incidence of divorce by providing a husband with increased opportunities for extramarital involvements which may be destabilizing to his marriage. An increase in the divorce rate due to an increase in extramarital involvements for husbands makes divorce a more common occurrence, and this in turn may encourage by example other couples to divorce, who might have stayed together had divorce been more exceptional.

While there seems little question that the availability of birth control tends to erode traditional habits and institutions regulating sexual behavior, the effect of easily accessible contraception and abortion on the number of "fatherless" children is a complex one. Contraception and abortion will, of course, prevent the births of some out-of-wedlock children. However, by reducing the *proportion* of cases in which extramarital intercourse leads to pregnancy, contraception may have the effect of increasing the number of such acts to such an extent that there may be a resultant increase rather than a decrease in the *number* of extramarital births. To the extent that premarital sex for women proves destabilizing to existing marriages, many of the children of those marriages will become economically "fatherless" through the failure of the divorced husbands to make child support payments. To the extent that more premarital sex for women reduces the incentive for men to marry, and thus reduces the chance that a woman may have of finding a satisfactory marriage partner, the number of unmarried women who elect to carry a pregnancy (perhaps due to contraceptive failure) to term may increase.

On the other side, we may speculate that the availability of birth control reduces the numbers of children born in marriages that eventually end in divorce, and thus reduces the number of children who are made economically "fatherless" by the failure of divorced fathers to make child support payments. The availability of safe and legal abortion may have an impact on child support institutions which goes beyond its effect on the numbers of births to unmarried women and the numbers of births to women who will eventually be divorced. We will take it for granted that abortion is a procedure which ought not to be done without the consent of the pregnant woman. If this is granted, then once a pregnancy starts, termination is possible, but the woman has veto power over that termination. The effect of this veto is to make the woman appear to be solely responsible (from at least some points of view) for the appearance of the baby in this world, or, if not solely responsible, at least more responsible than the baby's father. For our purposes, we need to ask whether "more or solely responsible for the appearance of the baby" is the moral and/or practical equivalent of "more or solely responsible for the economic burden of raising the child."

As things now stand, a man who can be shown to the satisfaction of a court of law to have fathered a baby out of wedlock can be ordered to contribute to its support. This has no doubt been based on a belief in the mother's inability to provide adequate material support, and a reasoning that the mother and the father of the baby had equal responsibility for the baby's appearance. However, as the law courts digest the new fact of the availability of abortion and the increasing ability of the mother to provide for the child unaided (discussed below), support orders against out-of-wedlock fathers may be harder to obtain, in the absence of legislation mandating them. Ironically, the availability of abortion may have the effect in the future of giving to marriage vows a new importance as the only legal basis on which support may be extracted from a man for the children which come from any sexual union he may engage in.

TECHNICAL PROGRESS AND ITS EFFECTS ON CHILD SUPPORT ARRANGEMENTS

For the lower animals, the amounts of goods and services which can be "produced" by a single individual, relative to the needs of the young, will determine in part the "social" arrangements with respect to the transmission of goods and services from adult animals to young ones. Changes in environmental conditions presumably have their major, perhaps their sole, effect on the behavior of the adult animals through the natural selection of those genes controlling behavior which conduce best to reproductive success under the new conditions.

Human beings themselves, through their own ingenuity, change the conditions under which they produce goods and services. That adaptations in social arrangements as well as economic arrangements tend to occur when technological changes in the mode of production occur is something we have been aware of since Marx. (However these changes in social arrangements do occur, they do not do so through genetic changes, as the time spans are far too short.) Since the start of the industrial revolution, the West has been in a period of constant technological change, which has had the effect of raising the productivity of the economy and raising year by year the amount of goods and services which can be purchased with the average wage earned in a day of work. Women workers' wages (corrected for price changes) have been rising along with men's wages, for the same reason. They have not been gaining on men's wages, remaining at about 60 percent of men's wages. In the United States in the postwar period, the productivity rises on which rises in real wages are based have gone on at a rate of 2.3 percent per year.[3]

The rise in women's real wages may well have an important effect on child support practices in our society. The most obvious effect of the rise in women's wages has been to alter traditional thinking concerning the suitability of paid work for married mothers, and to cause more and more married women with young children to seek and occupy paid jobs. The rise in labor force participation of married mothers, and in particular the increase in the number of women who maintain a fairly continuous attachment to the labor market, seems to have brought in its train new thoughts about appropriate occupational goals for women and new opinions (and laws) about the right of employers to treat women differently from men with respect to job availability and wages, which may in time succeed in narrowing the gap between men's and women's wages.

The increasing orientation of married women toward paid work, while reducing the birth rate of within-wedlock children, has probably had the effect of increasing the divorce rate (and thus the number of children living apart from their fathers), as the lessening in economic dependence on the husband has given wives more courage to terminate bad marriages and has reduced the guilt husbands feel about leaving wives and children and failing to contribute to their subsequent support. It may have also increased overt conflict within marriage, to the extent that the unchallenged dominance of the husband, based partly on his monopoly of access to money wages, reduced overt conflict in the past.

The rise in women's wages may also have implications for the number of out-of-wedlock children and the means by which they might be supported economically. The most important effect may be a reduction in the public's willingness to contribute support to the non-working mothers of such children out of the public purse. Up to now, welfare policy has been based on the idea that welfare mothers should have the same right as middle class women with husbands have to choose to make child rearing and homemaking their sole occupation. Such a claim is bound to sound outlandish to an increasing proportion of American adults, as more married mothers take jobs.

Because of rising real wages, a considerable proportion of women are now capable of earning enough money to support themselves and their children at above the poverty level as officially defined, unaided by a man. In 1976, the median money earnings of a woman who worked full time year round was $8,099. This is far below the 1976 median male money earnings of $13,455.[4] However, the rate of productivity increase has been such that employed women now have real wages that are about what men's real wages were on average twenty-two years ago, wages which allowed men to be the sole financial support of their families. The average male wage levels of twenty-two years ago did not provide families with the vacation trips, the extra cars, and the extra bathrooms which men's wages provide today, but they did provide decency. Since women have reached this level of financial capability, it will no doubt be tempting for separated fathers (and for policymakers) to continue to let a high proportion of single and divorced mothers bear the burden of supporting their children without male help.

Toward a New System of Support for the Young

NUMBERS OF "FATHERLESS" CHILDREN IN THE UNITED STATES AND THE LEVEL OF MATERNAL PROVISION IN THEIR FAMILIES

As of March 1977, 9.5 million children, or one of six children in the United States, were living with women who had no husband present, up dramatically from the ratio of one in ten observed in March 1970. About 80 percent of the increase in the number of such families between 1970 and 1977 was due to divorce or separation, while about 20 percent of the increase was due to an increase in first births to never-married women.[5]

One out of three "fatherless" families in 1977 had money income below the official poverty line. However, placement of "fatherless" families above or below the poverty line gives an incomplete and biased picture of their material situation. It leaves out of account the fact that a single parent who is working full time is going to experience an acute shortage of adult person-hours available for domestic tasks—such as shopping, cooking, going to the doctor, companionship with and supervision of children.[6] Even more importantly, the rationale on which poverty lines for various kinds of families are based includes no allowance whatever for cash payments for child-care services. In the case of husband-wife families, the minimal budget is understood to take care of cash outlays for food, clothing, shelter, and other necessaries, and the assumption is made that the mother will look after the children. In computing the minimal budget for a family without a husband, the assumption is made that the requirements for food, etc., diminish, but no increase is provided for child-care expenses.[7] This may be reasonable in the case of the non-jobholding single parent. However, a minimal poverty budget for the family of a working single parent should include the cost of child care to such a family. If a poverty-line budget tailored to such a family had been promulgated we would have recorded a considerably higher proportion of "fatherless" families living in poverty.

We turn now to sources of monetary support for the families of single and divorced mothers. Little direct information has been available breaking the income of such families down by source.[8] Using information about government expenditures for the program of Aid to Families with Dependent Children, and material from the Current Population Survey about earnings by family members, one can piece together the following orders of magnitude:

1. The women's own earnings account for roughly 50 percent.[9]

2. The wage income of other family members, such as the woman's mother, accounts for 15 to 20 percent.[10]

3. Transfer payments from the government, excluding in-kind transfer, make up roughly 30 percent.[11]

4. Payments from the children's father may account for 5 to 10 percent.[12]

To bring the one-third of "fatherless" families who are in poverty up out of poverty would require a doubling of current total income of such poor families, so we can further roughly estimate that absent fathers are making a contribution on the order of 4 to 8 percent of the sum required for a decent level of life in the families in which their children reside. By contrast, only one out of eighteen families in which both the husband and the wife were present lived in poverty, and the husband's wages accounted for about 80 percent of the financial base in husband-wife families.[13]

The estimates given above relate to *monetary* contributions from fathers to the *families* in which their children live. If we want to make an estimate of the proportion of the *total* material resources consumed by *children* that absent fathers contribute, we need to include as part of the resources that the children consume the value of the unpaid services of their mother, but exclude that part of family income which goes for the mother's consumption. We can make these adjustments in a rough way by putting the value of the mother's unpaid services to the child at 25 percent of the money income, and the part of family money income devoted to children's consumption at 40 percent of the family money income. On these assumptions, the absent father's 5 to 10 percent share of money income to the family translates into 7 to 15 percent of the child's consumption of goods and services (including unpaid services). These numbers also imply that the total monetary contribution which fathers make to children living apart from them averages only 2 to 5 percent of the total of absent fathers' income.

POST-DIVORCE ECONOMIC FLOWS

The increasing incidence of divorce has probably increased the proportion of divorces which occur to people in the lower and middle strata and has certainly increased the number of such divorces. In the United States, this has raised the number of children who will receive little or no economic support from their fathers. The reason lies in the manner in which child support orders are enforced in divorce cases. When a divorced father is ordered by a court to make payments for support of his children, the court in most jurisdictions sets in motion no governmental mechanism that sends him bills, notes his payments and delinquencies, and moves against him if he is delinquent. The woman who is to be the recipient of the payment must move against him by legal action in the case of delinquency and will in most cases require the help of a lawyer to do so. By the nature of the case, she will be very short of funds to pay a lawyer, and a lawyer's prospects of collecting the amount owed from the man, out of which his or her legal fees would be taken, are low if the delinquent man is not a person of very substantial property and income. In the United States, the problem of the legal pursuit of a delinquent ex-husband may be further complicated by the move of the man to another state. The net result of this situation is to discourage attorneys from taking on and pursuing child-support cases.[14] Even if, after a long legal process, the delinquent father has been ordered by a judge to make good, he may shortly thereafter become delinquent again and must be legally pursued anew. The process is so cumbersome that obedience to support orders can almost be said to be voluntary. The practical result of this system is that in about 80 percent of all cases, mothers who have support orders experience delinquency in the payments due them.

Data relating to 1973 from the Michigan Panel Study of Income Dynamics analyzed by Jones, Gordon, and Sawhill show that of families with children with absent fathers, 55 percent received no payments at all from the children's father, another 20 percent received less than $1500, and another 14 percent received $1500–3000. Of mothers who were judged by the researchers to have had child support awards, 34 percent in a given year were likely to receive not a single payment.[15]

It is commonly conjectured that most of the fathers defaulting on child-support payments have low income, but the data do not bear this out. In the Panel Study group about 60 percent of fathers with earnings below $5000 paid nothing, about 50 percent of fathers with incomes between $5000 and $10,000 paid nothing, and about 52 percent of fathers with more than $10,000 in income paid nothing.

HOW SHOULD "FATHERLESS" CHILDREN BE SUPPORTED AND AT WHAT LEVEL?

The possible sources of support for a child living apart from his or her father are those we listed above: the mother, the father, other relatives, the state. Mothers currently provide the biggest share of such support. Let us start by asking whether there are any circumstances which would justify allowing the mother to assume the entire burden of the support of a child out of the proceeds of her own (paid and unpaid) productive activity?

Many such mothers are, of course, currently doing so, and a common answer would be that it is right for them to do so if they have access to well-paid employment and if the father is unknown or poor.

In considering such a proposition, it must be remembered that it is unlikely that a single mother can find someone who will do all the domestic work of her household for no pay except free room and board plus a clothing allowance. This is the "deal" which many men get from their wives, and the fact that it is not available to women means that the single mother is not as well off in terms of material provision as a married man making the same salary. She does not have access to sources of material production on the same basis at the same prices. The possibility that the single mother will have to pay cash for child care is only one of the sources of the disparity in the situation of the working single mother and the working married man. It thus becomes reasonable to consider the working mother who makes a salary equal to a particular man's salary as deprived relative to him. When we add the fact that only 8 percent of women who work full time have wage income as high as the average wage income of the men who work full time, it follows that there are very few single mothers who could be pointed to as people who can fairly be left without help from any source.

Let us turn now to the fairness of getting help from absent fathers. The easiest case is fathers of children born in wedlock. Marriage has in the past been considered tantamount to a promise to contribute to the economic support of any children born. There may be, of course, some special cases which some would now consider sufficient for the abrogation of such a promise. For example, if both spouses have married with the understanding that neither wanted children and would take active steps to prevent their appearance, and if such steps were not taken (by the mother) when she might have done so without danger to her health, then it might be claimed by some that the father was under no obligation to contribute to those children's support. Such an argument might make sense, but one would want to restrict its applicability to cases in which legally binding agreements to take steps to prevent the appearance of children were made at the time of the marriage.

A second line of argument absolving some absent fathers of the obligation to support might hinge on the fact that an absent parent may get less enjoyment from a child than does the parent who is caring for the child. This argument ignores the fact that caring for children affords both enjoyment and pain, and that the balance of pleasure and pain that will be struck in the relationship of a child to a parent is one that cannot be predicted at the time the decision to have the child is made. What can be predicted, however, at that time is that the child will be the occasion of considerable expense on the part of whatever adults or adult are responsible for it. If the father is absent because of his own wish and against the wish of the mother, it seems unfair for him to be allowed to saddle her with all of the economic costs of a child whenever he decides that the prospective pleasures and pains of a life separate from the child are more attractive than the pleasures and pains (financial contributions included) of a life together with the child. Where the father is absent because the mother wants to be apart from him, and she has gained custody of the child, the case is more complex, and some might argue that the ethical judgment as to the financial obligation of the father may hinge on such issues as the "fault" of each party in the breakup.

I would tend to argue that important interests would be served by interpreting marriage vows as a promise to contribute to the support of children born of the marriage except in exceptional circumstances. Resolving most doubtful cases in the direction of requiring contributions from absent spouses in effect gives the benefit of the doubt to the child, who will receive support from both parents in that case.

A somewhat harder case is that of fathers of children born out of wedlock. There is, first of all, the identity problem. In recent years, biological testing processes have improved so that the proportion of non-fathers of a particular child who will be excluded from the possibility of being the biological father of that child on the basis of blood tests is better than 90 percent.[16] Despite the technical excellence of current methods of paternity testing, problems remain. The reluctance of a mother to name candidates for the paternity test might be legitimately tolerated under certain conditions. If we consider cases where there is no identity problem, either because the man has freely admitted paternity or because a (possibly forced) test has proven non-negative, one might make an argument along the following lines that the father should be compelled to pay: Releasing fathers of children born out of wedlock from support obligations makes the situation of married fathers more onerous as compared to that of other men. Unmarried men are able to enjoy the companionship of a woman and their children with no long-run financial commitment. The result would be a reduction in the incentive for men to marry, and a further devolvement of burden of the support of children onto the mother and the state.

How much should absent fathers give? Sawhill has suggested a formula which sums the income of a man and his former wife and allots to him for his own use a share equal to $1/(2+n)$ of the sum of the combined incomes, where n is the number of children.[17] All the rest is for the use of the wife and children, which leaves a father's contribution of

$$Y_f - \frac{Y_f + Y_m}{(2+n)}$$

where Y_f and Y_m are the money income of the father and mother respectively. Sawhill allows modifications to take account of the cost of establishing two households, the fact that children require less upkeep than adults, and any subsequent support obligations the man may incur, all of which have the result of reducing the recommended payment. Even with these modifications, Sawhill's formula strikes most people to whom it is presented as unrealistically generous to the ex-wife and children. A formulation suggested by Judith Cassetty[18] would equalize "the relative economic well-being of the household in which the child resides and that of the absent parent.[19] In practice, this would give much the same result as Sawhill's (modified) formula.

An alternative formula would establish a level of "need" rather than a sharing process as the guiding principle. A further characteristic which might be built into an alternative formula would be the segregation of the children's needs and their satisfaction (including paid care and the value of unpaid care) from the satisfaction of the mother's needs, in a way that Sawhill's or Cassetty's formulas do not do. (Sawhill explains that the mother and children are going to have the same standard of life—the ex-husband cannot provide a steak for the children and none for the mother because she will inevitably eat part of it. The net result is that Sawhill's formula mandates supplying both the mother's and children's upkeep out of the support payment.)

A formula incorporating these alternative ideas might start out by computing the resources to be devoted to the child's support as

$$U + M$$

where U is the money value of the unpaid services the child will receive, and M is a sum of money required for the purchased goods and services necessary to a modest but adequate standard of life. The standard contribution of the absent father would be

$$\tfrac{1}{2}U + \tfrac{1}{2}M$$

all in money and the caretaking mother would be responsible for U in services, and

$$\tfrac{1}{2}(M - U)$$

in the form of a money contribution.

Unlike the Sawhill or Cassetty formula, the formulation I suggest above does not depend on the income of the parents. A well-off father would owe the same amount as one less affluent. Moreover, the contributions suggested are not intended to subsidize the mother's living expenses, but to take care of the extra expenses she incurs by having the child with her. The mother's own expenses would be expected to be taken care of out of the proceeds of paid work or unemployment insurance or government relief payments. If paid child care were required, the amount M in the formula above would include an allowance for such expenses. Exclusive of child care expenses, the order of magnitude of M I would be thinking of would be $3000 per year for a single child not requiring specially expensive care for medical, educational, or psychological reasons. More children would require some lesser amount per child. This is not out of line with the *average* results of Cassetty's formula.[20]

It seems plausible to suggest that government should supply three things: *(1.)* subsidized high-quality child care to repair the inability of the single mother to buy the economic services of a "wife" as cheaply as a man can; *(2.)* cash payments to bring provision for the child to a minimal level of decency if either of the parents are judged incapable of meeting the above standards of provision for the child, and, perhaps most important of all; *(3.)* a mechanism for the collection, monitoring, and disbursing of payments by fathers living apart from their children. The mechanism for collecting from absent fathers should work on the principal of the withholding tax and could be taken care of by the Internal Revenue Service, and/or the Social Security Administration. Entry into such a system should not await delinquency, but should be from the very start of the separation.[21]

Harold Watts has suggested a tax on absent fathers, which would be earmarked for support of all "fatherless" children.[22] Whether one favors a scheme in which each absent father pays for his own children and simply passes the funds through IRS, or a Watts-type scheme under which he pays into a general fund which is then distributed to all "fatherless" children, depends on whether one believes that the child's provision should be higher if his father is more affluent, and also which scheme one views as giving more positive psychological dividends to the people concerned.

Conclusion

The burgeoning welfare rolls and the dissatisfaction felt with the amount of tax dollars going to welfare are really just the tip of the iceberg of the social problem created by the atrophy of long-standing human institutions which kept children under the economic support of their fathers. Much suffering and unfairness caused by the drying up of the flow of resources from adult males to children is not reflected in the welfare budget. The burden is born in part by millions of women and children who never see a welfare dollar. The social institutions which in the past served to channel resources to children from their fathers are unlikely to be revived in their old forms, nor should we wish them to be. These institutions kept women in a grossly inferior status and ruined many lives by preserving unhappy marriages which should have been dissolved. The problem is that we have not yet developed institutions that serve some of the positive purposes of the old institutions and that are felt to be just and adequate.

An unavoidable part of any solution is that the government should take a more active role in policing the flow of private resources from adults—absent fathers—to children. This would do more than help the direct beneficiaries. If some of the "fatherless" children could be removed entirely from the welfare rolls and some supported privately, at least in part, resources would be freed which might be used to give more generous help to those remaining on the rolls, might be used to help some poor persons not now on the rolls, or to lower the burden on taxpayers, or some combination of all of these desirable actions.

Notes

1. Comments on an earlier draft from Paul Vernier, Peter G. Brown, Conrad Johnson, Harriet Presser, Sandra Tangri, and Paul Wonnacott were helpful.

2. For documentation, see E. O. Wilson, *Sociobiology, The New Synthesis* (Cambridge: Harvard University Press, 1975).

3. For data on trends in men's and women's earnings and productivity, see the *Statistical Abstract of the United States*, 1975.

4. *Current Population Reports*, "Money Income in 1976 of Families and Persons in the U.S.". U.S. Bureau of the Census, series P-60, No. 114. July 1978

5. See B. L. Johnson, "Women Who Head Families, 1970–77: Their Numbers Rose, Income Lagged," *Monthly Labor Review*, February, 1978, pp. 32–37.

6. See C. Vickery. "The Time-Poor: A New Look at Poverty," *Journal of Human Resources* 12, no. 1 (1977): 27–48.

7. For current poverty lines, see *Current Population Reports*, U.S. Bureau of Census, Series P-60, No. 115.

8. The Census Bureau Special Study, *Divorce, Child Custody and Child Support* (Special Studies: Series P-23, No. 84, June, 1979) became available as this paper was being edited, and its information does not appear to contradict the range of estimates made in the text. More complete information will become available when results of a supplemental current population survey in April 1979 on child support and alimony become available.

9. See Johnson, "Women Who Head Families."

10. *Ibid.*

11. Data on aggregate welfare payments from *Statistical Abstracts*.

12. By subtraction.

13. *Current Population Survey*, Series P-60, No. 115.

14. See M. Gates, "Homemakers into Widows and Divorcees: Can the Law Provide Economic Protection?", in J. Chapman and M. Gates (eds.), *Women into Wives: The Legal and Economic Impact of Marriage* (Beverly Hills: Sage Publications, 1977). Also see J. Cassetty, *Child Support and Public Policy* (Lexington: Lexington Books, 1977).

15. For accounts of the economic and social plight of divorced and separated women see the following: R. Bradwein, C. Brown, and E. Fox, "Women and Children Last: The Social Situation of Divorced Mothers and their Families", *Journal of Marriage and the Family*, August 1974, pp. 498–514. L. Shaw, "Economic Consequences of Marital Disruption for Women in their Middle Years." Center for Human Resource Research, Ohio State University, June, 1978. K. Bradbury, S. Danziger, E. Smolensky, and P. Smolensky, "Public Assistance, Female Headship and Economic Well-Being," Institute for Research on Poverty, Discussion Paper, pp. 536–578. S. Bould, "Female Headed Families: Personal Fate and the Provider Role," *Journal of Marriage and the Family*, May 1977, pp. 339–349.

16. For a technical discussion of this issue, see *Child Support and the Work Bonus*, Hearing before the Committee on Finance, U.S. Senate, September 25, 1973, pp. 275–282.

17. See I.V. Sawhill, "Developing New Normative Standards for Child Support and Alimony Payments" (Washington: The Urban Institute, 1977.)

18. See Cassetty, Ch. 4.

19. *Ibid.*, p. 122.

20. See Cassetty, p. 103.

21. Such a system is also recommended by Cassetty, Chapter 6.

22. The suggestion is reported in I. Garfinckel, Testimony on Welfare Reform to Human Services Committee, Wisconsin State Senate, August 14 and 16, 1978.

PART THREE

The Question of Welfare Rights

Introduction

Closely connected to issues about the authority and proper goals of the state, and to assigning weights among competing objectives, is the question of welfare rights. If all persons in genuine need of assistance have a *right* to that assistance, then it is not only a proper goal of some other person or persons to provide that assistance; it is a mandatory goal. For example, if it is true that needy persons have a right to assistance from the government, then it is a mandatory goal for the government to provide this assistance. Such a goal would then not be a matter of discretion for the organs of government, as are such goals as, say, building a military installation in one area rather than another, or seeking a reduction of inflation via a tax cut and reduced expenditures rather than through wage and price controls. If there is a right to the assistance from the community via the government, then it is no more a matter of discretion for the government than it is a matter of discretion for a parent, within the traditional institution of the family, to give support to his or her children.

There are very few reflective persons—whatever their fundamental convictions may be—who hold that it is not good or admirable or somehow desirable that those who have plenty give to those in need. Even a libertarianism of the most strongly individualistic kind can make room for the idea that it is good, even admirable, to give to the needy. But controversy begins to develop if we add to this idea that it is *(1.)* a *duty;* and controversy becomes increasingly sharp if we add further that the needy have *(2.)* a *right* to the assistance. Let us examine each of these in turn.

(1.) That there is a duty to help those in need. It is one thing to claim that it is better to give to the needy than never to give, that it is a good thing or an admirable thing; it is quite another to claim that such giving is a duty. If giving is a duty, then not giving makes one the appropriate object of criticism, censure, and blame. Further, if giving is a duty, then a person who has a well-developed conscience will feel guilty about not giving. But if giving is no duty at all, then one who fails to give is not the appropriate object of such external sanctions as criticism and censure, and such a person has no reason to feel guilty in the privacy of conscience. This is clearly a substantive difference. It is likely to be a difference with significant practical consequences, too, if we think of morality as a code to be taught and reinforced in various ways. For to teach that giving is not only desirable but a duty, that one is properly subject to criticism and the pangs of guilt feelings upon failing to give, is likely to have an important effect, for good or bad, not only on the extent to which people help one

another, but on the ways in which they tend to regard one another. Many hold that it is a duty to help others, especially those in need. But the existence of such a duty of benevolence does not by itself imply that anyone has a *right* to assistance from anyone else or from the community as a collective entity. To claim this involves taking an additional and more controversial step, one that some have been unwilling to take.

(2.) *That those in need have a right to assistance.* Both philosophers and jurists have often made a distinction between duties of *perfect* obligation and those of *imperfect* obligation. The main idea usually is that the former, though not the latter, are linked to some person's *right*. For example, if you and I have reached an agreement that I am to pay you a specified sum of money in return for one hundred pounds of potatoes, then on delivery of the potatoes you have a right to that specific amount of money from me. Your right is against me alone, and not against some stranger who happens to be in the vicinity and to have that amount of money. And your right is to that specific amount and not a bit more. If I decide, out of generosity, to give you more, that might well be a good thing, but it is not part of my duty to you. There are also duties of imperfect obligation. Those who resist the idea that anyone has a right to anyone else's help, but who nevertheless believe that giving to others is a duty, sometimes cite the duty to be benevolent as an example of a duty of imperfect obligation. On this view, we have a duty to help others, but we have great latitude in choosing the times, circumstances, and objects of our benevolence. (However, anyone who *consistently* fails to give under *any* circumstances has not lived up to the duty of benevolence.) Using this general line of thought one might argue that no one, however needy, really has a right to the help of others, though everyone has a general duty to be helpful.

If assistance to those in need is solely a matter of individual charity, then the idea that benevolence is a duty only of *im*perfect obligation seems to be on fairly solid footing. Except for those situations in which it is perfectly clear that a person in dire need can only be helped by a specific individual who in turn could give the help without bearing an enormous risk or cost (e.g., an adult near a baby who is drowning in shallow water), it would probably be chaotic, and would multiply acrimony and criticism, to have a social system in which every person in need had a right against each and every person who could help. The costs of conforming to, and enforcing, such a moral (to say nothing of legal) code would be enormous.

But it is a fact that, today at any rate, much of the support given to those in need either is or can be institutionalized as one of the functions of the state. This fact cuts in opposite directions, depending on one's fundamental philosophical convictions. For those who think it of fundamental importance either that the least-advantaged be provided with basic needs or that inequalities of income generally ought to be reduced, the existence of institutions making these goals possible is an opportunity that in justice ought to be seized. For those who think either that the state already exceeds its moral authority or that to strengthen it further is dangerous, the idea that individual needy persons have a right against the community, via the state, is an idea especially to be resisted.

The four papers in this section touch on these and other matters about rights and explore some issues in some detail. Paul Vernier's paper gives an introduction to the notion of a right as it applies in the area of welfare policy. Vernier's discussion shows some of the ways in which the notion of a right to some level of well-being has gained currency in recent years, and he attempts as well to link the idea of a right to welfare to particular conceptions of levels of well-being.

Allen Buchanan's paper has as its strategy to show libertarians (and others who agree with libertarians that there are rights of the kind Buchanan lists) that they are at least implicitly committed to welfare rights as well. Buchanan holds that such rights as the right to participate in political processes, the right to freedom of expression, and the right to the benefits of the legal system, are rights from which one can derive a right to welfare, and that this is a right against the government primarily, though derivatively against the citizens living under that government.

Baruch Brody's paper defends the claim that while those who are in need have a right to collective assistance, society has a collective right, and indeed a duty, to impose work requirements in return for welfare benefits. He defends work requirements in a large setting of a philosophical theory about property and the just distribution of wealth. Brody holds that those who are in need have a right to certain benefits due them as rent paid by the more affluent for the use of natural resources, but that the receivers of the rent who are able to work may be required to do so in order to conserve resources for others who are unable to work.

A. I. Melden, in his paper, takes the position that there are no moral rights to welfare. At the same time, he holds that we ought to act generously toward others. Melden's position is closely akin to holding that we have a general duty to be benevolent, but that no one has a right to that benevolence. In staking out his position, Melden provides what he takes to be the contours of the concept of a right, particularly a moral right.

CJ

11

Rights to Welfare as an Issue in Income Support Policy

PAUL VERNIER

The rights of those who need or depend upon welfare benefits have been the subject of intense interest among social philosophers in recent years. It is also a subject of substantial importance in any consideration of conceptual and moral issues in welfare policy today.

Philosophic discussions of welfare rights, generally speaking, are more concerned with questions of broad moral principle than with concrete policy issues in the field of welfare per se. This is no criticism of social philosophy, of course, since elucidation of the principles of social morality is what one needs and wants from social philosophers. At the same time, there are urgent policy questions for welfare planners and decision makers that bear on the subject of rights as discussed by philosophers, jurists, and political scientists. A general lack of connection between welfare policy planning and scholarly discussion of rights has served, I believe, to limit the potential contribution of scholars to policy formulation to the general detriment of welfare programs.

My purpose in this paper is to try to draw together the subject matter of these two fields in such a way that the work being done by rights theorists might have a more direct impact on policy considerations than has so far been the case. To that end, my discussion will be largely expository, and I shall not be arguing for or against any particular moral or political theses. I want to show, in a general way, how the question of rights is linked with welfare policy, and why it is an important subject for decision makers in this field. I shall begin by offering a brief characterization of the concept of a right in general and of the particular features of a right to income support. Next, I shall offer a short historical background concerning rights and welfare policy, to be followed by a more intensive examination of the ways in which welfare rights are most likely to influence and condition welfare policy decisions.

I

We live in an age in which questions about people's rights rise quickly out of the welter of public issues to receive public attention. What is it, however, to have a right to something? What is meant when the rights of some group, such as racial minorities and women, are invoked? Social philosophers, jurists, and political scientists have written at length on the answers to these questions, and several basic conceptions appear to be generally agreed upon in what has been written.[1] I shall make use of them in the characterization of rights with which my discussion begins.

The assertion that a person has a right to something embodies three distinct, but closely related, ideas. First, to have a right is to have a claim of a special kind to possess, or do, or be something. The claim is one of entitlement to the object of the right without having to secure the permission or consent of anyone else. Second, having a right to something implies, in most instances, a corresponding obligation or duty upon some other person, group, or institution. The object of a right cannot arbitrarily be withheld or denied to the right-holder by those upon whom such a duty is imposed. Third, both a right and its correlated duty are sanctioned by a governing set of rules or principles which are binding on those involved.[2]

To invoke an individual's rights, therefore, is to make the following claim: that he or she is entitled to possess or enjoy something (e.g., choice of religious worship) in accordance with some set of valid rules or principles, and that some organization or other individual is obligated under the same rules to satisfy that entitlement. If there is a right to welfare, therefore, some set of individuals is entitled to the benefits of welfare, yet to be described, as a claim against others, in accordance with some set of valid rules. These governing rules may belong either to the realm of law or to that of moral principle. Sometimes they fall in both realms. For example, the Declaration of Independence calls for liberty as a moral right, and the Bill of Rights of the U. S. Constitution guarantees us certain specific liberties, such as freedom of speech.

While this distinction is generally familiar to professional groups such as lawyers, philosophers, and political scientists, it may not be as well known to the wider public engaged in the debate about welfare reform. It is of central importance in this debate, however, because certain welfare rights are already contained in law, while others are claimable solely on grounds of moral principle. Unless the distinction is kept clearly in mind, and we know which of the rights under discussion are legally sanctioned and which are not, our debates on this subject will not be well informed.

Another distinction needs to be kept in mind: whether a right is to non-interference in one's activities or is, on the other hand, a right to receive something. It is important because traditionally we have been concerned mainly with rights to non-interference, such as those guaranteed in the Bill of Rights of the U. S. Constitution. Articulation of rights to receive something, for example, a minimum standard of living, educational opportunities, and medical care, is a more recent development. For this reason, the notion that there are rights to welfare is not as familiar as the notion of forbearance rights.[3]

Rights are seldom absolutely enforceable in every situation. In specific circumstances, they can often legitimately be overridden. In Oliver Wendell Holmes's famous example, the right of free speech does not extend to shouting "Fire!" in a crowded theater. If there is a moral right to income support, there are clearly circumstances in which it cannot be honored. For example, in time of famine, there may be no resources for responding to need. From the viewpoint of welfare policy, the recognition of a welfare right thus entails the further question of the circumstances in which it can be validly overridden.[4]

There is a great deal more that one might say about the nature and scope of rights.[5] However, for purposes of an introduction to the subject of welfare rights, the points I have made seem to be the important ones. To summarize briefly, a distinction needs to be made between moral rights and legal rights in considering rights to welfare. A further distinction between forbearance rights, like the right to privacy, and positive social and economic rights is likewise important. And finally, the question of circumstances in which rights can be legitimately overridden must be taken account of. I turn now to a brief characterization of welfare rights, and specifically of rights to income support.

What is meant by a right to income support? Based on the preceding discussion of rights in general, I want to offer a particular construal which links the notion of such a right directly to practical policy issues concerning eligibility for aid and levels of payment to be provided by an income support program. According to this construal, a right to income support is the right to the economic resources needed to bridge any existing gap between an individual's own resources and those required to achieve some agreed-upon standard of living. The central concept here is that of a deficit between standardized need and an individual's resources. If there is a right to income support, it is the right to exist at some level or standard of living. Those who have the correlative duty are obligated to supply what is needed to fill the gap between that level and any individual's own resources. Presumably, everyone has such a right, but it actually accrues for any individual only when his income falls below the established level.

The crucial factor in determining income support rights, if this construal is accepted, is the standard to be used in determining when someone's right accrues, and what his benefits should be. Such a standard can vary from one of meager survival to a much higher level of well-being and opportunity for realization of individual potentialities. In Section III I shall examine this range of possibilities in some detail. Understood in this way, it should be noted, a right to income support is equivalent to a right to a minimum standard of living or income "floor" for everyone, fixed at whatever standard is decided upon. This follows from the circumstance that the right to income support would accrue for an individual if and when his or her resources fall below the level of expenditure which has been set. The amount of the entitlement would be the amount required to enable each individual to enjoy the established standard.

Although this account concerns only income support, the same formula can be extended, I think, with suitable modifications, to other welfare services, such as medical care and day care for children. There are, of course, other ways of defining a welfare benefit right, such that income testing is not the crucial factor. For example, the family allowance system, which is not based on need, might also be used to generate a definition of a welfare right. One advantage of my definition is that it fits current welfare reform proposals, which are income-tested in basic structure.

II

Before going further into the content of a right to income support, let us look for a moment at the historical record on this subject. To what extent and in what ways has the rights issue in welfare been a subject of debate and legislative enactment in earlier periods? Is it a long-time issue, or one of recent emergence? And how far has the concept of a welfare right been implemented in our welfare programs up to now?

According to a well-informed writer on this subject, A. D. Smith, writing in the *Harvard Law Review* in 1949, "historically and traditionally . . . there was no legal right to public assistance."[6] A major obstacle to its legal recognition, he says, was the firm conviction of many people that the claim to subsistence is "a claim to what can only be a gratuity." Aid to those in need, according to this view, can never escape its origin as a "charitable benefaction." Changes in the economy of the nation in the last century, according to Smith, led to the possibility of a different view about the relation of individuals and the economic mechanisms of society than the highly individualistic one of earlier times. The newer outlook made possible the passage in 1935 of the Social Security Act, with its emphasis on providing economic security through social insurance. Part of the Social Security Act was the enactment of public assistance for special groups of needy people—dependent children, the aged, and the blind.

A major purpose of the Act, and hence of the public assistance titles of the Act, according to Smith, was to "give enforceable legal rights of participation." These rights were brought into existence by requiring an opportunity for a fair hearing for dissatisfied applicants and recipients. How far did this take us along the road to the establishment of legal rights

to income support? Those special groups who qualify under these programs do have legal entitlements to assistance, as Smith holds. This was
confirmed in an opinion of the Supreme Court in *Goldberg v. Kelly* in 1970:
"Such benefits [i.e., AFDC] are a matter of statutory entitlement for
persons qualified to receive them."[7] The courts have also, in recent years,
articulated certain rights of welfare recipients to due process and equal
protection under the law, as illustrated by the ruling in *Goldberg v. Kelly*
that recipients whose assistance is being stopped and who have appealed
are to remain on the rolls pending the hearing decision.[8]

These are all steps in a cumulative recognition of rights of welfare
recipients, but they do not add up to a general right to benefits for those
unable to support themselves. In the first place, these programs are based
upon statutes that can be amended or discontinued by legislative act.
Moreover, persons eligible for the programs that provide entitlements are
a limited class of those who are poor (i.e., families with dependent
children, the aged, blind, and disabled).

Several related developments, since the passage of the Social Security
Act, are also of some interest and importance in the field of welfare rights.
These are expressions of policy and opinion outside the legislative and
judicial context. First, President Roosevelt's famous declaration during
World War II of the "Four Freedoms" included the right to freedom from
want. Next, the Universal Declaration of Human Rights of the United
Nations was adopted in 1948 and includes the right to a minimum
standard of living. Even though this is an international declaration that the
United States has not ratified, it has frequently been cited by writers on
welfare rights (e.g., by Wayne Vasey in a paper entitled "Social Welfare
as a Human Right"[9]). A few years ago, the national association of welfare
recipients adopted as its name the "National Welfare Rights Organization." And recently, Secretary of State Cyrus Vance stated as United
States policy that "There is the right to the fulfillment of such vital needs
as food, shelter, health care, and education."[10]

These instances do not, it is true, add up to a major groundswell. Yet it
is fair to say that they reflect something more than a random, unrelated set
of occurrences. They express a point of view about rights of the poor
which would not have been found prior to the 1930s.

III

The issue of rights to income support, as we have already observed, is
closely connected with the designation as a matter of policy of some
standard or level to which entitlement applies. This is true whether we are
speaking of moral or legal rights. In the discussion of this subject which
follows, the close link that exists between abstract questions of rights and
programmatic requirements of policy determination comes clearly to
view.

It makes a great deal of difference whether we are talking about rights to a level of bare survival or to a level which permits a mode of life exceeding survival. This relativization to some specific level of existence is required for two reasons. First, it is only by such means that we are able to identify the content of what a person may have a right to. Second, the grounds for asserting moral rights to welfare are not the same for different levels. For example, one possible argument for rights at the level of survival is that such rights are part of what we mean by the right to life. That is to say, if there is a right to life, as the Declaration of Independence asserts, one possible argument for support at the survival level is that such support is part of what we mean by the right to life because it may be required for remaining alive. However, if the asserted right is to some level of existence beyond mere survival, the argument from the right to life is no longer sufficient taken by itself. Other arguments will be needed, e.g., that everyone ought to have equal access to what he needs to successfully pursue his life interests, including a reasonably adequate level of economic goods. Moreover, the arguments for rights at one level of benefits might be significantly more persuasive than those at another. It is also possible that rights might be strongly justified at one level, but that there are other powerful motivations, such as achievement of certain social ideals, for providing support, without reference to rights, at some higher level.[11]

Standards of living relevant to income support policies can be viewed as constituting a continuum along a dimension extending from the barest level of survival upward. Points along the continuum, however, must be selected in order to focus discussion. A number of possibilities are presented. For example, Benn and Peters, in *The Principles of Political Thought*,[12] offer a threefold set of levels as follows: *(1.)* the biological level, which defines the requirements for simple survival; *(2.)* the level of basic needs, which are those that must be satisfied for enjoying what the authors call a "decent sort of life" at any particular time and place; and *(3.)* the level of functional needs, defined by those requirements that a person must satisfy as a condition of performing his or her particular job or task in the community. A virtue of this classification is that it gives us a hold on some important stages along the continuum of individual and family needs. I shall offer a somewhat different, two-level classification, however, partly because it appears to be more directly relevant to welfare policy considerations, and also because the kinds of arguments that can be made in support of welfare rights may, I think, relate somewhat more directly to these levels than to others. The two levels or standards are *(1.)* a level of subsistence, which differs in an important way from Benn and Peters's biological level; and *(2.)* a level of minimal well-being. Both levels are broadly characterized in the discussion that follows.

THE LEVEL OF SUBSISTENCE

Subsistence, as I shall understand it, is a level of minimum economic security which encompasses the elements of biological survival, but goes beyond them. This level of subsistence, taken from an analysis of subsistence needs by Henry Shue,[13] provides the economic means to live a healthy and active life of more or less normal duration. This level exceeds that of bare biological needs in specifying certain positive conditions of health and activity as well as introducing a durational component. Survival, as a concept of living, implies more a day-to-day meeting of primitive needs without explicit consideration of one's state of health or longevity.

At the same time, the concept of subsistence or minimal economic security clearly does not extend to a standard that is comparable to Benn and Peters's "decent sort of life." That level not only enables an individual to subsist, but to live in a certain manner, i.e., one that is considered minimally acceptable within the community of one's abode. The notion of subsistence, while going substantially beyond survival in a biological sense, is nevertheless not to be identified with any particular manner of life. Subsistence needs would be met, for instance, by one's having warm clothing and shelter in winter even though these might be quite different from one's neighbor's clothing and shelter, and of a less desirable character by accepted community standards.

THE LEVEL OF MINIMAL WELL-BEING

Achievement of the level of subsistence just described is a necessary condition for the continuation of life in any sense but that of mere survival. It is by no means sufficient, however, for the level I shall call "minimal well-being." Achievement of this level requires not only economic security on the subsistence level, but also a set of opportunities for living in a more comprehensive sense. Three such opportunities are essential to this conception of well-being. One is that of being able to have what Benn and Peters call a "decent sort of life," that is, of living in accordance with what is minimally acceptable in one's community so that one is not looked upon as different or outside the established patterns of community life. Second, at this level an individual can participate in the general range of ordinary community activities such as church-going, modest entertaining of one's friends, and taking part in political and community affairs. Third, one can achieve a sense of one's value as a human being, and enjoy some confidence in the ability to plan one's life and fulfill these plans.[14] A life which meets these specifications would, I suggest, be regarded by most Americans as meeting a test of minimal adequacy. More important, a life which did not provide such opportunities would be considered seriously deficient.

It would perhaps be more accurate to designate this level as one of opportunity to achieve minimal well-being, since the actual achievement would depend on a complex set of factors which extend beyond economic and educational resources to their utilization by each individual. The level of economic support which is linked with minimal well-being, as I have characterized it, is an enabling instrumentality, rather than constitutive of that condition in its full sense.

The characterization I have offered here is extremely general, and requires further elaboration in several directions. For example, circumstances under which well-being in this sense can be achieved differ markedly for different groups of people. Children and the elderly have clearly diverse prospects in life, and the kinds of opportunities needed by children as they are growing up are not those of their grandparents. Other distinctions apply to breadwinners in contrast with family members who are not in the job market. Despite its generality, however, and taking account of the need to relativize it to different groups of individuals, the central notions of minimal well-being as a level of existence, as I have described it, can be grasped from this delineation.

What level of resources is needed for the achievement of minimal well-being? Stated in terms of an income support program, what would have to be provided to an individual who lacks resources of his or her own? A specification of the needed goods and services is far beyond the scope of this paper. In general, however, it seems clear that food, shelter, and clothing within standards accepted by one's community are needed. The ability to utilize educational and health resources, insofar as they are available generally, and the requirements for holding employment (e.g., work clothing, transportation) are further necessities. This listing is only illustrative. A full listing would add further similar items. If there is a right to income support at the level of minimal well-being, as I have described it, such a right is to the goods and services noted above.

THE OFFICIAL POVERTY LINE

In 1969, the federal government adopted an "official" poverty line or threshold as a measure of economic insufficiency.[15] In the past decade, this poverty threshold expressed in dollar amounts has been in general use as a base for establishing levels of income support in proposed welfare programs. For example, the payment level in a given proposal may be computed at 75 percent of the poverty threshold. Because this quantified measure of economic need plays such an important role in contemporary policy formulation, we should take time to look into its relation to the various living standards I have been discussing in conceptual terms. One point of interest comes to light at once: Although the poverty line is expressed in dollar figures based on empirical research into what people are thought to need for food and other requirements for living, its use in policy formulation is normative and reflects moral judgments regarding the level of existence which a support program should sustain. When we have located the poverty line, as well as we can, at a point along our continuum of living standards, we shall observe that it designates a conceptual standard which calls for moral justification as the standard selected for purposes of setting payment levels. From the viewpoint of rights to income support, the poverty line either implies a description of what people have a right to, or else it is not to be construed as descriptive of such rights. If the former, it requires moral argument to justify its selection. If the latter, its selection conflicts with people's rights, if there are such rights.

The concepts and premises that lie behind the poverty line computation are complex and, in some respects, highly controversial. We need not enter into these difficulties here, however, since our interest is only in the question of where the official poverty line falls along the continuum of possible standards of living. The primary component of the official poverty line is the economy food diet issued by the Department of Agriculture. This is described as minimally adequate for nutrition, although not for long-time use. The first step in the computation is to price this diet for families of differing composition. The second step is to use this dollar cost for food as the basis for computing the total cost of all items of living expenses. This is done by multiplying food costs by a certain factor (for a family of three or more, the factor is three). This formula is based on empirical studies of actual expenditure patterns of American families concerning the proportion of expenditures for living expenses that goes for the purchase of food. The poverty line is the dollar figure obtained by carrying out this computation.

Because the method of computing non-food costs gives no clue as to what can be purchased, we cannot place the poverty line on our standard of living continuum with too much precision. However, the use of a minimally adequate diet as the basic component gives us some grounds for the view that it should be considered roughly comparable to the level of subsistence which I described above. There seems no reason to place it higher on the continuum, and possibly it should be placed somewhat lower, because the Department of Agriculture has recommended that diet only for temporary use.

IV

What can be said, now, about the impact of the rights issue on the actual formulation of income support policy? First, I think it is clear that in setting policy, the central issue is that of moral rights to income support rather than legal rights. Whatever legal rights are secured for recipients in law, they are the outcome of political decisions already made, and their implementation is a technical problem. From the policy planning viewpoint, therefore, the important concern is with moral rights. Moral rights, in the context of legislative planning, are expressions of what ought to be the case in law. They are moral directives to legislators. If moral rights are recognized and accepted as valid, it follows that one responsibility of decision makers is to identify the nature of these rights and the conditions under which they accrue. Based on this identification, decision makers would then seem to have an obligation to make policy decisions that reflect these results. If these rights are denied validity, on the other hand, another set of motivations for providing income support would be determining.

Even if the validity of moral rights to income support were accepted by policymakers, of course, there are other motivations which are present and will play an important role. The difference made by non-recognition of the validity of moral rights is that, in this case, the other motivations would stand alone. The role of rights in policy formulation is not to displace these other motivations entirely, but to serve as one important factor in the process.

Let us look for a moment at some of these other motivations to the provision of income support. We cannot discuss them in any detail in the present setting, but several may be identified. Humanitarian concern for those in need is one motivation. A second is the desire to provide greater equality of opportunity. Another is concern for the well-being of the community at large. That is, poverty, with its associated crime and ill health, is seen as a pathological condition affecting the entire community and therefore needing to be controlled. A fourth motive is desire for social stability and security from possible social disruptions.

Whatever motivations are operative in policy formulation, they will each have some effects on program policies. If one of these motives is an acceptance of some set of moral welfare rights, then policies will, to this extent, reflect the views of policymakers regarding the substance of these rights, who has them, and the conditions under which they would become effective. These views about rights will not be the only motivating factors at work, but they should give important direction to the kinds and levels of benefits provided, the groups of individuals who are to be eligible, and the limitations to be imposed on eligibility. For these reasons, the question of whether there are rights needs to have attention in this project on moral issues in welfare reform.

V

To conclude this survey of the nature and ramifications of welfare rights in the field of income support policy, I want to raise four questions which require consideration in deciding whether or not there are moral rights to income support, and to whom they apply. First, how can it be shown that there are moral rights to income support? We can verify the existence of legal rights by consulting the actual laws of a society. We cannot, however, find a similar empirical basis for showing that there are moral rights unless we resort to polling public opinion. Except for ethical relativists, however, philosophers have not found this kind of test persuasive. Another approach to showing that we have such rights is that of John Locke and other natural-law theorists, who attempted to find the ground for moral rights in purported laws of nature; but this line of justification has not proved convincing. One task of the advocate of moral rights, therefore, is to formulate persuasive arguments to justify them. This is a task to which social philosophers in recent years have devoted considerable time and effort.

The second question concerns the identification of the persons or organizations having the duty or obligation correlative to a moral right to income support. A necessary condition for the ascription of a right to someone is that we can point to someone else who has the correlative duty. In the absence of an agent so obligated, ascription of the right is empty. It is not easy to identify the holder of the obligation that is correlated with a moral right to income support. If no government authority now has legal responsibility for providing assistance to some class of needy people, who is obligated? Professor Brandt has asserted that if an individual is in dire need and we are the only ones in a position to help, then we have a moral obligation to do so. But in a larger sense, as Brandt also recognizes, we are not each individually responsible for helping everyone who is in need, even though we may have a duty to help some individuals. Where, then, does the obligation rest?[17]

Third, there are potentially serious problems of resource allocation to be met. If there is a right to income support at some accepted living standard, the simple obligation is to provide the funds needed to finance a program which meets all such needs of those whose resources fall below the minimum level. In times of affluence, this may not be a source of problems, but when resources are limited in respect to demands for services which may have comparable priority (e.g., education, police protection), difficult moral issues of allocation are raised. The proponent of welfare rights must have answers to these challenges as a part of a comprehensive and persuasive account of such rights.

Fourth and last of the questions requiring consideration if moral rights to income support are claimed is that of defining the obligations of the right-holders themselves. A frequent response to the assertion of a right to income support is to say that what is really important is the obligation of the needy individual to take care of his or her own needs. It is the general wisdom that an individual should work to support himself or herself if able to do so and if there is a job available. If someone simply wants to live a life of leisure or finds work distasteful, would he or she have any assertable right to support? I take it, from the viewpoint of formulating policy, that the problem is not whether recipients of support have responsibilities as well as putative rights, but what these responsibilities are. The responsibilities can, in theory, range from almost nothing at all to requirements that are recognizably extreme, like requiring a mother of several children to submit to sterilization as a condition of eligibility. There are serious moral issues to be faced in determining what these conditions should be and the advocate of income support rights must provide some answer to them as part of the characterization of the right.

These are all difficult questions, but they are not, I believe, unanswerable. One task for social philosophers is to identify and consider the possible answers to these and questions like them across the spectrum of moral issues in welfare policy.[18]

Notes

1. See Joel Feinberg, *Social Philosophy* (Englewood Cliffs, N.J.: Prentice-Hall, Inc., 1973), ch. 4 and 6, for a comprehensive discussion of characteristics and types of rights.

2. "To have a right is to have a claim against someone whose recognition as valid is called for by some set of governing rules or moral principles." Joel Feinberg, "The Nature and Importance of Rights," *Journal of Value Inquiry*, Winter 1970.

3. Although this distinction is important to a clear understanding of the issues under debate, it also needs to be kept in mind that positive government action is equally required to ensure the enjoyment of both kinds of rights. This point has been forcefully argued by Henry Shue in *Basic Rights: Subsistence, Affluence, and U.S. Foreign Policy* (Princeton: Princeton University Press, 1980), ch. 1 and 2.

4. Rights that can be set aside in certain circumstances have been characterized by some philosophers as "prima facie" rights. Gregory Vlastos has adopted this characterization in "Justice and Equality," *Social Justice*, ed. Richard B. Brandt (Englewood Cliffs, N.J.: Prentice-Hall, Inc., 1962). A. I. Melden, however, rejects this account, holding that it incorrectly undermines the authoritative status of a warranted right. Cf. *Rights and Persons* (Berkeley: University of California Press, 1977).

5. In addition to the volumes by Feinberg, Brandt, and Melden already cited which deal with rights, see also A. I. Melden, ed., *Human Rights* (Belmont, CA: Wadsworth Publishing Co., 1970).

6. A. D. Smith, "Public Assistance as a Social Obligation," *Harvard Law Review*, V. 63, 1949.

7. *Goldberg v. Kelly*, 397 U. S. 254 (1970).

8. Other Supreme Court decisions which have reinforced the rights of welfare recipients to equal protection and due process include *King v. Smith*, 392 U. S. 309 (1968); *Shapiro v. Thompson*, 394 U. S. 618 (1967); *Weaver v. Doe*, 404 U. S. 987 (1971); and *Wheeler v. Montgomery*, 397 U. S. 280 (1970).

9. Wayne Vasey, "Social Welfare as a Human Right," *Social Values*, ed. Katherine A. Kendall (New York: Council on Social Work Education, 1970).

10. Cyrus R. Vance, "Human Rights Policy" (Washington: Office of Media Services, Bureau of Public Affairs, Department of State, April 30, 1977).

11. Recognition of this need to formulate distinct arguments in support of welfare rights at different levels of economic and social adequacy is to be found in contemporary social philosophy. As examples, see Frederick Rosen, "Basic Needs and Justice," *Mind*, January 1977; S. I. Benn and R. S. Peters, *The Principles of Political Thought* (New York: The Free Press, 1965), ch. 6; Hugo Bedau, "The Right to Life," *The Monist*, October 1968; and Henry Shue, *Basic Rights*.

12. S. I. Benn and R. S. Peters, *The Principles of Political Thought* (New York: The Free Press, 1965), ch. 6.

13. According to Shue's account, subsistence is equivalent to "minimal economic security," by which he means, "unpolluted air, unpolluted water, adequate food, adequate clothing, adequate shelter, and minimal preventive health care." The basic idea, he says, is to have "available for consumption what is needed for a decent chance at a reasonably healthy and active life of more or less normal length. . . ." Henry Shue, p. 23.

14. In *A Theory of Justice* (Cambridge, MA: Harvard University Press, 1971), John Rawls identifies these conditions as necessary for achievement of what he terms "self-respect." (See p. 440.)

15. See Mollie Orshansky, "Counting the Poor: Another Look at the Poverty Profile," *Social Security Bulletin*, v. 28 (1965).

16. See Frank I. Michelman, "In Pursuit of Constitutional Welfare Rights: One View of Rawls's Theory of Justice," *University of Pennsylvania Law Review*, May 1973, for a comprehensive consideration of the question of whether there are constitutional rights to income support.

17. Richard B. Brandt, *Ethical Theory* (Englewood Cliffs: Prentice-Hall, Inc., 1959), p.

439. One possible answer to the question of who is obligated to respond to welfare needs is the following: Although we cannot individually be held responsible, except in very special circumstances, we are jointly members of a society which has certain public and private institutions in which we participate. Our obligations, on this view, are to be met through these institutions (e.g., the public welfare departments of government).

18. This paper has benefitted substantially from criticisms and suggestions made by Peter G. Brown, Conrad Johnson, Douglas MacLean, and Henry Shue.

12

Deriving Welfare Rights From Libertarian Rights

ALLEN BUCHANAN

I

The aim of this essay is to examine and support the thesis that certain welfare rights can be derived from certain widely accepted libertarian rights.* The libertarian rights in question are (*1.*) the right to freedom of expression and (*2.*) the right to the benefits of the legal system. The right to freedom of expression is the right to communicate through various media and is not restricted to speech in the narrow sense. The right to the benefits of the legal system consists of a cluster of due process rights, the right to legal counsel, and the right to legal representation. Both the right to freedom of expression and the right to the benefits of the legal system are to be understood as *negative* rights—rights not to be interfered with in certain ways as one engages in certain activities. My right to freedom of expression, thus conceived as a negative right, is a right not to be interfered with by violence or the threat of violence, as I engage in certain communicative activities. As a negative right, my right to freedom of expression is *not* a right not to have my communicative activity limited in *any* way whatsoever. For example, if I somehow gain access to a broadcast microphone without paying for air-time, you, the owner of the network, may cut off the power. In such a case you would be interfering with my communicative activity, but not in a way which violates my right to freedom of expression. Similarly, my right to the benefits of the legal system is only a right against certain sorts of interferences —it is not itself a positive right to be provided with legal services.

The point of calling these negative rights "libertarian rights" is to

233

emphasize that they are held to be genuine rights by libertarians. By "libertarians" I mean those who hold that the only morally justifiable state is one whose functions are limited to the enforcement of voluntary contracts, and to protecting citizens against bodily injury, theft, and fraud. Libertarians contend that any state which exceeds these minimal functions violates individuals' moral rights. According to libertarians such as Robert Nozick,[1] there are no welfare rights and any state which engages in welfare functions is illegitimate.

The libertarian view on rights of political participation is rather complex. Clearly, libertarians reject unlimited majority rule, since it would violate libertarian rights—for example, the right to property. But some variants of libertarian theory can include a right to run for office and to vote in elections to determine who shall be the officers of the minimal state. In what follows I will be concerned with the relation between (1.) the right to freedom of expression, (2.) the right to the benefits of the legal system, and (3.) the right of political participation, on the one hand, and welfare rights, on the other. Whether or not the right to political participation, like the other two rights, is a *libertarian* right is of little importance to my argument. For the sake of brevity I shall usually use the phrase "libertarian rights" to refer to all three, but the reader is invited to restrict its application to the right to freedom of expression and the right to legal benefits if he thinks this is fairer to the libertarian. My point in calling the right of political participation a libertarian right is to emphasize that it, too, is a negative right.

The point of saying that there are *rights* to freedom of expression, to legal benefits, and to political participation is complex. There are four basic elements in the concept of a right as I understand it here. First, a person who has a right to something has a *valid claim* to it—he is *entitled* to it. He may demand it as his due, rather than merely request it as something beneficial. Second, the fact that a person has a right to something implies a *corresponding obligation* on the part of others. Third, claims of right *take precedence over considerations of utility maximization.*[2] Fourth, rights are *enforceable*—coercion may be used to protect rights where other methods are inadequate.[3] The libertarian or minimal state theorist, as well as most of the rest of us, adds a further feature: It is the *state* which is the proper enforcer of the rights in question.

For purposes of my argument I make a further assumption: The coercively backed, state-enforced, negative rights in question are to be understood as *equal* rights. They accrue to all citizens (or at least to all competent adult citizens). The question of whether there are rights is distinct from the question of whether there are equal rights. I shall simply assume that there are equal rights to freedom of expression, to the benefits of the legal system, and to political participation, where these rights are understood to exemplify each of the features listed above. The question I shall attempt to answer can now be posed with greater precision: Granted that there are (equal) libertarian rights to freedom of expression, to the benefits of the legal system, and to political participation, where these are negative rights to be enforced by the state, are there also (equal) state-enforceable welfare rights?

Three more points must be added before the question can be fully specified. First, it is important to note that the libertarian rights are to be understood as *moral* rights, and that the question is whether they give rise to *moral* welfare rights. *Moral* rights are to be distinguished from *legal* rights, i.e., rights actually established in the positive law of a society. In this essay I am not concerned with the question of whether, granted that our legal system includes the libertarian rights, it follows that it also includes certain welfare rights. Second, I am not assuming that either the libertarian rights or the welfare rights to which they may give rise are that special sort of moral rights called *human rights*. By a "human right" I mean a moral right which accrues to all human beings simply by virtue of their being human, and hence which all human beings have regardless of the social, political, and economic circumstances in which they live. It is absurd to assume that every moral right is a human right. For example, even if there were a moral right, say, to periodic holidays with pay, or more generally, to income, this could not possibly be a human right, since not all human societies have reached a level of development at which it would even make sense to claim such rights. For one thing, not all human societies compensate labor through money. Similarly, it might be argued that the right to vote and to run for office could not be human rights since the very notion of such rights presupposes a rather complex background of social institutions not present in all human societies. Consequently, I shall make only the weaker assumptions that the libertarian rights are moral rights, and I shall argue that if there are such moral rights, there are also certain moral welfare rights.

One last term in our question requires clarification. What is meant by "*welfare* right"? A comprehensive definition may be hard to come by, but for now, illustration and rough characterization must suffice. The right to income support or the right to be provided with certain health care services or legal services are examples of welfare rights. In general, a welfare right is a right to be provided with cash or with certain material goods or services, either without charge or at a subsidized rate below their market value.

II

The importance of the thesis that welfare rights can be derived from libertarian rights now becomes apparent. Libertarians, by definition, believe that coercion may only be used to prevent or retaliate against coercion or fraud and to enforce contracts, and that consequently there are no welfare rights, though there are rights of free speech, legal benefits, and political participation. If it can be shown that welfare rights can be derived from rights which the libertarian himself recognizes, it will follow that the libertarian position is incoherent.

The attempt to derive welfare rights from libertarian rights is quite important, however, regardless of its implications for libertarianism. Whether they are libertarians or not, many who recognize the rights to free expression, to political participation, and to legal benefits reject welfare rights. The strategy of deriving welfare rights from libertarian rights, then, is a very powerful one: If it succeeds, it provides an indirect argument for welfare rights which should convince those who are unmoved by direct arguments. If successful, the derivation of welfare rights from libertarian rights has the virtue of establishing the controversial by appeal to the uncontroversial.

Further, if the indirect or derivative approach to the right to cash or goods or services succeeds, it calls into question the appropriateness of calling these rights *welfare* rights. For often a welfare right is taken to be simply a right that serves to secure or increase a person's welfare, where "welfare" is equated with the possession of material wealth. Libertarians sometimes encourage this interpretation by suggesting that welfare rights are advocated by those who view persons as passive consumers of utilities—utilities in the form of material goods and services. The libertarian then presents his defense of libertarian rights and his rejection of welfare rights as being grounded in an alternative conception of the person as a free agent. For the libertarian, increases in welfare—gains for the person as a consumer of utilities—cannot compensate for losses of freedom. It becomes tempting, then, to see the debate over the existence of welfare rights as a controversy rooted in two opposing conceptions of the person. Yet if welfare rights can be derived from libertarian rights, and if libertarian rights are rooted in the conception of the person as free, then this way of understanding the controversy over welfare rights is profoundly misleading.

III

I shall now explore one attempt to derive welfare rights from libertarian rights. It may be called the argument from fairness. The argument begins with a distinction between equal rights and equal effectiveness in the exercise of those rights.[4] Consider the right of political participation. Assume that all citizens equally possess the right to vote and to run for office, and that this right is impartially enforced by the state. Recall that this right is a coercively backed guarantee against certain sorts of interferences—interferences by violence or threat of violence. Yet even where each has an impartially enforced equal right of political participation there may be vast inequalities in the effectiveness with which different individuals can exercise their equal rights. Due to inequalities in wealth, in access to health care, and in educational opportunities, some persons are able to exercise their right of political participation much more effectively than others in pursuing their goals, whatever these goals happen to be.

Here is one example which nicely illustrates the divergence between equal rights and unequal effectiveness in their exercise for both the case of political participation rights and the right of freedom of expression. Suppose that a certain Mr. Jones is the commentator on a state-wide television news program in state X. For years Mr. Jones uses his unique position as a commentator to set out his political views. His success in becoming a Senator is due in large part to the fact that he was able to make his views widely known and to build up a large constituency years in advance of any official campaign. Even more interestingly, Jones happens to be the owner of the television station on whose news program he appears. Indeed, there is good reason to believe that Jones would not have been hired as commentator had he not been on such intimate terms with the owner. Mr. Smith, on the other hand, is an unemployed migrant worker who can't afford a television set, much less a television station. Both Jones and Smith have equal rights of political participation and freedom of expression. Yet there is an enormous inequality in the effectiveness with which the two can exercise their equal rights.

Differential access to mass media is only one of the more dramatic instances of gaping inequalities in the effectiveness of the exercise of equal rights to freedom of expression and political participation. Poor nutrition and lack of health care, compounded by the cultural deprivation and inferior public education prevalent in inner cities and many rural areas, produce millions of "citizens" who are illiterate, uninformed, and unable to communicate effectively their own interests.

Differences in wealth, educational opportunities, and access to health care also contribute to striking inequalities in the effectiveness of the equal right to the benefits of the legal system. The most cynical comment on these inequalities in the criminal law is the remark that "capital punishment" means you can avoid the punishment if you've got the capital. Leaving aside the role of poverty in the etiology of crime, there is strong evidence that poor persons who commit crimes are more likely to be prosecuted, if prosecuted are more likely to be convicted, and if convicted are more likely to get stiff sentences.[5] All of this is presumably due, at least in part, to the fact that the poor often suffer from severely restricted access to sound legal advice and able legal representation.

The disparity between equal rights and inequalities in the effectiveness with which they can be exercised is not, of course, restricted to the criminal law. In civil as well as criminal cases, those who are wealthier and better educated are better able to identify situations in which legal advice ought to be sought, better able to obtain sound legal advice, and better able to press their claims through the services of able legal representatives.

The argument from fairness can now be outlined. The system of libertarian rights has a crucial feature which the libertarian tends to overlook. The institutions which provide the libertarian rights constitute procedures by which individuals may pursue their goals and defend their interests and rights. But these procedures are inherently monopolistic: They impose severe limits on the ways and means by which an individual may pursue his goals and defend his rights and interests. The system of libertarian rights sharply restricts the ways in which a person may express his views, participate in the selection of political leaders and the resolution of public issues, and press his claims against others. The libertarian tends to view my possession of the equal rights in question strictly as a *benefit* for me. And, of course, coercively backed guarantees against violent interference with the freedoms in question are great benefits. But the price of these benefits is a system of rights which places me under serious liabilities. It is not simply that I have the *right*, for example, to protect my rights and interests through litigation: The system of legal rights precludes me from attempting to protect my rights and interests in certain other important ways. The state—even the minimal state—claims a monopoly upon enforceable adjudication, specifies the procedures through which such adjudication is to occur, and thereby puts me in an awesome condition of dependence upon these procedures.

A concrete example may be helpful. Suppose that I am a black activist. My right to free speech—if duly enforced by the authorities—enables me to pursue my goal of informing complacent liberals that the struggle for civil rights is not over. In exercising my right, however, I am required to recognize the same rights of others—including the Propaganda Minister of the Ku Klux Klan. The benefit of being able to express my views in safety comes at the price of a liability to suffer from the racial hatred which may be generated by others' exercise of this same right. The correlative of my enforced right is an enforced obligation to refrain from certain means of defending my rights and interests against attack. The system of equal rights precludes me from fighting racism in certain ways. If I have sufficient funds to secure access to effective media of communication, it may be reasonable for me to accept this liability and it may be fair for others to require me to accept it. But if illiteracy and poverty prevent me from being able to reply effectively to the Klan's racist propaganda, it may be neither reasonable nor fair. At least where certain extreme inequalities exist, compliance with the system of libertarian rights requires too much from some persons. They are unfairly expected to accept a system of procedures that significantly limits their resources for defending their rights and interests, without receiving the compensating benefits that others enjoy.

A libertarian such as Nozick might raise an important objection at this point. He would contend that the options precluded by the system of libertarian rights simply ought not to be counted as costs and that hence the question of whether they are adequately compensated for does not arise. It is true that the black activitist is precluded from using violence or threats to counteract the harmful effects of the Klan's racist propaganda. But the black activist cannot legitimately complain that he is barred from defending his rights and interests in *these* ways because his use of coercion would be morally wrong. The black activist cannot complain that he is unfairly prevented from doing that which he has no right to do.

Although this reply has a certain charming simplicity, it will not stand scrutiny. Even a libertarian like Nozick admits that prior to the establishment of the state as an effective protector of libertarian rights claiming a monopoly on the use of coercion, individuals have the moral right to protect themselves, through coercion if necessary. Consequently, the libertarian cannot block the argument from fairness by simply denying that the individual may count as costs the liabilities he incurs when the system of rights precludes him from defending himself in certain ways. The individual can be expected to relinquish his right to defend himself and forego those options only if the system of rights provides an effective set of procedures for defending his rights and interests. And the system of rights cannot perform this function where certain gross inequalities exist.

The libertarian might reply that all that fairness requires is that the loss of these options for self-defense actually be outweighed by the gain in security which the state-enforced system of libertarian rights provides. He would then contend that we are all much more secure and much better off under the minimal state than we would be were there no state. So no one can complain of unfairness, even if there are vast inequalities in the effectiveness with which different individuals can exercise their equal rights. It is true that a rich man can exercise his right to the benefits of the legal system much more effectively than a poor ghetto youth can. But even a poor ghetto youth is better off in a system that includes such a right than in one that does not. Hence, the libertarian concludes, it is not unreasonable or unfair to require the poor to accept the liabilities imposed by the system of rights.

This reply is flawed because it does not take the requirement of fairness seriously enough. The requirement of fairness might be satisfied if the only practicable alternatives were a Hobbesian state of nature or a system of unrestrained inequalities in the effectiveness of the exercise of libertarian rights. But unless the libertarian can show that these bleak alternatives are the only possibilities, fairness at least demands that we consider ways of insuring that the system of rights does not place unacceptable burdens on the poor.

The next task facing us is to see whether this sketch of the fairness argument can be developed into an argument for welfare rights. It is one thing to say that the argument supports the conclusion that certain inequalities violate a basic requirement of fairness. It is quite another to show that the argument generates a clearly formulable principle which specifies a determinate welfare right. It is yet a further step to ascertain what institutional arrangements would be needed for putting the welfare right into effect.

IV

It is tempting to conclude that the argument from fairness shows that all citizens must be able to exercise their equal libertarian rights with *equal effectiveness*. One could then argue that certain welfare arrangements are necessary to ensure equal effectiveness for the libertarian rights.

This temptation, however, must be resisted. One must not jump to the conclusion that if equal rights are desirable, then equality in the effectiveness of the exercise of rights is a reasonable goal. The argument from fairness at most makes a strong prima facie case for the conclusion that inequalities in effectiveness are unacceptable. This conclusion must be weighed against countervailing arguments which come to light as soon as we examine the goal of equal effectiveness.

The effectiveness with which an individual can exercise rights in the pursuit of his goals, or, more broadly, his conception of the good, depends upon many quite different factors. Some of these factors we have already noted: wealth, educational opportunities, and access to health care. But those who argue that equal rights require equal effectiveness in their exercise overlook the simple fact that there are other factors, including intelligence, motivation, personal qualities such as physical attractiveness and, most importantly, *the nature of one's goals*. Clearly, whether one can exercise one's right to free expression or one's right to political participation so as to achieve one's goals depends in part upon whether those goals are ambitious or modest, reasonable or unreasonable, popular or unpopular. Similarly, whether one can effectively exercise one's rights to the benefits of the legal system in the pursuit of one's ends will depend in part upon what one's ends are.

Once these other factors are recognized, it becomes clear that the demand for equal effectiveness in the exercise of rights cannot be satisfied by any welfare arrangements, no matter how radical. For even if radically egalitarian schemes for the redistribution of wealth were implemented, this would not suffice for achieving equal effectiveness, so long as individuals differ in motivation, intelligence, personal qualities, and goals. There are, unfortunately, measures which might be taken to equalize these other factors. Persons with superior motivation, intelligence, or personal qualities might be handicapped in various ways, and certain techniques of indoctrination and socialization might be used to produce homogeneity of goals.

Regardless of whether the goal of equal effectiveness is actually attainable, any serious attempt even to approximate it would require intolerable violations of individual freedom. Further, though I shall not belabor the point here, I suspect that any serious attempt to achieve *equal* effectiveness in the exercise of rights would require the abandonment of the commitment to equal rights. For example, the most effective way to insure that individuals with different goals and capacities can use their rights of political participation or their rights to legal benefits with equal effectiveness might be to accord them different rights. Those with superior capacities or more easily attainable goals would be accorded more restricted rights. If this suspicion is well founded, then the argument from equal rights to *equal* effectiveness undermines the commitment to equal rights on which it is based.

V

The argument of the preceding section shows that if a welfare right can be derived from the libertarian rights, it cannot be a right to whatever goods and services are required for equal effectiveness in the exercise of the libertarian rights. Is there a more plausible welfare rights principle which can be gotten from the fairness argument? John Rawls's Principle of Equality of Fair Opportunity presents a possibility worth exploring. This principle requires that persons with equal skill and motivation have equal chances of attaining social positions or offices, regardless of whether they are rich or poor, or come from families which occupy high or low social positions.[6]

The virtue of Rawls's principle is that it focuses on a particular goal—the attainment of a particular office or position—rather than upon the individual's goals or life plan in general. This particular restriction is not, of course, appropriate for addressing the *general* problem of inequalities in the effectiveness of the exercise of libertarian rights, because in many cases the individual is not attempting to attain any *office* or social *position* through the exercise of these rights. Yet the idea of restricting the notion of effectiveness may be crucial for deriving a welfare-rights principle which avoids the excesses of the principle of equal effectiveness discussed in the preceding section. That principle was unrestricted in the sense that it required that different individuals be able to exercise their equal rights with equal effectiveness in the pursuit of their goals in general, or more holistically, their life plans.

Examples will indicate how a restriction on the ideal of equal effectiveness might work. Suppose that Jones and Smith both desire to campaign for Congress on the platform of lowering property taxes—they are both one-issue candidates and they hold virtually identical positions on the same issue. Jones is extremely rich and well educated and is able to buy many hours of expensive media coverage to get his message across to the voters. Smith, on the other hand, is very poor, was forced to leave school at the age of fourteen to support his family, and is functionally illiterate. To conclude that equal rights of political participation are not by themselves adequate, one need not argue that Smith is unable to use his rights as effectively as Jones in the pursuit of his goals in general, whatever they happen to be. There is no need to ascertain the general goals or life plans of either Smith or Jones. We need only focus on a much more limited and manageable context of comparison. The pertinent question is whether it is fair that factors such as wealth and educational opportunities should be allowed to make such a tremendous difference in the chances which two individuals have for achieving *the same limited goal*—in this case, a successful campaign for Congress on the platform of property-tax cuts. We must ask whether, other things being equal, Jones would have a much greater prospect of winning this particular race on this particular platform if it were not for his great wealth and superior educational opportunities.

This way of approaching the issue of whether inequalities in the effectiveness of equal rights are unacceptable has two advantages over the approach which condemns all inequalities in the effectiveness with which different persons can use their rights to pursue their goals in general. First, it limits the goals with reference to which the question of effectiveness is raised. In the case at hand, we are concerned only with the very restricted goal of winning a certain election. We are not asked to gauge the effectiveness with which Jones can exercise his rights in the pursuit of his life plan and to compare this with the effectiveness with which Smith can pursue his life plan. Such ambitious comparisons are avoided by suitably restricting the scope of the notion of effective exercise. Second, we are asked to focus only on the role that certain factors, in this case wealth and educational opportunities, play in determining the effectiveness with which certain individuals can exercise their rights in the pursuit of the suitably restricted goal. We need not be concerned with every factor that may contribute to inequalities.

Similarly, to ascertain whether existing inequalities in the exercise of the right to legal benefits are unacceptable, we can again invoke a restricted notion of effectiveness and again consider actual and hypothetical cases. We may ask, for instance: other things being equal, would the defendant have been found guilty of this crime, on the basis of this evidence, if he had been able to buy the services of a skillful defense lawyer? If, on consideration of many such cases, we conclude that differences in wealth or educational opportunities or access to health care should not be allowed to make such a difference in the effectiveness with which different persons can use their rights in pursuing the same limited goals, then we can proceed to the problem of determining what sorts of institutional arrangements would be appropriate for remedying or at least ameliorating the situation. For example, the more extreme inequalities between persons such as Jones and Smith might be diminished by some combination of public campaign financing and programs for increasing educational opportunities for the poor. This way of proceeding is much less likely to commit us to the impalatable measures dictated by the much more demanding goal of ensuring that different individuals can exercise their equal rights with equal success in pursuing their life plans or goals in general, whatever they happen to be.

In the next section I will attempt a classification of the main institutional forms by which unacceptable inequalities in the effectiveness of libertarian rights might be reduced. Before exploring possible institutional arrangements, however, it would be helpful to get clearer about what exactly they are supposed to achieve. To do this, it will be helpful to review the argument so far. First, I distinguished between equal rights and inequalities in the effectiveness of the exercise of rights. Second, I argued that unrestrained inequalities in the effectiveness of the exercise of libertarian rights violate a basic requirement of fairness for institutional procedures. Third, I argued that this conclusion must be modified once it is realized that attempts to achieve (unrestricted) *equal* effectiveness would involve unacceptable restrictions on individual freedom. In the light of this third point, the fairness argument was viewed as an argument for the conclusion that inequalities in effectiveness are prima facie unfair, at least as far as they are due to differences in wealth, educational opportunities, and access to health care. Fourth, I suggested a much more restricted notion of equal effectiveness, along with a procedure for considering concrete cases of unequal effectiveness, as a way of making reasonable judgments about whether certain inequalities are in fact unacceptable.

I am not at all certain whether the argument thus far is capable of yielding any clear, crisp *principle* specifying welfare rights derivative upon libertarian rights. I am confident, however, that is has ruled out one attempt to specify the welfare right in question. A principle requiring that institutions be arranged so as to ensure that individuals can exercise their libertarian rights with equal effectiveness in pursuing their goals, whatever they may be, is wholly unacceptable.

The following principle seems to do a far better job of capturing the intuitive judgments about fairness which I appealed to in the concrete cases discussed above.

Institutions are to be arranged so as to minimize significant differences in the effectiveness with which different individuals can exercise their libertarian rights in the pursuit of the same particular goals, insofar as these differences in effectiveness depend upon differences in wealth, educational opportunities, and access to health care.

Whether this principle or something like it turns out to be plausible can best be ascertained by considering some of the ways in which it might be implemented. Our intuitions about specific institutional arrangements may be clearer and firmer than our judgments about abstract principles.

VI

There are two main types of institutional arrangements for coping with the problem of inequalities in the effectiveness of the libertarian rights. The one may be called the *particularistic* approach, the other the *global* approach. The particularistic approach focuses on the particular phenomena in which inequalities in effectiveness are manifested. For example, public funds might be provided for political activities, for access to media, and for legal services, so as to diminish the influence of private wealth. A global approach, in contrast, would attempt to minimize inequalities in effectiveness by ensuring some minimum standard of living for all.

The distinction between global and particularistic approaches cuts across the familiar distinction between universal and needs-tested welfare programs. Public funding for political activities or for access to media might be provided to those who qualify for it by falling below some minimum income level, or a fixed sum of cash might be given to everyone, regardless of income level, in the manner of a "demogrant." Neither of these methods, however, would be effective by itself, since those with great wealth might still be at a great advantage. Measures for providing the wherewithal to the poor would presumably have to be combined with measures to limit the amounts that the rich may spend on political activities.

One advantage of the particularistic approach is that it allows us to target our efforts more closely. One disadvantage is that it seems incapable of getting at the root of some of the more extreme inequalities in the exercise of libertarian rights. Needs-tested or universal funding for political participation may be extremely helpful to poor persons who are sufficiently informed, educated, and motivated to use it. Such particularistic measures may prove ineffective, however, if significant numbers of the poor are so uneducated, uninformed, and habituated to political passivity that they are not likely to utilize the means for political participation even if they are available. Similarly, so long as large segments of the population are illiterate, malnourished, and impeded by the lack of adequate health care, it is very unlikely that they will be willing or able to take full advantage of free or subsidized legal services. The advantage of the global approach is that it attempts to improve a person's general condition up to a point at which his exercise of libertarian rights can be augmented by more particularistic measures. Presumably some combination of approaches would be most effective.

Both global and particularistic measures would qualify as programs providing welfare rights in the broad sense stated at the outset of this paper. Both types of arrangements would provide cash or material goods or services free of charge or at a subsidized rate, as a matter of enforced right. But if such rights are grounded on the considerations adduced in the fairness argument, it might be more appropriate to call them "citizenship rights" than "welfare rights."

VII

I have sketched an argument from the commitment to certain libertarian rights, via the idea that the system of libertarian rights must constitute a fair system of procedures, to a commitment to welfare rights. I have also discussed briefly the main types of arrangements by which those welfare rights might be provided. It is now time to consider very briefly one of the most basic objections which might be raised against any attempt to derive welfare rights from libertarian rights. In its simplest form, it is the libertarian objection that any significant welfare program aimed at minimizing the more extreme inequalities in the effectiveness of the rights of political participation, freedom of expression, and the benefits of the legal system would violate another basic right, the right to property.

The objection from an alleged right to property is not, of course, an objection only against welfare rights allegedly derived from the three libertarian rights discussed above. It is the standard libertarian objection against any sort of welfare right, derivative or nonderivative. As an objection against derivative welfare rights, however, it seems to me to be especially unconvincing. There are several difficulties which the libertarian must overcome if the objection is to have any force. First, the right to property must be specified as such a strong right that it can be seen to be incompatible with any significant redistributive measures aimed at minimizing the more extreme inequalities in the exercise of the other three libertarian rights. Clearly, not just any property right will be incompatible with such measures, since most, if not all, of these measures could be implemented through a system of taxation and transfers and since such a system is compatible with a wide range of stronger or weaker property rights. Contrary to Nozick and other libertarians, it is simply not obvious that all such taxation and transfer schemes are incompatible with stable and substantive property rights. Second, the libertarian's strong property right must not only be shown to be a genuine moral right; it must also be shown to be so basic that it overrides the plausible requirement that the other libertarian rights are to form a fair system of procedures.

Though I cannot pursue the point here, I believe that there is no defensible notion of a property right that is strong enough to block the derivation of welfare rights from libertarian rights. This is not to say, however, that considerations concerning the proper scope of a right to property will not play an important role in determining what measures are appropriate for minimizing inequalities in the effectiveness of the exercise of equal rights.

Notes

*I would like to thank Peter G. Brown, Norman Daniels, Gerald Dworkin, Conrad Johnson, Rolf Sartorius, and Paul Vernier for helpful suggestions on an earlier version of this paper.

1. Robert Nozick, *Anarchy, State, and Utopia* (New York: Basic Books, Inc., 1974), pp. 3–280.

2. This conception of a right as a claim which "trumps" considerations of utility (or welfare) is what Ronald Dworkin calls the strong conception of a right. *Taking Rights Seriously* (Cambridge, Mass.: Harvard University Press, 1977). Rawls advances essentially the same conception when he says that "Each person possesses an inviolability founded on justice that even the welfare of society as a whole cannot override." *A Theory of Justice* (Cambridge, Mass.: Harvard University Press, 1971), p. 3.

3. I am not assuming that every right may be coercively backed. Other sorts of sanctions—public opinion, peer pressure, etc.—may sometimes be appropriate where coercion is not. For the sake of my argument, I am assuming that the libertarian rights listed above may be backed by coercion where necessary.

4. Norman Daniels examines Rawls's related distinction between equal liberty and equal worth of liberty and argues that Rawls's concern with it indicates a serious flaw at the heart of his system. Daniels argues that if the parties to Rawls's hypothetical social contract would, as Rawls argues, choose greatest equal liberty, they would also choose equal worth of liberty. Daniels's argument differs from mine in that his does not rest on considerations of fairness and in that it is constructed as an ideal contractarian argument. Norman Daniels, "Equal Liberty and Equal Worth of Liberty," *Reading Rawls*, ed. Norman Daniels (New York: Basic Books, Inc., 1976).

5. For a provocative presentation of some of the relevant statistics, see R. Quinney, *Class, State, and Crime* (New York: David McKay Company, Inc., 1977), pp. 136–39.

6. Rawls, pp. 83–89.

13

Work Requirements and Welfare Rights

BARUCH BRODY

This paper presents an argument for the following thesis: while those who are indigent have a right to certain welfare benefits, society also has a right and (in most cases) an obligation to impose work requirements on some of those indigent recipients of benefits. The work requirement should include three obligations for the recipient: an obligation to seek employment, to accept any job offered at or above the minimum wage, and to work in the interim at some public service job.

This presentation is divided into four sections. The first consists of a series of arguments against these work requirements, some based upon the right to welfare and some based upon other considerations. The second and third sections show why these arguments are invalid and, in so doing, shift the account of why there should be welfare rights into a larger context being developed elsewhere as part of a major project on the redistribution of wealth. The fourth section briefly introduces the question of the relationship between theory and practice.

I

The first objection to work requirements is based upon a particular conception of the right of human liberty, as evidenced in part by how reluctant we normally are to impose work requirements. If I have voluntarily incurred a great many debts, society allows me to go bankrupt to clear them up. No one suggests that I be compelled to work for a period of time to satisfy those debts. If I sign a contract under which I voluntarily accept certain obligations, our law rarely requires that I actually fulfill those accepted obligations. To be sure, I am liable for certain damages which result from my nonperformance, but even if I cannot pay the damages (even if I am judgment-proof), I am rarely enjoined to perform. This is sometimes due to the difficulty of enforcing performance, but even when performance is relatively easy to enforce, it is rarely imposed. In this respect, our legal system differs vastly from the civil law systems where performance is normally mandated, and damages are awarded only in cases where performance is difficult to monitor.

Why, even in cases in which I have voluntarily accepted obligations, am I not compelled to do what I have agreed to do? A standard answer is that our social value-scheme places a high value upon human freedom. To make people work off their debts or otherwise perform what they have agreed to do is to impose upon them a form of servitude, and we are not prepared to do that. Why, then, should we treat those who are indigent differently? To make available attractive possibilities of employment that will encourage those receiving welfare to become employed might be a highly laudable scheme. But compelling people to accept work (or even to search for work) seems to be a denial, at least for the indigent, of that right to freedom which we prize so greatly in other cases.

Many might find this argument objectionable. They would insist that since welfare payments are a privilege which we offer those in need, we have a right, as a condition for making those payments, to require the recipients to seek work or to accept public service employment. Now, I have no objections to the rights-privileges distinction. Even if the courts have correctly pointed out that this distinction is irrelevant in the context of denying procedural due process—even if they point out that once a privilege has been extended it cannot be denied to a given individual without due process—this should not prevent us from using the distinction in our policy decisions on how to structure aid for the indigent. Nevertheless, the distinction is of no help for us in this context. Our fundamental assumption is that welfare is a right of the indigent, and not a privilege, so no appeal to the rights-privileges distinction can justify enforcement of the work requirement.

The second, more policy-oriented objection to work requirements is that they don't work. A number of points are normally made here. On the demand side, it is pointed out that we are living in a period of relatively high unemployment, and it is unclear where the jobs for the indigent are to come from. On the supply side, it is pointed out that the indigent seeking welfare support lack the education, the training, the job record, the health, etc., to successfully enter the private labor market. The conclusion is therefore drawn that the requirement to seek employment in the private market and to accept any job offered is irrelevant. There remains only the requirement that recipients do public service work. But is this work really of any social benefit? Experience suggests that people performing such work rarely acquire the training, habits, and attitudes required to find meaningful work in the private labor market. So the whole program seems to be an exercise in futility.

This second objection can also be put as follows: our ultimate social goal is to see that people live from the fruits of their labor and not from public support. We desire this in part to save society from the burden of supporting those who are not supporting themselves and in part because we believe that such a life is better than a life of being supported by others (a view, by the way, which seems to be shared by most welfare recipients). Obviously, this goal cannot be fully met, because any society will have some people incapable of working or, at least, incapable of working given certain social values and others who need help temporarily between periods of employment. We would like to make as much progress as possible toward meeting this goal, which is also the goal of the work requirement program. The trouble is that the program doesn't seem to accomplish its purpose, and it should therefore be dropped.

The third objection combines a rights argument and a public policy argument, postulating the fundamental value of autonomy as a right of the individual and, simultaneously, as a social goal to be pursued. The autonomous decision maker is, roughly speaking, one who, free of coercion, chooses his life pattern and his activities according to his own values. All social coercion is, of course, an infringement on autonomy, although some such infringements are obviously commendable (possibly because in the long run they promote still greater autonomy). The right to be an autonomous decision maker is a fundamental human right lying behind such ideas as the right to privacy and the right to control one's own body. Moreover, the promotion of autonomous individuals has seemed to many to be a fundamental social goal. If we envision a society of free individuals, then the attainment of that vision seems to require the promotion of autonomy. Now, work requirements of the type we have been discussing seem in direct opposition to both the right of autonomy and the social goal of a society of autonomous individuals. After all, to stipulate that one cannot receive the help to which one has a right and which is desperately needed unless one accepts either any job that pays the minimum wage or a public service job is to compel individuals to make certain decisions, is to violate their right of autonomy, and is to weaken our efforts to develop a society of autonomous individuals.

From the perspective of this last argument, work requirements look very much like those traditional requirements that welfare recipients must spend the funds they receive in accordance with patterns laid down by their case workers. One of the fundamental objections to this older approach was that it violated the recipients' rights of privacy and autonomy and that it encouraged dependency rather than autonomy. It is this same objection that is raised against the work requirement. To be sure, this objection could be met by showing that, as suggested above, work requirements are commendable because in the long run they promote greater autonomy. But our third objection insists that the burden of defense is now upon those who defend work requirements.

These three objections comprise a serious battery of reasons for skepticism about work requirements. In the next section, I shall, nevertheless, argue for these work requirements. I shall do so by rooting the right to welfare in a certain conflict about the right to property. The resulting right will, it shall be argued, have the flexibility to allow for, and perhaps even require, a work requirement.

II

There are those who derive welfare rights from the assumption that we all equally need certain basic goods. Their argument runs roughly like this: since we all have an equal need for these basic goods, we therefore have an equal right to them. But since the operations of the market lead to an uneven sharing of these basic goods, society itself must redistribute wealth so that these basic goods are equally possessed by all. I have never seen the force of this argument since it assumes that the need generates a right and leaves this crucial assumption totally unsupported.

There are those who derive welfare rights from the assumption that the existence of such a system of transfers maximizes general welfare. Their argument proceeds as follows: any reasonable assumptions about the diminishing marginal utility of money, even when combined with assumptions about the need of monetary incentives to maximize production, lead to the conclusion that utility will be increased by the distribution of welfare payments to the indigent. The indigent therefore have a right to these payments. I have never seen the force of this argument, either. Its crucial difficulty is how it moves from the maximization of utility to the existence of rights. Despite the ingenuity of Mill and others who have followed his theory of rights, it would seem that rights are moral considerations independent of considerations of general utility, in that policy A might lead to a maximization of utility without entailing a right to the carrying out of policy A.

There are also those who derive the existence of welfare rights from the existence of other rights. Their argument runs roughly like this: the effective enjoyment of these other rights presupposes the possession of a certain basic set of goods. Since everyone has these other rights, it follows that everyone also has a right to the possession of this basic set of goods. But not everyone possesses these basic goods. Therefore, society must distribute wealth so that the basic goods are available to everyone. Again, I have never seen the force of this argument. Its crucial difficulty is the assumption that if everyone has certain rights, it follows that they also have the right to what is required for the effective enjoyment of these rights, an assumption left unsupported by the argument.

It seems to me, nevertheless, that there are welfare rights. In my current work on the moral basis for the distribution of wealth, I have developed a different argument for these rights, one that ultimately derives from certain eighteenth-century followers of Locke (e.g., Thomas Paine and William Ogilvie). Let me sketch this argument.

The theory of the just distribution of wealth, by my account, is best approached by looking at Locke's labor theory of the origin of property rights. From our perspective, the crucial idea in Locke's theory is that labor does create entitlements to the value produced by that labor, and any theory of the just distribution of wealth must respect these entitlements. At the same time, however, some of the wealth that exists is simply the initial value of natural resources, and Locke never really explained why anyone should have an entitlement to that wealth. To be sure, as Locke pointed out, no one will be able to enjoy the value created by his labor unless he can appropriate the natural resources, but that does not explain why he has a right to do so. The theory that I want to offer suggests, following Ogilvie and Paine, that the simultaneous existence of both property rights and welfare rights emerges out of this difference in the types of wealth and in the possibilities for entitlements. To see how this works, let us imagine an initial position of a social contract. (I leave aside for this paper the important question as to who is involved and its implications for questions of international aid.) All those forming the contract recognize the existence of initial equal rights to use the natural resources. They also recognize that allowing exclusive property rights is economically efficient. What I argue for elsewhere is that such people would agree (1.) to allow for the formation of exclusive property rights (either private or socialized) over natural resources as well as added values, (2.) to compensate those who would lose their rights to use the natural resources assigned to property holders, and (3.) to provide that compensation in the form of guarantees of minimum subsistence if things go wrong, i.e., in the form of socially recognized welfare rights. In short, property holders owe compensation for their usurpation of natural resources, however socially desirable that usurpation may be (with respect to efficiency and increased opportunities), because not all will be beneficiaries of those gains from usurpations, and the system of welfare transfers is the appropriate way of paying that compensation.

I have found it useful, in thinking out the implications of this approach, to imagine the terms of the social contract running something like this: the natural resources of the earth are leased to those who develop them, or to those to whom they transfer those leases. In return, they owe a rental to everyone. That rental is collected as taxes and paid into a social insurance fund which covers everyone equally. In this respect, since we are all covered equally, the rent payment to everyone is equal. The social insurance fund insures us against destitution, making payments to those who are destitute. As with all insurance funds, all are equally covered, but not all receive equal payouts. In short, on this approach, all welfare programs are replaced by a program of social insurance.

Naturally a full exposition and defense of these claims lies beyond the scope of this paper. What I want to do now is to draw out some of the most relevant implications of this approach for our problem:

1. *The level of welfare payments.* Most of those who have argued for the existence of welfare rights have not really drawn out the implications of their approach for the crucial question of the level of benefits to which people are entitled. Some of the implications are staggering. If, for example, welfare rights are based upon equal need, then in a less affluent society with many needy, the resulting rights may exhaust the total pool of goods available to be distributed. Or if, for example, welfare rights are based upon the effective enjoyment of other rights, then, depending upon which other rights there are and how effective the enjoyment is, it may turn out that even in our society the resulting rights will exhaust the total pool of goods available to be distributed. What happens to entitlements based upon labor? The defenders of these approaches are required to make ad hoc balancing decisions so that the level of assistance will vary with the degree of affluence of the society. The utilitarian is, of course, exempt from this critique of the ad hoc, because the needed balance between distribution and incentives is built into his approach. On our approach, the question of level of benefits looks very different. The pool of resources to be distributed at any given time in any given society depends upon the wealth of the society, and is only some reasonable percentage of it (roughly, the rental rate given the value of the opportunities to exploit the natural resources). The actual level of benefits is determined by the total of that pool and the total number of recipients; the fewer the recipients, the higher the level of benefits.

2. *Raising the rates by lowering the number of recipients.* This last point gives rise to an important observation. Putting people to work, so that they no longer require part or whole payments from the insurance fund (welfare payments), does not save society money. Rather, it frees funds so that the level of payments to the remaining recipients can be raised. This means that measures taken to get people off welfare should, in a just society, be beneficial to others in need.

3. *Clauses in the original social contract.* Consider once more the people forming the original social contract. Recognizing the points we have made so far, they see that there is an important option open to them. They can raise the probability of getting an adequate payment—if they are truly in need and cannot work—by agreeing to modify the contract so that to receive benefits one must seek work and even accept it providing that certain minimal conditions are met (e.g., it pays a minimum wage). Now, given that the whole idea behind receiving the compensation in the form of an insurance policy is that we protect ourselves against those disasters which can destroy us and to which all are vulnerable, it seems reasonable to accept this additional clause so as to raise our level of protection rather than to fritter away our protection by retaining the right not to work.

We can summarize this crucial line of argumentation in the following way: most who have written about work requirements have supposed that any money saved would revert to society. Some have applauded, bemoaning the heavy burden of taxation to support welfare; others have been critical, claiming that it shows the heartlessness of those who would force people into demeaning work to save this pittance, thereby stigmatizing them because they are needy. This whole discussion is, I believe, irrelevant. In a just society, the level of the pool available for need-based redistribution should be set independently, on other considerations, and the sole goal of the requirements to seek work and accept it is to make more available for those who are truly needy. This goal combines the practical desire to conserve funds with the ideal of offering more generous help to the needy by using the funds conserved to aid the needy.

We are now ready to reexamine the initial arguments against work requirements. As we saw, some of those objections are based upon the rights of welfare recipients to autonomy and to liberty from servitude. Those who raise such objections assume that the requirement to seek work or to accept employment is an other-imposed infringement upon liberty and autonomy, where people are coerced into doing things by a threat to deny them basic goods to which they have a right. By our account, the work requirement is part and parcel of the right to receive payments. The statement that payments are conditioned upon fulfilling that requirement is not a threat to deny a right but merely an affirmation of the conditions under which the right in question exists. The other objections, as we saw, were based upon the assumption that the goal of the work requirement is to find ways to get people permanently off the welfare rolls. Given the types of work available, and the skill levels of those on welfare, that seems an implausible goal. We feel that the work requirement has far more modest goals. It merely seeks to free some funds for distribution to those in need who cannot help themselves at all. Given the more modest goal, this program might have some hope of success (more on that below).

In all of our discussion, we have been emphasizing the requirement to seek work and to accept minimally acceptable employment. We have said very little about the requirement to work off one's welfare payment by performing public service employment. Again, if the goal of such a program is to provide meaningful employment that will take people permanently off the welfare rolls, the critics of the requirement win. Can we find any justification for this requirement if we approach it with different goals? I believe that we can under some conditions. Suppose there are some socially useful tasks that we do not fund because we, as a society, cannot afford them, meaning that the cost of having these tasks performed by normal employees working at the minimum wage is x and the performance is only worth n% x (o $<$ n $<$ 100) to us. (Here, "worth" means what we as individuals would be willing to pay for that performance either in a private exchange or in a benefit-based taxation system with honest revelations of what we are willing to pay for that benefit.) Here, I suggest, we have an opportunity for a justifiable use of a public service requirement. After all, suppose welfare recipients are required to perform that work at the prevailing minimum wage. Then, some portion of their wage (n% x) is what we would pay out of nonwelfare funds to have the job done, and only the remaining portion of their wage (100 − n% x) would come from the welfare pool. Providing that that remainder is less than what they are entitled to receive, then it is socially desirable to require them to do the work. The tasks are being provided at a cost to our general funds equal to their worth to society, and the welfare pool is saving on the payment to the recipient who is performing the task, a saving that can be passed on to other recipients. An example might help to illustrate this point. Suppose that, at the prevailing minimum wage, it would cost $100 to clean up a Staten Island ferry, but that cleaning it up is worth only $50 to the commuters. In a rational society (but perhaps not in the real world) the task is not performed. Suppose, however, that the job is done by a welfare recipient who would normally receive a $75 welfare payment. If he is paid $50 by the Staten Island Ferry Company and $25 by welfare, the job is done at a cost to the commuters equal to its worth to them and the welfare pool is ahead $50. These are the types of conditions under which the public service requirement is justified.

I have, in this section, argued that in a justly organized system of welfare payments, work requirements are justified. But, of course, not all such systems are just. One major injustice which we have already noticed is the use of any savings from the work requirement for nonwelfare purposes. Since my goal is only to argue for a work requirement in a just system, I want to sketch in the next section an outline of a just system.

III

In the theory I am developing, a just system of welfare rights is part of a more general system for the distribution of wealth. The theory of that system contains three basic elements: a general outline of distributive justice, a theory of taxation, and a theory of welfare rights. Let me outline each of these:

THE GENERAL THEORY OF DISTRIBUTIVE JUSTICE

Nozick has usefully distinguished patterned theories of distributive justice from nonpatterned theories. A patterned theory of distributive justice is one in which justice means a particular distribution of wealth in society. Thus, "to each according to his needs" or "according to his marginal contribution" or "according to his merit" . . . are all slogans for patterned theories of distributive justice. A nonpatterned theory of distributive justice is one which does not identify justice with a particular distribution but rather with the process by which a given distribution came about. Thus, to say that a given distribution is just because it came about by legitimate transfers from legitimate acquisitions is to adopt a nonpatterned theory of justice.

Our theory of distributive justice is a mixed theory, containing both patterned and nonpatterned elements. The reason for this is very simple. The heart of our theory is its insistence that there is a fundamental distinction between the wealth that results from people's labor and the wealth that is the value of initial natural resources. About the former type of wealth, we have accepted a nonpatterned approach. That wealth should, in justice, belong either to those who produced it or to those to whom it was transferred by legitimate acquisitions (including labor contracts between employers and employees). On the other hand, the wealth that is the value of the initial natural resources should, in justice, belong equally to all. In this respect, we have accepted a patterned approach. We have argued, however, that instead of distributing that wealth equally, we funnel the income from it into a pool for distribution to those who are most needy. So, we have a mixed theory of distributive justice.

THE THEORY OF TAXATION

For reasons that are best understood historically rather than justified morally, we have come to accept the proposition that the only good taxes are those that are progressive on income. Taxes other than progressive income taxes (e.g., property or sales taxes) are weighed against a number of considerations, some technical and some moral, with the progressiveness on income of their impact being the crucial moral factor. With the exception of defenders of the expenditure tax and conservative admirers of Blum and Kalven, this belief in progressive income taxes is nearly universal.

In my current work on the distribution of wealth, I challenge the dependence on the progressive income tax. My chief objection is that different forms of governmental activities, undertaken because of different market failures, ought to be financed in different ways. In some cases (public goods like lighthouses, as well as such goods as could be provided privately but are provided publicly like national parks), user fees or beneficiary fees could and should be used. In other cases, other forms of taxation are needed. One obvious case—which is relevant for our purposes—is the case of funding redistribution through the welfare system. Obviously, beneficiary fees should not be used since our whole purpose is to redistribute wealth *to* the beneficiaries. How, then, shall we fund redistribution through the welfare system?

Our basic model provides an answer to the question. Those who pay should be taxed in proportion to the natural-resource value of the property which they have appropriated (or received from others who have appropriated it). The failure of Henry George's single tax plan makes us realize that some other answer is required in the real world and that we must find the best surrogate for that ideal answer. Progressive income taxes, looked at in this way, seem less attractive than they normally do. Perhaps proportional taxes upon wealth (or at least upon wealth based upon natural resources, excluding patents, copyrights, etc.) would be a better surrogate.

WELFARE RIGHTS AND WORK REQUIREMENTS

As we have already suggested, the distinctive feature of our welfare system is that the total dollars to be distributed should be an approximation of fair compensation for the use of the natural resources, and that the overall sum is independent of the number of recipients. One variant is that the poorest should receive the dollar amounts required to raise them to the level of the next to poorest, the resulting group receives such dollars as are required to raise them to the level of the next to poorest, the resulting group receives such dollars as are required to raise them to the next income level of the next to poorest, the resulting group receives such dollars as are required to raise them to the next income level, etc., until the pool of welfare dollars is exhausted. Another variant is that everyone below a certain level (say, the poverty level) is given an equal sum of money, where that sum is determined by the total dollars in the welfare pool, divided by the number of recipients. And still other variants are possible. Whether all of these systems are just (because they would be acceptable to our social contractors) or whether one is uniquely just is a question for further research. It would depend upon whether or not only one of the possible systems would be acceptable to our contractors. Further questions are raised by variants in which goods rather than dollars are distributed.

It is in the context of this system of welfare rights that our work requirements are introduced, on the basis of the arguments given in section II. Certain fundamental questions arise in connection with these requirements, perhaps the most important being who should be required to work. The short answer is "those who are capable." But that answer leaves too many questions open—such as the salary at which people can be required to work, the type of work they can be required to do, and whether single parents should be required to work and put their children into some form of day care.

The answer to the latter question is normally thought to depend on whether or not it is desirable to place children in day care, on the costs of day care versus the income from the working parent, and so on. From our perspective, two points should be noted: (1.) Our goal is to save money for the welfare pool. Since we have little hope for programs to get people permanently off the welfare rolls, we must weigh the savings in this case (often modest, given the jobs available) against the considerable job-related costs, especially adequate day care. It may not pay. (2.) More attention should be paid to the views of the particular single parent, rather than of society at large, about day care and surrogate child-rearing. The right to make this type of determination about how one's child is to be raised is a precious right, and it seems likely that the initial contractors would be concerned to protect it when the social insurance contract is formulated.

There is one objection to our system that deserves notice even in this brief sketch. Some object that any version of the work requirement would impose administrative nightmares, since it could not be administered without violating due process. Some would inevitably be cut off from welfare payments because they were not working, even though they deserved to receive the benefits because they really could not work. To answer this question would require an essay about due process, so I will only say for now that due process is not supposed to guarantee perfectly accurate results, just a fair process, and that nonmechanical judgments (such as judgments about eligibility) must be allowed in any adequate theory of due process.

IV

One final issue remains: the question of the relationship between theory and practice. We have argued that in a certain ideal system of distributive justice some welfare recipients should be required to seek employment, to accept any employment if certain minimal conditions are met, and if necessary, to work off their welfare by accepting public service jobs. But should those work requirements be introduced in the real world, where less than ideal systems exist?

There are several important reasons for answering this question in the negative. Work requirements in the current system differ from what they would be in our ideal system in several ways. The most important differences are that the welfare pool is not a fixed amount, and that savings from the work requirements (if there are any) do not revert to the rest of the welfare recipients. Moreover, the work requirement is complicated in the current system by the desire to provide *meaningful* employment that will permit recipients to leave the welfare rolls permanently. All of these factors undercut the argument for the work requirement. However, while the full system of distributive justice outlined above is hardly realizable politically, responsibility demands our noting that it may be politically possible to develop a welfare system in which recipients who truly cannot work receive more because those who can work are treated in accordance with the work requirement plan outlined above. That seems enough to justify the imposition of the work requirement. Thus, if this goal can be realized politically, its realization would be an important achievement for a philosophically grounded welfare reform.

14

Are There Welfare Rights?

A. I. MELDEN

In this essay I assume without argument at the outset that there are good moral reasons for instituting programs of public assistance for the needy. My concern here is with the claim that the needy have a moral right to that assistance, that this is a moral right that they have as human beings. For moral rights are quite special moral grounds for conduct—there are considerations other than rights that serve as moral grounds. But while I shall argue against the view that there is no human right *as such* to welfare support, the human rights that the needy have in common with all others are in fact relevant considerations that may be brought to bear upon the moral claim that they ought to receive welfare support.

Some Cautions

There are many things we ought to do, morally speaking, which involve no issue of rights. For example, we ought to act generously, but no one has any right to our generosity. Wherever possible, we ought to relieve those in pain, but it seems queer to say that, generally at least, those in pain have a right to the relief we may be able to provide—the fact that they are in pain is itself good and sufficient reason for the help we can provide. And if those who have transgressed against us have provided evidence of their remorse and determination not to repeat their offenses, we ought to forgive them. But do they have a right to our forgiveness? And, while it may be reprehensible when distributing candies to a group of urchins or pieces of pie to those seated at one's dining table, to do so in such a way that some get more than others and some get nothing at all, it will hardly do to assert that all such forms of maldistribution involve any deprivation of rights.

It is enough in such cases to say that one ought not to act in such ways. Why? Because of the unfairness involved. Indeed, what some have labeled "distributive justice," which calls for equity in the distribution of benefits and burdens—some distributions clearly being fairer and therefore better or more desirable than others—need involve no violation of any rights.

This last point, frequently overlooked, can be brought home by considering morally askew arrangements which fail to satisfy Rawls's difference principle. That principle, it will be recalled, states that social and economic inequalities are permissible only if they are to the advantage of the least advantaged members of our society.[1] For suppose—what clearly and sadly is untrue in the world in which we live—that no one in our society needs any income support in order to maintain a tolerable and decent existence, and that some individuals manage to accumulate, quite legally, great wealth without thereby adding in any way to the well-being of those less favored by fortune. For the Rawlsian-minded, at least, such a distribution would appear to be unfair—why should some prosper in ways that do not add to the well-being of others? Such an arrangement might well have an unfortunate tendency to create envy and jealousy. Besides, there is the Kantian point that if these high peaks in the fortunes of the favored few are associated with substantial deficiencies in moral virtue, it would be better if they had not occurred at all.[2] In any case, such a distribution of income or resources might well strike us as being less than the best.

Some might label such an arrangement "social injustice," the so-called injustice perpetrated by a fortune that is blind to moral merit and desert. But does it involve any infringement, deprivation, or violation of rights? Here some might say that the favored few have no right to the benefits they have received. But what does this mean? That rights have been violated in that clear and straightforward sense in which there is a violation of a right when someone, who has no right to do so, invades another's privacy? To say that the favored few have no right to the goods a morally blind nature has lavished upon them can only be a misleading way of saying that they do not deserve the goods they have acquired, that it would be better if either they had not acquired them or those with superior moral merit had been favored instead of them. It is only muddying the waters, in my view, to raise the issue of moral rights whenever maldistributions of benefits and burdens have occurred.

The point I have been making is that both philosophers and non-philosophers have been much too inclined to engage in rights-talk in support of their moral views; this is especially clear in two such instances I want now to mention before going on to discuss the question of welfare rights. Animals obviously do feel pleasure and pain, at least those now being raised for human consumption; and we ought, surely, to avoid causing them pain when we hunt them, or maintain them in confined quarters, or ship them to slaughterhouses for butchering. But, not content with these undebatable claims, some have gone on to buttress them with the conclusion that animals enjoy rights just as human beings do, and that all of the various practices in which humans engage, from the eating of meat to those practices this encourages—the hunting, breeding, raising, and slaughtering of animals—violate animal rights.

Such a claim succeeds only in obscuring the need to make good a number of claims that stand in need of examination: that all of the practices mentioned above are and of necessity must be cruel to the animals destroyed for human consumption; that the raising of oysters, clams, and snails for human consumption is inherently cruel along with the gathering of snakes, locusts, grasshoppers, and bees now being consumed in certain parts of the world by human beings; that agriculture does not have any deleterious effect upon those animals in the fields, meadows, orchards, and surrounding territories who would intrude and devour the food being raised for human consumption; and, not by any means of minor importance, that cruelty and/or the killing of animals is a deprivation of moral rights. There is some reason for an inclination to ascribe moral rights to dolphins, whales, chimpanzees, gorillas, and family pets, but this is enormously distant from the conclusions urged by some vegetarians that we shun the eating of animals. Even less lacking in any rational support is the claim made by some who urge upon us a view that can be described only as frivolous, that we ought to protect and cleanse the environment in which we live on the ground that it—the environment that consists of such inorganic ingredients as earth, air, water, rocks, mountains—is the possessor of rights.

But enough of the need for arguments to offer rational support for this kind of environmentalist claim, and for a vegetarianism that starts with an appeal to our humane feelings about the imposition of cruelty on animals.[3] The question we need to ask is why in fact there is this temptation to appeal to moral rights without any apparent realization on the part of those who make such an appeal of the need to provide rational grounds for their conclusion. For of course we ought to avoid cruelty toward animals; surely the fact that something is cruel is good enough reason for eschewing it. And we ought to protect the environment and to take steps to cleanse it from the pollution human activities have produced—and for a variety of good and sufficient reasons.

But why has it been felt necessary to buttress such good/ought-talk by invoking the language of rights? The answer, I venture to suggest, is that our deepest moral feelings are evoked by the idea that there has been a violation of moral rights. This gives rise to the understandable temptation to evoke these feelings in order to buttress one's cause as strongly as possible. To succumb to this temptation in the two extreme cases I have just cited is to provide a way of saving oneself the necessity of doing what is far more difficult, namely, adducing considerations that serve as rational grounds for the cause one has endorsed. Perhaps we ought not to eat animals, but the case is not proven by citing the fact that cruelty toward animals is offensive. And in the case of environmentalism, it is ludicrous that any appeal to moral rights is felt to be necessary when there are in fact a number of supporting considerations that can be cited without too much difficulty, despite complications of cost and convenience.

It is not enough, therefore, to claim that there are moral rights. Considerations, at least of the sort Mill described in another context as being capable "of determining the intellect," are also needed; for the issue of whether any moral right is involved in any moral claim that is made is surely one that lies, as he put it, "within the cognizance of the rational faculty." Of course, I do not wish to assert or imply that the appeal to welfare rights in support of public assistance programs is or must be as farfetched as either of the last two cases I have mentioned in which moral rights have been alleged to obtain. I wish only to comment on the manifest excesses to which an uncritical appeal to moral rights *can* give rise in order to emphasize the point made earlier, that both philosophers and non-philosophers have been much too disposed to engage in rights-talk in cases in which the relevance of such talk is at best problematic. If it is claimed that there are welfare rights, discussion is needed to support the claim. Specifically, we need, first, to examine some of the distinctive features of our concept of a right, and second, to adduce considerations designed to show whether or not rights, thus understood, can reasonably be cited in justification of social or public programs of income support.[4]

The Distinctive Nature of Rights

Some philosophers have attempted to elucidate the concept of a moral right in terms of what it is that ought to be done. One such attempt is to be found in Chapter V of Mill's essay *Utilitarianism*, where he declares that "to have a right . . . is . . . to have something which society ought to defend me in the possession of." But what is it that one *has*, in the possession of which society ought to defend one? Surely not *that* to which one has the right, for one may have a right to something one will never gain, but, rather, the right that society ought to defend one in the possession of. A defender of Mill might retort that defending one's right means insuring that one will obtain *that* to which one has a right. Still, the tacit reference here to the right in this exegesis provides at least the appearance of circularity. In any case, persons have rights by virtue of the transactions in which they engage with one another or the relations in which they stand to one another, and it will hardly do to claim that they have these rights only if society ought to do whatever is needed in order to protect them.

Not every case of a broken promise that violates the right of the promisee, an untruthfulness that breaches the right that persons have to truthful declarations from others, or an unwarranted interference with the right one has to take a drink, or, minimally, to rub one's itching nose, would warrant invoking the protection of society. Individuals have rights sometimes by engaging in transactions with, or standing in relation to, other specific individuals, and sometimes, as in the case of the last two instances I have enumerated, simply as individuals who have the right, or liberty, to do certain things without any interference from others; but it would be excessively heavy-handed, at best, to call upon society with its social pressures and the penalties of the law for protection. Further, if society ought in point of moral fact, as Mill claims, to defend a person's possession of what he can earn in fair professional competition, because "society ought not to allow any other person to hinder him from endeavoring to earn in that manner as much as he can," surely this claim can only be based on the presumed right that persons have to earn what they can in fair competition.

Mill intends to avoid the logical circle by appealing at this point to the principle of utility—society ought not to allow persons to hinder others from earning what they can in what we describe as fair professional competition because this breaches the fundamental principle of morality specified by utilitarianism. But this is to invoke a philosophical doctrine I see no reason to accept and far too many reasons to reject. There is, of course, the legal right that persons have to engage in fair competition in the pursuit of their economic interests, but this legal right, established as it is by statute and judicial interpretation, is morally justifiable, in my opinion, because of the conception of a person embodied in our constitution as the possessor of certain rights which would be infringed by unfair competitive practices.

There are, however, more general points that can be made against any reductionist analysis of rights-talk in terms of ought-talk, the talk about what ought to be done. Why, for example, ought one to keep one's promise? Surely one good reason, insufficient as it may be in a special case, is that in doing so one would be meeting one's obligation. But to say that one ought to meet one's obligation is *not* to utter the complete triviality that one ought to do what one ought to do. It is rather to cite an obligation that one has *to a person*, in the present instance because of the promise given to him. The obligation to that person is the very same thing, viewed from the point of view of the person considering what is to be done, as the right the other person has against him; it is, as it is commonly put, the correlative of the right conferred by that paradigm of a right-conferring act, the making of a promise. One ought to keep one's promise because, in doing so, one will be according someone the right that person has against one. It is therefore the right (and its correlative obligation) that explains the ought, i.e., what ought to be done—not the other way around. The attempted reduction of rights-talk to ought-talk, in reversing the proper logical order, simply puts the cart before the horse.

The unsatisfactory character of Mill's definition of a right and the implausibility in general of the attempt to reduce rights-talk to ought-talk will be apparent as soon as we consider the conceptual complexity of the notion of a right. Rights, it has been pointed out, involve correlative obligations, in some cases to do (or to forebear from doing), as in the case of the rights created by promises; generally, these rights call for perform-ances on the part of the promiser, although in special cases the obligation involved may be to abstain from performances, this being the subject of the promise-locutions. Some rights are mere liberties, as in the case of the right one has to smoke in the privacy of one's study, a right with respect to which no one else has any right to interference; here the correlative obligation is the obligation not to interfere.[5] And there are finer distinc-tions that can be and have been drawn.[6]

But this is only the beginning of the story that needs to be told. For rights may be acquired by entering into specific transactions with or relations to others, as in the case of those who receive promises from others and in the case of family members; and so, too, may they be forfeited by relevant circumstances, as in the case of a father who forfeits his paternal rights by failing to meet even the most elementary of his responsibilities. Some rights may be relinquished, and those who are bound by them are released from their obligations; although what sense can be ascribed to any talk of relinquishing one's right as a human being is another matter. And some rights may be waived without being relin-quished or forfeited, as in the case of someone who waives the right he has acquired as the recipient of a promise, although the same caution about "waiving one's right as a human being" needs to be made, and for the same reason. But if there are those rights that can be called "special," because they arise in the special circumstances of human life, e.g., the occurrence of promises, the arrangements of family life, and even some of the forms of communication in which there is the right to truthfulness and the correla-tive obligation to be truthful, then there are rights that human beings have simply by virtue of their status as moral agents.[7]

Yet even this is not enough in order to indicate the scope of the conceptual ramifications of the concept of a moral right. For rights, special or human, may be infringed, justifiably or unjustifiably; and they may be exercised reasonably or unreasonably. Rights are not like bank drafts that are cashable on demand; that is to say, they may not be exercised, or accorded, regardless of any circumstances.[8] But even when an agent reasonably infringes the right of another, the agent is responsible to the person whose right has been infringed; that is to say, he is accountable to the latter and owes him an explanation, and if the infringement has caused him moral damage (as is the case when the right is a matter of importance to him as he pursues his interests), reparation, if possible, and even a sense of guilt for the damage for which he was responsible, are in order. And if the infringement is unjustified—that is to say, if the right has been violated—guilt has surely been incurred. The appropriate emotion here is not shame, for this may occur when, for example, one has been cowardly without in any way infringing upon the rights of others, and the remedy in the case of shame calls for something that only the person who feels the shame can provide, namely, remaking his character and having done so, hoping that the incident will be erased from his memory.

But in the case of the guilt suffered, and rightly so when the right of another agent has been violated, moral healing can be effected by the remorse suffered, the reparation paid, and the determination not to repeat the offense; these considerations should compel the victim of the offense to forgive the offender, thus restoring the trust that had existed before the offense had been committed, and thereby preparing the way for further good moral relations with him. But to forgive in this way is possible only for the person who has suffered the moral injury. As Locke put it, "He who has suffered the damage has a right to demand in his own name, and he alone can remit."[9] That is to say, the possessor of a right is endowed with a certain authority in his moral relations with others: to hold them to account as necessary and to forgive them when required. And as the possessor of the rights he has as a human being, he has sufficient authority to comport himself with a dignity apparent to others by the way in which he deals with them, be they high or low, in terms of moral equality with them, and prepared in ways they can observe from his demeanor that they must answer to him for any violation of his rights. Indeed, as the possessor of rights it is incumbent upon him, as circumstances warrant, to stand up and, by asserting his rights, display openly the dignity he has as the possessor of rights in common with everyone else.[10]

Space does not permit the full story that must be told in any adequate elucidation of the concept of a right—the possible rational grounds for waiving or even relinquishing certain of our rights, which serve also to justify infringing rights and, correlatively, refusing to meet one's obligations; the moral requirements or burdens imposed upon those who possess rights and those who are under the correlative obligations; the conceptual connections between rights and goods; the moral background or logical substratum of rights and obligations; and the rationale that operates in the way in which moral agents can reasonably weigh competing considerations of rights, obligations, and goods in arriving at their moral decisions. These are topics that cannot be discussed within the brief compass of a single paper, but I mention them here only in order to reinforce the points made earlier, that it is hopeless to attempt to reduce rights-talk to talk about what ought to be done, specifically, that the explanation offered by Mill of what a right is, notwithstanding the appeal it has had for some, is impossibly anemic.

The 'Basis' of Moral Rights

I turn now to the question of the 'basis' of moral rights. Here, as in some of the allegations that there are certain moral rights justifying certain sorts of conduct, there is a decided tendency among philosophers to offer views without adequate discussion or argument.

One frequently encountered ploy is to assert that individuals have moral rights by virtue of certain moral rules or principles. Unfortunately, the suggestion, coming as it does from a presumed analogy between moral and legal rights, is never explored. For if we ask, "What are the rules or principles in question?" it is difficult to see what possible candidates can do the trick. Our familiar moral precepts can hardly serve as the analogs of the statutes by which legal rights are established. For even if *one ought to keep one's promises* were a rule or principle that established the possession of the rights of promisees and the correlative obligations of promisers— which clearly it does not do[11]—it is too slender a reed to support the complex conceptual structure of our concept of a moral right. Nor would any principle that takes the form of a declaration that there are certain rights, as the Declaration of Independence, serve as the analog of the statutes, common law, and judicial pronouncements that have the force of law. For the declaration that there are certain rights is the *assertion* or *claim* that there are certain rights; but it does not itself *establish* the existence of these rights in the way in which statutes and judicial pronouncements do. Legal statutes, together with a body of common law and judicial interpretations, serve to explain not only the existence of legal rights, but also the complex implications such rights have in legal affairs; but there are no such moral rules or principles that do this trick for moral rights.

Why then do we ascribe moral rights as we do? The answer, I have argued elsewhere, lies in the conception of a person as a moral agent. For even Locke, who speaks of the laws of nature and reason that is that law, as he phrases it, when he attempts to explain the natural rights we have, appeals not to such laws but to considerations of quite a different nature: the allegedly self-evident claim that individuals have a right to their own persons and the further claim that by mixing their labor with what God has given them in common, they acquire rights to what they thereby obtain, by making them parts of their own persons.[12] There are, to be sure, serious difficulties in this account, but we would do well to follow Locke in abandoning any effort to employ the analogy with legal rights by claiming, as do some writers today, that there must be moral principles that explain the moral rights persons have.

We need, clearly, to distinguish between special and human rights. The former depend upon the latter and arise, as I have argued elsewhere, when there is a mutual understanding of the support that one person is to provide for the agency of another as the latter engages in the pursuit of interests that define the good or goods he seeks to achieve.[13] A promise is a formal device for establishing a special right, but there are other rights, e.g., the right to truthfulness and the complex distribution of rights, along with their correlative obligations, among the members of a family. In my view, what operates as a fundamental human right, without which none of these special rights can arise, is the right that human beings have to engage in the pursuit of their interests, interests defining goods that enable them to achieve lives worth living.

It is human rights and the claim that some sort of basis can be found for them with which I am now concerned. I shall put off, for the moment, the question of the extent and variety of such rights, and mention only one more claim concerning their basis. And once more, as in the case of the appeal to moral principles on the analogy of those principles or statutes by which legal rights are established, we find only the flat assertion without any of the argument and discussion needed to support the dictum. For it is widely thought and often said that moral rights—the rights that human beings as such possess—derive from the autonomy of human beings. I shall be brief at the risk of appearing dogmatic in dealing with this echo of Kantian thought.

By autonomy is intended, I believe, the ability of persons to choose and decide for themselves on the basis of reasons they can understand and invoke. But surely we ascribe rights to those unable or unwilling to decide for themselves: the pathetically submissive wife who accepts the choices and decisions made for her by a domineering husband, the slave who is content with a lot he has no role in fashioning, and the young child. And for most of us there is only more or less autonomy—those of us for whom orthodoxy, tradition, and the will of our parents and friends are a comfortable substitute for the disturbing insecurity threatened by any attempted self-criticism or departure from received opinion. And how much autonomy has the frightened patient who is told by his physician that he must freely give his assent to surgery—it is his right to decide whether or not to submit to the surgeon's knife—in order to remove a cancerous growth? And our autonomy varies with our moods and the medications we take.

We can go on and on in this way. Yet submissive wives, obedient slaves, patients trembling with fear in their physicans' offices, and you and I on our off-days and moments have rights as the human beings they and you and I are. Besides, by what logical hocus-pocus is it possible to squeeze the rich and complex structure of moral rights—a structure I was at pains to sketch earlier in this essay—out of a pallid rationality and the ability to bring it to bear in the decisions we make? For supposing we avoid circularity by stipulating that this rationality is not that reasonableness that is exhibited by persons who weigh rights and obligations, their own and those of others, in deciding how to conduct themselves, how can we derive rights from mere rationality?[14]

But enough of the moves designed to find some firm foundation for moral rights. For a right can be derived from nothing less than a right, e.g., the right to life from the right of agents to pursue their interests. And if we look to those features in human beings for a so-called basis for moral rights, nothing will do except what is manifest to the observer (not something hidden, for how else would it be possible for us unhesitatingly and reliably as we do to ascribe such rights to individuals)—specifically, those features that human beings exhibit when they proceed as responsible beings in meeting the normative requirements imposed upon them by their rights and those of others, or, when because of fault or necessity they do not meet those requirements, their responses to their own omissions and commissions: the explanations and excuses they offer to those who may hold them to account, the guilt and the remorse they suffer, and the remedies they recognize they are called upon to make, whatever it is possible for them to do so, for the moral injury for which they are responsible. In other words, what alone can be provided as an explanation of moral rights is not some basis or Cartesian foundation from which the possession of rights can be deduced, but only a more detailed description of those features of human beings relevant to the role that rights and obligations play in our common moral life. Explanations of rights can only take the form of more detailed descriptions of the ways in which to a greater or lesser degree and in the endlessly varied circumstances of human life rights play their role in our thought, feeling, and action.[15]

Welfare Rights—Arguments Pro and Con

I turn now to the question of whether or not there are moral welfare rights—the rights that individuals have to the income support, of some sort or another, needed to bridge the gap between whatever income, if any, they may have and that income level or its equivalent necessary for some minimal but acceptable level of well-being. I shall not attempt to discuss the complex and difficult questions involved in any attempt to specify such a level, or whether in fact it is possible to do so without taking into account such highly variable factors as cost of living, individual interests, aptitudes, and life-styles, age, state of health, and so on. But however that notion of an acceptable level may vary with relevant circumstances, we do have at least a rough conception of what a minimal standard of decent human life would be in specific cases. And however variable this conception and however difficult the problems of administering any program of welfare which attempts to take account of such variability, it is clear that many individuals are unable to muster enough income by their own efforts and need assistance from others in order to maintain decent conditions of life.

Since we can no longer accept the view that those unable to fend for themselves in tolerably decent ways have only themselves to blame, and that the assistance to be given them in order to improve their wretched lot is to take the form of charity, some programs of public assistance are clearly needed in order to provide these individuals with minimal but morally acceptable conditions of life. In recent years the claim that individuals have rights to the satisfaction of certain basic human needs has been implemented by legal and administrative measures designed to insure that these basic human needs are met. We do not question, I trust, that there are good and sufficient moral reasons for measures of this general sort; the only question we need to ask is what sort of moral reasons are in order. Are these moral reasons the welfare rights that individuals deficient in income levels possess?

If there are welfare rights, are these special rights that individuals have, as in the case of the rights of promisees, by viture of the transactions in which they engage with one another, or, as in the case of parents or children, by virtue of the relations in which they stand to one another? The answer would appear to be in the negative. For if there are rights of welfare recipients these would appear not to depend upon their relations to or transactions with others. Nor is there any mutual understanding of the support that others are to give them upon which the alleged welfare right depends; certainly welfare programs were instituted when no such understanding existed. It is, rather, the fact that individuals are presumably unable by their own efforts to satisfy their basic needs, and, accordingly that they are compelled to live below minimally acceptable standards of human decency. It would appear, therefore, that if there are welfare rights, these must be rights that they have as human beings.

But here we are faced with the prospect of adding one more to a large and growing list of putative human rights. If we look to what one writer has described as "the most complete of currently authoritative declarations of human rights, that passed by the Assembly of the United Nations in 1948,"[16] reaffirmed in recent days in the Helsinki agreement and in the public pronouncements of those deploring the trials of dissidents in Russia, we cannot fail to be impressed by the manner in which the list of such rights has grown since the days of Locke and Jefferson and by the change that has taken place since the days of Jeremy Bentham, for whom the doctrine of natural or human rights seemed to be "nonsense upon stilts."[17] The climate of opinion has indeed changed when not only philosophers but moralists and persons in government cite not only the rights to life, liberty, the pursuit of happiness, property, security, and resistance to oppression, but a wide variety of other alleged human rights, such as the rights to freedom of movement, to leave and to return to one's native land, to work without discrimination, to equal pay for equal work, etc., etc., including the right to rest, leisure, periodic holidays with pay, not to mention those rights in Article 25 of the *Universal Declaration of Human Rights* which call for a broad variety of social welfare programs.

I have no desire to denigrate an historically important document or to minimize the moral importance of the many things to which the title of "human right" is given in this document of the United Nations. But why not go on to add to these? Surely it would be mistreating human beings in factories not to permit them to leave their workbenches in order to answer the periodic calls of nature or to lay down their tools for coffee breaks. Shall we then say that workers in factories have, among their basic human rights, the rights to go to the toilet and to take midmorning or midafternoon coffee breaks?

There are those who may be undaunted by this apparently endless proliferation of human rights. And why not, since this seems to be in keeping with the currently fashionable talk about human rights at the highest levels of government? But the reply to this is not merely that we need to refrain from multiplying human rights beyond necessity, but that there are certain substantive considerations about the nature of human rights that tell against this proliferation.

For human rights, first, are fundamental in the sense that without them there could not be the variety of moral rights that depend for their existence upon the quite special circumstances within which individuals conduct their affairs with one another. The rights of the recipient of a promise, for example, arise with the mutual understanding of the support which a promiser is to provide for the agency of the promisee, but such a mutual understanding *by itself* is unable to generate any moral right the promisee has to the promised performance (or abstention); at best, the failure of the promiser to act in accordance with the mutual understanding that exists between promiser and promisee would be merely defeating the expectation of the latter, unless there is some right of the promisee that is breached with the breach of the mutual understanding created by the promised transaction. And, as I have argued elsewhere, this right that must exist independently of the promised transaction is the right that any agent has, as moral agent, to pursue his interests and thereby, it is hoped, to achieve the goods these define. For it is only on the assumption that there is such a right that the mutual understanding of the support the promiser is to provide the agency of the promisee, during the course of some line of conduct in which he intends to engage, can have this logical consequence, namely, that a failure to carry out the terms of that understanding and make good the assurance contained therein is to subvert the agency of the promisee in that line of conduct to which the promised action (or abstention) is essential, thereby doing him moral injury by failing to accord him his right.

So, too, with the relation between members of a family in which there is a characteristic distribution of rights and obligations that constitute the moral relations in which they stand to one another. The mutual understanding of the support each is to give to and receive from others serves to generate rights and obligations only if the members of the family have as a matter of human right the right to pursue their interests.[18] Throughout, therefore, this fundamental moral right of human beings is presupposed by the special rights they have against one another when the mutual understandings of the support they are to provide one another arise in the course of their transactions with and relations to one another.

Second, human rights are rights that persons have simply as human beings. They are rights they have in common without regard to the enormous differences in their circumstances or in their character, interests, or in any other features they exhibit as individuals. In respect of human rights, therefore, persons are on terms of equality.

Third, human rights are important and morally basic in that the recognition of their possession by individuals establishes that they are beings capable of entering into these special moral relations with other human beings, relations constituted by the special rights and obligations they have with respect to one another. To recognize others in this way is to recognize them as members of the moral community, as individuals with whom good moral relations are possible in principle, difficult as it may be in practice to achieve them. The alternative can be only to exclude them from the moral community, to regard them as beings devoid of rights whom we may treat kindly but against whom we need, as in the case of psychopaths, to adopt measures to protect them from the retaliation others may seek in response to the damage they may cause them, and to protect ourselves from the harm they are apt to do us. But for those to whom, unproblematically, we do ascribe human rights, there are moral requirements that stem from their rights; and I shall comment later on some of these in connection with social welfare programs.

We need at this point to examine whether the alleged human right of the needy to a minimal and decent level of income support exhibits the features of human rights I have enumerated, and, if not, what kind of moral grounds there are for such programs of income support.

First, how could one show that the alleged right to income support is basic or fundamental? Clearly, by showing that special moral rights, separately or collectively, imply the existence of such a right, that in the absence of such a right, there could not be the moral relations between individuals constituted by the rights that they have against one another. But it is wildly implausible to maintain, for example, that there could not be the right established by a promise, or the right of one member of a family with respect to another, without the right that any of these persons have to income support. For even if any of these persons were in need of the support required for them to enjoy a decent mode of life, with at least minimally adequate food, clothing, shelter, and other necessities, this would establish not that any of their rights could not exist without a right to income support, but something quite different, namely, that they could not enjoy such a life without receiving the required support.

The case is quite unlike that which obtains, for example, in the relation between the right persons have to pursue their interests and the right they have to life itself. For it is a truism that pursuing one's interest implies being alive, and it follows, accordingly, that if one has a right to the former, one will, necessarily, have a right to the latter. And the case is quite different from that of a paradigm case of a promise in which the promised performance is essential to an endeavor in which the promisee intends to engage, and in which there could not be any right he has to the promised action, unless he has a right as moral agent to engage in lines of conduct in which he pursues his interests and hopes to achieve his good.

The arguments for the alleged right to income support take quite a different form; they attempt to show, usually, the necessity of providing such support in order that the needy may achieve those goods that make life for them worthwhile and worthy of human beings. But this is far removed from the conclusion they seek to establish. In any case, it does not show that the alleged right is basic or fundamental in the required sense. For, unless one supplies the premise that individuals have a right to a decent form of life, the consideration that income support will enable certain individuals to achieve such a life simply does not establish that they have a right to the required support; we need to show not only that persons ought to enjoy lives worthy of human beings, but that they have a right to some of the things necessary for them to achieve this. And we need, further, to show that if any of them have a right as human beings to the income support needed in order to achieve such a life, that this right is basic or fundamental in the required sense.

I shall later consider one more argument for the view that the needy have a right to income support. But for the present I wish to turn to the second of the three features of human rights I mentioned earlier. Human rights, as we have seen, are invariant with respect to the circumstances and individual characteristics of human beings. They are, in addition, unalienable; that is to say, they cannot be waived or relinquished. And while an individual may cease to have the rights that human beings have in common, this is possible only if that being is transformed into something less than the human being he has been. By the same token, human rights cannot be acquired by any human being, for as a human being he already has them; there is nothing he can acquire in the form of human rights if he is already a human being with the features of a moral agent, just as there is nothing he can lose in the form of human rights as long as he remains the moral agent he is.

Now, the idea that persons have, among their human rights, the right to vacations with pay is incoherent, for this is a right that human beings have not in common with any other human beings but only as employees. Such a right, if indeed it is a moral right, can be acquired by becoming gainfully employed. But human rights are invariant with respect to the circumstances of human beings, and they can neither be acquired nor lost by human beings. In the same way, the doctrine that the needy have as their human right the right to income support, in order to bring them up to some satisfactory level of income that would provide them with certain goods essential to a minimally desirable form of human existence, would appear confused: this is a right that only the needy have, not those who are affluent. Further, such a right can be acquired by those who suffer severe economic losses that reduce their income below certain levels; and it can be lost by those who acquire the necessary income to enable them to escape from the deprivations they have previously suffered. It would appear, therefore, that whatever welfare rights may be, they cannot be human rights.

The reply to this argument is that welfare rights have been needlessly restricted to those who are in dire need, in the same way in which the right to vacations with pay *is* restricted to those who are employed. But why not formulate the doctrine of welfare rights so that what it asserts is that any human being has the right to a certain minimal level of well-being, whether or not in any given case supplementary support is necessary in order to bring the person to that level of well-being? If persons already enjoy that level of well-being by virtue of their own income, well and good—they have the morally desirable level of well-being and they need no help from any external source. It is only if they fall short of the required level of well-being that income support is needed in order to accord them the right to well-being they have as human beings. In short, whether or not they are in dire need, persons have as their human right the right to a certain minimal level of well-being. And this is a right they can neither acquire nor lose as long as their status as human beings remains unchanged.

Still, we need some argument to show that there is such a human right, for the mere fact that a certain level of well-being is morally desirable is hardly enough. Now, it has been argued by Henry Shue that there is a right to physical security that is basic on the ground that "no one can fully enjoy any right . . . if someone can credibly threaten him or her with murder, rape, beating, etc., when he or she tries to enjoy the alleged right. . . . No rights other than a right to physical security can in fact be enjoyed if a right to physical security is not protected."[19] And Shue goes on to argue that "subsistence, or minimal economic security . . . can also be shown to be as well justified for treatment as a socially basic right as physical security is—and for the same reasons."[20]

The argument is unlike the one stated previously which moves from the right to pursue one's interests to the right to life. For that argument proceeded on the basis of an entailment relation holding between the pursuit of one's interests and being alive. The present argument proceeds from the fact that there are certain basic human rights to the conclusion that there must be a right to minimal economic security, on the ground that otherwise there could be no *enjoyment* of these basic human rights. But the conclusion surely does not follow; for what is required in order that these human rights may be enjoyed is *not* that there be a *right* to this minimal economic security, but that there *ought* to be this minimal economic security. Otherwise an indefinitely large series of basic rights is threatened. For in the same way one could argue that in order to enjoy the right to minimal economic security there must be a basic right to the legislation by means of which alone it is possible to enjoy this right. And in order to enjoy the basic right to this legislation, there must be a basic right to institute proceedings to pass such legislation by means of which alone, etc., etc. And this is not only to launch a regress of basic or human rights, it is also to elevate to the status of human rights, rights that go beyond the nature of human beings as such since they relate to the structure of our political institutions.

But no such regress need be initiated. Granted the moral folly of ascribing rights to persons which admittedly they cannot possibly enjoy, what is required by the ascription of basic human rights to individuals is that there be the settings appropriate to those rights within which these may be enjoyed. Given then that there are such basic human rights, it follows not that there are basic rights to whatever is needed in order that these rights may be enjoyed, but, rather, that we ought to provide, by whatever means we can effectively and efficiently do so, the settings in which individuals may enjoy their rights as human beings, including the minimal economic security they need in order that they may go about their affairs, pursuing their interests and achieving the goods that make life worth living for them.

The situation here is by no means peculiar to human rights; it also holds true of special rights. For moral rights do not exist in vacuo, without regard to a setting appropriate to their exercise. For the moral rights established by the mutual understanding that exists between, e.g., a husband and wife, call for a setting appropriate to these rights; otherwise that moral understanding, in the case of a morally askew conception shared by a domineering husband and a submissive wife, of the roles they are to play with respect to each other, can only preserve the morally objectionable treatment by the husband of his wife, in which he is brutalized and she lives a life that is not worthy of a human being, however willingly she may accept it for herself. If we are to think of the moral rights of husband and wife as unproblematic, we must assume a setting that is appropriate for them, in which interests and capacities of both parties are allowed to develop and flourish in ways that enable the support that each is to provide the agency of the other, a support understood by both parties to be forthcoming, to contribute to making the lives they have joined worthy of them as the human beings they are.

And in the same way, if there are rights that persons have as human beings, a setting for their exercise and enjoyment is called for in which, among other things, there is a certain minimally acceptable level of economic security that will enable those capable of it to achieve their proper development in the societies in which they live, and thereby obtain for themselves the goods that make their lives worthy of the particular human beings they are.

The argument, therefore, that there is a fundamental right to a certain minimal level of income support, on the ground that without it no fundamental rights can be enjoyed, confuses two quite different matters: the fundamental rights we do in fact have and the conditions of their enjoyment, or, as I have put it, the settings within which such rights may be enjoyed. Granted that rights, fundamental or not, do not exist in vacuo, that they call for settings within which they may be exercised and enjoyed, and that, in the case of fundamental rights, there are moral requirements we must bear to ensure, as far as it is possible for us to do, that human beings live in the settings called for by such rights—granted all this, it simply does not follow that, by rejecting the claim that human beings have as one of their fundamental rights the right to an adequate level of income support, we are in effect reading the needy out of the moral community of persons. Our fundamental moral rights are enough to establish them as full-fledged members of the moral community without including among these a fundamental or human right to income support.

Conclusion

Are there fundamental or human rights to welfare? No. But there are serious moral requirements we must bear because of the settings called for by the fundamental rights of human beings, settings within which alone it is possible for persons to acquire and to pursue interests worthy of human beings so that their lives may be worthwhile. Hence it is *because* of the fundamental rights of persons—their human rights—that we must provide the needy with adequate levels of income support in order that it may be possible for them and for their children to live lives worthy of the human beings they are. And if we fail to do what we can in providing this assistance for those in dire need, our fault is no mere lack of generosity, kindness, or sympathy for those who encounter difficulty and need our assistance in order that they may succeed in their endeavors. Our failure to help is not an occasion for mere shame on our part; it is, rather, one that calls for a sense of guilt, because of our failure to contribute our assistance in providing them with a setting appropriate to the rights they have as human beings, just as was the case for those law-abiding or conforming individuals in Nazi Germany who went about their private affairs with the stench of burning human flesh in their nostrils or at the sight of Nazi bully-boys beating up defenseless Jews, as if these were matters that were none of their business.

The Founding Fathers of this nation, like John Locke before them, were wise in restricting the list of unalienable or natural rights to a very small number of items. For those who in recent years have expanded the catalog of natural or human rights were mindful, not of the *rights* which individual human beings have as individuals, but of the necessity of implementing such rights, given the radically altered social circumstances of human life in our contemporary society. Hence the talk of rights to travel freely from one community to another, to vacations with pay, and so on. For even if welfare rights are defined as rights to a certain minimal level of income support, the thinking here is in fact about a right that individuals are supposed to have as the beneficiaries of certain social services, which implies that this right, like the rights to paid vacations, to travel freely, and so on, are rights that individuals are alleged to have, not as the individuals they are because of their nature as human beings, but in virtue of their situations in the social circumstances in which they live.

This is not surprising, since the reason for claiming that there are such rights is the conviction, sound as it is, that unless some acceptable level of income support is assured to all who live in our present technologically developed and complicated social and political world, the rights that Locke and the Founding Fathers ascribed to human beings are likely to be, for many of us, empty moral possessions, as much so as the title of "Vice President in charge of . . ." that may be assigned to the most menial of employees. The motivation is clear, but the move is unnecessary, given the distinction I have drawn between rights and the requisite settings for their enjoyment. And the move may well prove to be counterproductive by fostering the suspicion, on the part of those who have any doubts at all that there are unalienable natural or human rights, that those of us who do talk about human rights are employing an inflated rhetoric that serves only to buttress our strong moral convictions.

Notes

1. John Rawls, *A Theory of Justice* (Cambridge, Mass.: Harvard University Press, 1971), p. 60.

2. See Kant's *Foundations of the Metaphysics of Morals*, at beginning of Sec. 1.

3. I shall not discuss those arguments for or claims made in support of vegetarianism based on quite different considerations: religious convictions about the sacred nature of all life or philosophical appeals to our kinship with fellow inhabitants on mother earth.

4. In this respect I fully endorse the view expressed by Paul Vernier in his chapter, "Rights to Welfare as an Issue in Income Support Policy," that advocates of moral rights should provide persuasive answers to these questions.

5. Cf. *Fundamental Legal Conceptions* (New Haven: Yale University Press, 1923).

6. For some of these, see H. L. A. Hart, "Are There Natural Rights?," *The Philosophical Review*, April 1955.

7. See my *Rights and Persons* for this and other claims made concerning the complex features of moral rights.

8. In this connection see my comments concerning the oft-repeated but mistaken claim (in no small measure fostered by Bentham's fierce and injudicious attack, in his *Anarchical Fallacies*, on the French Assembly's *Declaration of the Rights of Man and of Citizens*, an attack many have supposed must apply to Locke's views as well) that Locke held the absurd view that absolute rights may be exercised no matter what the circumstances may be, that they cannot be justifiably infringed. See in this connection my *Rights and Persons*, pp. 12–13.

9. *Second Treatise of Civil Government*, Ch. II.

10. See in this connection pp. 22–26 in my *Rights and Persons*. Dignity is not some esoteric attribute of a rationality invisible to the eye, as Kant thought, but manifest in the behavior of human beings in the public forum.

11. What this precept conveys is that the keeping of a promise is as such a reason for the relevant promise keeping act. It serves usually as a reminder to one who has promised that he or she does have a good moral reason, one that may be overridden (hence the familiar locution, "One ought to keep one's promises, but . . ."). But as it stands it offers no reason for why it is that it is a reason; that is to say, it does not itself cite any right as the underlying reason for the keeping of promises.

12. See my discussion of the issue of the alleged analogy between moral and legal rights in my *Rights and Persons*, pp. 227ff.

13. See my *Rights and Persons*, especially Chapters II and III in which I discuss a variety of rights, beginning with those established formally by means of promises.

14. Even if, with Kant, we were to concede that rational nature exists as an end in itself, and for *this* reason is worthy of our respect, how does *this* enable us to deduce the possession of moral rights, rights we ascribe not only to those whom, as we say, we do *not* respect because of their serious moral flaws, but also to those whom we do respect—not because of some abstract rationality that they have in common with scoundrels, but because of their manifest moral merit, in which the former are lacking?

15. It is not possible, because of lack of space, to do more than indicate the direction in which such explanations of rights must go. I have tried to provide a more detailed account in my *Rights and Persons*, pp. 199–206.

16. Cf. Gregory Vlastos in his essay, "Justice and Equality," published originally in *Social Justice*, ed. R. B. Brandt and reprinted with minor excisions and the addition of a concluding footnote in *Human Rights*, ed. A. I. Melden (Belmont, California: Wadsworth Publishing Co., 1970).

17. In *Anarchical Fallacies;* the selection in which this characterization occurs can be found in *Human Rights*, ed. A. I. Melden, pp. 28–39.

18. This is not the whole story, of course. Later, I shall remark upon one important feature of the logical substratum of rights, in addition to the point being made here that a human right is presupposed by the special rights that human beings have against each other.

19. In his paper, "Foundations for a Balanced U. S. Policy on Human Rights: The

Significance of Subsistence Rights," pp. 6–7. An expanded version will appear as Chapter 1 in Henry Shue, *Basic Rights: Subsistence, Affluence, and U.S. Foreign Policy* (Princeton: Princeton University Press, 1980).

   20. *Ibid.*, p. 9.

PART FOUR

History and Prospects of Welfare Reform

Introduction

Any thoughtful study of basic issues in income support policy must take account of changing social and economic circumstances, past and future. Policies which successfully effectuate some set of social objectives in one period of history may not succeed in another. While there have been significant numbers of poor people in the United States since colonial times, the demographic characteristics of the poor have undergone major shifts from period to period, as have social and economic conditions associated with poverty. The advent of industrialism at the end of the last century provides a dramatic instance of such a change.

This concluding section is concerned with income support policy issues from the historical perspective, beginning with colonial times and extending into the foreseeable future. Two of the four papers take as their subject matter the nature and outcome of the most recent effort to accomplish a major reform of the present system, that sponsored by the Carter administration in 1977–78. It will be noted in these two papers that the term "welfare reform" is frequently used. The term "welfare" has, in recent years, become synonymous with "income support," even though the real scope of welfare programs extends far beyond the range of income support provisions. However, the term "welfare reform" has been retained because it was given this name throughout the period of debate over reforming the income support system, beginning with the Nixon Family Assistance Plan in 1969–72.

Wayne Vasey's paper, which begins the section, examines the history of our basic social welfare policies from colonial times to the present day. Vasey's thesis is that a set of fundamental conflicts in public views about the poor and programs to help them have complicated and usually hampered the development of income support policies and programs. These divergent viewpoints, he holds, have been held mainly in respect to (1.) the extent to which need is individually or socially caused; (2.) the appropriate role of government, especially the federal government, in providing for economic need; and (3.) the effect on needy individuals of providing income support—the fear that dependency will be fostered by such programs. We need to be well informed regarding such conflicts in viewpoint, Vasey points out, if we are to understand the forces that have shaped our policies and that may be expected to have an important effect on them in the period ahead.

In the second paper, entitled "An Assessment of Major Welfare Reform Proposals of the 95th Congress," Robert Fersh examines four important legislative proposals for replacing or modifying the existing income support system that were put before the Congress in 1977–78, including a Carter administration bill. His main interest is to appraise the extent to which any of these proposals would, if enacted, have represented

281

significant changes in the social values underlying our income support policy. He concludes that the basic features of the existing system would have remained intact. These features are the commitment *(1.)* to provide government support to the needy; *(2.)* to provide support on the basis of a means test; *(3.)* to provide different programs and services for different groups of the poor; and *(4.)* to enforce work requirements for those deemed able to work. In the second part of his paper, Fersh examines the moral consequences of giving priority to financial work incentives over adequacy of benefits when the two objectives come into competition. This problem is illustrated in the Carter administration's welfare reform proposal in the following way: Two-parent families would have received reduced benefits under that proposal for the first two months during which an active job search was to be carried out. Fersh argues that adequacy of benefits should be given priority on moral grounds in this set of circumstances.

Henry Aaron's paper, entitled "Welfare Reform: What Kind and When?" follows. It is also an account of the Carter administration's welfare reform effort, but from a different perspective. In his position as Assistant Secretary of the Department of Health, Education and Welfare in 1977–79, he was the principal architect of the administration's welfare proposal. Although reform legislation failed to be enacted, he contends that a basic consensus regarding the nature of needed reforms emerged from the effort. Although the prospects for future major reforms are not bright, this consensus, he believes, does mean that they are better than they have been in many years.

The principal elements of this consensus, according to Aaron, are the following: *(1.)* a national minimum level of benefits for AFDC families; *(2.)* coverage of two-parent families in the income support system beyond the present very limited inclusion; *(3.)* a requirement that able-bodied adults work if not needed at home, together with creation of jobs for recipients to the extent needed; *(4.)* increased benefits from the Earned Income Tax Credit for low income families; and *(5.)* fiscal relief to states and localities by expansion of the federal contribution.

The last paper, James Rotherham's "Impact of Future Social and Demographic Change in Programs for Reducing Economic Dependency," identifies and appraises the probable effects of a number of anticipated changes in social and demographic circumstances which will have an important bearing on income support policy in future decades. His paper makes it clear that social welfare planning that does not take expected changes into account is likely to produce policies that are poorly adapted to a changing world. Rotherham's principal conclusion is that the non-aged population most likely to be economically deprived in the years ahead are those minorities that are particularly subject to discriminatory treatment in the field of employment—blacks, Hispanics, and women.

PV

15

Recurring Themes in the Income Support Policy Debate—Obstacles to Change

WAYNE VASEY

We do some things well and other things badly in this country, but we do few things as badly as we do welfare reform.—Meg Greenfield in *Newsweek*, May 9, 1977.

For more than a decade, welfare reform has been high on the list of stated national domestic priorities for successive administrations, but thus far has eluded all efforts to bring it about. It is the premise of this paper that welfare, public aid to the needy, has been one of the most controversial of all areas of domestic public policy because of conflicts over moral and conceptual issues that have long historical roots. At the heart of the problem is not poverty per se, but poverty resulting in public dependency. It is the act of asking for help that attracts criticism, not the condition that causes it. It was not until the 1960s that poverty itself became the declared business of the national government.

Moral and conceptual issues that arise in connection with welfare include the following:

1. The cause of welfare dependency. Is it individually based or socially caused? Does it arise out of some defect of character, or individual and personal failure of performance, or out of failure of the social institutions to function satisfactorily? In other words, has the individual person failed—or been failed?

2. The role of government as a welfare provider. How far should

government at any level go in meeting welfare needs? Does welfare foster the very dependency that it is supposed to treat? The issue of the role of government is complicated, especially in the past fifty years, by the question of the relations among the levels of government—federal, state, and local—in supporting or providing welfare.

3. The relation of welfare to work. In welfare policy, this has been expressed in the form of the use of a requirement of work for relief as a test of the authenticity of need, and as a preferred method of providing aid to able-bodied needy persons.

These are not issues that are quickly and simply resolved. They are too deeply imbedded in the American traditions and values with respect to all of the members of this society. But they have a special application when applied to the status of a person seeking public aid in this country. This is not intended as a history of welfare in America. Rather, its purpose is to identify some points at which these three issues or strands have appeared and reappeared. It is assumed that while this kind of review will not provide solutions to the problems of welfare, it may help to put these problems in some perspective and may offer a background for some of the current difficulties with welfare reform.

Welfare Under the Poor Law

This account begins with the English Poor Law brought by the early colonists from the mother country. The poor law survived in both principle and practice through more than three centuries of American life. Even the first welfare reform, the Social Security Act of 1935, has a number of residual features of the old poor law.

The English poor law was enacted in the reign of Elizabeth I, in 1601. It included the following provisions: It identified three classes of dependents, the able-bodied vagrant or presumably willfully idle, the involuntarily unemployed or "impotent poor," and the helpless—those whose condition of age or disability rendered them incapable of employment. It assigned responsibility for providing aid to the local unit of government, then the parish, and authorized it to raise such taxes as were required and to enforce the obligation of support. Administration of aid was put into the hands of an official called the "overseer of the poor," appointed by the local justices of the peace. The parishes were empowered to levy taxes for support of the poor. Funds could be used to develop and maintain almshouses for the able-bodied, and to provide aid in their own homes for the blameless, i.e., the helpless poor. The able-bodied could be set to work, and tax funds could be used for that purpose. Primary responsibility for support rested with the family—children were obligated to care for parents and grandparents; parents and grandparents were liable for support of children and grandchildren. Children could be set to work or could be bound out as apprentices if parents were unable to provide for them.

Justices were empowered to "commit to the House of Correction or common gaol such poor persons as shall not employ themselves to work, being appointed thereto by the overseers."[1]

The poor law provided a further precedent for American policies and practices by serving purposes that were ancillary to aiding the destitute. In fact, one historian suggested that the ordering of priorities of purpose of the law was as follows: "first, the suppression of vagabondage and violence—conjointly with some relief for the destitute by means of charitable or enforced contributions—then, the relief of destitution from whatever cause, and lastly, the relief of destitution and want in such a manner as that, while effective for that object, it shall not weaken the incentive to independent exertion on the part of individuals or of the laboring classes, or of the public general."[2] Caring for the poor was described as "an act of the greatest civil prudence and political wisdom, for that poverty is in itself apt to emasculate the minds of men, or at least it makes them tumultuous and unquiet."[3] The poor law affirmed a limited and firm conception of public responsibility. It represented an attempt "to create a new statutory relationship of status, in which the responsibility for poor persons was laid first upon relatives to whom the poor belonged and, failing that, upon the place to which the poor belonged."[4] While the poor law clearly enunciated the principle of governmental obligation to provide aid, it did not establish the status of the right to receive it.

As early as 1642, the statutes of the Plymouth Colony stipulated that "Every township shall make competent provision for the maintenance of the poor according as they shall find it most suitable and convenient for themselves by an order and general agreement on townmeetings and notwithstanding the permission that all such person or persons as are now resident and inhabitant within the said towns shall be maintained and provided by them."[5] Throughout the colonies, and later the nation, the local obligation for aid to the poor was enunciated as a responsibility of town, township, parish, district, or county. Local responsibility was reinforced by the influence of another English statute, the Law of Settlement, in 1662. This law had two purposes: first, to ascertain the locality to which the person belonged, and to place the obligation on that place, and second, to establish barriers to acquisition of settlement by persons whose circumstances suggested that they might at some future date become public charges, or who might be deemed undesirable for other reasons. This permitted the practice of shipping the poor back to their place of original domicile, or of simply waving or warning them out. It was also used to protect the local community from the unwelcome onslaught of alien influences.

In his history of the poor law in Massachusetts, Kelso has pointed out that the reasons for "closing the gates upon the stranger" included incompatibility of religious belief. The settlement law was used, among other purposes, to protect the Massachusetts towns from "the horrid apostasy of the Quaker." Without struggling for historical parallels, it is not too strenuous an exercise of comparison to relate to a later period, when efforts to exclude or expel the individual or family stemmed from differences in other characteristics, such as race or ethnicity.

The interest of the colonial settlements in limiting aid to their own established members is not hard to understand. "The margin of subsistence was so narrow that starvation stalked through the dreary months of more than one chill winter. There was urgent need, therefore, that the settlers guard their hearth fires against the indigent and the incompetent."[6]

Attitudes toward Dependent Poverty

In the early treatment of the poor there was not much evidence of distinction between those who were dependent by reason of physical or mental problems and those who were able-bodied and, presumably, in the labor force. "Anyone who was in need of help for a longer or shorter period was a pauper irrespective of the reasons."[7]

By the second quarter of the nineteenth century, the dominant practice of providing aid was care in local almshouses. This was intended originally as a reform of previous practices of contracting with householders for relief of the dependents, auctioning off the services of the poor person to the highest bidder, and indenturing or "binding out" the children of the poor. However well intended, the almshouses, or poorhouses, or county farms, as they were termed in various parts of the country, "were the repositories of misery in its most varied and abject form. The abandoned child, the aged respectable widow, the unemployed farmhand, and the unmarried mother and her infant shared quarters with the prostitute, the senile, and the feeble-minded, misfits of all kinds, whose personal problems, though of long standing, were understood neither by themselves nor by those who were responsible for their care." The kind of care was characterized as marked by "filth, squalor, inadequate food and clothing, lack of privacy, and exposure to the most degrading influences."[8]

Another indicator of the low esteem for the dependent poor was the quality of the official entrusted with their care. The late Karl de Schweinitz described the official in these words:

The official, perhaps most often cited as an illustration of incompetence, was the overseer of the poor. Everybody knew him as the man who managed the almshouses and supplied outdoor relief . . . to the people who could not support themselves. The inefficiency of his administration was notorious, a combination of neglect and petty despotism.

The defects of administration were ascribed to conflicts of attitude within the community that supported the system. The overseer might be considered to have been as much the victim as the villain, playing a role that was never clarified, reflecting the uncertainties and doubts that have consistently beset the administration of aid to the needy. According to de Schweinitz, "While his treatment of the persons entrusted to him was usually all the public thought it to be, and worse, he himself was largely the victim of a society that did not know what it wanted." On the one hand, there was recognition of the necessity for providing for the poor, which implied "humane administration." On the other hand, people wanted their property protected, which required stern measures, "and public relief before the twentieth century was administered as a function of the police power of the State."[9]

While the indiscriminately harsh treatment of the poor by the local officials may not have seemed to reflect distinctions between the helpless or blameless and the able-bodied, categorical distinctions were made in other ways. The development of special institutions for the care of selected classes of the dependents was the earliest of such measures.[10] The interest was not so much in reforming the poor law as in removing certain groups from its jurisdiction. Similar categorical distinctions were made in the first three decades of the twentieth century by the enactment in a number of states of programs of cash assistance to persons in their own homes for preferred classes of dependents. This followed the time-honored practice of separating the impotent or blameless poor from those thought to be able but unwilling to provide for themselves.

By 1931, forty-five states had enacted legislation for dependent children (mothers' aid), and by 1935, more than half the states had made statutory provision for cash assistance, euphemistically called "pensions," for the aged and the blind. Slight use of state funds was made for these purposes. In many cases, no appropriations were made, and in those that made provision, the appropriations were too small to meet the costs. Depending largely on local funds, they provided for only a fraction of those in need in the selected categories.

The enactment of mothers' aid, however sparing its use among the states, is an indication of some change of attitude toward children of the poor. Over the years, as the dangers of exposing these children to the degrading influence of the almshouse became clear, special institutions or orphanages had seemed the best way to provide for them. In the latter part of the nineteenth century, a blend of biological determinism and social Darwinism fostered the view that the institution was the best way of combining care and control. Indenture of homeless children who had been placed in institutions over time evolved into arrangements for foster care.[11]

In 1909, at the first White House Conference on Children, called by President Theodore Roosevelt, the principle was enunciated that no child should be removed from his or her own home solely because of poverty. This was the principle that formed the basis for mothers' aid legislation, and subsequently for the aid-to-dependent-children category in the Social Security Act of 1935. As an expression of public policy and purpose, these special categorical measures were important. By frequently using the term "pension," they suggested the principle of risk and entitlement, and acknowledged the existence of social and economic causes of poverty on circumstances external to the character and behavior of the individual poor person.

Right up the Great Depression of the 1930s, the prevailing policy was a poor law but little changed in more than three centuries of American history. The general objective was one of keeping relief expenditures as low as possible. Little effort was made to secure accurate information about recipients. "To be 'on the town' or 'on the county' was the lowest state outside prison to which a member of the community could descend."[12] Many states required pauper's oaths. Lists of persons receiving aid were available for public scrutiny, in official reports of county or township governments in weekly or daily newspapers, and on lists posted on courthouse or town-hall bulletin boards.

This necessarily brief summary of the persistence of a poor-law philosophy that reflected a harsh and uncompromising view of the dependent poor does not sufficiently acknowledge the continuing existence of a view widely at variance with the belief that the poor were the sole authors of their condition. Throughout the history there were critics and crusaders who believed that the poor were as much sinned against as sinning. One of these believers was Joseph Tuckerman, a Unitarian minister, who believed in the superiority of preventive measures over both public relief and private charity. He was born in Boston in 1798, entered the ministry after graduation from Harvard, and, after twenty-five years of parish life, became a missionary among the Boston poor. "Recognizing the economic causes of poverty, he became a champion of social reform."[13]

But accounts of the history of the first half of the nineteenth century suggest that the problems of the poor, while they were not unnoticed, "did not attract much reforming zeal." The "deserving poor" were those who could be elevated from their condition by personal influence designed to strengthen their moral fiber and to stimulate their wish for independence. One of the leaders of an earlier movement toward this end, the New York Association for Improving the Condition of the Poor, was Robert Hartley, whose initial interest was in the temperance movement and religious education. Inspired by the chaotic growth of private relief efforts during the depression period and aversion to the harshness of the poor law, he attempted, by the use of volunteers, to provide moral aid rather than financial relief. In time, however, the society became a relief-giving agency and was in some respects the prototype of the later private relief agency, with its stress on investigation and individualization of treatment of need, combined with efforts to improve the housing and health of the poor. On the other hand were those who believed strongly that both private charity and public aid were not only destructive in their influence on the lives and character of the poor, but also destroyed the impulse to find other means.[14]

In the last quarter of the nineteenth century, a major institutional development was the growth of organized private philanthropy. While it was developed completely outside the public poor relief system, it had a profound effect in later influence on public assistance.

The Charity Organization Society, imported from England in 1877, had as its initial purpose the elimination of indiscriminate unorganized relief giving, and the development of means of assisting the poor to remove themselves from the condition of poverty. Beginning in Buffalo, the movement spread in fifteen years to more than ninety cities in the United States. Their methods involved many of the same approaches that had characterized the earlier AICP: friendly visiting, individual investigation of need, and in addition, a registration or clearance procedure, to avoid duplication of relief among the various charitable agencies. Over the years, the methods of "scientific charity" evolved into the practice of family-oriented casework. Early volunteers or "friendly visitors" worked under the influence of paid agents, and in the course of time salaried workers were added and gradually replaced the volunteers.

The charity organization societies in the larger cities largely replaced the smaller private relief-giving agencies. They came to believe that private philanthropy was the answer to the problem of poor relief. They fostered the concept of "scientific charity" and contributed to the growth of the profession of social work. While seeking better ways of individualizing treatment, however, they continued to press for action designed to alleviate the effect of external influences on poverty.

Private philanthropy was largely confined to urban communities, leaving the countryside to the not so tender mercies of the overseer of the poor. Even in the cities, local public relief continued without any significant evidence of cooperation or communication with the private philanthropic system. As late as 1929, three-fourths of all aid was provided by public poor-relief offices even though the view persisted that they were inherently corrupt and incurably inefficient.

Role of Government

There were some exceptions. In 1910, the first municipal board of public welfare was established in Kansas City, Missouri. Following that beginning, more than one hundred boards of similar kinds and purpose were put into operation throughout the country. In 1917, North Carolina established by law a state-wide system of county boards of public welfare. Some few states, notably Alabama and New Mexico, created special state and local departments of public welfare. In these days of general rejection of the term "welfare," it is interesting to review the high hopes that were held for this emerging form of public administration. The late illustrious sociologist Howard W. Odum, of the University of North Carolina, emphasized that by "public welfare," not simply "welfare," or "human welfare," or "social welfare," the responsibility of government was affirmed for redressing the balance of opportunity for "unequal folk in unequal places."[15] The idea of putting the administration of aid in the hands of experts was perceived as vastly superior in both form and purpose to the traditional method of poor relief.

Prior to the 1930s, the states had only a minor role to play in the administration of welfare. As has been noted, early in the nineteenth century, some state governments began to assume the obligation for institutional care for certain classes of paupers. While the objective might have been humanitarian, there is also the possible explanation that some kinds of dependents were too few in number in a given locality to justify a local institution. The first categories of dependents to be given care in state institutions were the insane, followed by the mentally deficient, then the deaf. Later other categories were added. In 1863, Massachusetts created the first State Board of Charities. Other states followed this example. Their duties were largely visitational and inspectional, rather than administrative, and could extend to inspection of local almshouses and prisons. They had no responsibility for outdoor poor relief except for the unsettled poor.

The view that public aid was outside the limits of federal authority was enunciated in 1854 by President Franklin Pierce, in his veto of a measure enacted by Congress, authorizing the giving of millions of acres of land to the states for the purpose of providing institutions for the insane. This measure had been the result of a persuasive and moving appeal by a pioneer reformer, Dorothea Lynde Dix. This episode of history, and the subsequent veto message of the President, is cited often as a definitive statement of federal limitation of power which persisted long after its time. In his message, the President maintained that the welfare clause of the Constitution (Article I, Section 8) did not confer the power on Congress to provide for the indigent insane, and raised the specter of a precedent which might extend to all classes of poor persons, indigent for whatever reason. This might, in the language of the President's message, "transfer to the federal government the charge of the poor in all states." This, he feared, would lead to a condition in which the "fountains of charity will be dried up at home and the several states, instead of bestowing their own means on the social wants of their own people, may themselves . . . become humble supplicants for the bounty of the federal government."[16]

It is interesting to compare this statement with one from President Herbert Hoover seventy-seven years later, on December 8, 1931. Confronted by the growing pressure of mass destitution, President Hoover nonetheless clung to the earlier principle enunciated by his predecessor in office. President Hoover declared in his message to Congress, "I am opposed to any direct or indirect government dole; if the individual surrenders his own initiative and responsibilities, he is surrendering his own freedom and his own liberty."

There are other instances of the strength and tenacity of the view of public assistance as outside the authority and responsibility of the federal government. There were, however, other welfare activities, which included a variety of services, but these were of a highly specialized character. One of the most significant of the federal welfare functions in the pre-depression period was vested in the U. S. Children's Bureau, established in 1912. It was directed by Congress "to investigate and report . . . upon all matters pertaining to the welfare of children and child life among all classes of our people." Placed within the U. S. Department of Labor, the Bureau in its discharge of its function had an impact on national life that went far beyond this seemingly innocuous responsibility. Its research and fact-finding were backed by the force of personality of its successive chiefs and by the excellence and quality of its research. Its standards of care had an immeasurable influence on child welfare practices. It influenced the passage of federal legislation in certain areas of policy, including child labor regulation, and maternal and infant care. It was charged with the enforcement of laws against child labor in interstate commerce. With respect to public aid, it undoubtedly had a strong influence in the enactment of state mothers' aid legislation, and advised states on these programs, as well as on those programs concerned with child care and protection, and juvenile delinquency. It undoubtedly established a federal presence that would be influential in subsequent welfare reform.

Explanations for the persistent limits on the welfare function of national government are not to be found in legalistic constructions of constitutional policy. As later events demonstrated, these can be set aside when there is a sufficient degree of national interest in doing so. What seems more logical in the perspective of historical development is the relation, some might say confusion, between economic and political theory in the developing structure of the American economy.

"In 1776, American statesmen proclaimed 'the equality of all men' before the law. That proclamation did not establish the doctrine. In the same year, Adam Smith proclaimed the equality of all men, women and children before the job. This proclamation did not establish the fact." In the long period that the doctrine of laissez-faire dominated the political thinking of this and other Western societies, "Political equality and economic equality became so completely identified and fused in the thinking of political and industrial leaders that few were able to escape from its confusion."[17] This statement, written in 1923, presaged much of the conflict and uncertainty seven years later, when national response to a nationwide disaster came only after a long period of struggle. The relation between freedom of the marketplace and welfare of the individual remains a complex and troublesome question.

Work and Welfare

When the Nixon administration spokesmen assured the country in 1969 that their welfare reform proposal, the Family Assistance Plan, was "workfare not welfare," they were reflecting the persistence of what is perhaps the most baffling and difficult to resolve of the historic issues of welfare policy. The "work ethic" was built into the poor law from the beginning. The use of the workhouse, the apprenticing of children of the poor, the farming out of the able-bodied adult were the earliest forms, as we have seen, and some of these practices persisted over the years.

American practice of relating welfare and work was reinforced by ready hospitality to the British Poor Law "reform" of 1834. This measure included a requirement that local administrators erect workhouses and establish a "workhouse test" with a view to discouraging the able-bodied person from choosing welfare as an alternative to work. One of the most influential of the new poor-law doctrines was the principle "that the condition of the pauper ought to be, on the whole, less eligible than that of the independent laborer."

The association between work and welfare continued to be close in American practice. In 1931, it was reported that "work relief has long been and is still regularly used by certain public welfare departments in this country in place of outright relief grants to unemployed applicants for charitable aid."[18] In both the almshouse and in the administration of outdoor relief, the recipients of aid were often set to work. Arguments past and present for requiring the able-bodied to work for their welfare have long had a plausible ring. It is alleged to be better for the morale of the individual person to do something in return for what he or she receives. Getting something for nothing is bad for character. The out-of-work person is stimulated to make extra effort to get a job if access to public aid is not too easy. The working taxpayer has the satisfaction of something to show for the dollar spent on aid. But there is another side to this. Drawbacks include the greater cost and lowered efficiency of work for relief. It is difficult to assign the work to those who most need it. It has a deleterious effect upon competitive wages, unless the work is kept strictly noncompetitive with private industry. It has a similarly deleterious effect on the workers if it extends over time.

In early times, the nature of the work often consisted of some useless task. The woodyard was frequently attached to municipal lodging houses. In later times, hastily opened workrooms "where sewing, bandage-rolling, or similar tasks were performed" were the practice. The results were "disappointing." "The work was not particularly useful or of permanent value, and there was real danger that it might interfere with the channels of trade and industry if developed on a large scale. Clients were likely to regard it precisely for what it was—a make-believe, a sugar coating for relief."[19]

It is not entirely clear in much of the current welfare reform debate what proponents of the work requirement have in mind. There is, of course, a sharp distinction between work relief and public works, viz., jobs in government for public projects—regular work for regular pay, without any test except that of qualifications for the work to be done. But there are two types of welfare-related work—work relief and work-for-relief. The former is one in which the welfare applicant or recipient is given the work, but at regular pay. This is often designed for the marginally employable, those with some handicap of disability or lack of specific skill. The accent is on the work rather than on the value of the product. The dilemma that confronts the administrators is this: The work must be sufficiently useful to avoid the charge of "boondoggling, but not so valuable that it can be criticized for competing with business."[20]

A brief historical note on the relation of work to the ADC mother is in order here. In mothers' aid and later in aid to dependent children there was enunciated the value of preserving the role of the mother as homemaker and as caretaker of the children, but the idea was selectively applied to those whose dependency arose from impeccable circumstances, viz., widowhood of the mother. While mothers' aid presumably provided for families in which the mothers were divorced, deserted, separated, or who had never married, county judges or other administering officials often raised moral questions of the fitness of mothers who were not widowed. They were often referred to work or to work-oriented relief programs. "If they could not support their families . . . the children went to public institutions or to foster homes."[21]

Work used solely as sugar coating for relief may have the consequence of degrading work without upgrading the worker. The difference may be the extent to which the work has a definite relation to the value of its labor.

Welfare Reform in the Great Depression

Massive unemployment during the Great Depression of the 1930s and the resulting condition of widespread dependency on public and private relief challenged the concept that financial need was the result of individual, personal failure. While the nation had gone through many depressions in its history, and while poverty certainly was not new, the problem in the 1930s was unique in its magnitude. It forced a reexamination of traditional attitudes toward the poor. Historic explanations of the causes of poverty and dependency continued to exert a strong influence, but did not provide a satisfactory reason why, during the period of from 1933–1938, the number of persons who were obliged to accept some form of public aid reached a staggering total of twenty-eight million.

The view that welfare was not a proper national responsibility was reluctantly relinquished. The Hoover administration clung tenaciously to its belief in the superiority of private philanthropy over public relief, and its conviction that the latter, if necessary, was strictly a matter for local action. Meanwhile, unemployment dramatically increased in a short span of time to four million in January 1930, five million in September of that year, seven million in December, and by spring, 1933, from thirteen to seventeen million. Neither the public nor the national administration was prepared for a problem of this dimension. Neither were the resources of local poor relief and private philanthropy equipped to deal with the emergency. Mutual aid and neighborly help, although extolled by national leadership, were scarcely an adequate resource, especially when neighbors, friends, and relatives were themselves in straitened circumstances. Personal savings were soon exhausted by millions of formerly self-supporting people.

The first break in the tradition of opposition to federal action came during the Hoover administration in the passage of the Emergency Relief and Construction Act in July 1932. This act empowered the Reconstruction Finance Corporation, which had been established primarily to assist industry and agriculture, to provide funds to states for relief work. These funds were dressed up as advances or "loans," however, in an effort to disguise the role of the federal government. The New Deal under President Franklin Roosevelt ushered in a series of measures between 1933 and 1935. These included the Civilian Conservation Corps to provide work opportunities for young men in the conservation of natural resources, the Rural Resettlement Administration, later the Farm Security Administration, which provided grants and loans to needy farmers, and the National Youth Administration to provide relief, work relief, and aid to needy students.

Probably the most significant of the New Deal measures from a welfare standpoint was the Federal Emergency Relief Act of 1933, which authorized funds for grants to states for relief of unemployment. This authorization, followed by an appropriation of $500 million, marked the entry of the national government into cooperative relations with the states in the provision of aid and required that the states set up administrative organizations to administer the services, or to utilize those already in being.

One of the most important of the programs of the New Deal was the Works Progress Administration (later the Work Projects Administration), enacted in January 1935. This was a large-scale program of relief through employment on publicly sponsored projects. Eligibility was based on the financial need of the family or individual, certified by the local public welfare agency. It was established in 1935 by executive order of President Roosevelt and began operation in the summer of that year. The WPA represented an effort to steer a course between work relief and public works. Over time, however, pressure from the public and from Congress moved the program considerably in the direction of work relief. Stricter measures were required. Agencies were required to make sure that workers were not refusing jobs in private industry. They were required to report their earnings, including any from private employment. Re-certification of need from time to time was demanded. Employment was restricted to only one member of any household. The term of employment was limited.

These measures of federal support and administration of aid to the needy were clearly earmarked as "emergency" in nature, and did not signal the permanent acceptance of federal governmental responsibility for action in this area of public policy. There was the implicit, and in some instances the explicit, assumption that they brought the government into "this business of relief" only for the duration of the crisis. The Social Security Act of 1935 marked the permanent entry of the federal govern-ment into the field of welfare. This act laid the foundation for the programs of public assistance that currently are the subjects of debate over welfare reform. In 1934, by executive order, President Roosevelt created a Committee on Economic Security. This committee was authorized to recommend a national program to provide what he, in his own words, had called "safeguards against risks which cannot be wholly eliminated in this man-made world of ours."[22]

The major features of the committee's report were recommendations for protection against a range of misfortunes by means of public works as a part of employment assurance, unemployment compensation, "non-contributory old-age pensions, compulsory contributory annuities and voluntary contributory annuities," "aid to fatherless children," a system of local services for the protection and care of "homeless, neglected, and delinquent children," for maternal and child health services, especially in rural areas, and, as has been noted, health insurance and grants to states for public health. The report was the basis for the Social Security Act, although the measure in its final form did include some features which were not in the committee's recommendations and excluded some that were.

The Social Security Act became effective on August 14, 1935. It enacted the following programs: grants to states to aid them in providing financial assistance to aged people, dependent children, and the blind; a federal system of old age insurance; a federal-state system of unemploy-ment insurance; grants to states to enable them to improve their services in maternal and child health, in crippled children's services and in child welfare; grants to states for public health services; and grants to states for vocational rehabilitation. Social insurance was regarded as the primary method of providing against want, as the keystone of the system. It was recognized, however, that there would be a need to supplement this means of protection against want in some cases by public assistance.

The expectation was that public assistance categories would be "both residual and transitional. They would be residual in the sense that they would provide income support to that limited number of households which had little expectation of self-support—female-headed families with children, the aged, the blind, the disabled—and that were not covered by the contributory social insurance programs. They would be transitional in that they would shrink in size as the social insurance programs expanded in coverage."[23]

Provisions of all of the public assistance categories represented a considerable departure from previous treatment of the needy applicant. These differences included the stipulation of the right of the person to apply for aid, thus protecting against arbitrary refusal without any form of administrative "due process" or prompt evaluation or adjudication of the merit of the request, and the right to an appeal and a fair hearing for a dissatisfied applicant or recipient. Certain limits were placed on eligibility requirements for residence and citizenship that could be imposed without foregoing or forfeiting federal assistance for any of the categories of assistance. The protection of the identity of the person receiving aid was provided by requirements of confidentiality of all information concerning the application for aid, or the receipt of assistance.

The Act specified the requirement of "money payments," or aid in the form of cash to needy recipients. These requirements were in marked contrast to the traditional and prevailing practices of the poor law. Except for the meager minimal programs of pre-depression state categorical aid, the dominant form of relief had been "in kind," the grocery or rent order, or the order on the public commissary. No poor person under traditional local poor relief practices had any "right" to request aid or to have his request reviewed. The only "right" to any form of appeal, unless history has been widely misinterpreted, was to the moral conscience of the poor-law official. As for confidentiality, there is no evidence in documents and accounts of poor-law practices of any official concern with protecting the anonymity of the poor person. There is contrary evidence that exposure of the fact of being "on the county" or the municipal dole was viewed as a means of keeping down the numbers on the relief rolls.

Without laboring the point of whether public assistance in the form specified by the Act was a major departure from the old poor law, or just an improved version, it is true that it was definitely more humane in intent and practice, provided a considerable degree of protection of the poor person from arbitrary exercise of power or prejudice by unrestrained local officials, brought the national government into the program, and provided safeguards against any of the centuries-old humiliating and degrading practices which preceded the Social Security Act, and persist to this day in many state and local general assistance measures in some areas. In this sense, it was a welfare reform. But it did not eliminate all of the philosophy of the poor law. Perhaps the picture was summed up most accurately by a prominent leader in the development of public welfare, the late Edith Abbott, former dean of the School of Social Service Administration of the University of Chicago, in these words in 1937:

Public assistance, in the second quarter of the twentieth century, is a strange assortment of things old and new, often with threads and patches underneath, and then some grand and quite new outside garment; the old pauper laws of the State underneath, and the new Social Security program with glittering promises for the top layer.[24]

The feature of the Social Security Act which most qualifies it as a welfare reform was the entrance of the federal government into an area previously reserved to the states, and largely relegated to local government by the states. By breaching the barriers to federal action under the Constitution in this sphere of public policy, the door was opened to a vast area of social legislation measures in the ensuing years.

Recent Experience

From 1950 to 1970 the number of recipients of AFDC more than quadrupled, rising from 2,233,000 in 1950 to 9,660,000 in 1970. The greatest increase took place between 1960 and 1970, during which the numbers of persons receiving family assistance (AFDC) trebled. Other programs of assistance did not follow this trend. By contrast, they showed either a decrease in numbers or a small increase at the most. Old Age Assistance, for example, became smaller in numbers aided over this period, moving from 2,736,000 in 1950 to 2,082,000 in 1970. State and local programs of general assistance increased marginally in numbers aided, growing from 886,000 in 1950 to 1,056,000 in 1970.

The fact that the AFDC rolls rose sharply during the 1960s, when business was good and unemployment was low, exacerbated public discontent. This was the first time in history that the numbers receiving public aid had not gone up or down with the level of economic activity. The experience seemed to flout the lessons of experience and to raise in many people's minds some serious questions about the behavior of the people who administered aid as well as the character of those who received it and to generate pressures for sweeping and drastic action. Proposals for action took off in different directions. Some advocated cracking down on recipients and on welfare offices to weed out the ostensibly ineligible or willfully eligible, while others suggested a comprehensive alternative in the shape of a guaranteed minimum income or negative income tax to encompass the financial problems of all the poor, including the working poor. Another point of view, particularly of social service professionals, called for intensification of efforts to rehabilitate families receiving aid and for a "service strategy" to serve both humanitarian and economic interests by helping people work their way off welfare.

This recommendation was embodied in 1962 in welfare amendments to the Social Security Act which included financial incentives to states to develop social service rehabilitative programs. Congress was convinced to pass this measure by the assurance that the process of individual rehabilitation was a way of moving people off the rolls. Failure of the rolls to go down after the enactments of these amendments led to Congressional disenchantment with the experience and to the subsequent measure in 1967 which featured a carrot-and-stick approach to welfare policy. This later measure included a work-incentive program, which liberalized an existing policy permitting working recipients to retain earned income and instituted a compulsory work and training program for recalcitrant recipients. A carrot was offered in the shape of day-care centers and other social services for working mothers, but a stick was proposed to be used on state welfare agencies by establishing a "freeze" on the number that could be federally aided in this program within each state.

Each of these so-called "new directions" reflected old biases and conflicts over the cause and nature of the problem of welfare dependency. While it provided for a federally aided floor for payments throughout the country, it also permitted states with more generous provisions to continue higher payments for AFDC recipients who had been receiving aid and who continued to qualify. Administration spokesmen insisted that the plan was "work-fare and not welfare." Then Secretary of Labor George P. Shultz declared, "The plan, contrary to the misunderstanding of many, is not a proposal for a guaranteed minimum income. Work is a major feature of the program."[25]

The fact that the 1962 and 1967 welfare policy initiatives did not meet expectations and that the 1969 Nixon Family Assistance Plan was not enacted reflected the fact that general dislike of a welfare program will not necessarily lead to general agreement on a different one unless there is at least a working consensus on cause and cure of the allegedly defective condition. Defeat of the Family Assistance Plan in the early 1970s was brought about by a combination of diverse forces described by Daniel P. Moynihan as a coalition of "welfare professionals, black militants, and conservatives," whose chorus of dissatisfaction reached a "liturgical consonance."[26] To illustrate further the point that the plan had in it potentiality for dislike from many quarters, another critic described it as having been framed "by careful Calvinists and careless reformers."[27] Perhaps it is in the nature of legislation which confronts divergent and emotionally charged ideological bias that what pleases one segment of sharply divided opinion will almost certainly alienate another; hence, what is designed to placate everyone will please no one.

Another significant factor in conflict over AFDC was the change in family characteristics among the numbers receiving aid. Mothers' aid had been aimed at widowed homemakers. While aid could be given to dependent children of mothers who were divorced, separated, unwed, or deserted, it was stipulated that these mothers must be morally fit to rear children. In practice, relief was given to widows by decision of local administrators, who generally ruled that only widows were fit and proper for such responsibility. In AFDC, federal aid to states was authorized for dependent children for reasons other than the death of the father, including continued absence from the home or physical or mental incapacity of the parent.

The characteristics of families in this category of assistance changed markedly over time. The proportion of AFDC families whose fathers were dead or disabled dropped from nearly three in five in 1948 to fewer than one in five two decades later. By 1968, the proportion of families whose fathers were dead or disabled had dropped from a majority of the load, to fewer than one in five. The proportion of living but absent fathers in families receiving aid increased to nearly three-fourths of all AFDC families. The proportion of unmarried mothers doubled.[28] During this period, opposition to the program intensified because of the increase in the proportion of non-whites, which reached a level of nearly one-half during the 1960s. Under these circumstances, it was quite possible to cover the fact of racial prejudice with a mask of pious disapproval of the alleged misbehavior of the recipients. A collateral influence on welfare policy during the period was reflected in the change in emphasis on work for pay and on work incentives for the AFDC mothers. When the program was enacted as part of the Social Security Act in 1935 during the Great Depression, a period of widespread unemployment, the primary concern was to find jobs for the able-bodied males. The emphasis in recent times has been on policies encouraging the welfare parent to accept training and to seek work.

Costs rose most dramatically in the urbanized northern states, and widows were replaced on the rolls by families in which the prinicipal cause of dependency was abandonment of the children by the fathers. To many critics, it seemed that AFDC-supported black mothers, many of them unwed, were traveling north with their illegitimate children to take advantage of high-benefit states.

Recent experiences with welfare reform highlight the difficulties in bringing about change in such a controversial area of public policy. These are persistent and remarkably consistent in content and substance. The rhetoric may be different, but the arguments are strikingly similar to those which might have been advanced over the span of many years on the issues of the cause of the welfare problem and measures to cope with it. The echoes of the past are quite audible in the polemic of the present. The growth of public expenditures for welfare in the past decade seems to belie the rhetoric of opposition, however, and raises some interesting questions respecting apparent disparities between what is said and what is done.

The cost of programs of assistance to the needy, including cash payments, in-kind transfers, e.g., health and medical care (Medicaid) and Food Stamps, have shown a considerable increase. Food Stamps, for example, increased sevenfold in cost between 1969–70 and 1974–75.[29] The continuing rise in this program has sparked strong sentiment in the Congress and in the country to find some measure of control, but thus far the proposals seem marginal in their likely effect on the continuing growth of this program. A continuing rise in the level of cost and support is also shown in cash assistance payments, in medical care, and in social services, for the needy. In the past ten years, cash assistance and services for the aged, the disabled, and families with children have grown substantially, under varying conditions of recession and prosperity.

The federal government became the senior partner in the welfare enterprise in this decade, providing more than half of the total public support. Social welfare is a far larger part of the annual GNP, and accounts for a much greater proportion of all governmental expenditures, then it did ten years ago. Meanwhile, the programs continue to exclude large numbers in poverty, including many whose need is as great as that of people receiving aid: the working poor, the underemployed, and needy families excluded from categorical forms of aid for reasons other than low income. One-half or more of the families below the poverty line in this country subsist without aid.

Other factors continue to spark sentiment for a complete federalization of welfare, to follow the lead already taken in replacing the federally aided but state-operated programs of public aid for the adult categories with the present federally administered program of Supplemental Security Income. Advocacy continues for extension of family assistance to those now excluded by categorical limitations. Critics of the present system point to wide disparities among the states in the liberality of eligibility requirements for AFDC and the amounts paid to those who qualify. The disparities are great in average payments, by family and by individual recipient from state to state, and reflect widely varying degrees of willingness and capacity to provide the state and local share of these payments. The federal share totaled $5.7 billion of a total of $10.1 billion nationally, for an estimated 11.4 million recipients in fiscal year 1977, or more than half, but the proportion of federal funds among the various states ranged from 50 percent to more than 80 percent. States with higher standards of aid and more liberal conditions of eligibility expended larger proportionate amounts of their own funds.

Although federal aid for state payments for families with the unemployed breadwinner in the home have been authorized since 1962, only twenty-six states, the District of Columbia, and Guam have enacted enabling legislation for this purpose.

During the 1960s, the large-scale movement from the rural areas to the cities of the industrial north was reflected in large increases in numbers aided and in program costs in areas on the receiving end of the migration. In that period, public assistance to needy families became "metropolitanized." States with large industrial cities continue to have a disproportionate number of persons and families receiving public aid. In fiscal year 1978, six states (California, Illinois, Michigan, New Jersey, New York, and Pennsylvania) accounted for more than 40 percent of the national total of persons receiving AFDC.[30]

Long-standing differences in views on welfare continue to press against conditions and forces which suggest basic change in the welfare system. It may be that changes will take place, over time, which will result in a system with the characteristics envisioned in the calls for reform— federalization of the system, extension of coverage to the families of the working poor, imposition of a uniform national minimum standard for aid, and other features hotly debated since the subject became a major focus for public policy concern. But the inhibiting forces are also still present, and traditional conflicts still make this a complex, baffling area of public policy in the issues of welfare.

It may well be that these issues are too controversial and too deeply imbedded in traditional attitudes, values, and folkways to permit their resolution in a single, statesmanlike enactment. This does not rule out the possibility of incremental changes within the present system which over time will add up to piecemeal reform. Much of this has already happened. The very fact that questions of "horizontal and vertical equity" are being raised is a sign of considerable progress. In the past, disparities in payments among states and localities wouldn't even have been raised as a public policy question. It doesn't take too much of a leap of imagination to anticipate the possibility of extending to AFDC the action already taken in 1972 to federalize the erstwhile "adult categories" under Supplemental Security Income. Whether this comes about as the result of fiscal relief for states and localities or from humanitarian concerns is perhaps beside the point.

Even though there are still recurrent calls for purging the rolls of ineligible persons, of eliminating fraud and waste, in food stamps as well as other forms of welfare, there are also demands for greater fairness, adequacy in meeting family needs, concern over possible suffering from higher energy costs, and other indicators which show a considerable "commitment to welfare." The moral and conceptual issues of welfare are far from being resolved, but at least they are being posed in considerably different terms. What seems to be the case now is one of programs in search of policy.

Notes

1. An Act for the Relief of the Poor, 32 Elizabeth, c. 2 (1601).

2. Sir George Nicholls, *A History of the English Poor Law* (1854) "Reprint of British Economic Classics" (London: Augustus M. Kelley, Publishers, 1967), pp. 14–19.

3. *Ibid.* p. 19. A more modern expression of the uses of welfare as an instrument of social control is in Frances E. Piven and Richard Cloward, *Regulating the Poor* (New York: Vintage Books—Random House, 1971). They contend that "Relief arrangements are ancillary to economic arrangements." Their function, according to the authors, is to regulate labor by initiating or expanding relief programs to quell revolt in times of turmoil, and then, as the turbulence subsides, to contract the system by expelling those needed in the labor force. The remainder, the aged, disabled, and mentally ill, are accorded treatment so degrading and punitive that the laboring masses are left in fear of what could happen to them "should they relax into beggary and pauperism" (p. 1). This use, the authors state, is made necessary by the inherent strains and instabilities of a capitalist economy.

4. Hasseltine Byrd Taylor, "Nature of the Right to Public Assistance," *The Social Service Review* XXXVI, no. 3 (Sept. 1962): 265.

5. Robert Kelso, *History of Public Poor Relief in Massachusetts* (Boston: Houghton Mifflin, 1922), p. 36.

6. *Ibid.*, p. 37.

7. H. L. Lurie, "The Development of Social Welfare Programs," *Social Work Yearbook* (Washington, D.C.: National Association of Social Workers, 1957), p. 22.

8. Hilary M. Leyendecker, *Problems and Policy in Public Assistance* (New York: Harper and Brothers, 1955), p. 38.

9. Karl de Schweinitz, "The Development of Public Welfare in the United States," *Public Welfare, Journal of the American Public Welfare Association* 6, no. 8 (August 1948): 147.

10. Special institutions for care of selected groups of dependents were developed under both public and private auspices, beginning in the colonial period of American history. They included orphanages, hospitals, and special facilities provided by religious and ethnic secular groups, particularly for the care of their own members, but these were not widespread or significant prior to the American Revolution. "It was only after the 1830s, however, when people began to demand the removal of children from almshouses, that the number of such institutions multiplied." (Walter I. Trattner, *From Poor Law to Welfare State*, 2nd ed. (New York: The Free Press, 1979), p. 98.) In the first half of the nineteenth century, the institutional ideal for care "was not confined to county poorhouses; the founding of houses of refuge, or orphanages, penitentiaries, and mental hospitals during this period was part of the same movement." (*Ibid.*, p. 54.)

11. Special categorical treatment of children outside institutions evolved in the last half of the nineteenth century. The development of the Children's Aid Society in 1853 by Chas. Loring Brace featured the "placing out" of children, chiefly city children, often sent great distances to rural areas. "So great was the need that both orphanages and child placing agencies increased in number and size after the Civil War. To complicate matters, state after state adopted the principle that children should be removed from almshouses, and that, if a child was removed to an orphanage, that orphanage should be of his parents' faith. James Leiby, *History of Social Work and Social Welfare in the U.S.* (New York: Columbia University Press, 1968), p. 84.

12. Josephine C. Brown, *Public Relief: 1929–39* (New York: Holt, Rinehart, Winston), p. 15.

13. Trattner, p. 63.

14. Lurie, p. 23.

15. Howard W. Odum, "Newer Ideals of Public Welfare," *The Annals of the American Academy of Political and Social Science* CV, no. 1 (January 1923).

16. Congressional Globe, 33rd Congress, 1st Session (May 1854), pp. 1061–1063.

17. Joseph K. Hart, "Public Welfare and Our Democratic Institutions," *The Annals* CV, no. 1 (January 1923): 31–32.

18. Ralph G. Hurlin, "Use of Public Works in Treatment of Unemployment," *Proceedings of the National Conference of Social Work* (New York: Columbia University Press, 1931).

19. Joanna C. Colcord, William C. Koplivitz, and Russel C. Kurtz, *Emergency Work Relief* (New York: Russell Sage Foundation, 1972).

20. Leyendecker, pp. 229–230.

21. Joel F. Handler and Ellen J. Hillingsworth, *Work, Welfare and the Nixon Reform Proposals*, University of Wisconsin, Institute of Research on Poverty: Reprint No. 60, p. 908.

22. Report to the President, *Committee on Economic Security* (Washington 1935), p. v.

23. Robert H. Havemann, *Work Conditioned Subsidies as an Income Maintenance Strategy*, (Madison: University of Wisconsin Institute for Research on Poverty, August 1973).

24. Edith Abbott, *Proceedings of the National Conference of Social Work* (New York: Columbia University Press, 1937), p. 3.

25. George Shultz, "The Nixon Welfare Plan," *New Generation*, National Committee for the Employment of Youth, Winter 1970.

26. Daniel P. Moynihan, *Politics of a Guaranteed Income* (New York: Random House—Vintage Books, 1973), pp. 309–321. Moynihan is critical of the so-called "welfare professionals" for, among other things, allegedly holding fast to a service strategy of welfare administration, which he alleges would sustain their control over the welfare system.

27. Alvin L. Schorr, *Social Welfare Forum*, Proceedings of the National Conference on Social Welfare (New York: Columbia University Press, 1970).

28. This information on changing characteristics is derived from Sar Levitan and David Marwick, "The Mounting and Insurmountable Welfare Problem," *Current History* 61, no. 363. An excellent account of efforts at welfare reform is an article in the same issue: "Welfare Reform: A Persistent Quest," by Wilbur J. Cohen, former Secretary of Health, Education, and Welfare. His recommendations included a strategy to reduce the factor of welfare dependency by economic and institutional reforms embodied in a ten-point plan to cut down on the need for dependency on welfare.

29. *Annual Statistical Supplement*, Social Security Bulletin, Dept. of Health, Education, and Welfare, 1977.

30. Social Security Bulletin, Dept. of Health, Education, and Welfare, Vol. 42, No. 3, March 1979.

16

An Assessment of Major Welfare Reform Proposals of the 95th Congress

ROBERT J. FERSH

Introduction

The first part of this paper argues that despite proposals to repackage the current array of public welfare programs and other significant policy innovations, none of the major welfare reform proposals of the 95th Congress, if enacted, would have represented a fundamental shift in American values as they are expressed in programs which currently serve the poor. Most of this argument is developed by comparing the so-called "comprehensive" reform bill proposed by the Carter administration with the current welfare system. The second part of the paper attempts to raise certain value considerations which the author believes are of importance in the formulation of welfare policy.

At the outset, it should be stated that it is extremely difficult to state definitively what values are, in fact, reflected in current public welfare programs or proposals to reform them. Congress rarely enacts a piece of legislation with single-minded purpose. Persons with vastly differing value orientations may favor the same policies. For instance, in the field of welfare reform, the concept of a negative income tax (NIT) has been endorsed by both conservatives and liberals. Some conservatives[1] see it as a mechanism by which to gain control over welfare costs. Consolidating the many welfare programs of today into one program would limit the political pressure points the poor now have to seek greater benefits. The NIT is also seen as a way to cut administrative costs and increase work incentives. To liberals, the NIT represents a way to guarantee adequate income to poor people and to provide it in an efficient manner without serious social stigma. The increase in benefit adequacy would result in higher costs. The NIT example thus illustrates the treacherousness of trying to identify the values which underlie such proposals.

This paper will focus on several of the major welfare reform bills introduced in the 95th Congress: the administration bill (H.R. 9030, S. 2084), the bill of the House Subcommittee on Welfare Reform (H.R. 10950), the Baker-Bellmon bill (S. 2777), and the bill proposed by Representative Ullman (H.R. 10711). Any future reference to "comprehensive" proposals alludes to the very similar administration and subcommittee bills (the latter representing a modified version of the former). The term "incremental" is used to refer to the Ullman and Baker-Bellmon bills and could as well describe the bill (S. 3498) introduced by Senator Kennedy late in the 95th Congress and the administration bill (H.R. 4321, S. 1290) which was actively considered and passed the House with minor modification.

It is not easy to distinguish between what constitutes a "comprehensive" and what constitutes an "incremental" welfare reform plan. The terms are used as a shorthand way to describe the general thrust of various proposals and the classification of a proposal as one or the other is somewhat arbitrary. The blurriness of these concepts was aptly expressed by Senator Moynihan when he described the Baker-Bellmon proposal as a "rather comprehensive incremental program."[2] In general, the term "incremental" is used to describe proposals which build on existing programs, without significantly altering the structure or roles of those programs. The Baker-Bellmon and Ullman proposals, for instance, would retain all of the current welfare programs, but improve individual features of and coordination among these programs. The term "comprehensive" is used here to describe proposals which would significantly reorganize the current array of public welfare programs. The administration and subcommittee bills call for a consolidation of several major federal welfare programs, with greater centralization of their administration. It is this type of wholesale change in the structure of the welfare system and the manner in which benefits are delivered which, above all, earns the label "comprehensive" for certain proposals.

The term "comprehensive" should be used advisedly, because none of the welfare reform proposals discussed here addresses the full range of human needs served by the current welfare system. Only in a peripheral way are the needs of the poor for medical, housing, and nutritional assistance and social services addressed by any of these proposals. To the extent that any proposal is described here as "comprehensive," it is comprehensive in its approach to what may be best described as the "income maintenance" aspects of the current welfare system.

To make the statement that none of the major welfare reform plans discussed in this paper would fundamentally reorient the current welfare system may come as no surprise when made in relation to incremental reform plans. These plans would, after all, leave the current welfare system largely intact and are unlikely vehicles for expression of a major shift in attitudes toward poor people. However, the same is true for the comprehensive reform plans. The sleek new packaging of welfare programs proposed by the administration (and ratified by the House Subcommittee in 1978) may have misled some people into believing that the welfare system would undergo a fundamental change in character if the Carter proposal were adopted. Some persons, including those very much familiar with welfare programs,[3] expressed a belief that the administration plan would constitute the first guaranteed annual income for all Americans, which would surely constitute a fundamental shift in our society's approach to aiding the poor. In the paragraphs below, more detailed arguments are presented which attempt to show why this line of thinking is off the mark. In addition, it will be argued that, for the most part, the major reform proposals of the 95th Congress reaffirm, by effect if not intent, three important recent trends in welfare policy: (1.) a growing acceptance of the notion that need is often beyond the control of the individual; (2.) a reduction in the paternalism inherent in providing "in kind," rather than cash, benefits; and (3.) a growing acceptance of the need for minimum standards of benefit adequacy.

Comparison of Current Welfare System and Reform Proposals

EXPENDITURE OF PUBLIC MONEY

The current welfare system[4] includes a variety of programs enacted over the years for differing purposes. One unifying feature is that it reflects a strong American commitment to the expenditure of public money for those in need, although, as discussed below, the extent of this commitment varies among categories of the poor. There seems to be very little sentiment for a return to a system of family support and private charity only.[5] There can be no question that both the comprehensive and incremental reform plans evidence a strong commitment to the expenditure of public money to assist the poor. In fact, in their first full year of operation, the Congressional Budget Office has estimated the federal costs of the administration and subcommittee bills would have been approximately $17–21 billion more than the costs of continuing current programs.[6] The incremental bills were estimated to cost somewhat less,[7] but would still constitute a commitment to spend a significant amount of additional public monies on the needs of the low-income population.

SEPARATE PROGRAMS FOR THE POOR

Another feature of the current welfare system is that the poor, whether considered "worthy or unworthy," are served through separate means-tested welfare programs. These programs sometimes impose unique conditions upon the poor and tend to treat them as a distinct segment of the society. While it is true that universal programs like Social Security may do much to alleviate poverty, the basic point is that the poor in the United States have not been integrated into a comprehensive, society-wide, income policy which might be achieved by such proposals as a demogrant, negative income tax or a children's allowance.

The incremental reform plans would not alter the current arrangement. The comprehensive proposals would also continue separate, means-tested programs for the poor (although they would probably be administered at the federal, rather than the state/local, level and would consolidate the current AFDC, SSI, and Food Stamp programs). Other than an expansion of the earned income tax credit (which is not available to everyone), there is no attempt to deliver benefits through a universal mechanism like a negative income tax or demogrant. And perhaps most importantly, despite increased coverage and liberalization of benefits for some groups of participants, the comprehensive plans do not provide income which is guaranteed to recipients any more so than by current programs. Virtually all of the same eligibility conditions, such as those relating to work (see discussion below) and providing information for child support enforcement purposes, would remain in effect. There would be no guarantee of income to an individual or family simply by virtue of citizenship or residency in the United States.

DISTINCTIONS AMONG GROUPS OF THE POOR

The existence today of many different welfare programs results in differential treatment among different groups of the poor. Since 1974, aged, blind, and disabled poor persons have been the only recipients of a federal cash benefit guarantee. The creation of the Supplementary Security Income (SSI) program cemented their position as the most "worthy" of the American poor. No work requirements are imposed on SSI recipients because, presumably, they are so old or so infirm that they are unable to work. Single-parent families with children, served by the Aid to Families with Dependent Children (AFDC) program, receive no federal income guarantee, and their receipt of assistance is conditioned upon satisfaction of many requirements (including those relating to work and others relating to child-support enforcement) beyond a means test. Two-parent families with children, served by the AFDC-Unemployed Father program, have similar conditions placed upon receipt of benefits. And such families receive no federal cash assistance in almost half the states, since participation in that aspect of the AFDC program is left to state option.

The only federal assistance program which serves all needy individuals, regardless of family composition, is the Food Stamp program. But this program provides only limited assistance to augment food purchasing power and its benefits can be used only for that purpose. Participation in the Food Stamp program is also conditioned upon satisfaction of certain requirements, such as those relating to work, in addition to means and assets tests.

By definition, the incremental reform proposals would retain the current differential treatment among groups of the poor. What might not be quite as clear is the fact that the comprehensive proposals would also continue to distinguish among groups of the poor by establishing varying benefit levels and eligibility requirements for them. This point may have been obscured for some by the consolidation of current programs into the one large program envisioned in the comprehensive bills. However, within that one program, the benefit levels, work requirements, and work opportunities would differ among (1.) the aged, blind, and disabled; (2.) single-parent families with children; (3.) two-parent families with children; and (4.) single individuals and childless couples. For instance, assuming no state supplementation, a one-parent family of four with no other income in 1978 would have initially qualified for cash benefits paid at an annual rate of $4,200. A two-parent family of four with no other income would have qualified for benefits paid initially at an annual rate of $2,300. This is a distinction that even the current welfare system, at least in states with an AFDC-UF program, does not make. Other examples of differential treatment abound.

Despite the fact that differential treatment would remain under the comprehensive bills, their proposed consolidation of current programs could have the effect, whether intended or not, of blurring some of the "deserving versus nondeserving" distinctions which the current, separate programs make among groups of the poor. The fact that a large degree of differential treatment among groups of the poor would remain after program consolidation tends to undercut an argument that framers of the comprehensive proposals viewed a reduction in the distinctions made between "worthy" and "unworthy" poor persons as a priority concern. Administrative simplicity and uniformity was undoubtedly a major concern of those proposing program consolidation. However, regardless of intent, the proposed consolidation could well have the effect of reducing the distinctions made among groups of the poor. Some of the negative stereotypes that are prevalent in the public's perception of AFDC and Food Stamp recipients might be muted if participants in those programs were to be merged in one program with elderly, blind, and disabled persons.

CASH VERSUS IN-KIND BENEFITS

The major reform plans include proposals which would have moved in opposite directions from current programs in terms of the types of benefits—e.g., cash, in kind, vouchers—that they would provide. Representative Ullman's plan would not vary the amount of cash assistance provided by family size. Instead, his plan would adjust Food Stamp allotments only, increasing them with family size. The result is that a large proportion of benefits under the Ullman plan, particularly those paid to larger families, would be provided in the form of an in-kind benefit— Food Stamps. For instance, the mix of annual cash and Food Stamp benefits which would have been provided in 1978 to a Louisiana family of six (mother and five children) with no other income would have been $2,550 in cash and $2,538 in Food Stamps. In Oregon, a similar family of six in 1978 would have received $4,333 in cash and $2,161 in Food Stamps under the Ullman plan compared to the $6,552 in cash and $1,227 in Food Stamps they received under current law programs.[8]

While other considerations may have played a primary role in the decision to structure benefits in this way, this feature of the Ullman plan would result in more paternalistic treatment of the poor.[9] As the proportion of benefits which can be utilized only for prescribed purposes rises, the flexibility afforded to the poor to spend their resources as they see fit diminishes. In-kind benefits, other than medical care, are often criticized as reflecting a distrust in the ability of low-income persons to judge what is best for themselves. In the past, efforts to establish in-kind benefit programs (such as Food Stamps) were justified by some advocates as a strategy to increase overall incomes for poor people. It was thought Congress would be more responsive and generous when particular needs of the poor, such as freedom from hunger, could be documented and the benefit to be provided could be fully targeted on those needs. However, in the Ullman plan, the increased reliance of Food Stamps is not a result so much of a strategy to increase benefits to the poor as it is a redistribution in the way in which benefits would be delivered. The Ullman plan would likely result in modest benefit increases for a relatively small number of low-income people.

If anything, Representative Ullman's plan would appear to be going against the grain of recent legislation. The Food Stamp Act of 1977 eliminated the purchase requirement in the program and in so doing, freed up the resources of a great many low-income people. Prior to the 1977 act, a Food Stamp household contributed a certain percentage of its income for an allotment of Food Stamps which varied only according to family size. A family of four with a moderate amount of outside income might have contributed, say, $90 to receive $162 in monthly Food Stamp coupons. Under the new law, the family would receive only the "bonus value" in Food Stamps, in this case $72 (assuming the benefit schedule remained the same), leaving the former purchase price ($90) free for other uses. So, the elimination of the purchase requirement not only makes access to the program much easier, but it also significantly affects the form in which benefits are delivered.

One other lesser-known example of a Congressional preference for cash benefits was expressed in a Senate vote in the fall of 1977. The Senate Finance Committee had reported a bill to the Senate floor which would have allowed state welfare agencies to increase the number of cases in which they made direct payments to landlords and utilities on behalf of AFDC recipients.[10] Also, the bill would have allowed more two-party checks (made out to both the recipient and the service provider) to be issued by the welfare departments. A floor amendment to delete these provisions was successful. While there were several other important considerations affecting the outcome, one of the central concerns was that of denying recipients the opportunity to manage their own scarce resources.

By "cashing out" Food Stamps and providing all income maintenance benefits in cash, the administration and subcommittee bills would have taken a large step away from in-kind benefits. While concerns about paternalism and stigma may not have been paramount in the decision to provide cash benefits only, the proposals nonetheless would have the effect of providing benefits to the poor in a less paternalistic fashion by allowing low-income people to manage cash resources. While neither proposal would have attempted, for a variety of political and policy reasons, to "cash out" the value of Medicaid and social services provided to the poor, it should be noted that the unpredictability of the health-care and social service needs of a particular individual or family causes them to be far less susceptible to (and perhaps far less desirable subjects for) payment in cash than the Food Stamp program.

WORK ORIENTATION

The current welfare system contains rather strong paper requirements that those who are able-bodied and without direct responsibility to care for a dependent must satisfy work requirements as a condition of eligibility for assistance. While there is some question as to the effectiveness of these requirements and the ability of government to enforce them, they seem to reflect a deeply held American belief that those able to work should be required to do so as a condition of welfare eligibility, even if elements of coercion may be involved. One indication of the strength of the belief in work requirements is found in the current Food Stamp law,[11] which disqualifies an entire family from benefits for two months if an adult member fails to comply with the applicable work requirements.

A strong case can be made that all of the major welfare reform bills discussed here would tighten work requirements in comparison to current law. For instance, for one-parent families, both comprehensive bills would exempt from work requirements only those families in which the youngest child is six years of age or less. While this corresponds to current AFDC law, the Food Stamp program exempts one-parent families from the work requirement when the youngest child is twelve years or less. Furthermore, the comprehensive bills place single parents with the youngest child 7–13 years of age in a category where they are "expected to work" part time. These features, in combination with job search requirements, generally would strengthen the work requirements compared to those currently in federal assistance programs.[12]

Perhaps the most important factor which distinguishes the latest batch of welfare reform proposals from their predecessors is their emphasis on work opportunity. Although each of the proposals suggests different approaches to the problem, ranging from large public sector jobs programs to incentives for private hiring, all would take concrete steps to improve employment opportunities for low-income people. These proposed jobs programs and employment strategies could signal an important change in attitudes toward the poor. Namely, it is possible to see such proposals as a further abdication from a widespread belief that the cause of poverty can be firmly placed only on the shoulders of the poor themselves. The recognition, in proposals put forth by Republicans and Democrats alike, that increased job opportunity is needed conflicts with the notion that poverty is due mainly to the personal shortcomings (i.e., laziness) of those on the dole. Even though mandatory work requirements would remain, job creation strategies seem to be indicative of a belief that the issue is not merely one of coercing freeloaders to work.

The various proposals' emphasis on work raises some other important value questions. The administration bill, in particular, attaches tremendous importance to work incentives. While such a design may increase the chances for voluntary work-force participation, the administration clearly opted, in some instances, to trade off benefit adequacy in favor of work incentives. This value choice will be more fully explored in the final section of this paper.

The entry of welfare reformers into the area of jobs program design brings new value questions to the fore. For instance, some criticism has been directed at the administration's proposal to create about 1.4 million minimum wage (or slightly higher) jobs intended for the heads of low-income households. Rather than viewing this ambitious proposal as true work opportunity, these critics see the program as establishing a distinct class of low-wage workers, divorced from the mainstream of employment. Because they think many of the jobs would be "make work" rather than "meaningful" jobs, they question the value of creating such jobs, seeing them more as a way to satisfy the society's work ethic than as an attempt to be truly helpful to the poor. They see these jobs as an attempt to make people work for the sake of work and would prefer to use the money for more adequate cash benefits. Defenders of the jobs program deny that the jobs would be "make work." They point out that even if the "make work" charge were partially true, the availability of any type of work can be helpful to many low-income persons in enhancing their self-image and developing skills necessary to succeed in the job market. They also suggest that the jobs can be seen as an alternative form of income maintenance to cash assistance. Under the administration's overall plan, persons accepting a minimum-wage job would always receive greater combined income from employment and cash assistance than those who do not work. Perhaps the most telling argument that jobs program proponents make is that many poor persons will want the jobs. Esoteric arguments about the creation of a pool of "second-class" workers have little relevance, they contend, for low-income persons who see minimum-wage jobs as an improvement over their current situation.

The debate over the jobs component raises some of the same questions addressed in the discussion above of "universal" versus "categorical" cash assistance programs. To what extent should the poor be treated as a separate, distinct class of people? Does the establishment of separate programs stigmatize the poor? Does it tend to reinforce an image (both to the poor and the rest of society) that the poor are really very different from the remainder of society?

COVERAGE

All of the major welfare reform proposals would broaden the coverage of federal cash assistance programs. Both the comprehensive and incremental plans would liberalize the coverage of two-parent families beyond that currently provided by AFDC-UF. That program is available in slightly over half of the states and has eligibility restrictions, in terms of prior work history and limits on current work force attachment (the 100-hour rule),[13] which are considerably tighter than the regular AFDC program. All of the welfare reform proposals would loosen the current eligibility restrictions and provide coverage to two-parent families in all states, although programs for two-parent families would generally be less generous than those for one-parent families.

The comprehensive proposals would increase coverage by extending eligibility to the "breakeven,"[14] as well as by providing federal cash assistance coverage to single individuals and childless couples for the first time. Only the Food Stamp program provides federal assistance to these groups at the present time. The incremental plans would basically retain the current Food Stamp program and would not provide cash assistance to single individuals and childless couples.

From an historical perspective, the broadening of federal cash assistance coverage flows logically from prior developments. Originally, the Social Security Act of 1935 provided for ADC (Aid to Dependent Children). In 1950, the title of the program was changed to AFDC (Aid to Families with Dependent Children), reflecting the fact that single parents (mostly mothers) living with the children also needed and utilized the assistance. In 1961, the Unemployed Parent (later called UF—Unemployed Father) program was instituted, providing limited coverage to needy two-parent families, at state option. In 1966, the Food Stamp Program was initiated. The program was gradually expanded nationwide and now offers assistance in kind to all needy persons who meet eligibility guidelines.[15] These developments reflect a steady broadening in coverage of different groups of the poor. Proposals to broaden cash assistance coverage even further in the late 1970s thus do not seem to reflect a dramatic change in policy, especially when one realizes that many states and localities fund and administer general assistance programs to fill in the gaps in coverage left by federal cash assistance programs. Perhaps one conclusion which can be drawn from the movement to expand coverage is similar to the one drawn above in relation to the expansion of employment opportunity: the expanded coverage may reflect a recognition that not all people, not even the able-bodied, may be able to provide adequately for themselves at all times in our complex society. Expanded coverage can have the effect of reinforcing the notion that environmental forces, as well as the qualities of the individual, play a significant role in the ability of individuals to subsist.

BENEFIT LEVELS

The level of cash (or cash plus Food Stamps) benefits which would be provided in the various proposals does not represent a decision to alter significantly the adequacy of benefits provided under current programs. All of the proposals would leave the benefit levels provided to aged, blind, and disabled persons through the SSI program virtually unchanged. For most of the remainder of recipients,[16] the minimum payment standard suggested by each of the proposals is about 65 percent of the poverty level (although the Baker-Bellmon plan would not achieve this level until 1985). This minimum payment standard would require only a handful of states to increase benefits above what they now provide in combined AFDC and Food Stamp benefits.[17] And, in most instances, the increase in benefits would not be dramatic. (In all of the proposals, it is expected that states currently providing more than 65 percent of the poverty level in combined AFDC and Food Stamp payments would continue to pay benefits at their approximate current levels.)

To be sure, the various proposals could result in significantly greater resources being provided to the poor. The public sector jobs proposed in the administration and subcommittee bills could result in a large rise in income, in the form of earnings, for many low-income families. Also, the assumption of a larger share of benefit costs by the federal government, as proposed in all of the major plans, might encourage states to raise benefits above what they currently pay. However, this decision would be left to the states and would occur only if a state were willing to exchange fiscal relief for greater benefit adequacy. Overall, then, the major welfare reform proposals of the 95th Congress would not achieve a significantly greater level of adequacy in public assistance benefit payments.

Even though the establishment of a 65 percent of poverty payment standard would not result in widespread benefit increases, it would establish an important principle—that of a uniform, nationwide, minimum benefit level. Aside from the minimum federal benefits assured to aged, blind, and disabled persons by the SSI program and the limited federal benefit guarantee of the Food Stamp program, no federal minimum benefit standards currently exist. Payment standards in the AFDC program are left wholly to state discretion, resulting in enormous disparities in benefits from state to state. While the Food Stamp program serves to reduce the variation in benefits provided in the different states, large differences remain. The 65 percent minimum benefit would, for the first time, provide a guarantee to many public assistance recipients that their benefit payments could not fall below a specified level. This principle is perhaps of greater significance than the level of benefits actually proposed, since only a small minority of recipients stand to gain from the proposed 65 percent of poverty minimum payment standard.

SUMMARY

The preceding discussion attempted to place major welfare reform proposals of the 95th Congress in perspective in relation to the current welfare system. An examination of various features of these proposals supports the conclusion that none of the proposals would have represented, if enacted, a fundamental reorientation in the manner in which low-income persons are served by the current welfare system. While some opponents of the administration's proposal sounded fears that it would institute a fundamental change in the form of a guaranteed annual income, this was really not the case. By and large, basic features of the current welfare system—a commitment to spend public money, serving the poor through separate means-tested programs, differentiation among different groups of the poor, and enforcement of work requirements—were reaffirmed and reinforced by the welfare reform proposals of the 95th Congress.

The argument that none of these proposals, if enacted, would have amounted to a fundamental reorientation in the philosophy of the current welfare system is not intended to understate the importance of many of the reforms presented in these proposals. The increased benefit levels, coverage, and work opportunities presented by these proposals could have made a significant difference in the lives of many low-income people. Other suggestions, such as the consolidation of programs, could have resulted in a major overhaul in the administration of programs. To characterize these proposed changes as less than "fundamental" is not intended to imply that these proposals would not bring significant change or are not worthy of serious attention. By discussing some of the details of the proposals, this paper attempts to cut through the oversimplified labels which are often attached to welfare proposals and provide a more accurate picture of their potential effects.

The Question of Benefit Adequacy

ADEQUACY AND THE ADMINISTRATION'S "LOWER TIER"

It is widely understood that there are certain trade-offs inherent in the formulation of welfare policy. The nearly universally accepted policy objectives of providing adequacy, equity, and work incentives[18] in the welfare system cannot all be met without running up against the political and economic reality of keeping costs within reasonable limits. Perhaps the clearest trade-off is that between adequacy and work incentives. If minimum benefits are set relatively high, the work incentive must be curtailed so that the "breakeven" is kept at a reasonable level. The higher the "breakeven," the more persons there are eligible for assistance, resulting in higher costs. Once overall budgetary constraints have been established, the design of a welfare reform proposal can vary dramatically, depending upon which of the different policy objectives are given the most emphasis. The argument presented here is that, given finite resources, the provision of adequate benefits should be accorded primary emphasis, at least until a threshold of adequacy has been met.

The reasoning behind the call for a minimum threshold of benefit adequacy is quite simple: There is so much riding on it for the individual recipient or family. For many program participants, their sole source of available income is public welfare programs. Certainly a humane society should carefully consider the implications of failure to provide enough income support for food, clothing, and shelter for low-income families. Failure to provide enough assistance has clear real-life effects. The failure to provide for adequate work incentives or to make the welfare system fully equitable in its benefit structure seem to be rather academic and distant concerns in comparison to the direct effect of hunger and substandard housing on human beings. When one considers that the welfare of children, who cannot control their living environment or income level, is often at stake, the argument for benefit adequacy is further strengthened. Although no welfare system can guarantee all persons freedom from want of life's necessities, a system which maximizes sensitivity to these concerns would seem to be expressive of some fundamentally important human values.

This is not to say that designing a welfare system that maximizes work incentives and equitable treatment is unimportant or morally indefensible. Policymakers should not always opt for adequacy over other objectives. No welfare system will be effective without the encouragement of self-support and the enforcement of fairness. However, if these other objectives are to be served, great caution should be exercised if the price is jeopardizing benefit adequacy. It is far too easy for program analysts, particularly those at the federal level who are several steps removed from welfare's front lines, to arrive at casual trade-offs among competing policy objectives without focusing on the critical effects of their decisions on individual families.

For instance, the administration bill proposed that eligible two-parent families with children be provided with significantly lower benefits than one-parent families of the same size for the first eight weeks they receive cash assistance. During this eight-week period, at least one of the two parents would be expected actively to seek employment. If no job was found by the time eight weeks have elapsed, the family's benefit would be raised to the level of one-parent families. For instance, in a state where no supplementation of federally mandated benefits would occur, the administration bill would have provided benefits to a one-parent family with three children at an annual rate of $4,200 a year (or about $350 a month) in 1978. In contrast, a two-parent family would receive benefits during the first eight weeks at an annual rate of $2,300 (or about $192 a month). After eight weeks, they could receive $350 a month in benefits if no employment was found.

The "lower tier" was justified on the basis of assumed work-force participation and work incentives. It was assumed that two-parent families certainly had at least one adult who could or should be working (special exemptions for families with disabled or incapacitated adult members were provided), and that such families were far more likely to be able to supplement their incomes during the initial eight-week period. If benefits were kept relatively low, it was thought that the job search activity might be more productive. The higher the cash benefit provided, the less incentive an individual would have to supplement his family's earnings and the more fussy he or she might be about the type of employment considered acceptable.

These arguments for a "lower tier" have some plausibility. Two-parent families, on the whole, should be far better able to manage their households and arrange for child care than one-parent families. It would appear that they would have a far greater likelihood of outside earnings. Also, given the low level of benefits provided, two-parent families certainly would feel a greater need to supplement their incomes than those who receive higher benefits.

While these justifications for a "lower tier" do seem plausible, they certainly do not exhaustively address the concerns that a "lower tier" proposal raises. If one assumes that the payment provided to a one-parent family with three children represents a minimal standard for that state designed to meet the family's most basic needs, it is clear that an attempt to survive on a payment slightly more than half that size is likely to impose a hardship on a two-parent family of four members. The administration's scheme raises the question, "What happens to a family which does not find work in the initial eight-week job search period?" Certainly the administration bill designers must have assumed that this would be the case for many program participants. Otherwise, it hardly would have been necessary to propose, as the administration did, that 1.4 million jobs be created to be filled largely by those who had completed their eight-week job search. Apparently, the administration made the choice that it was more important that an exceptionally strong work incentive exist for two months or more than to provide to many families the level of benefits (65 percent of poverty) which the bill otherwise establishes as a minimum national threshold of benefit adequacy for those in need.

The strength of the administration's belief in the importance of work incentives is highlighted further by the controversial "52 percent rule." This rule would have required that states choosing to supplement the minimum federal benefit retain a substantial differential between benefits paid to one-parent and two-parent families, at least during the initial eight-week job search period. In the current AFDC program, states which cover two-parent families in the AFDC-UF program pay the same amount of benefits to eligible families of the same size and income, regardless of the number of parents present. However, the administration bill was designed to prohibit states from opting to provide greater benefit adequacy to two-parent families, even at their (the states') own expense. For two months, states could not pay two-parent families the minimal level of benefits which states establish as necessary for a family of a given size.

The administration's decision to emphasize work incentives through a "lower tier" of benefits virtually assured that many adults and children would have to survive for two months (or more) on less money than it is acknowledged they need for minimal subsistence. Aside from the questions about the effectiveness of work incentives to begin with and whether a sufficient work incentive could have been maintained without such a clear sacrifice of adequacy, there is the basic concern that some persons would be subjected to live at such a low level of income for two months or more. Given what is at stake for those people, a policy decision to provide admittedly inadequate benefits should be driven by concerns of overriding importance. It is not clear that the administration could satisfy that standard.[19]

SUMMARY

There has been no attempt here to define what constitutes benefit adequacy. It is difficult to quibble with the notion that poverty is a relative concept. Because of the importance of public assistance benefits to destitute individuals, an argument can be constructed that provision of adequate benefit levels should be given great weight in the balancing of the competing objectives inherent in designing a welfare system. At a minimum, once standards of minimally adequate benefits are established, only concerns of overriding importance should impair the delivery of this level of benefits. Welfare program designers, particularly those far removed from hardship on a first-hand basis, should exercise great caution in proposing features that might jeopardize the adequacy of benefits provided.

Notes

1. See Casper Weinberger, "The Reform of Welfare: A National Necessity," *The Journal of the Institute for Socioeconomic Studies*, Summer 1976, pp. 1–27.

2. "Hearings Before the Subcommittee on Public Assistance of the Committee on Finances," U.S. Senate, Ninety-Fifth Congress, Second Session, Part 3 of 5 Parts (Washington, D.C.: U.S. Government Printing Office, 1978), p. 581.

3. The July 1979 issue of *The Socioeconomic Newsletter* quotes House Ways and Means Chairman Al Ullman (D-Oregon) as follows: "In the last Congress we rejected the initial guaranteed income recommendations of the President." *The Socioeconomic Newsletter* IV, no. 7 (July 1979): 1.

4. For purposes of this paper, the term "welfare system" refers to a variety of federal means-tested cash assistance programs and Food Stamps. Included among the cash assistance programs are the Aid to Families with Dependent Children (AFDC), AFDC-Unemployed Father (UF), and Supplementary Security Income (SSI) programs, and the earned income tax credit (EITC), which provides benefits to low-income families through the tax system. The paper discusses the issues of welfare reform from a federal perspective and thus pays little attention to state-run general assistance programs. It also recognizes that the term "welfare" could easily encompass a far broader range of programs, such as nutrition programs, housing assistance, medical assistance, social services and veterans' pensions, but the discussion has been limited to the major programs which the welfare reform proposals would affect directly.

5. See Nancy Jaffe, *Attitudes Toward Public Welfare Program and Recipients in the United States* (Welfare Policy Project, The Institute of Policy Sciences and Public Affairs of Duke University, The Ford Foundation, 1977), p. 3, and Martin Anderson, *Welfare* (Stanford, California: Hoover Institution, Stanford University, 1978), p. 68 for evidence of the minimal public support for a return to private charity.

6. Congressional Budget Office, Congress of the United States, *The Administration's Welfare Reform Proposal: An Analysis of the Program for Better Jobs and Income* (Washington, D.C., April 1978), p. xxii. See also James R. Storey, "The Need for Welfare Reform," an unpublished paper presented before the Conference on Federal Affairs of the Tax Foundation, April 17, 1978, p. 15.

7. Storey, p. 15.

8. All of the statistics provided in relation to the Ullman bill are taken from an unsigned paper dated February 7, 1978 entitled "Summary of Ullman Welfare Reform Proposal," which was prepared by Representative Ullman's staff.

9. One major rationale offered to explain the lack of variance of cash benefits by family size in the Ullman bill is the fact that family size is not ordinarily a consideration in determining the level of wages or unemployment benefits. Variation of cash benefits by family size in welfare benefits could be seen as a "reward" for having larger families. This reward is not available to families who rely on wages or have a work history and receive unemployment compensation.

10. The bill in which this provision was included was H.R. 3387, reported by the Senate Finance Committee in August of 1977 and debated on the Senate floor October 17, 1977. The bill, as amended, later became Public Law 95-171.

11. Public Law 95-113, Stat. 958, Title XIII, Section 6, approved September 29, 1977.

12. Congress has recently acted to strengthen work requirements in the AFDC program. Public Law 92-265, enacted June 9, 1980, provides for employment search by certain AFDC recipients for a period not to exceed eight weeks a year.

13. In addition to a means test, AFDC-UF applicants must prove that the father either worked six or more quarters in any 13-quarter calendar period ending within one year prior to application or received or was eligible to receive unemployment compensation during the year prior to application (Section 407(b) of the Social Security Act). In addition, the AFDC-UF participants cannot be employed over 100 hours a month, even if earnings from

working over 100 hours a month would not have otherwise disqualified them on a means-tested basis. The 100-hour rule is found in regulation 45CFR 233.100.

14. The "breakeven" refers to the level of gross income where, after all allowable deductions are taken, a family becomes ineligible for assistance. The AFDC program currently does not provide for eligibility to the "breakeven" for applicants. When first applying, AFDC applicants are not allowed to deduct the "30 + one-third" work incentive from gross income in order to determine whether their income is low enough to receive assistance. (They can deduct actual work-related expenses.) Only if otherwise eligible can an applicant receive the benefit of the "30 + one-third" deduction for purposes of determining his benefit amount. The comprehensive bills would extend eligibility to the "breakeven" by allowing applicants to take the full work-incentive deduction in determining initial eligibility. Under the comprehensive bills, one-parent families applying for assistance would be allowed to deduct 50 percent of their earned income (assuming no state modification of benefit reduction rates) in determining whether they are eligible for cash assistance. The allowance of such a deduction would increase the population able to qualify for assistance.

15. The only major missing piece from this chronology of welfare programs is the SSI program, enacted in 1972. This program replaced long-standing categorical programs of aid to the aged, blind, and disabled. Coverage of these groups has never been a matter of controversy.

16. The reference to most of the remainder of recipients refers mainly to one-parent families with children. They comprise the vast majority of the AFDC program. In all of the proposals, two-parent families would be likely to receive lesser benefits than one-parent families, although only for an initial two-month period in the administration and subcommittee bills.

17. CBO estimates that the benefit level proposed in the administration bill would exceed the combined Food Stamp and AFDC benefits in nine states. Congressional Budget Office, p. 6, 150–151.

18. See Michael C. Barth, George J. Carcagno, John L. Palmer, *Toward an Effective Income Support System: Problems, Prospects and Choices* (The Institute for Research on Poverty, University of Wisconsin—Madison, 1974), pp. 39–42.

19. Additional arguments could be made that other features—the six month accountable period and mandatory retrospective accounting—of the administration bill also would jeopardize the adequacy of benefits provided to recipients. These features would not affect the benefit payment standards but could impair another aspect of adequacy: program responsiveness. Both features would have the capability to delay or diminish benefits to persons very much in need of assistance. While there are reasons why these features might be favored from the perspectives of maximizing program equity and assuring administrative efficiency, there is no question that their operation could result in destitute persons receiving for a month or more lower benefits than the established payment standard. Certainly this possible impact and its consequences for individual families should be carefully weighed against the assumed benefits of these proposals.

17

Welfare Reform: What Kind and When?

HENRY AARON

A minor paradox is unfolding. Welfare reform languished over the last decade, a period during which real federal expenditures rose 40 percent. Presidents Nixon and Carter could not push their plans through Congress. President Ford decided not to submit the plan prepared for his consideration by Secretary Weinberger. Now, with the nation wracked by Proposition 13 fever, suffering from a remarkably stubborn case of inflation, and slowed by a debilitating shortage of gasoline, and with Congress and the President agreed that a cut in real domestic governmental expenditures is good medicine, the prospects for Congressional enactment of welfare reform, while not good, seem better than they have been in years. Why have the prospects of welfare reform improved?

Two developments explain this paradox. The first is the emergence of a core of agreement about a common approach to welfare reform, perhaps the most surprising aspect of the debate precipitated by the Program for Better Jobs and Income. Though surprising, its existence cannot be questioned. The administration's proposal, a modified bill approved by the special subcommittee created in 1979 to act on welfare, chaired by Congressman Corman, the proposals of Senators Baker, Bellmon, Danforth, and Ribicoff, of Congressman Ullman, of the New Coalition, and of Senator Kennedy all embodied certain common elements. This common core represents the area of overlap among more ambitious proposals advanced previously. The second development is more predictable, the growing interest of states and localities in the fiscal relief that welfare reform can bring. The direct pressure on state budgets from cash welfare payments is smaller than it was in the early 1970s because welfare caseloads and real benefits are rising less rapidly now or are falling, while both were increasing rapidly then. However, the volume of pleas from constituents for lower state and local taxes is far louder today than in the early 1970s. The first section of this paper describes these common elements and distinguishes these elements from previous proposals and suggested approaches. The final section asks whether the kind of bill Congress is most likely to pass would be a good thing and whether it deserves support or opposition from advocates of the interests of the poor.

The Unexpected Consensus

During the past two years a rather unexpected consensus has emerged about the form of desirable changes in the welfare system among most politically relevant actors. What are the elements of that consensus and why has it emerged?

ELEMENTS OF THE CONSENSUS

Any welfare reform plan that passes Congress in the next several years is very likely to have some or all of five major components and may have a number of minor ones. These elements include the following:

National minimum in AFDC. The best bet for inclusion in any welfare reform bill is a national minimum under Aid to Families with Dependent Children (AFDC). Combined benefits for one-parent families under AFDC and Food Stamps remain quite low in many states. In six states benefits are less than 55 percent of official poverty thresholds, in fourteen states they are less than 65 percent, and in twenty-nine states they are less than 75 percent of poverty thresholds. Moreover, the federal cost of establishing a federally mandated minimum at these modest levels is surprisingly low—less than $100 million for a floor at 55 percent of the poverty threshold, $280 million for a floor at 65 percent, and $700 million for a floor at 75 percent. The price tag on this liberalization is surprisingly low because most states with very low benefits are small.

Coverage of two-parent families. Most two-parent families with low incomes do not qualify for AFDC. Although twenty-six states, including all of the more populous ones, provide aid to unemployed fathers under AFDC, restrictive rules have limited eligibility to only about 160,000 families. Fathers must have been working in at least six of the preceding thirteen quarters and they currently must be working fewer than 100 hours per month. Mandating the program for unemployed parents and relaxing these restrictive rules could be achieved at a cost of $100 million. This change would remove one of the most glaring apparent inequities in the present system—the fact that parents in intact families can often best serve the economic interests of their spouse and children by leaving them.

Jobs. Cash assistance to two-parent families is unlikely to be extended without a work requirement because of the widespread view that able-bodied adults should work if they are not needed at home to care for young children or for disabled relatives. To make sure that this expectation can be fulfilled, a key element of the present consensus is that welfare recipients should be required to work and that jobs should be created for welfare recipients. Work requirements are not new. The Talmadge amendments of 1967 created the Work Incentive (WIN) program which requires recipients of AFDC to register for work if their youngest child is six or over, provides them some training and assistance in finding work, and offers modest incentives to employers to hire welfare recipients. The present consensus departs from previous attempts to encourage employment by welfare recipients in recognizing that more jobs suited for welfare recipients than are now available must somehow be created to make work requirements meaningful.

There is some disagreement about how these jobs should be created. The government could create the jobs directly through the prime sponsors established under the Comprehensive Employment and Training Act (CETA). Alternatively, WIN agencies could expand services they now offer, and tax incentives to private employers to hire welfare recipients could be increased. Whether the private or the public approach to job creation will prevail is not clear, but it seems quite likely that any welfare plan that is proposed and enacted will take steps to encourage employment in welfare families that contain a member expected to work. If the route of direct job creation is pursued, the public cost is roughly $10,000 per job. The cost of providing a job for all welfare families with two healthy adults or one parent not needed for the care of young children would run from $2.4 billion to $4.5 billion, depending on the height of any floor under AFDC and the degree to which coverage for two-parent families is broadened.

Earned income tax credit. The current consensus on welfare reform rests both on an awareness of the importance of financial incentive to work and on a commitment to work requirements. Since 1974, workers with low earnings in low-income families with children have been entitled to claim a tax credit of up to $400 per year. Legislation in 1978 increased the maximum credit to $500. Under present law, the credit equals 10 percent of the first $5,000 of earnings and is phased down at the rate of 12½ percent of adjusted gross income between $6,000 and $10,000. It would be desirable to increase the credit percentage for workers with low earnings in order to increase the financial incentives to work. Costs could run from $700 million to $2.2 billion. Disagreements remain about the exact form and the justifiable cost of any such change.

Fiscal relief. For both political and programmatic reasons, fiscal relief to states and municipalities is an essential component of welfare reform. Such relief can be provided directly by increasing the proportion of the costs of cash assistance which the federal government meets or it can be provided indirectly by reducing the number of families requiring assistance or by reducing the amount of assistance they require (for example, by providing them jobs or by increasing the earned income tax credit).

It is politically essential, because no politically powerful organized group views welfare reform as a top priority objective other than the organizations representing states, counties, cities, and state legislatures. The poor have rarely been organized. The National Welfare Rights Organization all but vanished after the death of its charismatic leader George Wiley. Organized labor has supported welfare reform, but never as a bread and butter issue. But state and local officials can vote lower taxes or increased public services if welfare reform provides fiscal relief. The interest of these groups is heightened by the fact that some part of the fiscal relief would go to municipalities such as New York City and states such as California that face serious fiscal problems. The fact that most of these problems are self-inflicted and that other devices for aiding these and other jurisdictions are available may seem relevant on the impartial scales of justice, but has only limited bearing on the political situation. Fiscal relief is certain to be part of any enacted welfare reform proposal. The only question is the price, which could run from a few hundred million dollars on up.

Other elements. The major difference between "comprehensive" and "incremental" approaches to welfare reform is the degree of program consolidation sought. The Carter administration proposed extensive program consolidation in 1977, but Congress was unwilling to pay the cost of comprehensive reform. The major surviving candidate for program consolidation is to eliminate the Food Stamp program for the aged, blind, and disabled who receive supplemental security income (SSI) and to provide them cash instead. To "cash out" Food Stamps for SSI recipients would cost about $.5 billion because roughly half of SSI recipients eligible to receive Food Stamps do not claim them.

Any welfare reform plan will raise questions about whether and how Medicaid rules should be changed. At present, Medicaid eligibility is available automatically to all AFDC recipients in every state but Arizona, which does not have a Medicaid program. If welfare reform increases the number of families who receive cash assistance, it would tend to increase the costs of Medicaid. Because of the importance of assuring states fiscal relief, it may be necessary to modify eligibility rules for Medicaid.

Whether or not Congress enacts welfare reform, it is quite likely that a number of administrative changes will be made in the system. The present practice of basing assistance on clients' forecasts of their future income is likely to be replaced with a system under which payments are based on the actual income clients received in an immediately preceding month. Together with such a change, clients are likely to be required to report actual income on a regular, periodic basis. This change in administrative procedures has a major impact on welfare costs. It also requires that some form of emergency assistance be provided to the relatively small number of families whose income drops sharply and who require immediate aid.

Another change in the AFDC program likely to be included in any welfare reform package is the requirement that welfare agencies use the same formula for determining initial eligibility that they use for determining continued eligibility. At present, initial eligibility in most states requires that family income be lower than is necessary for continued eligibility. As a result, a family receiving benefits may live next door to a similar family with the identical income that is ineligible for benefits. Furthermore, present rules increase the "risk" of earning enough to escape welfare, because eligibility can be regained only if income drops substantially.

The net additional cost of this consensus proposal could range from $5 to $12 billion, depending on the height of the federal minimum in AFDC, the number of jobs created for welfare recipients, the generosity of the earned income tax credit, and the amount of fiscal relief.

PAST PROPOSALS

The welfare reform proposals of the early and mid 1960s emphasized social services to enable actual or potential recipients to become attractive to potential employers or to free potential recipients from burdens of child care that prevent them from working. Welfare reform proposals of the late 1960s and early 1970s—the plan recommended by the President's Commission on Income Maintenance (The Heineman Commission), President Nixon's Family Assistance Plan, Secretary Weinberger's Income Security Plan—were all unadorned negative income taxes without much emphasis on social services or job creation. The House-passed version of the Family Assistance Plan, in fact, combined these two approaches, linking a negative income tax to greatly expanded social services. The present consensus is marked by the linkage of proposed reforms of cash assistance, work requirements, and direct job creation, but without much attention to social services within the welfare reform plan itself.

In addition to the proposals advanced in the political arena, two other approaches have enjoyed some scholarly support. A long line of social thinkers, drawing on a European tradition, have advocated some kind of demogrant—a payment made to *all* citizens or to *all* members of a broadly defined group, such as families with children—regardless of income or need. France pioneered with children's allowances in the early twentieth century and most European countries now have them; American supporters of this approach included Daniel Patrick Moynihan, Alvin Schorr, and others. An even more sweeping version of the demogrant was supported by Professors Earl Rolph and James Tobin, by Democratic presidential nominee Senator George McGovern, and by Director of the Wisconsin Poverty Center, Irwin Garfinkel. Under this approach—sometimes called a "credit income tax"—all citizens would be entitled to a refundable tax credit and would be subject to tax on all income. Persons with little or no income would receive a payment from the government because the credit would exceed their tax liability. As income rose, taxes would exceed the credit by increasing amounts.

Despite the appeal of family allowances abroad, no form of the demogrant has appealed much to Congress or the executive branch of government, probably because a demogrant is a particularly costly way of helping the poor. Much of the budgetary cost of any demogrant goes for benefits paid to people or households who are not needy. The net cost of a demogrant and its overall impact on income distribution can be altered to any desired final pattern if changes in the tax system accompany the proposed benefits. But such an approach compounds the difficulty of welfare reform by adding in the quite distinct and independent headaches of tax reform and requires the involvement and cooperation of another large and influential bureaucracy, that of the Treasury Department, in arriving at a plan.

More recently, a number of economists have supported wage rate or earnings subsidies as an instrument of welfare reform. By providing a bonus to low-wage workers in addition to the earnings they can achieve unaided in the market place, it is hoped that low-income families can achieve economic independence. In a very limited form, Congress has already enacted an earnings subsidy—the earned income tax credit. In addition, Congress has put in place two credits payable to employers to encourage them to hire welfare recipients and other low-income or disadvantaged workers. But experience with these credits makes it clear that they can solve only a portion of the welfare problem. Many actual or potential welfare recipients cannot work and will not be aided by any form of wage or earnings credit. Because welfare will continue to be necessary, whatever form of wage or earnings credit may be enacted, one cannot escape the question of whether and how welfare should be reformed.

The consensus approach to welfare reform described above is not a straight negative income tax because of its emphasis on job creation; it is not a demogrant because it provides payments on a needs-tested basis and proposes no changes in the tax system (other than slight modifications in the earned income tax credit); and it relies only to a minor degree on earnings subsidies because of the need to retain a welfare system for those incapable of working.

REASONS FOR THE CONSENSUS

The present consensus shows no signs of any major change in underlying attitudes toward the poor or about the ethics of redistribution. The United States has never given large-scale, no-strings cash aid to the poor. It has assisted people during periods of unemployment (but only subject to a work test), disability, and old age. It has provided support for the dependents of people so afflicted and for the survivors of deceased workers. It has provided aid purely on the basis of need and without a work test, but only to subsidize the purchase of certain commodities deemed to be necessities, such as housing, food, and medical care. Rather than broadening the terms on which aid should be given to the poor, the present consensus would reaffirm past limitations. I believe that there are four reasons why the consensus described earlier has arisen.

The political events set in motion by President Carter's 1977 proposal are the first source of the consensus. Because it was so broad and costly, that proposal made it possible for elected officials of quite diverse political coloration to support more modest but still significant changes in the welfare system. According to the Congresssional Budget Office, the administration's welfare reform plan would have added nearly $20 billion to federal expenditures in 1982. This estimate differed from much smaller figures put forth by the administration, largely because the administration's estimate referred to an earlier year and because it presumed a number of offsetting reductions in expenditures and supplementary revenues that CBO held were extraneous to the welfare reform proposal. In fact, CBO and the administration were in substantial agreement about the total expenditures under the plan. In the end, Congress accepted CBO's way of presenting the costs and found the resulting $20 billion estimate horrifyingly large. The plans advanced by Senators Baker, Bellmon, Danforth, and Ribicoff, by Congressman Ullman, by the New Coalition, and by Senator Kennedy, all would have cost from one-third to a bit over half as much as the administration's proposal, or about $7 billion to $12 billion. In short, by presenting a comprehensive reform costing far more than Congress could contemplate, the administration inadvertently created an atmosphere in which modifications in welfare that were far from cheap seemed sufficiently modest to elicit the support of acknowledged conservatives as well as liberals.

Second, results from income maintenance experiments have broadened the appeal of linking cash assistance, work requirements for healthy adults without young children, and job creation. The experiments confirmed that the reduction in labor supply by such adults will not be large. For example, fathers reduced work effort from 1 to 11 percent under the various experiments. This method of presenting the results makes the decrease seem modest, but it is also true that from one-quarter to one-half of the cost of providing cash assistance to two-parent families would go to offset reduced wages from induced declines in work effort. Rather serendipitously, analysis based on results from the income maintenance experiments also indicates that a combination of cash assistance, work requirements, and direct job creation can actually increase work effort by welfare recipients. The proposal advanced by the Carter administration and most of the alternatives would increase work effort and earnings, not decrease them. Thus, the results of the experiments reinforce the tradition of placing conditions on aid to the poor.

The experiments do not indicate whether a policy of job creation is necessarily cost effective; whether, in other words, the work performed in the specially created jobs pays for enough of the wages and other associated costs so that they are cheaper than welfare. In fact, a recent Brookings conference and preliminary research findings on supported work in the United States raise some doubts about the value of the output from public service jobs.

In my experience many Representatives and Senators support work requirements for the poor and job creation whether or not such policies are cost effective. They seem to believe that a family owes society something in return for the assurance of a basic income. Somewhat paradoxically, no one has proposed similar work requirements and job creation for recipients of social security or unemployment insurance, although a significant part of the cost of these programs may go to replace reduced work effort or private savings. Indeed, social security imposes a retirement test that discourages work; and unemployment insurance requires only that a recipient accept "suitable" work. Both of these programs are regarded as "earned rights" derived from a history of significant labor force attachment to which most voters are entitled. Welfare, in contrast, is not an earned right, but rather largesse which the voting majority bestows on a group it regards as separate. Some critics of the welfare system continue to believe that a work requirement and direct job creation will be very costly to administer and are undesirable public policy; others argue that people capable of working should receive no cash assistance and that they should be provided work often at quite low wages. Senator Long, for example, has advocated employment for able-bodied adults with children at three-quarters of the minimum wage.

A third force underlying the consensus proposal is harder to specify. The perception that two features of the present system are particularly unjust and harmful seems to have become almost universal. The official income thresholds used in measuring poverty are generally regarded as quite strict (they are built up from the cost of diets considered adequate only for brief periods of time), but fourteen states paid AFDC benefits that in combination with Food Stamps amounted to less than 65 percent of those thresholds. I have found no one willing to oppose arguments that benefits should be at least 65 to 75 percent of those thresholds. The traditional sticking point, that some states are fiscally unable to pay such benefits, is laid to rest in all of the welfare reform proposals now under discussion by the assurance of fiscal relief to all states.

The second common perception is that the way in which two-parent families are treated is simply unjust. Many such families are not covered at all, so that a needy couple knows that if one spouse leaves, the other will be entitled to AFDC. Furthermore, if the family remains intact, and is eligible for aid, then it loses all aid once the father works 100 hours. The obstacle to dealing with this problem has been concern that assistance to two-parent families on more generous terms would lead to a reduction of work effort. As indicated earlier, this concern can be met if the two-parent family is confronted with a work requirement and provided a job when none can be found independently.

Finally, the consensus plan is an incremental modification of existing programs, rather than a comprehensive reform that creates a new program. The incremental approach has appeal for a variety of reasons. The great diversity of welfare systems across the fifty states means that the major advantage of comprehensive reform—program consolidation and simplification—must be seriously compromised at the outset. Combined AFDC plus Food Stamps benefit levels now vary from $3,516 per year in Mississippi to $6,516 per year in New York and Vermont for a four-person family. (Hawaii's $7,872 benefit is an outlier, explained in large part by its prices, about 10 percent higher than those on the mainland.) A comprehensive plan can promise to reduce those disparities—as President Carter's plan would have done—but, as a practical matter, cannot eliminate them. The budgetary cost of leveling benefits toward the top of the range would be prohibitive; the damage to the poor from leveling benefits at the lower end of the range also would be politically unacceptable. To accomodate wide variations in benefits within a comprehensive plan and to provide benefits on different terms to the aged and the non-aged and to two-parent and one-parent families requires complexities almost as great as those within the existing system. If comprehensiveness does not buy simplicity, why go through the bother of creating a wholly new system? In addition, comprehensive reforms of all kinds—energy, taxes, welfare—have not fared very well lately. The complexity of these questions and the brief period most elected officials can devote to any single issue means that comprehensive reforms must be taken on faith. And in America of the late 1970s, faith is in short supply.

Prospects for Reform

The fact that most of the discussion of welfare reform has converged on structually similar plans does not necessarily mean that the prospects for favorable action by Congress are good. It also does not mean that the consensus plan is necessarily a good one that deserves favorable action. All it means is that we know over what kind of a plan the debate will take place.

THE "MORNING LINE"

Jimmy the Greek does not quote odds on welfare reform. But, if he did, I think that his report in early 1979 would have been that the odds were about even on some limited form of welfare reform passing Congress before the 1980 presidential elections, consisting, at least, of a federal minimum for AFDC benefits and of some fiscal relief. The odds would have been about 3 to 1 against enactment of the full consensus proposal described earlier in this paper.

Some action seemed likely because rather powerful forces were working to obtain fiscal relief and because of the shared sense that the benefits paid to one-parent families in the least generous states are unconscionably low. The fiscal problems of New York City, one of the handful of cities that bears a heavy welfare burden, could be significantly alleviated through federal assumption of an increased share for welfare costs. New York City would have received about $206 million in fiscal relief under President Carter's proposal. A $7 billion package along the lines of the consensus proposal would provide New York City with roughly $60–$100 million. California, where Proposition 13 has increased the already intense interest in welfare reform, would receive a large proportion of fiscal relief from welfare reform. The interests of both California and New York receive added political substance from the fact that the three ranking Democratic members of the Public Assistance subcommittee of the Ways and Means Committee are from those two states. A floor under AFDC benefits at 65 percent of the poverty threshold and $1.3 million of fiscal relief could be implemented at a comparatively modest cost of about $1.5 billion.

Enactment of the full consensus proposal faced four serious obstacles. First, President Carter's tight 1980 budget foreshadowed an era of retrenchment in a broad range of federal programs in order to reduce federal spending and combat inflation. It will be difficult to increase aid to the welfare poor at the same time that programs for the middle class are being slashed.

A second major obstacle was Senator Long's opposition to extending cash assistance to two-parent families. He is clearly on record in support of providing jobs for such families, but at wages substantially below those proposed in President Carter's welfare reform proposal or in the major incremental alternatives. He led the successful fight to kill the Family Assistance Plan, and his presumed opposition to President Carter's plan inhibited negotiations to reach a compromise in the House of Representatives in early 1978. If refusal to accept proffered work triggered a loss of eligibility for cash assistance, it is not clear why Senator Long would resist the consensus proposal in principle. The linkage of jobs and cash assistance may be sufficiently attractive to garner enough support to pass both houses of Congress.

The third obstacle was the 1980 election. The sponsors of two of the major welfare reform bills, Senators Baker and Kennedy, and the ranking Republican member of the Finance Committee, Senator Dole, have all been mentioned as possible presidential candidates. Rivalries between them and President Carter and among themselves are unlikely to smooth the already treacherously rocky road to welfare reform. Presidential politics may make it harder for Republican members of the Ways and Means Committee to play as constructive a role on welfare reform as they have in the past. This problem is exacerbated by the death of Republican Congressman William Ketchum, a conservative member of the subcommittee on Public Assistance who worked hard for welfare reform, and his replacement by John Birch Society member John Rousselot.

Finally, key committees had a full agenda of other work that could delay consideration of welfare reform and put the issue into the 1980 presidential primaries and campaign.

SHOULD THE CONSENSUS PROPOSAL PASS?

Whether or not Congress enacts some form of welfare reform now, it is unlikely to confront the issue again for several years. Congressmen and staffs from both houses last year freely volunteered the opinion that Congress would have shunned the welfare issue if President Carter had not made it one of his major domestic priorities in 1977. Whether or not it acts on welfare next year, Congress is unlikely to return to the issue soon thereafter. Action will consign the issue to the end of the legislative queue for several years. Inaction after past strenuous and unsuccessful efforts would confirm that welfare is an issue best shunned. The question, therefore, is not whether a better welfare reform bill can be gotten in one or two years—it cannot—but whether the consensus proposal is enough of an improvement over the present system to justify its cost.

To answer this question it is helpful to regard the consensus proposal in its "schematic" form. Essentially, this proposal seeks to liberalize benefits for certain categories of households, to create jobs for some of these households and to enforce an effective work requirement on them, and to provide "fiscal relief." Whether the additional fiscal relief is desirable or not cannot be answered apart from an examination of other federal aid to state and local governments and the economic circumstances of the various sectors of the economy, none of which will be undertaken here. The one issue of principle at stake in the recent consensus, therefore, is whether it is justifiable to impose an effective work requirement on recipients of cash assistance. Many other issues are of great practical importance for the design of a welfare reform plan—for example, how fast benefits should be reduced as earnings rise, how the family unit should be defined, how income should be measured, and so on. These issues have been and will be of great practical significance, but they are not questions that raise the issue of fairness to the same degree as the question of whether people should be required to work in order to receive aid.

The consensus proposal is subject to attack from the left on the ethical ground that work requirements and job creation constitute a kind of "forced labor" to which the poor should not be exposed. It is subject to attack from the right on the practical ground that providing able-bodied adults with cash assistance will undermine their will to work. I do not think that either of these criticisms is persuasive.

The argument that a work requirement constitutes "forced labor" rests on the presumption *both* that the government ought to provide a guarantee against destitution *and* that nothing should be expected in return from the beneficiaries of that guarantee. While some would dispute the wisdom or the justice of providing such a guarantee, public opinion polls suggest that most Americans seem prepared to accord it. When pollsters ask whether people should be guaranteed adequate food and housing and assured a job, they receive overwhelmingly positive responses. When they ask whether welfare should be increased, they typically receive overwhelmingly nega- tive responses. As a practical matter, no increase in aid without strings can pass Congress. The issue is whether poor families demographically similar to those who, in late twentieth-century America, typically supply at least one full-time member of the labor force should be required to accept work at wages equal to or greater than federal statutory minimums.

The idea that as an abstract matter nothing should be expected in return for such a guarantee seems to me to have very little justification. Requiring recipients of an income guarantee to work if they are able to do so and if no serious harm results to their dependents seem quite reasonable and fair. Indeed, there is some evidence that steady employment is consistent not only with economic well-being, but also with family happiness and physical health. The chief question is a practical one—whether work opportunities can be provided at a reasonable cost.

Similarly, the idea that no cash assistance should be provided to two-parent families, even if the family is willing to provide a member to take a job but none is available, at the same time that we are prepared to provide aid without any work test to one-parent families with young children, seems to me to insist on an indefensible distinction. That distinction would seem to imply that we are unprepared to permit mothers and very young children to starve, but that we are prepared to let mothers, fathers, and older children go hungry.

The question once again is a practical one, whether jobs with decent working conditions can be created at a reasonable cost. If the answer is yes, then the concerns of both the left and the right should be laid to rest.

In that event, the work requirement will lead to increased employment. The same is true if the answer is no. In that event, cash assistance would be provided to all. The meeting ground of left and right should be the clear insistence that welfare families containing an able-bodied, non-aged adult, who is not needed at home for the care of young children or a disabled person, should accept a job paying at least the minimum wage if it is offered. Every effort should be made to create such jobs if the market does not create them, and benefits should be reduced or denied if such a job is refused. But, if for any reason such jobs are not available, there seems to be no reason why aid should not be available to both two-parent and one-parent families.

Opinions will differ on whether the consensus program and the basic and innovative principle on which it rests—that society owes families basic support and families owe society their work—is worth the cost of welfare reform. Whether half the House and Senate find it sufficiently attractive will become clear before voters go to the polls in November 1980.

18

Impact of Future Social and Demographic Change on Programs for Reducing Economic Dependency

JAMES A. ROTHERHAM

Introduction

The objective of this paper is to assess the implications of probable social, demographic, and economic trends over the next three to four decades for federal programs to reduce economic deprivation. This paper is organized into four sections. The first defines what economic deprivation is and discusses some of the methods by which the government seeks to reduce it. The second section describe some of the interrelationships since World War II between social welfare programs and major social, demographic, and economic trends. The third is a projection of probable trends which are likely to affect economic deprivation. The final section is a discussion of some moral implications of these trends for current and future programs to reduce economic deprivation.

A recurring theme in the survey of post-World War II developments and the projection of future trends is the extent to which certain groups in our society have been and are expected to remain at higher risk of economic deprivation than the rest of the population. Groups at higher risk include racial and ethnic minorities, primarily blacks and, to a lesser extent, persons of Hispanic heritage. Also traditionally at high risk of economic deprivation and likely to remain so more than the rest of the population are families headed by women. In contrast, since World War II the risk of economic deprivation has declined dramatically for aged

individuals and couples and for non-aged families in which both a husband
and wife are present. The risk of economic deprivation, however, remains
higher for these families if they are black or of Hispanic heritage.

An assumption in this paper is that the past and present higher risk of
economic deprivation for racial and ethnic minorities and for female-
headed families indicates a presumption of discrimination against these
groups. The nature of the discrimination against women is somewhat
different from that against minorities, however. It can be argued that the
lower incomes and higher unemployment rates of racial and ethnic
minorities simply reflect the fact that these groups tend to have lower
educational attainment levels than the rest of the population. It has been
repeatedly demonstrated that income and employment are positively correlated with educational attainment. This line of reasoning, however, begs
the question of whether there is an impact from discrimination, since the
lower educational attainment levels of minorities may reflect their lack of
equal educational opportunities or may be influenced by the socioeconomic level of their parents. Presumably, the socio-economic level of
parents, which has been demonstrated to have a major impact on educational attainment, in part reflects the legacy of past discrimination. A
fundamental premise of this paper is that when the burden of economic
deprivation and unemployment is not distributed among racial and ethnic
groups in something close to the proportion of these groups to the overall
population, the burden falls upon society to prove that economic deprivation among the members of these groups does not reflect the impact of
discrimination. Obviously, individual blacks and other minorities can
"make it" in American society through diligence, talent, and luck. On the
other hand, to infer from individual success stories that blacks and other
minorities have opportunity for success equal to the rest of society is
analogous to arguing that because some people can run a mile in less than
four minutes, anyone who cannot lacks sufficient application and diligence.

The dilemma for policymakers in our highly competitive society is how
to encourage individual effort without stigmatizing as undeserving those
who do not make it. Contemporary social welfare policy in the United
States is heavily influenced not only by vestiges of social and economic
Darwinism, including the often-described programmatic dichotomy
which separates the deserving from the non-deserving poor, but also by
vestiges of the philosophy behind the English poor laws which presume
that the needy have to be coerced away from idleness.

A past and projected legacy of discrimination is a higher probability of
being poor or unemployed if one is black or of Hispanic heritage. This
legacy raises several moral issues which will be addressed in this paper,
including the following: (1.) Should recipients of government transfer
payments be coerced to work even though their need for assistance may
reflect the legacy of past discrimination? (2.) Since discrimination is a

national problem, but its legacy of unemployment and poverty is not distributed evenly across the nation or equally within individual states, what financing arrangements and benefit structures for programs to reduce economic deprivation will be fair to both recipients and workers who finance the benefits? (3.) Should a distinction continue to be made between welfare programs and other programs, such as Social Security, which also reduce economic dependency? The programs traditionally considered to be welfare, such as Food Stamps and Aid to Families with Dependent Children (AFDC), will increasingly become programs which reach disproportionate numbers of blacks and other minorities compared with the overall representation of these groups in the population. At the same time, the burden of financing programs like Social Security is likely to become so great that the future debate on these programs could become similar in many ways to the contemporary debate about welfare programs. Issues could emerge, such as whether the able-bodied aged should have to work, and whether people who did not work and pay taxes in their younger years should receive benefits when they become old.

Families headed by females represent an increasing proportion of the population in need of assistance from social welfare programs. In part, this reflects the lower wages paid to women. Throughout this century, the median female wage has been about 60 percent of the median male wage.[1] This also reflects the increasing rate of marital disruption and illegitimacy. Both trends increase the risk that a woman will need assistance. Because of discrimination, she can on the average command lower wages to support a family than can a man. Her ability or willingness to work outside of the home may also be limited due to child-care responsibilities. When a marriage breaks up, the woman in contemporary American society normally assumes child-care responsibilities. Although from the perspective of controlling the cost of welfare programs, it would appear desirable not to provide incentives for families to separate, and public officials often proclaim family stability as a policy objective, the current welfare system provides significant incentives for family instability. A moral question discussed in this paper is whether social welfare programs should be structured to encourage specific family structure and living arrangements.

Economic Deprivation

Economic deprivation is defined as income less than society considers adequate for subsistence. No distinction is made between income from earnings and investment or income from public transfers on the grounds that individuals have only limited control over the source and amount of their income, particularly when there is less than full employment. Although data based on the Census poverty series are frequently cited in this paper, the Census definition of poverty is not used as a measure of economic deprivation. The Census definition is not relevant to a discussion of long-term trends because the poverty level is adjusted only for price increases, not for increases in real income. It is assumed that over the long run, the normal trend for average wage increases to exceed price increases will resume so that the income level under the census definition of poverty will be a gradually declining proportion of median wages. When society perceives the implications of this trend, there is likely to be a redefinition of what constitutes poverty.

The current and probable future federal effort to reduce economic deprivation is much broader than welfare. Indeed, there is not even a generally accepted list of federal welfare programs. Virtually all observers would agree that the Aid to Families with Dependent Children (AFDC) and the Supplemental Security Income (SSI) programs are welfare, but any consensus quickly evaporates as the list is expanded. For example, veterans' pensions, which cost about $3.8 billion in fiscal year 1979, are means-tested benefits provided to low-income aged and non-service disabled veterans and their families and survivors. Few recipients and even fewer spokesmen for veterans would consider these benefits welfare.

The largest programs which reduce economic deprivation are Social Security (Old Age, Survivors, and Disability Insurance) and Unemployment Compensation, which cost $114.6 billion in fiscal year 1979. Both are generally considered to be social insurance, not welfare. This distinction is based on the following characteristics of these programs: no means test, payroll tax financing, and benefits tied to previous earnings. Despite the distinction that these programs are social insurance, not welfare, many features of these programs have a substantial welfare component. The Social Security benefit formula has always been weighted to provide comparatively higher wage-replacement rates to low-wage workers than to higher wage workers, and this weighting has increased over the years. In addition, all workers who become eligible for Social Security benefits are guaranteed a minimum benefit of $122 a month. The original minimum benefit of $10 was instituted for administrative convenience, but over time it became an anti-poverty feature of the benefit structure. The minimum benefit should become less significant because the Social Security amendments of 1977 froze the initial minimum benefit for future beneficiaries.

A major Social Security benefit which appears increasingly like welfare is the spouse's benefit. An aged woman who is married to a covered worker or who is divorced after at least ten years of marriage is entitled to a Social Security benefit equal to 50 percent of the covered worker's benefit.[2] The spouse's benefit was instituted in 1940 when the norm was the nuclear family in which the husband was the breadwinner and his wife remained at home to care for the children. The labor force participation rate for women with children in 1940 was only 9 percent. As a result, the spouse's benefit reflected the economic dependency of married women at that time and was an appropriate extension of social insurance coverage. By the late 1970s, the nuclear family in which the wife remained at home to care for the children had become much less the norm. By 1978, 45 percent of married women were working outside of the home, as were 38 percent of married women with children under age six. Some observers have questioned whether the spouse's benefit remains an appropriate function of a social insurance program. Others want increased benefits for working wives, who in most cases receive benefits based on their husband's earnings and thus no return on their own Social Security taxes. The treatment of women under Social Security is likely to receive increasing attention over the next several years. This author does not believe that the debate on this issue should be kept separate from the debate on welfare.

The current procedures in both AFDC and social security favor women who do not work outside the home. AFDC recipients with children under age six are not expected to work outside the home even though more than one-third of the women in the general population who have children under age six do work outside the home. Married women who remain at home also receive preferential treatment under Social Security compared with their counterparts who work outside the home. As previously noted, a woman is entitled to 50 percent of her husband's benefit and, if divorced, her former husband's benefit when the marriage lasted at least ten years. This means that a woman who works outside the home receives no return on her payroll taxes if her benefit based on her earnings is less than 50 percent of her husband's benefit. If the benefit based on her own earnings exceeds 50 percent of her husband's benefit, her payroll taxes have yielded her a benefit which is only equal to the difference between her benefit and 50 percent of her husband's benefit. When both Social Security and AFDC favor women who remain at home, it seems incongruous to stigmatize AFDC as welfare while calling the spouse's benefit under Social Security a social insurance benefit.

Not only are efforts to reduce economic deprivation broader than narrowly defined welfare programs, but government transfer payments are only one way to reduce or forestall economic deprivation. Economic growth directly provides jobs and higher incomes which reduce the need for transfer payments. Plotnick and Skidmore have found a significant positive correlation between higher average pretransfer incomes and a reduction in poverty for non-aged male family heads. Conversely, for the same group, an increase in the unemployment rate leads to a significant increase in pretransfer poverty. Pretransfer poverty among female family heads is less well correlated with changes in the unemployment rate and average family income. This weak relationship appears to reflect the lower labor force participation rate of women with children and wage levels for women which rise more slowly than for men. Table 18.1 summarizes Plotnick and Skidmore's findings.[3]

A second way in which economic deprivation is reduced is the most traditional way in all societies—transfers from one member of a family to

Table 18.1   Effect of Macroeconomic Conditions on the Incidence of Pretransfer Poverty

	Percent change in the incidence of pretransfer poverty associated with a 1% rise in average family pretransfer income (average unrelated individual pretransfer income for unrelated individuals): Relative	Percent change in the incidence of pretransfer poverty associated with a 10% rise in the national unemployment rate: Relative
All Families	−.30	2.7[a]
White male head under 65	−.90	5.8[a]
Nonwhite male head under 65	−1.79[a]	2.1
White female head under 65	.84[a]	2.2[a]
Nonwhite female head under 65	−.02	−0.1
Male head over 65	−.84[a]	1.4[a]
Female head over 65	−.48	2.5
Unrelated individuals: All related individuals	−.50[a]	0.8
Males under 65	−.70	4.7[a]
Females under 65	−.34	1.4

[a]Statistically significant at .05 level.

another. A recent study by Morgan using data from the Michigan Panel Study of Income Dynamics estimated that intrafamily transfers amounted to about one-third of the gross national product in 1970 and 1976.[4] Although historical data are not available to test whether intrafamily transfers have declined as a percentage of GNP since World War II, the rising divorce and separation rates and the decrease in the number of extended families living together over this period make it probable that intrafamily transfers have declined.

A third way in which economic deprivation can be reduced is through private charities. As government transfers have increased, this method has become less significant in the United States.

A fourth way in which economic deprivation can be reduced is through what has been termed investment in human capital, such as education, employment and training services, social services. Considering the time required for the development of skills and modification of behavior, it is not reasonable to assume that economic deprivation will be reduced in the short run through human capital investment. The effectiveness of this approach over the long run is a complex and controversial issue which is beyond the scope of this paper.

The final way to reduce economic deprivation is through government transfer payments. The current effort is substantial. Total transfers from social welfare programs, including cash and in-kind benefits, such as Food Stamps, Medicare, and Medicaid, were $183 billion in fiscal year 1976. Even though not all of these transfers are targeted on low-income persons, this level of spending has a substantial impact on reducing poverty. The Congressional Budget Office has estimated that in the absence of transfer payments, 27 percent of families in the United States would have been poor in fiscal year 1976. Social insurance transfers reduced this percentage to 15.7 percent. Other cash transfers, primarily needs-tested cash assistance, reduced this percentage further to 13.5 percent. If in-kind benefits, such as Food Stamps and Medicare/Medicaid, were valued at their cost to governments, the Congressional Budget Office estimates that the number of poor families would have been reduced to 8.1 percent.[5] The Census poverty statistics do not include the value of these in-kind benefits. As a result, the series overstates the number of poor since these benefits have some value to recipients even though it does not equal the cost of these benefits to governments.

Trends Since World War II

While the experience of the recent past does not necessarily represent an accurate harbinger of future trends, it is useful to examine changes in both income distribution as well as social and demographic trends since World War II to determine what trends have emerged. A recent analysis by Reynolds and Smolensky of the impact of governmental expenditures and taxes on the distribution of income in the United States confirms what other analysts have also found: The distribution of income after taxes and governmental expenditures has not changed significantly since 1950. When the income distribution is measured before taxes and public expenditures, however, Reynolds and Smolensky conclude that it has become substantially less equal since 1950.[6] This does not mean that the tremendous increase in governmental transfers—from $14.3 billion in fiscal year 1950 to $183.0 billion in fiscal year 1976—simply kept everyone at the same point on a treadmill. This increase has enabled a substantial increase in the economic well-being of certain groups. Furthermore, the income distribution data may understate the increase in economic well-being since it includes only government cash transfers. Nearly one quarter of the fiscal year 1976 transfer payments were in-kind benefits, such as Medicare/Medicaid and Food Stamps. Were it possible to estimate the value of these benefits to recipients and include this in the income data, there might be a modest increase in income equality after taxes and transfers. Just the increase in cash benefits has been substantial for certain groups, however. For example, average monthly Social Security benefits for the aged increased by 117 percent in constant dollars over the period 1950 to 1976, and coverage was extended to virtually the entire population. The Congressional Budget Office estimates that in fiscal year 1976, 60 percent of families with a head age 65 or older would have been poor in the absence of transfers, but cash transfers reduced the poverty incidence to 16.7 percent. Social insurance programs, primarily Social Security, were estimated to lift about 64 percent of the aged poor over the poverty line.[7]

Similarly, substantially increased aid to the disabled was provided over the same period. In 1950, aid to the disabled was provided through state-administered programs. Average monthly payments of $104.36 (expressed in 1976 dollars) were provided to about 69,000 participants. Currently, aid to the disabled is provided through the disability component of the Social Security program, which was established in 1956, and the Supplemental Security Income (SSI) program, which in 1974 replaced the state-administered programs providing aid to the aged, blind, and disabled. By 1976, 2.5 million disabled workers and their dependents received average monthly benefits of $225.90 under the disability component of Social Security. In addition, the SSI program provided average monthly benefits of $141.72 to 2.1 million disabled recipients, about 35 percent of whom also received Social Security benefits.

Increased federal transfer payments were less successful in reducing the incidence of poverty among female-headed families. Between 1959, the first year in which data became available on the number of poor using the Census definition, and 1976, the number of persons in female-headed families below the poverty level increased by 29 percent. Over the same period, the overall poverty population declined by 43 percent. A breakdown by race of female-headed families indicates that families headed by a black female contributed disproportionately to the increase. The number of poor persons in such families increased by 83 percent over this period, while the number of poor persons in families with a white female head increased by 5 percent.[8]

This increase occurred despite a substantial increase in both the benefit level and the participation rate in AFDC, which is the primary cash assistance program targeted on families with a female head. In 1950, there were 2.2 million AFDC recipients. Over the next twenty-five years, the number increased to 11.4 billion, and the program reached about 90 percent of the eligible population. Expressed in 1976 dollars, average monthly payments per recipient increased from $49.30 to $77.35 between

1950 and 1976. The average monthly family benefit was about 57 percent of the poverty level in 1976 for the average AFDC family.[9] Comparisons of average monthly benefits in the AFDC program on a national basis to the poverty level are subject to three caveats, however. First, the use of national data masks significant variations in benefit levels by state. Average benefits range from about $47 a month for a family in Mississippi to about $370 a month for a family in New York. Second, AFDC recipients are also eligible for in-kind benefits, including Food Stamps and Medicaid, which are not included in the Census poverty statistics. Third, the AFDC benefits are reduced if the recipient has earnings or other income.

One group that has experienced a significant decline in poverty and has not experienced an increase in cash transfers comparable to that received by the aged, disabled, and female family heads is families with a husband and wife present. The number of poor persons in such families declined by 61 percent between 1959 and 1976 (the decline for white families was 60 percent and the decline for black families was 69 percent).[10]

The increase in income inequality before taxes and government expenditures since World War II may reflect the impact of two major changes in the structure of the American family—the increase in the number of female-headed households; and the decline of both three-generation families living together, and also childless couples living with parents. The increase in the number of female-headed households represents a trend which became evident after World War II and which has accelerated during the 1970s. Between 1970 and 1975, the number of female-headed households increased 50 percent—from 2.9 million to 4.4 million. During the same period, there was a 1.5 percent decline in the number of husband-wife families.[11] The increase in the number of female-headed households reflects both the increasing rates of marital dissolution and illegitimacy.

A basic question is whether the evolution of welfare programs since World War II has been a reaction to the increase in female-headed families or whether government policies, including welfare programs, have encouraged this trend. In his recent book, *Haven in a Heartless World: The Family Besieged*, Christopher Lasch attributes the breakdown of the family to intervention by modern industrial states.[12] This indictment is not only too sweeping but also denigrates many reforms, such as the abolition of child labor and the advent of compulsory education, which have benefited children as individuals. In addition, the family in the pre-industrial state may have been somewhat less utopian than Lasch implicitly assumes.[13]

Addressing the issue more narrowly, it is not clear how much the welfare system has contributed to the increase in female-headed families, even though the AFDC program provides substantial economic incentives for families to split up. In twenty-three states, a family cannot receive benefits if the father is present. In the remaining states, AFDC benefits are available if the husband is present only if he works fewer than 100 hours a month. A study of Marjorie Honig found a positive relationship between increased AFDC benefits and family splitting.[14] However, several subsequent studies have not supported the conclusion that the economic incentives for family splitting actually cause it to occur.[15] The moral issue is not whether AFDC has encouraged family splitting but whether the government should provide economic incentives for families to split up.

This issue is complicated by the results of the Seattle/Denver income maintenance experiment in which it was found that the three variants of a negative income tax that were tested all increased family splitting. A major factor in this outcome could have been that people who were already in unsatisfactory marriages found that the increased income from the experiment provided the woman with sufficient economic independence that the relationship could be dissolved.[16] Clearly the results from this experiment raise questions about whether a negative income tax will increase marital stability as some proponents of this approach hope. It should be emphasized that these experimental results cannot be automatically generalized to a national program. Furthermore, even if the results were applicable to a national program, it does not follow that a negative income tax would provide economic incentives for marital instability similar to the current AFDC program. To the extent that the government provides people with higher incomes either through the current AFDC program or through a negative income tax, recipients obtain incomes which meet some minimum standard established through the political process. If these higher incomes give the recipients more control over their lives and this control results in a higher number of divorces, the government has not created direct incentives for marital instability but has simply fulfilled its obligation to provide a minimum level of income support. In contrast, the current AFDC program provides direct incentives for husbands to leave their families. In a majority of states, AFDC benefits are not available if the father is present. Even in the states in which AFDC benefits are available when the father is present, there are contraints on the hours he can work to support his family that are not imposed on women.

Illegitimacy presents a similar moral issue. Here, as in the case of family splitting, there does not appear to have been a significant impact on illegitimacy rates from either higher AFDC benefits or the increased availability of abortions after the 1973 Supreme Court decision. The current restrictions on the use of federal funds to finance abortions will limit the availability of abortions for low-income persons. Whether this will have an impact on the illegitimacy rate is unclear.

A moral question, however, is whether it is appropriate for the government to limit the availability of means by which people can avoid unwanted births, whether legitimate or illegitimate. The argument can be made that when the government limits a low-income woman's access to an abortion on the grounds that human life must be protected from the moment of conception, the government also incurs an obligation to provide adequate support to the woman and her child. The rebuttal to this argument is based on a concept of parental responsibility, which was well described by John Stuart Mill in the following passage:

It still remains unrecognized that to bring a child into existence without a fair prospect of being able, not only to provide for its body, but instruction and training for its mind, is a moral crime, both against the unfortunate offspring and against society; and that if the parent does not fulfill this obligation, the State ought to see it fulfilled, at the charge, as far as possible, of the parent.[17]

The power which Mill would have granted to the state to enforce this concept of parental responsibility was awesome, not only by today's standards but also compared with the rather constricted role which Mill was willing to grant the state in other spheres. Mill supported compulsory labor when no other means were available to require a father to support his children. While this position is consistent with the premise underlying the work requirement in many contemporary assistance programs, the explicit advocacy of compulsory labor would be unacceptable in most contemporary political discourse.

Mill was willing to involve the state even more deeply in the area of familial responsibility than by his advocacy of compulsory labor to ensure parental financial responsibility. He believed it to be a legitimate power of the state to prohibit marriage unless the parties could show that they had the power to support a family. Few would advocate granting the state today such paternalistic authority over who can marry. Indeed natural parents assert such a power with decreasing frequency. But if one holds that the state has the power to enforce parental financial responsibility, it seems inconsistent to advocate also that the state should limit the access of low-income persons to abortions when the state provides other medical services free to low-income persons. Of course, this inconsistency is eliminated if one assumes that people should refrain from sex unless they have the financial resources to provide for children. While this attitude toward sexual behavior logically follows from Mill's position, it is hardly consistent with the sexual mores of contemporary America.

A second major change in family structure has been the decline since World War II in three-generational families living together. While increased mobility, higher incomes, and personal preferences have all been significant in this decline, the impact of the Social Security program has been substantial. Unlike the AFDC program, which provides economic incentives for a specific family living arrangement, higher Social Security benefits provide individuals with the income to determine their own living arrangements. The increase in Social Security benefits since World War II does not reflect a deliberate federal policy to encourage the aged to live apart from their children. It merely reflects the outcome of a politically popular strategy of raising benefits for the elderly, a group which is not only considered needy but one which also votes at a higher rate than the rest of the population.

Because of Social Security, the responsibility of working-age adults to care for their aged parents has been transformed from an individual responsibility into a collective responsibility. The Social Security program operates as an intergenerational transfer system in which the taxes paid by working-age adults are used to finance the Social Security benefits of their parents' generation. In turn, working-age adults anticipate that their retirement benefits will be financed with their children's taxes.

From the end of World War II until 1977, this intergenerational compact worked quite well. Even though the number of aged persons increased dramatically, an expanding economy enabled the aged to receive increasingly higher benefits. The Social Security Amendments of 1977 may well have symbolized the rewriting of the intergenerational compact, however. By 1977, the Social Security trust funds had serious financial problems. The most immediate problem was that revenue was less than spending because of high unemployment, which caused a drop in revenues, and inflation, which generated higher benefit levels. The system was also projected to incur long-term deficits even if the economy approached full employment with stable prices. Two factors were primarily responsible for these long-term deficits. The first was the projection of an increase in the proportion of aged in the population. The second was an unintentional flaw in the way Social Security benefits were adjusted for cost-of-living increases. This flaw caused an over-compensation for inflation because annual cost-of-living increases were provided to retirees but effectively also to current workers, whose future benefits were increased whenever benefit increases were provided to current retirees. Current workers were thereby over-compensated because their future entitlement to benefits is based on their current wages which tend to increase with inflation. If this flaw had not been corrected in the Social Security Amendments of 1977, certain groups of workers in the next century could have received higher retirement benefits than their earnings immediately prior to retirement.

Although this flaw was a highly technical issue, its correction in 1977 represented a substantial reduction in future Social Security benefits. The willingness of Congress to make this correction and the fact that both a Cabinet officer in the current administration and also influential Republican members of the Committee on Ways and Means have recommended raising the retirement age indicate that the intergenerational compact on Social Security may be renegotiated even more as the burden of financing Social Security benefits increases.

The fact that this burden is high and will go higher was evident in the tax provisions in the Social Security Amendments of 1977. By 1985, the rate which workers pay on earnings subject to the Social Security tax will increase 20.5 percent over the 1977 level. Over the same period, the maximum tax liability of high-income workers will increase 178 percent. Even these tax increases as well as additional increases in the next century provided under the Amendments will not make the system self-financing over the next seventy-five years, according to the projections of the Social Security Administration's actuary. This projection could turn out to underestimate future costs since it is based on reasonably optimistic long-term economic projections (annual rates are projected over the next seventy-five years which will level off at 4 percent inflation, 5 percent unemployment and 1.75 to 2.0 percent real growth).[18]

Because of the anticipated deficits and the increasing burden of the payroll tax, enactment of some type of subsidy from general revenues is likely in the future. This will not solve the financial problems of the Social Security program, however. Instead, the subsidy will simply shift part or all of the financing burden from the payroll tax to income and corporate taxes, or to the deficit.

The shift in responsibility for care of the aged from an individual one of adult children to one through the government is also evident in the Supplemental Security Income (SSI) program, which in 1974 replaced the state-operated programs of aid to the aged, blind, and disabled. The new program effectively repealed the provision in a number of state-operated programs which had required adult children with adequate resources to assist in the support of their parents. The SSI program also contains two provisions which tend to encourage the aged poor to live apart from their children. First, benefits are reduced by one-third if an SSI recipient lives in another person's household. Second, SSI recipients are allowed to keep their homes and are not required to transfer the title to the federal government in return for benefits. Under the old state-operated programs, recipients could be required to transfer title to their homes to the state.

Future Trends

To summarize the first part of this paper, the overall themes in programs to reduce economic deprivation since World War II have been a substantial broadening of coverage and higher benefit levels, which have been increasingly targeted on the groups most affected by the changing family structure—the aged and female-headed households. The focus of the paper will now shift to some projections of future trends in family structure and also in economic, social, and demographic factors which will affect deprivation.

The most important trend will be the demographic shift as a result of the decline in the birth rate and the increasing proportion of aged persons in the population. The 1978 report by the Trustees of the Social Security Trust Funds includes a projection of future trends based on the assumption that the fertility rate of women will stabilize at the replacement rate (2.1 children).[19] (See Table 18.2)

Table 18.2   Projection of U.S. Population by Broad Age Groups

| | Population (in millions) | | | | Dependency ratio | |
	Under 20	20–64	65 and over	Total	Aged[a]	Total[b]
1977	76.0	126.1	24.1	226.2	.191	.794
1980	73.5	132.4	25.7	231.6	.194	.749
1990	72.8	148.2	30.7	251.6	.207	.698
2000	77.2	158.6	33.0	268.8	.208	.694
2010	77.4	169.9	36.0	283.3	.212	.668
2020	80.0	171.0	46.4	297.4	.271	.739

Note: Numbers may not add to totals due to rounding.
[a] Population 65 and over as ratio to population 20–64.
[b] Population 65 and over plus those under 20 as ratio to population 20–64.

Through the year 2000, the projections are already determined for workers and the aged since virtually all people who fall into these categories have already been born. The number of elderly persons will increase by nearly nine million, or 37 percent, between 1977 and the end of the century. Primarily because of the post-World War II baby boom, however, the dependency ratio between the aged and the working population will not increase substantially over the rest of this century, although it will surge during the first two decades of the next century as the post-World War II baby boom reaches retirement age.

If replacement fertility is assumed, the overall dependency ratio, including both the aged and those under 20 as a ratio of the population aged 20–64, will continue to decline over the next forty years. While, superficially, this should mean that the overall burden of providing for dependent groups in the population should be less, it might not work out that way because of the divided responsibility for the care of dependent groups in our federal system of government. Increasingly, the provision of cash transfers to the aged and disabled has become a federal responsibility, although state and local governments have a large and growing budgetary problem with their own retirement programs. The primary source of cash transfers to needy children is the AFDC program, which is financed with federal, state, and local funds. (The federal share currently averages about 55 percent of the total program cost.) The most important financial burden which children represent for governments, however, is not welfare but education. Despite significant increases in federal funding for education in recent years, most of the burden for the financing of public education in the overall dependency ratio is not likely to help the federal government's budgetary problems with retirement costs. In addition, if recent experience is any guide, stable or declining school enrollments will not produce stable or declining costs for state and local governments. During the period 1972 to 1976, state and local expenditures for education in constant dollars increased by 8.6 percent, while public school enrollment declined 3.5 percent.[20]

This demographic projection, like all projections, is subject to increasing uncertainties the further one looks into the future. The major uncertainties are the birth rate, net immigration, and life expectancy. Even though the birth rate is currently below the replacement rate, a change in societal attitudes could push it above the replacement rate. The post-World War II baby boom, which was not foreseen in the 1930s, is now considered to have been a temporary departure from the longer-term trend toward lower birth rates. Nevertheless, the post-war experience should give prognosticators pause before making unqualified projections.

The second major uncertainty is net immigration. The Social Security projections are based on net annual immigration of 400,000, which is the level of legal immigration in recent years. Thus, this projection ignores illegal immigration. The estimates of the number of illegal immigrants already in the United States range as high as 12 million. The Immigration and Naturalization Service in 1977 estimated the number of illegal aliens at 6 million and has since stopped providing public estimates.[21] In the short run, illegal immigrants do not appear to have a major direct impact on public assistance programs, probably because most illegal immigrants are reluctant to risk detection by applying for benefits. The more significant short-range cost may well be the displacement of American workers by illegal immigrants. In addition, there could be a long-run impact on participation levels in programs to reduce economic deprivation, since the children of illegal immigrants are American citizens if they were born in this country. These children may be less likely to need public assistance than native-born Americans, however. In a recent study, Barry R. Chiswick concludes that immigrants, both legal and illegal, in general improve the overall well-being of United States citizens. After ten to fifteen years, immigrant men earn as much as native-born Americans of similar age and education. After twenty years, the earnings of male immigrants exceed those of native-born American men. The earnings advantage of male immigrants appears to be passed on to their sons. Chiswick found that not all immigrant groups fare equally well, however. Because of discrimination, the earnings of Mexican immigrants do not catch up to the average earnings of native-born Americans, although after fifteen years they match the earnings of United States-born men of Mexican heritage.[22]

The third uncertainty in these projections is anticipated life expectancy. The Social Security projections are based on an improvement averaging 19 percent over the next seventy-five years. While this projection appears reasonable in light of recent HEW statistics on declining rates of death from heart attacks and cardiovascular diseases during the 1970s, breakthroughs in medical research could make the projection obsolete.[23] Obviously, any increases in life expectancy beyond this projection will accentuate the basic trend toward an older population.

The projected replacement birth rate should mean increased economic independence for women. In addition, continuing a long-term trend, the labor force participation rate of women is expected to rise. The Urban Institute's recent study of women at work, *The Subtle Revolution*, projects that the female labor force participation rate by 1990 will be 54.8 percent, which compares with a March 1978 rate of 49.1 percent.[24] Higher female labor force participation rates reduce the burden of financing programs for the aged and the young since the larger number of female workers will pay Social Security and other taxes. Increases in labor force participation by women, however, of the magnitude projected in the Urban Institute study will only lessen, not eliminate, the projected increased burden on the working age population of supporting the aged and the young. The Social Security Administration in its projections of the long-term cost of the Social Security benefits already assumes an increase in the labor force participation rate which by the year 2010 would level off at nearly 20 percent above the 1978 level. If the 20 percent assumed increase is phased in at a constant rate, the labor force participation rate in 1990 would be slightly higher (56.6 percent) than the Urban Institute's projection.

Despite increased labor force participation, women are unlikely to achieve either income or occupational equality with men—at least over the next forty years. One reason for this is that the largest increase in employment opportunities is likely to occur in the service sector where earnings traditionally have been lower than in production or construction. A second reason is that even when income and occupational equality is achieved for persons entering the labor force, the lower earnings of women who entered the labor market before equality was achieved will keep the average below the male average for forty to forty-five years.

The risk of economic deprivation for women will remain greater than for men not only because of the earnings disparity between the sexes but also as a result of marital disruption. Because of sex discrimination and child care responsibilities, marital disruption reduces available income dramatically for women. Female-headed households have incomes about one-third of husband-wife families. Even when the female head works outside the home, household income still averages less than 50 percent of the level for husband-wife families.[25]

There are three reasons why the rate of marital dissolution could level off, however, through the rest of the century. The first is the sardonic observation that if the 1970 to 1975 increase in the number of female-headed households were simply projected forward on a linear basis, the number of female-headed households would exceed the number of husband-wife households by the year 2000.[26] A second reason, which is not sardonic but perhaps wishful, is the renewed interest in the family as an institution. Although the family as an institution has changed, this

renewed interest may presage increased marital stability as couples develop patterns different from the traditional stereotype of a dominant male
breadwinner and a theoretically subservient wife who stays at home to
care for the children. A third reason is based on the well-known sociological finding that the rate of marital dissolution declines as income and
educational attainment increases.[27] The increase in educational attainment
which has occurred in the last two decades and rising average incomes
could over time reduce the rate of marital dissolution. If the prediction
that the rate of marital dissolution will remain relatively stable is borne
out, the caseload in the AFDC program should be relatively stable. The
Congressional Budget Office has estimated that if benefit levels were
adjusted only for cost-of-living increases, the caseload in the year 2000
would be 3.8 million, or only 7 percent above the current level. Even if
benefits were adjusted for overall increases in real income, which is
unlikely, the caseload is projected to increase 27 percent.[28]

Another trend with significant implications, not only for the programs
to reduce economic deprivation but also for the evolution of the United
States toward a just society, is the narrowing of the black-white income
differentials that has occurred since World War II, although during the
1970s the gap did not narrow because of the high inflation and unemployment over much of that decade. Between 1955 and 1975, the black-white
income ratios for males increased from .588 to .734.[29] For younger
workers, the wage ratios are somewhat closer to unity, reflecting the
impact of less discrimination and higher education levels among blacks.
The 1975 black-white income ratio for males of different education levels
who began work in 1967 are as follows: college graduates, .89; high
school graduates, .77; and those with only eight years of schooling,
.79.[30] With black education levels now approaching those of whites and
with a continued commitment to equal opportunity, black-white income
differentials should continue to narrow if there is sufficient economic
growth to allow increases in real wages.

The picture is not all bright, however. As with male-female income
differentials, black-white income differentials will remain for a generation
after the initial entrants into the labor market achieve income equality. In
addition, as long as racial earnings differentials remain, the rate of marital
dissolution is likely to remain higher for blacks than for whites. If racial
earnings equality were achieved, however, the differential between black
and white marital dissolution rates could disappear. This prediction is
based on a finding by Robert Hampton, based on the longitudinal data
collected by the Institute for Survey Research at the University of
Michigan, that the percentage of black families experiencing divorce or
separation is six percentage points less than for whites when income, home
ownership, and family size differences are taken into account. Of these
variables, Hampton found the most important to be income.[31] This has
significant implications for the racial composition of the AFDC program.

Until equal earnings capacity is achieved, black participation of this program is likely to remain disproportionate to the percentage of blacks in the population.

The burden of unemployment will continue to fall more heavily on blacks than on whites. The black unemployment rate remains nearly twice that for whites, and blacks continue to bear a disproportionate share of the unemployment increases during cyclical downturns. A specific problem with particularly serious long-term potential is black teenage unemployment. During the last two decades the white teenage labor force participation rate has been increasing, while the black rate has been declining. Over the same period, the black teenage unemployment rate has more than doubled.[32] For more than a year the reported unemployment rate among black youth has been around 37 percent. When the discouraged youth are added to the reported rate, Bernard Anderson has estimated the black teenage unemployment rate at close to 60 percent.[33] This shockingly high unemployment rate may limit the options of young black youth in their subsequent careers if their opportunity to go through the normal process of trial and error in settling into a career is forestalled because of unemployment. While the decline in the overall birthrate since 1970 will lessen the overall youth unemployment problem beginning in the next decade, the number of black youth is expected to continue rising at rates comparable to the 1960s because the black birth rate remains higher than the white rate.

Persons of Spanish origin suffer poverty problems similar to blacks'. In 1976, nearly 25 percent of persons of Spanish origin were poor, compared with 31 percent of blacks.[34] Like blacks, Americans of Spanish origin suffer from the legacy of discrimination, although not from the legacy of slavery. Two important differences between blacks and Americans of Spanish origin in terms of risk of economic deprivation, however, are: first, the rate of marital dissolution is lower for those of Spanish origin; and, second, during the 1970s, Hispanics made relative economic progress compared with whites, while black Americans did not.[35]

Inseparable from marital stability and racial/ethnic income differentials in assessing the problem of economic deprivation in the future is the health of the economy and the size and composition of the labor market. Assuming a reasonable rate of economic growth, it appears likely that the expansion of jobs will occur primarily in the services sector rather than production. This would continue the post-World War II trend. Since service jobs in general require less physical stamina than jobs in the production of goods, this trend should provide more job opportunities for women and the aged. A disadvantage of job expansion in the service sector, however, is that earnings in this sector tend to be lower than in production. This disadvantage is partially offset by the fact that earnings in the service sector are less affected by cyclical downturns in the economy than are earnings in the production sector.[36]

Over time, there is likely to be an increasing mismatch between the general educational level and the educational requirements for the labor force. By 1985, 36.3 percent of the labor force will have had some education beyond high school, compared with 27 percent in 1970. The rising education level will likely lead to a surplus of qualified applicants for professional and technical jobs. A recent estimate projects that the number of these jobs will increase by about 50 percent between 1970 and 1985, while the supply of qualified persons will increase by 66 percent. At the other end of the occupational spectrum, there is likely to be a shortage of workers for semiskilled and unskilled jobs.[37]

This mismatch could have several outcomes. The traditional view would hold that the labor market will adjust to the change in demand with many persons with substantial education shifting toward lower positions. Employers would likely respond to rising education levels, as they have in the past, by raising the minimum educational requirements for lower level jobs. An alternative possibility is that the United States could experience the phenomenon already found in many less-developed countries of high unemployment rates among youth university graduates who will not seek lower status jobs. The former outcome is probably more likely in this country. Since the status associated with higher education has traditionally been lower here than in other countries, a shift down in occupational status is less perceived to be a social stigma.

If the surplus of more educated workers generates an increase in educational qualifications for lower level jobs, those persons with the least education are likely to be crowded out of the labor market. Crowding out because of this trend as well as likely continued competition for the lowest paying jobs by illegal immigrants may create a pool of permanent unemployed workers with low educational attainment. Even though the educational attainment of Americans has increased substantially in recent years, a significant number of persons still have less than a high school education. For example, most persons age 44 or under will remain in the

Table 18.3   Percent of Persons 25 Years and Over
             With Less Than a High School Education

Racial/Ethnic origin	Percent by age group		
	25 to 29	30 to 34	35 to 44
White	13.2	17.4	24.2
Black	25.5	32.8	44.4
Spanish origin	41.9	51.0	59.0
Total	14.6	19.0	26.4

potential labor force for the remainder of this century. Table 18.3 indicates the percentage of persons between ages 25 and 44 who had less than a high school education in 1977.[38]

The fact that the percentage of whites in these age cohorts with less than a high school education is substantially less than the percentages for blacks and persons of Spanish origin indicates that the proportion of these minorities at risk of economic deprivation will remain higher than the proportion of whites.

To the extent that the supply and demand for education and training adjusts to changing labor demand, these discontinuities would be reduced. Based on recent trends in education and training, however, there are no particular grounds to hope that the training and educational system can respond quickly or that students are sufficiently aware of the demand for various types of training to avoid mismatches between training and the demand for specific jobs.

An emerging trend which is likely to facilitate higher labor-force participation of both women with child-care responsibilities and also the aged is the increased flexibility in work hours and availability of part-time work. Persons who work less than thirty-five hours a week now represent about one-fifth of the labor force. Over the past decade, the number of part-time workers has expanded three times as fast as the number of full-time workers. Currently, part-time workers are concentrated in lower paying jobs but over time part-time work may become more common in professional and technical jobs.[39] The Congress in 1978 enacted legislation requiring federal departments and agencies to establish timetables for increasing the number of part-time positions at every job level.

Just as economic deprivation is likely to become more concentrated among ethnic and racial minorities in the future, minorities are likely to be concentrated in specific areas.[40] Within central cities, particularly in the Northeast, the percentage of residents who are black will continue to increase. From 1960 to 1976, blacks as a percentage of central-city population increased from 21 to 24 percent. Even if everyone stopped migrating today, the concentration of blacks in central cities would continue to increase simply because the black population is increasing at a more rapid rate than the white. Although the well-publicized return of the white middle-class to the central city could reverse this concentration, this return up to now has been occurring in cities with strong economic bases and expanding opportunities for professional employment. Cities which lack these advantages are unlikely to experience a substantial influx of middle-class whites.

There are also likely to be increasing regional disparities in the population at risk of economic deprivation. The shift in the growth of metropolitan populations away from the mature industrial regions of the Northeast and lower Great Lakes to the "Sun Belt" is likely to continue. This is primarily a migration of highly skilled workers and, to a lesser extent, elderly persons with high incomes. This migration means that the population in the mature industrial regions will increasingly be composed of less skilled workers and aged persons with relatively low incomes. A second population trend which first became evident in the 1970s is increased migration to nonmetropolitan areas. Like the migration to the "Sun Belt," this is likely to increase the relative burden of economic dependency in metropolitan areas, particularly in the Northeast and lower Great Lakes.

Both of these migration patterns are likely to generate increased demands for federal assumption of a larger share of welfare costs. These patterns were also a factor in the debate during the 95th Congress on fiscal relief to state and local governments from public assistance costs. In 1977, the Congress approved with little debate a provision in the Social Security Amendments which provided $187 million in fiscal relief, using a formula that favored states with high benefit levels. The largest recipient was California, but the Northeastern states, particularly New York, also received comparatively high shares. A similar proposal which would have provided up to $400 million in fiscal relief was deleted on the floor of the Senate from the 1978 tax bill. A major issue in the debate was the extent to which states with low welfare costs should subsidize states with high welfare costs. It is likely that debates about sharing the cost of the welfare burden will continue.

Moral Issues

Based on these projections of likely demographic, social, and economic trends which will affect the population at risk of economic deprivation over the next thirty to forty years, some moral issues which welfare reform planners should consider are presented in the final section of the paper.

With a likely decline in poverty among whites and among husband-wife families of all races and ethnic backgrounds, the non-aged population at greatest risk of economic deprivation will increasingly be the groups discriminated against in our society—blacks, persons of Spanish origin, and women—and particularly black and Spanish-origin women. The fact that welfare is a form of compensation to victims of discrimination will become increasingly evident. Viewed from this perspective, the emphasis on work requirements in the Family Assistance Plan and the emphasis on work requirements and public service employment in the Carter administration's proposal may be misplaced. An extreme categorization of the work features in both programs is that they blame the victim for the crime. A more important objective than welfare reform is a full-employment economy that does not discriminate. Clearly, while seeking the objective of full employment without discrimination, the transfer system should not be structured to discourage work but the encouragement should include financial incentives, including benefit reduction rates which are low enough not to discourage work and possibly expansion of the Earned Income Tax Credit (EITC) with higher benefit levels and eligibility for all low-income workers, regardless of family status. Even though, as Hoffman has noted, such an expansion of the EITC would be costly and not efficient for the purpose of reducing poverty, it would be fairer than work requirements or mandatory public service employment which may simply substitute a new stigma for the stigma of welfare.[41]

A second moral issue which welfare reform planners should consider is whether the government should encourage any particular family structure. A major objective of the Family Assistance Plan (FAP) and an important objective of the Carter administration's 1977 proposal was to enhance family stability. On practical grounds, it is not clear that this objective can be achieved through welfare reform. In the HEW-OEO-funded income maintenance experiments, increased family splitting, not increased marital stability, was observed.[42]

This could have occurred because some recipients, knowing that the experiments would end, used the temporary increase in income to dissolve already unsatisfactory marriages. A second possibility is that the income guarantees under these experiments were not high enough to have an appreciable impact on marital stability. The Michigan Panel study found that the largest drop-off in the probability of separation occurred with average incomes of $7,500 or more over the period 1968–1973, which was 186 percent of the poverty level over the same period.[43] In the Seattle-Denver experiment, only the group which received an income guarantee of 150 percent of the poverty level did not experience a statistically significant increase in marital dissolution.[44] It is highly unlikely that income guarantees above the poverty level would be provided in a national program. A third possibility is that even though receiving transfer payments through the income maintenance experiments was substantially less degrading than the current welfare system, recipients still did not have an enhancement in self-esteem and efficacy that might result from a job which provided an adequate income. Although one cannot automatically generalize results from an experiment to an ongoing program, the results of the income maintenance experiments are evidence that providing transfer payments with the objective of enhancing marital stability is not likely to succeed.

Even if an ongoing program could have a positive effect on marital stability, there are significant moral issues in designing programs to encourage a specific family structure. The current AFDC program has been appropriately criticized for providing economic incentives for marital dissolution. It does not automatically follow, however, that it is preferable to encourage families to stay together. Although this arrangement lessens the need for cash payments, this is a budgetary rather than a moral justification. On moral grounds, it does not seem appropriate to encourage or discourage particular living arrangements. The objective of welfare reform should be to provide all economically deprived individuals with an adequate income, not to provide financial incentives for particular living arrangements. Parents, of course, should be required to support their children to the extent their financial resources permit, but this moral obligation should not be construed to force parents to live together.

The most appropriate role for the government regarding marital stability might well be what William Gorham has advocated: "intentionally neutral with respect to family type."[45] However, as MacDonald and Sawhill have noted, complete neutrality might be unattainable at acceptable cost.[46] The most neutral approach would be a universal demogrant, which would have a prohibitive cost if adequate guarantees and reasonably low benefit-reduction rates were provided. Absent complete neutrality, therefore, welfare plans should minimize economic incentives for particular living arrangements. This position is consistent with Martha Phillips's conclusion in her essay, "Favorable Family Impact as an Objective of Income Support Policy," that income support programs should be evaluated primarily in terms of fairness, equity, and adequacy. In Phillips's view, family impact concerns should dictate the design of income support policies only when unexpectedly large negative impacts on family structure or functioning occur.

Given the likely increasing concentration of economic deprivation in certain regions and in central cities in all regions, an issue with both political and moral implications in our federal system of government is what level of government should finance the cost of alleviating economic deprivation for the non-aged. If benefit levels were identical in all areas, the issue would be easily resolved. To the extent that the problem of economic deprivation among the non-aged reflects the legacy of discrimination, the financing should be federal since discrimination is a national problem. The regions of the United States that will have an increasing proportion of the economically deprived because of out-migration of skilled workers can argue on this basis that the burden should be a federal one. This argument is weakened by the fact that AFDC benefit levels between states vary by more than the interstate cost-of-living. Taxpayers in a state that has elected to pay low benefits have grounds to complain if their taxes support higher benefits in another state and they had no input into the political process that determined these benefit levels. In fact, taxpayers from the low-benefit states already help pay for higher benefits in other states through the federal share in the AFDC program. To allow taxpayers from low-benefit states an opportunity to make an input into the political processes which determine the benefit levels which their taxes help finance, any increased federal share of welfare costs should be accompanied by a commensurate increase in the federal power to determine benefit levels. The fact that overall federal spending in a low-benefit state may be greater than the federal taxes paid by the residents of that state does not eliminate the individual taxpayer's right to seek low-benefit levels for welfare programs if that is his preference. In fact, this principle of coupling increased federal financing with increased federal influence on benefit levels is included to a limited extent in the Carter administration's plan because states which supplement federal benefits above specified levels do so with their own funds.

As the aged become an increasing proportion of the population, the intergenerational compact on Social Security between the aged and the working-age population will most likely be renegotiated in such a way that the current distinction between means-tested welfare programs and social insurance will become moot. A major tenet of social insurance programs, which will probably be severely diluted within a decade, is the use of earmarked payroll taxes to finance benefits. In 1977, the Carter administration proposed limited general fund subsidies to the Social Security trust fund. Additional proposals for substantially greater subsidies are likely to be considered in the 96th Congress. Once ongoing general fund subsidies are provided to the Social Security trust funds, the concept that benefits should be related to earnings may be increasingly brought into question, and the level of benefits will be debated in terms of adequacy, as in welfare programs.

The moral issues about whether welfare recipients should be required to work in order to receive benefits are likely to have increasing parallels in the Social Security program. While it is highly unlikely that Social Security beneficiaries would be required to work in order to receive benefits, there is likely to be substantial pressure to eliminate early retirement benefits at age 62 and to increase the retirement age beyond age 65. The treatment of women who currently remain at home to care for their children, or who remained home in the past and thus did not become entitled to retirement benefits from their own earnings, will also be a work-related issue in both AFDC and Social Security.

On moral grounds, an end to the distinction between welfare and social insurance will be an improvement over the current system which implicitly divides the economically deprived population into the deserving and non-deserving poor. In theory, reform of the entire transfer system would be a more appropriate objective than reform of the welfare system. The history of welfare reform efforts over the past decade, however, indicates that even proposals to restructure a limited number of welfare programs may be too complex and comprehensive for the political system to digest. Nevertheless, to the extent that the welfare system is the legacy of discrimination, to continue the distinction between welfare and other transfer programs is to continue this tragic legacy.

Notes

1. Ralph E. Smith, "The Movement Into the Labor Force," in Ralph E. Smith, ed., *The Subtle Revolution* (Washington: The Urban Institute, 1979), p. 5.

2. Men are now eligible for the spouse's benefit without a means test but this benefit will be reduced by the amount of any public pension which the man receives. Both men and women who do not become eligible for public pensions by the end of 1982 will have future spouse's benefits offset by the amount of any public pension.

3. Robert D. Plotnick and Felicity Skidmore, *Progress Against Poverty: A Review of the 1964–74 Decade*. (New York: Academic Press, 1975), pp. 120–121.

4. James N. Morgan, "Intra-Family Transfers Revisited: The Support of Dependents Inside the Family" in Morgan and Duncan, eds., *Five Thousand American Families: Patterns of Economic Progrsess*, Vol. VI (Ann Arbor, Michigan: Institute for Social Research, 1978), pp. 355–356.

5. U.S. Congress. Congressional Budget Office, "Poverty Status of Families Under Alternative Definitions of Income," (June 1977), Background Paper No. 17 (Revised).

6. Morgan Reynolds and Eugene Smolensky, *Public Expenditures, Taxes, and the Distribution of Income*. (New York: Academic Press, 1977), pp. 74–75.

7. CBO, "Poverty Status."

8. U.S. Census Bureau, *Characteristics of the Population Below the Poverty Level: 1976*, Series P-60, No. 115 (July 1978), p. 5.

9. Average AFDC family size of 3.2 had monthly benefits of $229.70. Poverty level was extrapolated from Census 3 and 4 persons non-farm family poverty levels.

10. Census, *1976 Poverty Report*, p. 5.

11. Mayer N. Zald, "Demographics, Politics, and the Future of the Welfare State," *Social Science Review* 51 (March 1977): 116.

12. Christopher Lasch, *Haven in a Heartless World: The Family Besieged* (New York: Basic Books, 1977).

13. Nathan Glazer, "The Rediscovery of the Family," *Commentary* 65 (March 1978): 51–53.

14. Marjorie Honig, "The Impact of Welfare Payment Levels on Family Stability," in U.S. Congress, Joint Economic Committee, *Studies in Public Welfare*, Paper No. 12 (Part I), *The Family, Poverty, and Welfare Programs: Factors Influencing Family Instability* (Washington: GPO, 1973), pp. 37–53.

15. For a summary of the relevant studies, see Maurice MacDonald and Isabel V. Sawhill, "Welfare Policy and the Family," *Public Policy* 26 (Winter 1978): 105–119.

16. Michael T. Hannon, Nancy Brandon Tuma, and Lyle Groenevald, "Income Maintenance and Marriage; An Overview of Results from the Seattle-Denver Income Maintenance Experiments," Stanford Research Institute (April 25, 1980), p. 3.

17. John Stuart Mill, "On Liberty," in *Great Books of the Western World*, Vol. 43 (Chicago, Encyclopedia Britannica, 1952), p. 318.

18. U.S. Department of Health, Education, and Welfare, "1978 Annual Report of the Board of Trustees of the Federal Old-Age and Survivors Insurance and Disability Insurance Trust Funds," (May 15, 1978), p. 88.

19. *Ibid.*, p. 113.

20. U.S. Department of Health, Education, and Welfare, National Center for Education Statistics, *The Condition of Education: 1978 Edition* (Washington: GPO, 1978), p. 42, 66.

21. Cited in U.S. General Accounting Office, *Impact of Illegal Aliens on Public Assistance Programs: Too Little is Known*, GGD-78-20 (December 1, 1977), p. 1.

22. Barry R. Chiswick, "Immigrants and Immigration Policy," in William Feller, ed., *Contemporary Economic Problems 1978* (Washington: American Enterprise Institute, 1978), pp. 298–307. Chiswick's study analyzed the earnings patterns of white immigrants only.

23. U.S. Department of Health, Education, and Welfare, *Health, United States, 1976–1977* (Washington: GPO, 1977), pp. 157–159.

24. Smith, *The Subtle Revolution*, p. 14.

25. Zald, "Demographics, Politics, and the Future of the Welfare State," p. 116.

26. *Ibid.*

27. Robert Hampton, "Marital Disruption: Some Social and Economic Consequences," in Morgan and Duncan, eds., *Five Thousand American Families: Patterns of Economic Progress*, Vol. III (Ann Arbor, Michigan: Institute for Social Research, 1975), pp. 165–166; also, Heather Ross and Isabel V. Sawhill, *Time of Transition: The Growth of Families Headed by Women* (Washington: Urban Institute, 1975), p. 40.

28. U.S. Congress, Senate Budget Committee, *Growth of Government Spending for Income Assistance: A Matter of Choice*, prepared by the Congressional Budget Office, 94th Congress, First Session, (Washington: GPO, 1975), p. 17.

29. James P. Smith and Finis Welch, "Race Differences in Earnings: A Survey and New Evidence," Rand Study R-2295-NSF (March 1978), p. 3.

30. Finis Welch, "Testimony Before Task Force on Human Resources," Committee on the Budget, U.S. House of Representatives (September 25, 1978).

31. Hampton, "Marital Disruption," pp. 168–169.

32. U.S. Congress, Congressional Budget Office, "Youth Unemployment: The Outlook and Some Policy Strategies," Budget Issue Paper for Fiscal Year 1979 (April 1978), pp. 13–15.

33. Bernard Anderson, "Testimony Before Task Force on Human Resources," Committee on the Budget, U.S. House of Representatives (September 25, 1978).

34. U.S. Census, "1976 Poverty Report," p. 5, 183.

35. U.S. Bureau of the Census, "Number, Timing, and Duration of Marriages and Divorces in the United States, June 1975," Series P-20, No. 297 (October 1976): 1.

36. Kassalov, "Labor Futures," pp. 7–8.

37. *Ibid.*, pp. 9–11.

38. *Condition of Education: 1978*, p. 22.

39. Joann S. Lublin, "Firms and Job Seekers Discover More Benefits of Part-time Positions," *Wall Street Journal*, October 4, 1978.

40. Subsequent discussion on migration trends is based on: Peter A. Morrison, "How Demographics Can Help Members of Congress," Rand Paper P-6079 (March 1978), p. 14.

41. Wayne Lee Hoffman, "The Earned Income Tax Credit: Welfare Reform or Tax Relief?" Welfare Reform Policy Analysis Series: Number 5 (October 1978), Urban Institute.

42. MacDonald and Sawhill, "Welfare Policy and the Family," pp. 110–113.

43. Robert Hampton, "Marital Disruption," pp. 165–167.

44. Michael T. Hannan, Nancy Brandon Tuma, and Lyle P. Groenevald, "Income Maintenance and Marriage: An Overview of Results from the Seattle-Denver Income Maintenance Experiments," Stanford Research Institute, (April 25, 1978), pp. 10–11.

45. William Gorham, Preface to Heather Ross and Isabel V. Sawhill, *Time of Transition: The Growth of Families Headed by Women* (Washington: Urban Institute, 1975), p. xxi.

46. MacDonald and Sawhill, "Welfare Policy and the Family," pp. 101–102.

APPENDIX A

Brief Description of Existing Income Support Programs

The income support system currently in existence, commonly known as "welfare," is a collection of separate assistance programs providing varying kinds and amounts of benefits to different groups in the population. The only feature common to all programs is that recipients must be in economic need; that is, they must satisfy a "means test." The other eligibility conditions vary from program to program, as do the standards for determining the amount of benefits received.

The various programs are administered by a variety of different federal, state, and local agencies. Some are federally administered, some are state administered under federal grants in aid, and one, known as "general assistance," is financed and administered by states and localities without federal support. Each program has its own legislative base. There is no central coordination among the various programs making up the income support system.

Income support is a segment of a larger and more expensive system of income transfers to individuals and families. The most important part of this larger system is social insurance. This system comprises a set of programs based on contributions of individual workers and/or their employers. It includes Old Age, Survivors', and Disability Insurance; Unemployment Compensation; Medicare; Railroad Retirement; and Workmen's Compensation. Total expenditures for the social insurances far exceed those for income support programs.

Following is a brief description of the most important income support programs currently in operation:

AID TO FAMILIES WITH DEPENDENT CHILDREN (AFDC)

This program is administered by the individual states with federal financial grants in aid and under federal program standards. Those eligible include families deprived of parental support by reason of the death, disability, or continued absence of a parent; and, in twenty-seven states, by reason of the father's unemployment. This program was established in 1935 under the Social Security Act. States determine who is needy and establish levels of benefits, which vary from state to state.

GENERAL ASSISTANCE

General Assistance is the name given to the widely varying programs of state and local governments to provide support for those needy persons who do not qualify for federally funded income support programs. There is no typical pattern among these jurisdictions. In a few states, General Assistance is comprehensive in coverage and its benefits are comparable to those in AFDC. In some others, each locality makes its own arrangements and provides only short-time aid in cases of emergency. The remainder of the states fall between these two extremes. There are no federal funds in these programs.

SUPPLEMENTAL SECURITY INCOME (SSI)

The needy aged, blind, and disabled are aided by this program. It is federally financed and is administered by the U.S. Social Security Administration. It was established in 1935 by the Social Security Act as a federal-state program, and federalized in 1972. Benefits are paid in accordance with nationwide uniform standards of payment. States may supplement federal SSI payments from their own funds, and a number of states do so.

FOOD STAMPS

This program was enacted in 1964 to enable people with low incomes to purchase additional food. Economic need is the only eligibility condition, except that unemployed recipients must seek employment and accept suitable jobs. Those found eligible obtain Food Stamps from local outlets and exchange them for food in grocery stores and markets. Its benefits are therefore "in kind." The program is administered by the U.S. Department of Agriculture through state and local welfare offices. It has uniform nationwide payment standards.

MEDICAID

This program purchases needed medical care for recipients of AFDC and SSI. In about half the states, aid is also provided for the "medically needy," who are self-supporting but cannot afford to purchase medical care. It is a federally supported grant-in-aid program administered by the states under federal standards. It is the most expensive needs-tested program in the United States.

VETERANS' PENSIONS

Needy disabled veterans who have non-service-connected disabilities, and their dependents and survivors, are eligible for this program. It is administered by the U.S. Veterans' Administration. It is separate and distinct from Veterans' Compensation, which is for veterans with service-connected disabilities.

HOUSING ASSISTANCE

Beginning in 1974, there has been a program of rental supplementation for poor families that is federally funded and administered by the Department of Housing and Urban Development through local governments. Payments are made directly to landlords to cover a percentage of the rental costs of beneficiaries.

This list includes all of the major income support programs, but is not a comprehensive list of support and service programs currently in operation. A more detailed and comprehensive account of existing programs is contained in Sar A. Levitan, *Programs in Aid to the Poor* (Baltimore: John Hopkins Press, 1976), Chapters 2, 3 and 5.

See Table 4.1, Chapter 4, for summary data on the number of recipients of these programs and amounts expended for them.

Appendix B

Principal Criticisms of the Existing Income Support System[1]

In 1969, President Nixon described the existing income support system as a failure and attempted unsuccessfully to secure its replacement by a new and quite different system. Less than a decade later, President Carter tried again to accomplish essentially the same goal. What is so wrong with the system that efforts of this magnitude are thought to be necessary to correct it? An understanding of the criticisms that have been made is necessary to gain perspective on this issue.

When the most serious criticisms are identified, it becomes clear that they are of two opposite sorts. One expresses the view that too little is being done for the poor; and that, in general, the poor are being shabbily treated. The second is based on the belief that too many receive too much, and that the system needs substantial tightening up. Recent public opinion polls reveal some tendency for the same individuals to hold both sets of criticisms simultaneously, depending upon which aspect of the system is under scrutiny.[2]

One problem facing reformers of our income support system, therefore, is that while criticisms are many and widely held, they break down into these opposing viewpoints. In consequence, attempts to respond to one criticism bring reactions from those who criticize the system from a different point of view.

1. *Inadequacy of coverage and benefits.* For those who think that income support is not doing enough, the principal criticism is that benefit levels in some parts of the country and for some groups are too low to provide a decent standard of living. Morever, according to these critics, not all needy families and individuals are provided for. There are important segments of the poor who receive only food stamps in the way of support. The "working poor," i.e., those who work but earn too little, and most poor two-parent families are among those that fall within this group.

2. *Inequities among recipients.* Apart from questions of adequacy, there are numerous and striking differences in the treatment accorded individuals and families in circumstances of similar need. This is in part the consequence of the categorical structure of most income support programs, which results in preferential treatment to those who are viewed most sympathetically (e.g., the aged, blind, and one-parent families with children). A second major source of inequity is the variation in benefit levels among states in state-administered programs. (In 1978 average payments in the AFDC program ranged from $61 in Mississippi to $337 in Michigan.)

3. *Disincentives to socially desirable actions.* Several kinds of disincentives have been

identified by critics. In each case the criticism is that existing policies encourage some kind of unwanted behavior or discourage socially valuable behavior. It is asserted, for example, that the programs operate in such a way as to discourage people from seeking work and from leaving the rolls to become self-supporting. For example, recipients who work often have so much of their earnings deducted in computing assistance benefits that there is no strong incentive to continue working. Another criticism is that some fathers of needy families are encouraged by existing policies to abandon their families so as to make them eligible for assistance benefits for which they would not otherwise be eligible.

4. *Extension of benefits to those who ought not to receive them.* Some critics want to tighten up the system, holding that many recipients are really able to manage for themselves or should be required to do so. For example, it is asserted that some mothers in one-parent families are content to let the public welfare programs support them with no effort made to become self-supporting. Moreover, many believe that fraud and waste are widespread in these programs, and also that absent parents are evading responsibility for their children. This criticism is often associated with another criticism that the system is too costly in any event, and that taxpayers should not be expected to support such large numbers of recipients at the current levels of benefit.

5. *Complexity.* The income support system is widely criticized on all sides as being too complex and intricate in its categorization of groups of needy people, and in the kinds of benefits they provide (e.g., cash benefits, food stamps, housing subsidies, payment of medical bills). Even a cursory examination of the multiplicity of programs, eligibility conditions, and levels of benefit is likely to raise such questions.

6. *Demeaning treatment of the poor.* Many critics hold that the existing programs seriously reduce the self-respect of recipients and that they invade their privacy. The needs test is thought to be demeaning, and some eligibility requirements attempt to enforce conformity to moral standards of those who pay the tax bill. (At the same time, other critics think that getting income support should be made more difficult to discourage dependency, and that benefits should be kept meager to force recipients to act for themselves.)

Notes

1. This account is based on information contained in the following publications: Lester Salamon, *Welfare Reform—The Elusive Consensus* (New York: Praeger Publishers, 1978), ch. 2; Martin Anderson, *Welfare* (Stanford, Calif.: Hoover Institutions Press, 1978); and *Joint Hearings Before the Welfare Reform Subcommittee* (Washington, D.C.: U.S. Government Printing Office, 1977), pp. 2–7.
2. See Lester Salamon, Appendix B, pp. 221 ff.

NOTES ON CONTRIBUTORS AND EDITORS*

HENRY AARON is Senior Fellow at the Brookings Institution. He served for two years as Assistant Secretary for Planning and Evaluation at the Department of Health, Education, and Welfare. He has been Professor of Economics at the University of Maryland. His most recent book is *Politics and the Professor: The Great Society in Perspective*.

JODIE T. ALLEN is Special Assistant to the Secretary of Labor. She was formerly Senior Vice President of Mathematica Policy Research, Inc. and Assistant Vice President of the Urban Institute. She is the author of numerous articles and technical studies on the subjects of welfare, employment, and other income maintenance programs including "A Funny Thing Happened on the Way to Welfare Reform" and "Perspectives on Income Maintenance: Where Do We Go From Here and How Far?"

THOMAS A. AULT is Director for Policy Planning, Office of Income Security, under the Assistant Secretary for Planning and Evaluation, U.S. Department of Health and Human Services.

BARBARA R. BERGMANN is Professor of Economics at the University of Maryland and a faculty associate of the University's Project on the Economics of Discrimination. She has written widely on unemployment, occupational segregation by race and sex, the economics of sex-roles, and the computer simulation of economic systems.

RICHARD B. BRANDT is Professor of Philosophy at the University of Michigan. He is the author of several books including *Hopi Ethics: A Theoretical Analysis, Ethical Theory*, and *A Theory of the Good and the Right*. He has been president of the American Philosophical Association, Western Division; and John Locke Lecturer in Oxford University.

GEOFFREY BRENNAN is an Australian economist, now Professor in the Center for Study of Public Choice at Virginia Polytechnic Institute and

*This information was correct at the time of printing.

State University. He has written extensively on public finance theory, including a number of articles on "Pareto-desirable" redistribution. He is currently engaged in writing a book with James M. Buchanan, *The Power to Tax: Analytic Foundations of a Fiscal Constitution*.

BARUCH BRODY is Chairman of the Department of Philosophy and Director of the Program in Legal Studies at Rice University. His publications include *Abortion and the Sanctity of Human Life* and *Identity and Essence*, as well as numerous articles and textbooks.

PETER G. BROWN is co-editor of *Food Policy*, *Markets and Morals*, and *Human Rights and U.S. Foreign Policy*, and is the author of a number of articles and monographs. He is currently Director of the Center for Philosophy and Public Policy at the University of Maryland.

ALLEN BUCHANAN is Associate Professor of Philosophy at the University of Minnesota at Minneapolis. He has published papers in epistemology, ethics, and political philosophy.

NORMAN DANIELS is Associate Professor of Philosophy at Tufts University. He is author of *Thomas Reid's 'Inquiry': The Geometry of Visibles and the Case for Realism*, editor of *Reading Rawls*, and author of a number of articles on philosophy of science, and moral and political philosophy.

GERALD DWORKIN is Professor of Philosophy at the University of Illinois, Chicago Circle. He is the author of numerous publications in moral and political philosophy and is an Associate Editor of *Ethics*.

ROBERT FERSH is currently Confidential Assistant to the Administrator of the Food and Nutrition Service of the U.S. Department of Agriculture. He formerly served as Senior Analyst, Income Security, for the U.S. Senate Committee on the Budget and as Counsel, Government Affairs and Social Policy for the American Public Welfare Association. His prior publications include an analysis of the Carter administration's first welfare reform plan, "The Program for Better Jobs and Income"; and co-authorship of "Equal Protection, Social Welfare Litigation, the Burger Court," *Notre Dame Lawyer*, July 1978.

DAVID FRIEDMAN is Assistant Professor of Economics in the Center for Study of Public Choice at Virginia Polytechnic Institute and State University. He is also active as a libertarian writer and speaker. He is the author of *The Machinery of Freedom: Guide to a Radical Capitalism*, and *Laissez-Faire in Population: The Least Bad Solution*, as well as a considerable number of articles in both popular and scholarly journals. His principal current interest is the application of economic analysis to understanding political institutions.

CONRAD JOHNSON is Associate Professor of Philosophy at the University of Maryland, College Park. He has written numerous articles in philosophical and legal journals, has appeared on the American Issues Radio Forum, and has served as a consultant in the office of the Division of Public Programs of the National Endowment for the Humanities.

DAVID LINDEMAN is senior analyst in income security policy in the Office of Planning and Evaluation, U.S. Department of Health and Human Services. In that and previous capacities, he has participated in every major welfare reform endeavor over the past decade; and, more recently, in policy planning for social security and in the development of national health proposals. He was recently named Acting Director for Social Insurance Analysis in the above-mentioned office.

A. I. MELDEN is Professor of Philosophy at the University of California, Irvine. He has written numerous articles and a number of books on a wide variety of topics. The most important of his writings in moral and social philosophy are *Rights and Right Conduct* and *Rights and Persons*. Also, he is editor of *Philosophy Research Archives*.

MARTHA H. PHILLIPS is Assistant Minority Counsel of the Committee on Ways and Means in the U.S. House of Representatives, where she directs a special project to assess the family impact of various programs under the Committee's jurisdiction, including welfare, income taxes, and Social Security. She serves on several organizations and groups dealing with family policy.

JAMES A. ROTHERHAM is Deputy Associate Director for Human Resource Programs on the House Budget Committee. He was formerly a senior budget examiner at the Office of Management and Budget.

WAYNE VASEY is Professor Emeritus of Social Work, University of Michigan. He is currently Visiting Professor in the Aging Studies Program at the University of South Florida. He is the author of *Government and Social Welfare* and of a number of articles and studies of public welfare. In 1970, he wrote the official report on "Social Welfare and Human Rights" for the United States Committee of the International Conference on Social Welfare.

PAUL VERNIER is Research Associate, Center for Philosophy and Public Policy, University of Maryland. He was Chief, Division of Program Review and Evaluation, Assistance Payments Administration, U.S. Department of Health, Education and Welfare; now the Department of Health and Human Services, until his retirement in 1971. He is a member of the Academy of Certified Social Workers.

Index